ACCOUNTING AND AUDITING IN CHINA

To our families and colleagues

Accounting and Auditing in China

Z. JUN LIN
DAVID C. YANG
LIYAN WANG

Routledge
Taylor & Francis Group

LONDON AND NEW YORK

First published 1998 by Ashgate Publishing

Reissued 2018 by Routledge
2 Park Square, Milton Park, Abingdon, Oxon, OX14 4RN
711 Third Avenue, New York, NY I 0017, USA

Routledge is an imprint of the Taylor & Francis Group, an informa business

Notice:
Product or corporate names may be trademarks or registered trademarks, and are used only for identification and explanation without intent to infringe.

Publisher's Note
The publisher has gone to great lengths to ensure the quality of this reprint but points out that some imperfections in the original copies may be apparent.

Disclaimer
The publisher has made every effort to trace copyright holders and welcomes correspondence from those they have been unable to contact.

A Library of Congress record exists under LC control number: 97042933

Typeset by Manton Typesetters, 5-7 Eastfield Road, Louth, Lincolnshire, LN11 7AJ, UK.

ISBN 13: 978-1-138-61317-1 (hbk)
ISBN 13: 978-1-138-61318-8 (pbk)
ISBN 13: 978-0-429-46462-1 (ebk)

Contents

List of Figures and Tables   ix
The Authors   xi
Preface   xiii

1 Overview of Chinese Accounting and Auditing Developments   1
Historical review   3
Economic transition and accounting reforms   7
The perspective of further development   14
Organizational structure of the book   18

2 Regulation of Accounting Affairs   23
The system of accounting administration   23
The framework of accounting regulations   30
Qualifications and obligations of accounting personnel   36
Reform of setting accounting regulations   42

3 Accounting Standards   51
Accounting standards and the accounting regulation system   51
Development of accounting standards in China   54
Analysis of Chinese Accounting Standards for Business
Enterprises (ASBE)   58
Implications of Accounting Standards for Business Enterprises
(ASBE)   69

4 Securities Markets and Information Disclosure   73
Resurgence and expansion of securities markets in China   73
Regulation of securities markets   77
Requirements on prospectuses and regular reports   82
Comments on disclosure to securities markets in China   86

5 Cost Accounting and Managerial Accounting   89
Principles of Chinese cost accounting   89

Practices of cost management   97
The rise of managerial accounting in China   102
The practices of Chinese managerial accounting   105
Prospects of managerial accounting in China   109

6   Auditing   111
Overview of the Chinese auditing system   111
The regulatory environment of state audit supervision   114
Governmental auditing   118
Institutional internal auditing   127
Non-governmental (social) auditing   131

7   Public Accounting and the Profession   137
Historical evolution of public accounting in China   137
Qualification of certified public accountants   139
Formation and administration of CPA firms   144
CPAs' legal obligations   148
Professional ethics and auditing standards   151
Professional bodies of CPAs   156

8   Taxation and Tax Returns   161
Overview of the Chinese taxation system   161
Types of taxes   166
The tax system for business entities with foreign investments   183
Tax registration and tax returns   185
Preferential tax policies for regional development   188

9   Accounting for Governments and Non-profit Organizations   193
The administrative structure of budgetary accounting   193
Regulations for budgetary accounting   199
Basic characteristics of budgetary accounting   202
Financial reporting for governments and non-profit organizations   207
Prospects of budgetary accounting reform   210

10   Computerization of Accounting   215
Evolution of computerization of accounting   215
Characteristics of computerized accounting   218
Regulation of accounting software   222
Commercialized Chinese accounting software   227
Education and training in accounting computerization   230
Prospects for computerization of accounting in China   232

11   Accounting Education   235
The accounting education system   235
The curriculum of formal accounting education   243
Professional qualification examinations and continuing
education   252

12   Accounting Associations   261
The nature of accounting associations   261
The Accounting Society of China   262
The Chinese Institute of Certified Public Accountants   266
The China Society of Auditing   272
The Chinese Accounting Professors' Association   273
Accounting research and publications   273

13   The Environment of Business Regulation   277
Overview of the business environment   277
Summary of business regulations in China   280
Business laws for enterprises with foreign investment   291

Appendix A: The Accounting Law of the People's Republic of China   295
Appendix B: The Audit Law of the People's Republic of China   303
Appendix C: The Certified Public Accountant Law of the People's
            Republic of China   315
Appendix D: Accounting Standards for Business Enterprises   327
Appendix E: General Rules on Financial Affairs for Business
            Enterprises   343

Index   357

List of Figures and Tables

FIGURES

2.1	The system structure of accounting administration	26
2.2	Reform of setting accounting regulations (phase I)	45
2.3	Reform of setting accounting regulations (phase II)	47
3.1	The system of accounting regulations in China	53
3.2	Structural interrelation of Chinese accounting standards	56
3.3	Conceptual structure of Chinese ASBE	60
4.1	Securities regulatory bodies in China	79
4.2	Required disclosures for publicly listed companies	81
6.1	Structural framework of state audit supervision in China	115
6.2	Organizational structure of the NAA	120
6.3	Flowchart of procedures for governmental auditing	128
7.1	Structure of Chinese independent auditing standards	153
9.1	The system of state budgetary administration in China	196
9.2	The structure of budgetary accounting in China	200
9.3	Interrelation of journal entries under the fund receipt–disbursement bookkeeping method	206
11.1	The structure of the post-secondary education system in China	236
11.2	The structure of accounting education programmes	240
11.3	Functional cores of the accounting curriculum (before mid-1980s)	245
11.4	Subjects of core accounting courses	248

TABLES

3.1	Treatment of selected items in Chinese ASBE	64
3.2	Comparison of accounting elements of financial statements	67
4.1	Overview of national stock trading, 1991–7 (March)	75
4.2	B share issuing and trading in China by March 1997	76
5.1	Illustration of chart of product costing accounts	94

7.1	Statistics of national CPA examinations, 1991, 1993–6	141
7.2	Statistics of overseas candidates in national CPA examinations, 1994–6	142
7.3	List of Chinese independent auditing standards (January 1997)	155
8.1	Categories and rates of consumption tax	170
8.2	Categories and rates of operation tax	172
8.3	Tax rates for personal income (wages and salaries)	177
8.4	Tax rates for personal income (income from business profits)	178
8.5	Categories and rates of resource tax	181
11.1	Accounting core textbooks adopted in top accounting schools	249
11.2	Content of accounting qualification examinations	253
11.3	Subjects of the national accounting qualification examination (before 1996)	255
11.4	Professional grading for government auditors	257
11.5	Content of the national auditing qualification examination	258

The Authors

Dr Z. Jun Lin is currently an associate professor at the University of Hong Kong and the University of Lethbridge, Canada. He completed his education in China and Canada and received the first PhD in accounting in China in 1985. After teaching at Xiamen University, China for several years, he went to the University of Stanford and the University of Illinois as a visiting scholar sponsored by the Ford Foundation in 1988–90. Since August 1990, professor Lin has been teaching at the University of Lethbridge, becoming a tenured faculty member in 1994.

Besides teaching a wide range of courses in accounting and financial management, Dr Lin is active in research and is a well recognized scholar in the studies of Chinese accounting. He has published many articles with a variety of topics on referred journals, including *International Journal of Accounting, Journal of International Accounting, Auditing and Taxation, Journal of Business Education, The Accounting Historian's Journal, Financial Management and Accountability* and *Asian Profile*. Professor Lin has also published one booklet for the American Institute of Certified Public Accountants (AICPA) and chapters in several books in North America and Hong Kong. In addition, he published three well-received accounting and auditing textbooks in China and Taiwan during 1995–7.

Dr Lin is currently a CPA in the USA and China. He has had practical experience in North America and China. He is also a member of several academic associations, such as the American Accounting Association, The Academy of Accounting Historians, International Association of Accounting Research and Education, Canadian Academic Accounting Association, Hong Kong Academic Accounting Association and the Chinese Accounting Professors' Association – North America.

Professor David C. Yang received his BA degree from the National Taiwan University, his MBA degree from the University of California at Berkeley and his PhD degree from Columbia University. Specializing in financial accounting and reporting, financial analysis and international accounting, with a particular emphasis on Chinese and Asian–Pacific accounting systems, Professor Yang has been honoured with numerous awards for teaching excellence, including the Outstanding Professor Award by the Delta Theta Chapter of Beta Alpha Psi, the Dennis Ching/First Interstate Memorial Teaching Award and the University of Hawaii College of Business Administration Teaching Excellence Award. Professor Yang is a member of Beta Alpha Psi and Beta Gamma Sigma. His biography appears in *Who's Who in the World*.

In addition, Professor Yang has been involved in developing Financial Accounting Standards 33 and Financial Accounting Standards 36 financial accounting databases. He has received research grants from the US Department of Education and the Coopers & Lybrand Foundation. He is the President of the Chinese Accounting Professors' Association – North America (1997–8) and Associate Director of Beijing University's Research Center for International Accounting and Finance.

Professor Yang is currently the Director and Professor of the School of Accountancy and the Faculty Director of the China-focused Executive MBA programme at the College of Business Administration, University of Hawaii. Having taught at Beijing University and the National Taiwan University, he has consulted on financial and accounting management concerns for major firms in China and the United States.

Liyan Wang, PhD, CPA (China), is Professor of Accounting and Head of the Accounting Department at the Guanghua School of Management, Deputy Director of the Research Center for International Accounting and Finance and (from 1993) the deputy editor-in-chief of *Economics Science* at Beijing University, China. He completed his education at three universities in central, south-western and northern China, and received his PhD degree from Beijing University, with an emphasis on accounting and economic management theory. He is a council member of the Accounting Society of China (from 1996), and a member of the Chinese Institute of Certified Public Accountants. Professor Wang's research outputs have appeared in many academic and professional journals in China, including *Statistical Research*, *Economics Science*, *CPA Journal* and *Management World*, and in the proceedings of national and international conferences. Professor Wang is also a main author or editor-in-chief of several accounting textbooks and monographs. In recent years he has been focusing his research interest mainly on green accounting, ecomanagement and auditing. He spent the academic year 1996–7 in the United Kingdom as a visiting scholar to pursue his research on environmental issues.

Preface

China is currently in a transitional period, switching from a centrally planned economy into a partial market economy, or the so-called 'socialist market economy'. Corresponding to the changing economic and business environment, remarkable progress has been made in Chinese accounting and auditing in recent years. For example, the regulatory system of accounting has been modified, the qualification system for accounting personnel has been implemented, and the new national accounting and auditing standards have been promulgated recently. A legal framework of accounting and auditing is also in place. Internationally accepted accounting principles and practices have been gradually adopted. Reform of accounting education is under way and continuing professional education programmes are booming. As a result, the gap between Chinese accounting and auditing and their counterparts in the rest of the world has been narrowed significantly.

As the Chinese economy is moving rapidly towards an integration with the world markets, international investors and professionals have become much more interested in learning Chinese accounting and auditing in order to explore potential business opportunities in China. However little reading on recent developments of Chinese accounting and auditing is available outside China, particularly in the West. This book therefore aims to help the international business community to gain an understanding of the current state of accounting and auditing in China.

A fairly comprehensive delineation of the updated developments of Chinese accounting and auditing is presented in this book. All major aspects of Chinese accounting and auditing are examined, in respect of the most recent developments up to June 1997. The topics elaborated include the regulatory system of accounting, qualification requirements and responsibility of Chinese accountants, organization of accounting and auditing work, setting accounting standards or regulations, product costing and managerial accounting, securities markets and information disclosure, public accounting and the accounting profession, accounting for governments and non-profit organizations, the statutory auditing system, taxation systems and tax returns, the business environment and the legal framework, computerization

xiii

of accounting, accounting education, accounting associations and research, and so on. The perspective of further development of Chinese accounting and auditing in a foreseeable future is also highlighted.

The authors of this book are affiliated with higher educational institutions in North America, Hong Kong and China and have long been involved in studies of Chinese accounting and auditing. We have worked closely in the last two years to complete this book, based on a continuing observation of the accounting and auditing developments in China. Although the book is aimed mainly at business and professional readers, it can be used as a textbook or teaching supplement for full-time accounting education or vocational training programmes. We are educators ourselves and have been aware of the mounting demands for courses on Chinese accounting and auditing in recent years. This book should enrich the very small collection of books on Chinese accounting and auditing currently available for students in different parts of the world.

We acknowledge the unfailing support for the preparation of this book from our families and colleagues. We are grateful to Ashgate Publishing Ltd for its prompt processing and publication of this book. The editorial team, John Irwin, Sonia Hubbard, Ann Newell and Rachel Hedges, from Ashgate Publishing Ltd have done excellent work and their assistance is highly appreciated.

Finally we look forward to the feedback from readers. Critical comments or suggestions will be appreciated. Such comments will help us to revise the book in the light of further significant developments in Chinese accounting and auditing in the future.

Z. JUN LIN
DAVID C. YANG
LIYAN WANG

1 Overview of Chinese Accounting and Auditing Developments

China, with a total population close to 1.3 billions, is one of the largest countries in the world. With a great economic potential and immense domestic markets, China's developments have a significant impact on world economies and social developments.

The Chinese economy has demonstrated remarkable growth resulting from an ambitious and enduring course of economic reform which commenced at the end of 1970s. In the following two decades, the Chinese economy grew at a pace second to none in the world, with an average annual growth rate at about 10 per cent. According to the Chinese government's statistics,[1] the total amount of China's gross domestic product (GDP) was *Renminbi* (RMB) ¥6779.5 billion (RMB ¥8.2 = US$1) in 1996, more than double the GDP in 1978. The GDP per capita was about RMB ¥5600 in 1996. This level of GDP may not be impressive compared to the prevailing standards in most of the developed countries in the West; however, it represents a remarkable achievement in a relatively short period in such a large country as China. It is widely believed that China will become one of the major economic powerhouses in the world in the next century.

The Chinese economy has become increasingly integrated into world economies in recent years. Besides a steady increase in the volume of international trade, China has attracted a very large amount of foreign investments. From 1979 to 1996, about 283 800 foreign-capital affiliated entities, in the forms of equity or contractual joint ventures, or wholly foreign-owned companies, were given approval to set up operations in China. The total amount of direct foreign investments within China is over RMB ¥2000 billion. According to the World Bank's reports, China was the leading recipient of foreign investments among developing countries for four consecutive years from 1992. More and more international investors are interested in the potential business opportunities and markets in China.

Accounting is a common language of business. International trade and investment activities require relevance and reliable accounting information. The development status of accounting is vital to facilitate or deter the growth of business activities in any country. China is no exception. Chinese accounting, stemming from a highly centralized planned economy, differed substantially from its counterparts in most industrialized countries in the past. Poor understandability of Chinese accounting and its inconsistency with the accounting practices prevailing elsewhere in the world have been frequently cited by foreign investors as negative factors with regard to doing business within China.

Significant changes have, however, taken place during the current course of economic reforms. In particular, new accounting and auditing systems have been introduced by the Chinese government in recent years, as part of the efforts to improve the investment environment for international investors. The development of accounting and auditing has contributed positively to China's drive towards a market-based economy. The international business community and professional bodies have demonstrated increasing interest in Chinese accounting and auditing, following the rapid expansion of foreign investments in China in recent years.

This book aims at an updated introduction of Chinese accounting and auditing to international businessmen and professionals who are interested in learning the current state of Chinese accounting and auditing. Although more specific examination of the major areas of accounting and auditing development in China can be found in the rest of this book, this chapter delivers an overview of Chinese accounting and auditing in the past, present and future. In particular, an overall background regarding the environmental settings and the causes, processes and goals of the reforms of accounting and auditing currently taking place within China is presented.

Learning history helps to obtain a better understanding of present changes and a proper prediction of future progress. As well elaborated by A. Enthoven, in his recent observation of Chinese accounting developments,

> It is hard to comprehend accounting without a clear understanding of both its historical and recent (since 1949 and 1979) eco-political developments. These historical trends are extremely significant in trying to grasp the current Chinese accounting system, while Chinese accounting has its own characteristics resulting from these developments.[2]

Thus we will begin with a brief historical review of the evolution of Chinese accounting and auditing prior to 1980.

HISTORICAL REVIEW

China has a long history of accounting. In particular, ancient accounting in China was among the most sophisticated accounting systems in the early civilizations of the world.[3] But China fell behind the evolution of modern accounting which stemmed from the Industrial Revolution in the West, owing to a slow growth of industry and commerce in the country over a long period before the middle of the 20th century.

After the birth of the People's Republic of China in 1949, the Communist government adopted a former Soviet-style planned economy. The state ownership of all production means and a centralized economic administration were introduced. Accordingly, accounting was highly regulated or under direct governmental control, and was treated as a tool to facilitate centralized economic planning and control, aiming at directly serving various administration needs of the government.

Chinese accounting therefore evolved in a pattern quite different from its counterparts in most industrialized countries in the West prior to 1980. Some major characteristics of Chinese accounting and auditing during the period of 1950–80 can be summarized as follows.

Objectives of accounting

The government was the principal, if not the only, user of accounting information. In particular, the central government relied directly upon accounting to supply data for the preparation of various economic plans and the state fiscal budgets. In addition, accounting was required

- to review and evaluate the execution of national economic plans and state fiscal budgets across the country;
- to ensure the safety and integrity of the state properties entrusted to individual entities; and
- to monitor the implementation of the state's fiscal policies and financial regulations.

Accounting also had to serve a great variety of information needs of governmental administrative authorities such as public finance, taxation, banking, statistics and industry-specific government departments. Thus Chinese accounting was policy-oriented with the government's economic and social policies dominating accounting work. The accounting regulations or systems were altered quite frequently, corresponding to changes in the government's economic and social policies.

Regulatory framework

Specific governmental authorities were set up under the finance departments in each level of government to take charge of accounting regulation and administration. Mandatory and detailed accounting regulations and rules were stipulated and enforced by government authorities in charge. Accounting work in all entities had to comply with the compulsory accounting regulations. Fairly detailed procedures for accounting transactions were stipulated in the accounting regulations or rules, including specific requirements governing the chart of general and sub-ledger accounts and the detailed format of financial statements to be adopted by individual entities. In addition, government authorities imposed fairly specific and thorough financing rules or spending criteria on the expenditure or expenses incurred in all governmental units, non-profit organizations (NPOs) and business enterprises. Violation of government's fiscal policies and accounting regulations was prohibited.

Government authorities in charge of accounting administration maintained a direct control of accounting affairs in all entities, including the decisions on staffing and organizing accounting work within individual entities. Accounting personnel were entrusted to exercise accounting supervision, on behalf of the state, over operations within individual organizations. Accounting work in all areas was closely monitored, or sanctioned accordingly, by government authorities in charge.

Uniform accounting systems

Corresponding to a centralized regulatory environment, the government stipulated compulsory accounting systems (regulations) for all organizations. The authority of formulating accounting regulations was consolidated at the Ministry of Finance and a few industrial ministries under the State Council (Chinese Cabinet). In order to ensure that accounting data fitted the needs of the government's economic planning and budgeting, Uniform Accounting Systems (UAS) were installed by the government. However, the UAS were stipulated separately by types of industry (that is, segregated by manufacturing, merchandising, agricultural industry, transport, construction, and so on) and by business ownership (separated by state ownership, collective ownership, joint ventures with Chinese and foreign capital, listed companies and private business). There were over 50 sets of UAS effective within China before the new accounting system was introduced in 1993. Differences were obvious among those coexisting accounting regulations since they were designed by the Ministry of Finance and a few other ministerial authorities to satisfy various purposes of industrial administration. As a result of this, variance was substantial in accounting information generated under the multiple sets of the UAS.

Rule-based accounting

Under state ownership, all economic entities, regardless of whether they were government units, NPOs and business enterprises, were directly funded by government and all the revenues or profits generated by economic entities had to be submitted to the government. Product costing was regulated rigidly by the government's financing and taxation authorities. Specific rules were established to control the purpose, use and spending limit of the financial resources in each entity. Accounting procedures for many important transactions, such as inventory valuation, depreciation, revenue and expense recognition, income determination, and so on, were mechanically codified in the compulsory accounting regulations or rules. All accounting regulations or rules were based on the tax laws and the government's financing policies. Accounting process was restricted to performing a primarily bookkeeping function in compliance with the financing and accounting regulations laid down by government authorities. Within such a rule-based framework, accounting personnel were allowed to exercise no professional judgment in processing accounting transactions.

Ideological influence

Over a long period, accounting and auditing in China was dominated by the political or ideological doctrines adopted by the government. For instance, operations of business enterprises were barred from 'profit seeking', as the concept of 'profit' was labelled as a capitalist phenomenon incompatible with the socialist economy. Such were the concepts of 'capital' or 'owners' equity'. Thus income determination lacked significance and capital or equity accounts were excluded from Chinese accounting. In addition, the accounting convention of 'conservatism' or 'prudence' was strictly prohibited in China as the convention was criticized as a tool to facilitate capitalists in manipulating business income. Independent auditing functions were completely outlawed for their alleged incompatibility with the public (state) ownership of production means in a socialist economy. Furthermore, even the double-entry bookkeeping method with 'debit' and 'credit' entries was once banned in China, simply because of its origination in the capitalist world. During the ten years of so-called 'Cultural Revolution' from 1966 to

1976, the role of accounting was downgraded and accounting procedures were deliberately simplified in order to make accounting easy for ordinary people. The ideological influence is obviously one of the major factors causing Chinese accounting to depart substantially from accounting practices in most other countries prior to 1980.

Fund-based accounting

In light of strict government fiscal control, fund accounting dominated in Chinese accounting, whether in governmental or business accounting. The concept of 'fund accounting' is interpreted somewhat differently in China in comparison with the West. Since all programmes and expenses were funded by the government, accounting was required to keep books of account strictly based on the classification of funds specified by the government. The basic accounting equation underlying financial statements of all organizations was 'fund applications equal fund sources'. 'Fund applications' means employment of funds in acquiring property, goods and materials used in the process of operations, while 'fund sources' represents the various channels for obtaining operational funds. Subcategories of funds were designed under both 'fund applications' and 'fund sources', with strict distinctions for each type of fund. Interflows among different funds were not allowed. This kind of fund accounting is, however, inefficient for business entities. For instance, many business enterprises would encounter difficulty in supplying sufficient operating funds or would have to pay higher interest for short-term financing, even if they had a surplus in other types of funds on hand.

Financial statements were constructed on the basis of the concept of fund accounting, with all accounts being grouped into two categories, 'applications of funds' and 'sources of funds'. Balance sheets with classification of assets, liabilities and owners' equity were not available under the old accounting system before the mid-1980s. Profit and loss accounts were constructed with a focus on operating income before taxes. Net income was indirectly reported in another statement of 'income allocation', showing distribution of income between government (taxes and net profits after retained income) and business entities (that is the retained income based on the formula set out by government finance and taxation authorities, which became the special funds that must be accounted for separately from operational funds). In addition, financial statements were full of specific and detailed items required by different government authorities. This approach of fund-based accounting made Chinese accounting information hardly comparable to the internationally accepted norm.

ECONOMIC TRANSITION AND ACCOUNTING REFORMS

Without doubt, the accounting system in China prior to 1980s was quite inefficient and could hardly produce meaningful accounting information for users other than the government. Comparability of financial statements among different organizations was poor owing to the large number of coexisting accounting regulations segregated by various types of industry and business ownership. Frequent changes in governments' fiscal policies and accounting regulations also caused inconsistency in accounting practices. Reforms of accounting and auditing became inevitable especially when China started to abandon the centralized planned economy at the end of 1970s.

Economic transition

Immediately after the chaotic decade of 'Cultural Revolution', the Chinese government decided to launch overall reforms of economic structures in the late 1970s, aiming at rescuing the deteriorated national economy which was dominated by highly centralized planning and control. The economic reforms have proceeded smoothly over the last 18 years and have brought about remarkable changes in the Chinese economy.

Decentralization of economic administration

The central government relaxed, step by step, its control over economic and business activities from the beginning of economic reforms in 1978. Local authorities and business enterprises gained much wider autonomy in making economic or business decisions. Business enterprises were exposed to market forces and competition. Business management were required to bear the responsibility for profit seeking. The central government introduced measures to tie the benefits of management and employees to the performance of business enterprises. Salaries, bonuses and other fringe benefits to management and employees were, to a certain extent, linked to the operational results realized during each period (including the fulfilment of production quota and profit targets). Management have been induced to pay more attention to production cost, sales and profits of the products or services produced.

Emergence of diversified business ownership

Although almost every enterprise was owned by the government under the state ownership of production means before the economic reforms commenced in 1978, the Chinese government has relaxed the restriction on non-state ownership during the course of economic reforms. The sectors of non-state-owned business grew steadily over these years. Collective owner- ship (partnerships or ventures) and private business (proprietorships) emerged in practice, followed by experimentation with the share capital system (stock companies). Business entities with foreign capital increased dramatically as a result of the policy of opening to the outside world. By the end of 1996, the share of the state-owned enterprises had declined to about 48 per cent of the national economy, while collective ownership (including joint ventures and the listed corporations) had risen to 40 per cent. Even the private businesses, called 'individual industrial and commercial households', in- creased from almost nil before 1980 to 12 per cent of the Chinese economy by the end of 1996. Business entities with multiple ownership, such as various kinds of business venture among government agencies, private own- ers and foreign investors, significantly increased. As a result, the capital structures and sources of funding for business entities have expanded con- siderably in comparison with the situation before 1980. New forms of business entity thus required accounting systems or procedures different from the traditional models designed for the state-owned enterprises.

Expansion of stock companies and capital markets

One of the most significant developments resulting from the economic re- forms is the emergence of stock companies and capital markets in China. The share capital system experimented with in the mid-1980s led to an official endorsement of the stock companies by the central government in the early 1990s. Two stock exchanges were established in Shanghai and Shenzhen on 19 December 1990 and 3 July 1991, respectively. The number of listed companies increased steadily, from a total of 14 listed companies in 1991 to 570 by March 1997. Many state-owned enterprises have been restructured into stock companies in recent years. Public reaction to the reappearance of stock markets was overwhelmingly favourable among ordinary investors in China, although the risks of speculation were fairly high at this infant stage of the experiment.[4] Markets for the 'B share' (denominated in US dollars and specifically designated for foreign investors to subscribe) had also been devel- oped and well received. In addition, 29 Chinese listed companies had been successfully listed in overseas stock markets up to May 1997, such as in Hong Kong (H shares), New York (N shares) and London (L shares). Capital mar- kets for government and private bonds and other short-term or long-term securities have been experimented with. The growth of capital markets has generated the demands for accounting information and disclosure that could assist investors in making proper investment decisions.

Movement towards a partial market economy

The enduring economic reforms have switched the centrally planned economy to a partial market economy, called a 'socialist market economy' in China. A series of integrated reform programmes has been introduced, step by step, by the central government, in the fields of economic planning, fiscal budgeting, finance and banking, foreign exchanges, taxation, pricing, manpower administration, and so on. The central government has speeded up the process of formulating business legislation. A framework of business laws and regulations has been built. Business administrative systems compatible with the partial market economy are taking shape. Business enterprises are now operating in a much diversified business environment. Separation of ownership and management has been emphasized. A great variety of new operational patterns has appeared, such as business leasing, contracting, merger or business combination. Group companies or consortia have emerged, with consolidation of operations involving varied lines of business or different regions. Bankruptcy law has been officially introduced to terminate the inefficient or failing enterprises. Changes in economic and business environment have generated a significant impact on accounting practices. A series of measurement and disclosure issues relating to accounting for leasing, ventures or business combination, group accounts and business liquidation has appeared, while no solutions could be found in the traditional Chinese accounting system based on the centrally planned economy.

Accounting reforms

Chinese accounting evolves in this particular economic and business environment. In keeping pace with the growth of the partial market economy, reform of Chinese accounting was inevitable. Remarkable progress has been made in Chinese accounting and auditing through the process of reform over the last one and half decades.

Modification of accounting objectives

The accounting objectives have been modified as a result of an expansion of the user groups of accounting information. Nowadays many interested groups other than government, such as investors, creditors and the public, have their stake in business entities in an economy with much diversified business ownership. These interested parties' information needs are not necessarily the same as that required by government. Thus modified accounting objectives were incorporated into the new national accounting system introduced in 1993 to take into account the information needs of these expanded groups of users. Accounting in China must now serve three information needs:

- to assist governments in pursuing macroeconomic management;
- to assist related (interested) parties in making investment and credit decisions; and
- to assist management in making operational decisions.

Accordingly, the formats of financial statements have been redesigned in terms of the general information needs of all users. The balance sheet and income statement have been redesigned much in line with the internationally accepted norm. Business entities are encouraged to provide statements of change in financial position or cash flow statements for external investors and creditors in particular.

The experiment of accounting regulation for foreign-affiliated enterprises

The *Accounting Regulation for Joint Ventures with Chinese and Foreign Investments* (ARFJV) was formulated and enforced in July 1985 as a response to the needs for accounting system by enterprises associated with foreign capital. The introduction of ARFJV is an important landmark in the development of Chinese accounting during the period of economic transition. The enforcement of this accounting regulation heralds the adoption of internationally accepted accounting practices in China. By incorporating the internationally accepted accounting principles to a great extent, the ARFJV has generated a very positive impact on improving accounting practices, for it has not only been applicable to joint ventures and foreign invested enterprises, but has also cast light on the redesign of accounting systems for other domestic enterprises. In particular, the ARFJV has served as one of the major references in the formulation of the *Accounting Regulation for Enterprises with Share Capital System* in 1992, and the new national accounting system, *Accounting Standards for Business Enterprises* (ASBE), in 1993.

The rise of managerial accounting

Managerial accounting originating in western countries has been introduced to China since the beginning of the 1980s. With increasing responsibility for profitability, business management showed a greater interest in cost management and profit planning. Demands for managerial accounting mounted during the mid-1980s. Research in managerial accounting or cost management gained momentum. The subject of managerial accounting was added to the curriculum of accounting programmes at colleges and universities. Foreign instructors were invited to deliver lectures on the development of managerial accounting. Western textbooks and literature on managerial accounting were translated into Chinese and disseminated widely within China.

Restoration of the auditing system

The auditing functions were re-emphasized in the early 1980s. Although the auditing system was suspended entirely in China in the early 1950s, the Chinese government decided to rebuild a system of 'state auditing supervision'. State audit offices have been installed in the central and local governments, to exercise supervision through audit over the national economy. In addition, non-governmental auditing, or public accounting, has been restored and expanded rapidly, to satisfy the demands for independent audit services from domestic and foreign investors, creditors and other users. In the last decade, the standardized practices for public accounting have been implemented and the accounting profession has emerged. With the introduction of entrance qualification examinations, annual performance review and renewal of certificates and licensing, professional ethics and continuing professional education, the quality of public practitioners and their performance have improved steadily in recent years.

Establishment of an accounting legal framework

A legal framework for accounting and auditing has been established in the country. The Chinese government has promulgated several accounting and auditing laws since the mid-1980s, such as *The Accounting Law of the People's Republic of China* (1985, 1993), *The CPA Law of the People's Republic of China* (1993) and *The Auditing Law of the People's Republic of China* (1994). A series of national accounting regulations governing foreign invested enterprises, listed corporations and governmental or other non-profit organizations have also been formulated and implemented. In addition, many other business laws have been enacted with legal provisions on accounting and auditing requirements.

Accounting internationalization

The drive towards internationalization of Chinese accounting is in full swing. To adopt the internationally accepted accounting practices and promote the internationalization of Chinese accounting has been one of the goals of accounting reforms in China since the early 1980s. Many accounting procedures or practices prevailing in market economies in the West have been gradually incorporated into Chinese accounting. Inventory revaluation, accrued accounting, revenue recognition, accelerated depreciation, intangible assets and goodwill, capital and investment, bad debt allowance, and so on, are just some of the examples. Accounting standards have been introduced in China, while the *Accounting Standards for Business Enterprises* was issued in late 1992 and came into effect on 1 July 1993. In addition, a set of practical accounting standards are under development and the first piece of the practical standards was officially issued in May 1997. This new set of Chinese accounting standards is fairly similar to the International Accounting Standards (IAS). As a result of the enforcement of the new accounting standards, the gap between Chinese accounting and its counterparts in the rest of the world has been significantly narrowed, and the understandardability of Chinese accounting information has been dramatically enhanced.

Setting auditing standards

Auditing standards have begun to be developed in recent years. The National Auditing Administration (NAA) started the process of developing auditing regulations and standards for government auditing in the late 1980s. A total of 38 pieces of governmental auditing standards and rules were compiled and released by the NAA in December 1996. On the other hand, the auditing standards and practical guidelines for public accounting have also been developed. The Ministry of Finance and the NAA approved and officially released two batches of *Chinese Independent Auditing Standards* (CIAS) in late 1995 and 1996. The 24 pieces of CIAS that have been released are fairly close to the 'Generally Accepted Auditing Standards' (GAAS) in the West and will greatly facilitate a standardization of public accounting practice in China.

Development of accounting computerization

Computerization of accounting has grown rapidly in recent years. As the development of computer technology in China is a relatively new phenomenon, the application of computers in business administration is at an early experimental stage. But application of computers in accounting has gained momentum since the beginning of the 1990s. Commercialized accounting software has been developed, as have the markets for accounting software. The Chinese accounting profession has realized the urgency and importance of accounting computerization. Government authorities in charge have exercised long-term planning for promoting the computerization of accounting in China. Numerous education and training programmes on computerization of accounting are currently available, on both a regular and a part-time basis. Computerized accounting systems have been adopted in increasing numbers of government units, NPOs and business enterprises across the country.

Enhancing accounting education and training

The Chinese government has increased input for accounting education and professional training, aiming at fostering qualified accounting personnel to meet the needs of accounting developments in the changing economic environment. Reform of accounting education has been undertaken. Accounting curricula and teaching methods have been updated in the light of accounting developments in practice. Higher education programmes in accounting, both undergraduate and graduate studies, have been expanded remarkably. Professional training programmes mushroomed as a result of the increasing demands for on-job training for accounting personnel. The certification system of accounting qualification was established by government authorities to set minimum requirements for those pursuing accounting work. National accounting qualification examinations have been held regularly since the early 1990s. Accounting personnel are encouraged to take continuing education or training programmes, as well as the accounting qualification examinations to upgrade their professional skills and competence.

Expanding professional exchanges abroad

In view of the growth of international economic cooperation and trade, the Chinese accounting profession has actively pursued exchange with regional and international accounting professional bodies. Mutual exchange programmes have been established between the Chinese accounting profession and its counterparts in many other countries. In particular, the Chinese accounting profession officially joined the Confederation of Asian–Pacific Accountants (CAPA), the International Federation of Accountants (IFAC) and the International Accounting Standards Committee (IASC) in 1996 and 1997. Expansion of international exchanges has been very beneficial for the Chinese accounting profession seeking access to the advanced accounting knowledge and experience of western countries and to facilitate the smooth progress of accounting reforms. At the same time, the exchanges with accounting professions abroad have promoted the advance of internationalization of Chinese accounting.

THE PERSPECTIVE OF FURTHER DEVELOPMENT

Chinese accounting and auditing have grown rapidly during the current course of economic transition within the country. Accounting and auditing systems suitable for the emerging partial market economy have been established. This progress has, however, been made through an evolutionary process. Reforms of Chinese accounting and auditing will continue, for the following reasons.

- The growth of accounting and auditing cannot depart from the particular state of economic development. China has moved from a centrally planned economy to a partial market economy, but the original structure of highly centralized business administration has not yet been abolished; the new accounting and auditing systems adopted in recent years may not be in full operation, or some newly introduced accounting procedures will not function well until there has been further growth of the market-based economy.
- Although the new accounting system has been enforced nationwide since 1993, a certain period of experimentation is deemed necessary to integrate the new accounting standards based on the International Accounting Standards with the accounting reality in China. Resistance to change may last for a while and an education process is needed to ensure the acceptance and proper adoption of the new accounting system in the real world.
- Improvement of accounting practice could not be achieved without qualified accounting personnel. Currently, accounting education and training is falling behind the process of accounting reform in China. A significant portion of the existing accounting personnel in China were trained under the traditional system of accounting which stemmed from the centralized economic and business administrative systems. It will take time to retrain a great mass of accounting personnel to ensure a full implementation of the new accounting and auditing system in China.

Accounting practices are shaped by the developments in particular economic, social and cultural systems. Chinese accounting and auditing will therefore move further into a state compatible with the market economy that will eventually appear in China. Although it is premature to depict the destination of Chinese accounting and auditing, the direction of its movement can be confidently predicted in light of the trend of recent developments. The next phase of reforms in Chinese accounting and auditing will mainly focus on the following areas.

Modification of the accounting regulatory system

Government is the primary user of accounting information so long as state ownership dominates the Chinese economy. Accounting and auditing will thus remain under governmental regulation or control for the foreseeable future. The mechanism of governmental accounting administration may, however, be altered to a certain extent. It seems that governmental authorities may reduce direct involvement in accounting administration while some semi-governmental agencies or the accounting profession itself will be entrusted with the responsibility for self-discipline over accounting affairs. The compulsory and industry-specific accounting regulations or rules will be gradually phased out. Business entities will be allowed to design their own accounting systems in accordance with the national accounting standards. Nevertheless, the success of such a reform depends upon whether governments at various levels are willing to relinquish the power of accounting administration, and upon finding ways effectively to reconcile the interests of government and other users of accounting information.

Enforcement of accounting standards

Formulation of accounting standards is important but enforcement of standards is much more crucial. How to implement effectively the newly formulated accounting standards is certainly an issue to be handled seriously over the current transition period. Besides the *Accounting Standards for Business Enterprises*, as mentioned earlier, about 30 pieces of transaction-based practical accounting standards will be issued by the Ministry of Finance in 1997 and beyond. Enforcement of accounting standards may, however, be problematic. Most accountants in China have been used to complying mechanically with the compulsory and detailed accounting regulations or rules. Unlike previous accounting regulations, the accounting standards provide only guidance on accounting transactions. Professional judgment is required to apply the standards. Training accounting personnel to exercise professional judgment in light of the accounting standards is certainly an arduous task facing the accounting profession in China. In addition, some non-compliance may appear in practice since the new set of accounting standards is less than compulsory, compared to the formal accounting regulations or rules. Proper mechanisms should be developed to deter and sanction non-compliance with accounting standards – this is another issue to be resolved in the course of accounting reforms in the near future.

Application of managerial accounting

Generally speaking, most of the recent developments in Chinese accounting are related to financial accounting and public accounting. Progress in managerial accounting has been less impressive so far. Although most of the basic concepts and procedures of managerial accounting and cost management have been widely introduced through accounting education and research, the application of managerial accounting in the real world is at present rare. One of the reasons for this situation may lie in the fact that the majority of state-owned enterprises have not become really independent business entities. There is a lack of incentive for business management to place sufficient emphasis on cost management and profit planning. Another reason is associated with the underdeveloped state of commodity and capital markets in China. Inventory purchase and product sales are subject to governmental control instead of market forces. The sources of capital and the instruments of business financing are insufficiently diversified or flexible at the moment. Many managerial accounting procedures, though very effective in the West, could not be applied successfully in the different economic, legal and cultural environment in China. Thus a formidable task facing Chinese managerial accountants is to study the possibility of adapting management accounting to the Chinese business environment. Initial efforts are currently under way. For example, some managerial accounting techniques, such as CVP (cost-volume-profit) analysis, standard costing, responsibility accounting and flexible budgeting, have been integrated with the traditional practices of business financial management in China. New procedures like 'fixed-norm costing', 'internal banking system' and 'team accounting' have been experimented. Thus managerial accounting with Chinese characteristics will emerge in the near future, as a powerful tool to assist business management to enhance operating efficiency and profitability.

Improvement of public accounting

Significant development can be seen in Chinese public accounting in the last decade. As mentioned earlier, the accounting profession has taken shape in China. Standardized procedures have been implemented for the certification of public accountants, the administration of accounting firms and the continuing professional education of public practitioners. However, much more work must be done to improve the quality of public accounting. For instance, an adequate mechanism must be developed to enforce effectively the newly-issued *Chinese Independent Auditing Standards* and professional ethics. Enhancing the independence of accounting firms or public practitioners by cutting off their ties, financial and personal, with governmental sponsors is another thorny issue to be solved. In addition, how to specify professional accountants' responsibilities or legal obligations towards clients and other users, as well as how to deal with practising risks and materiality criteria in public accounting, are just two examples of unsolved issues requiring immediate attention and action by the accounting profession in China. Further liberalization of public accounting services is another dimension of accounting reform that will be needed to satisfy the demands for an increasing integration of Chinese economy with the world markets.

Reform of governmental accounting

Relatively speaking, governmental accounting lags behind recent developments in other branches of accounting. At present, 'budgetary accounting' is a synonym of accounting for governments and non-profit organizations in China. In comparison with the practices in other countries, Chinese budgetary accounting maintains many distinct characteristics, derived from the centralized state fiscal or budgetary administration system rooted in a planned economy. The traditional pattern of budgetary administration has, however, become outmoded as a result of the reform of fiscal or budgetary systems aiming at a decentralization of economic administration by the central government. Reform of budgetary accounting is currently on the agenda of Chinese accounting reforms. The Chinese government has set a timetable for experimenting and expanding the reform of budgetary accounting before the year 2000. The proposed reform of budgetary accounting will have very positive implications in enhancing the effectiveness of spending in the public sector, as well as increasing the accountability of government at all levels. The significance of budgetary accounting reform cannot be underestimated in a country with an immense governmental share in the national economy.

In summary, remarkable changes have taken place in Chinese accounting and auditing in step with the progress of economic reforms initiated in the late 1970s. In particular, the new accounting and auditing models compatible with the emerging market-based economy have been established or under experiment since 1993. The gap between Chinese practices and those in most industrialized countries has been narrowed significantly in recent years. However, Chinese accounting and auditing remains in a transitional phase. Many newly introduced accounting and auditing reforms need additional time for fine-tuning and further reform measures will be introduced in the near future. Readers may gain more detailed insights into the development of Chinese accounting and auditing from the remaining chapters of this book.

ORGANIZATIONAL STRUCTURE OF THE BOOK

The content of this book is structured in a logically integrated order. Most areas of Chinese accounting and auditing will be covered in detail in the following chapters, aiming at delivering a complete picture of the current state of accounting and auditing developments in China. The book also presents an analytical elaboration of the potential accounting reforms that will appear in the foreseeable future. Both the transition and the development of Chinese accounting and auditing will be examined.

The system of accounting regulation in China is examined in Chapter 2. Detailed discussions are provided of the regulatory pattern of accounting administration, the governmental authorities in charge of accounting affairs, the statutory requirements governing the qualification, rights and obligations of accounting personnel, and accounting functions within particular regulatory systems. Comprehension of the accounting regulatory system in the past and present is a prerequisite for an understanding of the unique characteristics of Chinese accounting and auditing.

Chapter 3 presents an analysis of Chinese accounting standards. While the framework of accounting regulations and standards will be depicted, the focus of this chapter is upon the major accounting principles, assumptions and concepts outlined in the new accounting standards which have been introduced since 1993. Comparison with the US Generally Accepted Accounting Principles (GAAP) is provided in order to help western readers to gain a better understanding of the Chinese accounting standards.

Chapter 4 examines the development of securities markets and information disclosure. The regulatory system of emerging securities markets in China is elaborated in detail. The statutory requirements on information disclosure, including prospectuses and regular reporting for publicly listed companies, will be introduced. The statutory requirements regarding the obligations of financial reporting and auditing are also discussed in this chapter.

Current practices of cost accounting and managerial accounting in China are presented in Chapter 5. The basic principles and methods of product costing and cost management prevailing in China will be examined specifically. In addition, this chapter introduces the rise of managerial accounting in China, with a brief discussion of the functions and existing practices of managerial accounting in the Chinese business environment.

Auditing is usually classified into governmental auditing and non-governmental auditing (or public accounting). These two branches of auditing in China have gone through the periods of dismantlement, restoration and expansion since the birth of the People's Republic of China in 1949. Chapters 6 and 7 are devoted to an examination of Chinese governmental and non-governmental auditing respectively. The organizational structures, statutory requirements, components of the state audit supervision, responsibilities and rights of state auditing authorities and the audit procedures for government auditors are introduced in Chapter 6. Chapter 7 focuses on the development of public accounting and the accounting profession in China. Detailed elaboration is presented on the subjects of the regulatory system of public accounting, the qualification of certified public accountants (CPAs), the scope of public accounting services and the Chinese auditing standards and professional ethics for public practitioners.

In China, accounting is taxation-oriented, with the tax legislation and regulations having predominant influences on accounting measurements and disclosure. Chapter 8 introduces the Chinese taxation system and tax policies, especially the new tax system and the major taxes introduced by the tax reforms of 1994. Tax administration and the procedures required for filing tax returns are elaborated. In addition, the government's tax policies, including the proposed changes in the preferential tax incentives for foreign investors, are discussed in detail.

Accounting for governments and non-profit organizations is a major branch of accounting. The significance of governmental accounting in China is obvious in an economic system dominated by a state ownership and centralized budgetary control. Although there is no clear distinction between accounting for governments and accounting for non-profit organizations, so-called 'budgetary accounting', as an equivalent to them both, is in operation with some unique characteristics in the Chinese environment. Chapter 9 elaborates not only the basic features of budgetary accounting, but also the proposed reform of budgetary accounting that is currently under way.

With the fast expansion of computer technology in business administration since the 1980s, electronic data processing has been introduced in Chinese accounting and auditing. The computerization of accounting, although still at an early stage of development, has generated a very positive impact on the rapid growth of Chinese accounting and auditing. The subject of computerization of accounting is addressed in Chapter 10, with an examination of the four evolutionary stages of computerized accounting experimentation in China. The development of commercialized accounting software and the regulatory process for the adoption of computerized accounting systems are discussed specifically.

Accounting education is vital to promote a high standard of accounting practice. Chapter 11 focuses on the development of accounting education in China. In a country with enormous demands for accounting personnel, accounting education plays an important role in producing qualified accountants. Both the full-time and professional continuing accounting education programmes are examined. The structure of the accounting education system, the development of an accounting curriculum for full-time education, the components of professional continuing accounting education and the national accounting qualification programmes are among the subjects elaborated in the chapter.

Chapter 12 presents a brief introduction to the professional associations and the research in accounting and auditing in China. The major national professional associations, such as the Accounting Society of China (ASC), the Chinese Institute of Certified Public Accountants (CICPA), the Chinese Society of Auditing (CSA) and the Chinese Accounting Professors' Association (CAPA), are briefly introduced. Major academic and professional journals in accounting and auditing in China are also highlighted.

Accounting is a tool for doing business. Thus Chapter 13 is devoted to a general introduction to China's business legislation. The major features of the Chinese business and legal environment are outlined and a series of important business laws in China are briefly elaborated.

Some selected accounting and auditing legislation and regulations are presented in the Appendices, aimed at providing direct and detailed references for those readers who are interested in learning more about the statutory requirements governing accounting and auditing practice in China. At present most Chinese accounting and auditing regulations or standards are available only in the Chinese language, English versions are virtually unavailable in the West. The accounting and auditing regulations and standards in the Appendices have been translated into English and will be a source of informative references for western readers.

In summary, a fairly broad coverage of the current state of Chinese accounting and auditing is presented in this volume in the light of the changing economic and business environment in China. Although the authors have made considerable efforts to incorporate the most recent developments in Chinese accounting and auditing, readers should be reminded that Chinese accounting and auditing is still undergoing comprehensive reform. The reforms move ahead at a pace faster than is generally expected. Thus some of the Chinese accounting and auditing practices described in this book may be altered or replaced as a result of reforms in the future. The authors are committed to keeping under close and continuing observation the growth of accounting and auditing in China and to providing a revised or updated edition of this volume in the future when significant further changes have taken place.

NOTES

1 The State Bureau of Statistics, PRC (1996, 1997), *China Statistical Year Book* (in Chinese), Beijing.
2 See A. Enthoven (1991), 'Accounting Auditing and Education in People's Republic of China', in C. Nobes and R. Parker (eds), *Comparative International Accounting*, 3rd edn, Sydney: Prentice-Hall.
3 See M. Chatfield (1977), *A History of Accounting Thought*, Huntington, New York: Robert E. Krieger Publishing Co. Inc., and M.A. Hoepen (1995), 'Accounting in China', in J. Blake and S. Gao (eds), *Perspective on Accounting and Finance in China*, London: Routledge.
4 The stock markets were very volatile in China, with stock prices moving up and down radically. Since the numbers of the listed companies are relatively very small at present, most stocks listed on the Shanghai and Shenzhen stock exchanges were oversubscribed. The Chinese government has, however, tightened up regulation and monitoring of stock markets since 1996, aiming at cooling down the overheated stock markets and ensuring a healthy development of the stock company system in China.

2 Regulation of Accounting Affairs

In a country like China where a centrally administered economy is in place, governments exercise comprehensive and rigid planning and control over economic and social activities. Since accounting serves as an important tool for business communication and economic management, the central government has long been relying upon accounting to provide data for preparing the state fiscal budgets and other economic plans, as well as for monitoring and control of the execution of governments' fiscal budgets or plans. Thus accounting is highly regulated in China, where all accounting work and accounting personnel are subject to direct governmental regulation or administration.[1]

The structure of accounting administration in China is determined by the government's needs for exercising economic planning and control at the macro level. As remarkable changes have taken place in China's economy, resulting from the ambitious and comprehensive economic reforms since the late 1970s, the system of governmental regulation over accounting affairs has also been reformed correspondingly in recent years.

THE SYSTEM OF ACCOUNTING ADMINISTRATION

Unlike the situation in most western countries, accounting work in both governmental and business organizations is subject to rigid governmental control in China. Governmental accounting administration was installed immediately after the birth of the People's Republic of China in 1949. Even today, in a partial market economy where relatively diversified business ownership has been established, accounting work remains under direct governmental administration.

Systems of accounting administration in China refer to the institutional arrangements for the central government to regulate and control accounting work and accounting personnel. The main elements of governmental accounting administration include (1) formulating accounting regulations or standards; (2) regulating accounting work such as establishing accounting set-ups and staffing with qualified accounting personnel in individual government bodies, non-profit organizations (NPOs) and business enterprises; (3) monitoring accounting transactions and events encountered in practice; (4) regulating the responsibilities and rights of accounting personnel working in individual entities or organizations; and (5) sanctioning the performance or behaviours of accounting personnel. Thus governmental authorities are involved not only in setting regulations but also in performing direct administrative duties over accounting affairs in China.

Statutory requirements for governmental administration

The Accounting Law of the People's Republic of China (the Accounting Law, hereafter), which was originally enacted in January 1985 and amended in December 1993, states:

> The Ministry of Finance under the State Council is the authority for nationwide accounting regulation and administration while the finance departments at lower levels of government are responsible for the administration of accounting affairs within their own jurisdictions. (Article 5)

> The uniform national accounting regulations shall be stipulated by the Ministry of Finance in accordance with this Law. Finance departments of government in each province, autonomous region and municipality administered directly by the State Council, of the ministerial authorities under the State Council, and the General Logistic Department of the People's Liberation Army, may formulate supplementary regulations or rules to implement the uniform national accounting regulations applicable within their own jurisdictions. The supplementary regulations or rules shall not be in conflict with this Law and the uniform national accounting regulations. A consent of, and reporting to, the Ministry of Finance under the State Council is required for the issuance of any supplementary accounting regulations or rules. (Article 6)

Judging from the quoted statutory requirements, the finance departments (for example, finance bureaux) at different levels of government are authorized to regulate the accounting work within their own jurisdictions, while the Ministry of Finance maintains the supreme administrative authority over accounting affairs at national level. Such a system of accounting administration is labelled as 'unified leadership and segregated management by different levels', which represents a major characteristic of the regulatory system of Chinese accounting.

Figure 2.1 depicts the organizational structure of governmental authorities in charge of accounting affairs, within the legal framework specified by the Accounting Law.

The Department of Accounting Affairs

Within the system of governmental accounting administration, the Ministry of Finance of the central government is the key player. Actually the administration of accounting affairs nationwide is mainly conducted by the Department of Accounting Affairs (DAA), under the Ministry of Finance. The DAA, the Department of Accounting Systems before the 1980s, is empowered to take control of accounting regulation and administration in China. Its mandates include the following:

- to analyse policies governing the accounting administrative system, accounting regulations, qualification and accreditation of accounting personnel, and the rights and responsibilities of accounting personnel;
- to prepare, on behalf of the Ministry of Finance, the drafts of national legislation or regulations governing accounting affairs;
- to stipulate the national accounting regulations and standards;
- to coordinate the accounting administration among various governmental authorities in the central and local governments;
- to monitor the implementation of national accounting legislation and regulations, including interpretation of the related accounting legislation and regulations;
- to exercise supervision over accounting work performed in individual business enterprises;
- to formulate the general working rules for accounting personnel;
- to coordinate the education and training of accounting personnel;
- to administer national professional qualification examinations for accounting personnel; and
- to exercise supervision over professional accounting associations.[2]

Before the reform of the financial accounting system in 1993, the nationwide regulation of accounting affairs was mostly under the direct administration of the Ministry of Finance (through the DAA). But the finance departments of a few ministerial authorities in the central government were allowed to take a lead in regulating accounting work within their own jurisdictions, under delegation of authority from the Ministry of Finance. For example, a few industry-specific accounting regulations, such as national accounting systems for business entities in banking, merchandising,

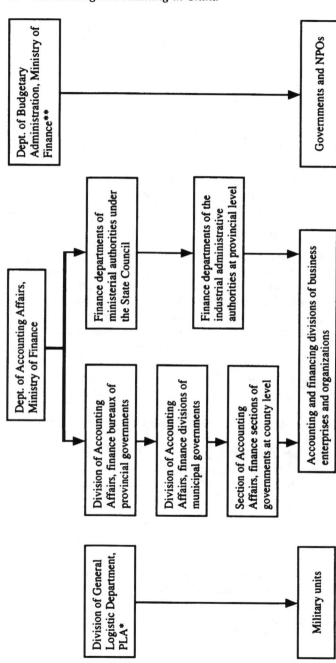

Figure 2.1   The system structure of accounting administration

Notes:

*   The accounting system for military units is administered by the General Logistic Department, People's Liberation Army, with delegation of authority from the Ministry of Finance.

**   Regulation of accounting for governments and non-profit organizations (NPOs) is run by the Department of Budgetary Administration, parallel to, but separated from the Department of Accounting Affairs, within the Ministry of Finance.

transport, railways, and so on were formulated jointly by the ministerial authorities overseeing those industries and the Ministry of Finance.[3] A very small number of highly specialized industrial accounting regulations were then formulated and enforced by the corresponding ministerial authorities exclusively.[4]

After the amendment of the Accounting Law, and particularly after the introduction of new national accounting systems in 1993, the Ministry of Finance had consolidated its statutory authority in regulating accounting affairs nationwide. In contrast, the involvement of other ministerial authorities and local governments in regulating accounting affairs has been relatively reduced. All uniform national accounting regulations, basic accounting principles and standards currently must be stipulated by the Ministry of Finance. Other governmental authorities could formulate only certain supplementary accounting rules or procedures for the purpose of implementing the national accounting regulations or standards.

It is too early to determine whether the new pattern of accounting regulation or administration will work effectively. A switch to a more centralized pattern of accounting regulation will enhance the uniformity of accounting work and promote comparability of accounting information across industry. But the centralized pattern itself may be a deviation from the course of decentralization-oriented economic reforms endorsed by the central government. Thus how to resolve potential conflict of interest among various levels of government involved in the accounting administration remains a knotty unsolved issue. A trade-off between uniformity of accounting procedures and decentralization of accounting administration is deemed necessary. Further changes will take place in restructuring the legal framework and the responsibility for accounting regulation and administration by governments at various levels; in particular, the mechanism of coordination between the Ministry of Finance and other governmental authorities must be worked out gradually.

The system of self-discipline by the accounting profession

Although Chinese accounting is currently under direct control of governments, some alternative patterns are under development. The existing structure of accounting administration may be altered substantially in step with the growth of market-based economic reforms in the future. An increasing number of Chinese accounting academics and practitioners have challenged the efficiency of direct governmental accounting administration, and lobbied actively for radical changes to the regulation or administration of accounting affairs.

Deficiencies of the existing administrative pattern

The existing system of governmental accounting administration has certainly enhanced the authority of governmental control over accounting work as well as the underlying business transactions in individual entities or organizations. It could have secured the government's needs for accounting and other data to serve economic planning and control. Two major deficiencies are, however, inherent within the existing framework of direct administration of accounting by government.

Firstly, governmental authorities could not exercise the administrative duties over accounting affairs in a fair or impartial manner. Governmental authorities in charge of accounting affairs, that is, the finance departments of the central and local governments, have not only become involved in the formulation and enforcement of accounting regulations and standards, but have also been engaged in performing certain accounting functions directly, such as preparation of governments' fiscal budgets and final accounts, as well as in administering the accreditation of professional qualifications for accounting personnel. Finance departments at different levels of government are actually performing the dual function of 'regulator' and 'executor' in accounting work. This dual status of government authorities would certainly impede their impartiality in accounting administration. For instance, government authorities in charge of accounting affairs might formulate or revise accounting regulations in terms of their own information needs and functional procedures, even at the expense of other interested parties. This would inevitably result in accounting regulations or standards biased towards governments' administrative needs, ignoring the management needs of individual economic entities and organizations.

Secondly, there is a severe shortage of manpower in government agencies in charge of accounting administration. According to government statistics, about 7000 staff were working for accounting administrative bodies within the finance departments at various levels of government across the country by the end of 1996. The total number of accounting personnel in China is, however, over 12 million. Governmental administrative agencies are overwhelmingly outnumbered in manpower by accounting personnel nationwide and thus can hardly exercise an effective administration of accounting affairs even though they intend to do so. In addition, a large proportion of staff in government agencies are lacking experience of actual accounting work because they joined government departments immediately after graduation from schools and obtained little training on accounting in the real world.[5] Inexperience of government staff could only worsen the inefficiency in governmental administration of accounting affairs.

The problems of governmental accounting administration have become more acute now that China is moving towards a market-based economy. Criticisms of direct administration of accounting affairs by government surfaced while demands for a substantial overhaul of accounting administration systems were heard continuously during the course of the comprehensive economic reforms. Reducing the government's direct involvement in accounting administration became a major theme in the Fourth National Conference on Accounting Affairs, held in Beijing in October 1995, under the auspices of the Ministry of Finance. The proposal of self-discipline by professional bodies instead of governmental accounting administration has gained considerable support.

The mechanism of professional self-discipline

According to the resolutions adopted at the Fourth National Conference on Accounting Affairs in late 1995, one of the major targets of accounting reform is to establish a functional system of self-discipline by the accounting profession within the governmental regulatory framework. A distinction has been made, however, between 'self-regulation' and 'self-discipline' in the Chinese literature. While the term 'self-regulation' is commonly used in western countries, it is irrelevant under Chinese circumstances where governments would not relinquish any authority over setting accounting regulations or standards. The proposed accounting reform aims to reduce the government's direct involvement in administering accounting affairs and to delegate the duties of supervision over accounting affairs to non-governmental accounting bodies. 'Self-discipline' may therefore be a better term to reflect the nature of the proposed changes in accounting administration in China.

Substantial reforms will be pursued to develop a new mechanism for effective professional supervision of accounting affairs. Professional bodies, instead of government authorities, would be entrusted with the responsibility for self-discipline of accounting work. The finance departments of governments will only play the role of regulator at the macro level instead of that of a direct administrator. The professional accounting bodies will represent accounting personnel in all economic entities and organizations across the country. Under delegation of authority from governments' finance departments, the professional accounting bodies should be able to exercise supervision over their members' performance based on the principle of 'self-discipline'.

Without doubt, changes in economic structures have resulted in much diversified business ownership and sources of funding for economic entities or organizations in China. It has become much more difficult for governments to exercise direct control of accounting affairs in recent years. Releasing governments from direct involvement in the administration of accounting affairs is consistent with the goals of economic reforms aiming at a decentralization of economic administration. In addition, the planned accounting reform towards professional self-discipline may also help to relax resource constraints facing the governmental administrative authorities in charge of accounting affairs.

The proposal is worthy of certain credits but the reform of governmental accounting administration remains at the planning stage at present. It is hard to predict when the proposed changes can be implemented. The main difficulty lies in the government's willingness to relinquish control of accounting affairs. Currently, there is no likelihood of the establishment of a mechanism of professional self-discipline in the foreseeable future. Its possibility, however, cannot be ruled out entirely so long as the process towards a market-based economy continues in China.

THE FRAMEWORK OF ACCOUNTING REGULATIONS

The Chinese government has established a legal framework to exercise rigid control over accounting affairs throughout the country. All accounting regulations and standards in China must be formulated by government authorities instead of by the accounting profession. Currently, multiple sources of accounting legislation and regulations are in place. They include the following.

1   The state laws governing accounting affairs, with nationwide enforceability, which have been enacted by the National People's Congress (NPC) or its Standing Committee.
2   The regulations on business financing and accounting affairs formulated by the State Council, such as *Regulations on the Responsibility and Rights of Accounting Personnel*, *Rules on Product Costing in Manufacturing Enterprises*, and so on.
3   The uniform accounting standards and industry-specific accounting regulations formulated and enforced by the Ministry of Finance.
4   Various regulations and rules issued by ministerial authorities of the central government, governing the implementation of related accounting legislation or regulations within individual ministerial jurisdictions.
5   Supplementary accounting regulations formulated by local governments.

Some of the major accounting legislation and regulations in China are briefly indicated below.

The Accounting Law

The Accounting Law of the People's Republic of China was enacted at the Ninth Council Meeting of the Standing Committee of the Sixth Plenary Section of NPC in January 1985. The law is the first state legislation governing accounting affairs in Chinese history. Six chapters are incorporated in the law under the headings of General provisions, Accounting calculation, Accounting supervision, Accounting set-ups and accounting personnel, Legal responsibility and Supplementary provisions. The law specifies the regulatory framework governing governmental administration of accounting, the requirements for the institutional arrangements and basic procedures of accounting work, the rights and obligations of accounting personnel, and so on. The Accounting Law came into effect on 1 May 1985. Amendment to the law was made officially in December 1993 at the Eighth Plenary Session of the NPC.

The introduction of the Accounting Law had a significant impact on the rapid development of Chinese accounting. In particular, the law has contributed to a restoration of order in accounting work after more than ten years of chaos resulting from the so called 'Cultural Revolution' before the 1980s. Other positive implications of this law for the growth of Chinese accounting during 1985–93 can be summarized as follows:

- it may lead to the establishment of a broad framework of accounting regulations. Several related national accounting regulations, such as the *Regulation for Certified Public Accountants* and the *Regulation for the Installation of Chief Accountants*, were formulated by the State Council and based on the Accounting Law;
- it may provide statutory support for the installation of the Grading Systems of Accounting Qualification, thus contributing to enhance the general quality or standard of accounting personnel;
- it may raise the social status of accounting and promote the involvement of accounting in economic and business management; and
- it may specify the statutory responsibility and rights of accounting personnel, thus enabling them to perform accounting duties effectively.

However, significant changes took place in the Chinese economy after the introduction of the Accounting Law in 1985. Growth of the market-based economy made the old pattern of accounting administration impracticable in respect of a changing business environment. In particular, some provisions of the Accounting Law have become outmoded during the current course of economic transition in China. For instance, the law was originally designed to fit the pattern of accounting administration with predominant state ownership of business enterprises. It became difficult to enforce the law in a much diversified economy with multiple forms of business owner-ship in the 1990s. In addition, the original version of the Accounting Law did not cover the areas of computerized accounting processing, public ac-counting and business consultations that have emerged in accounting prac-tice since the late 1980s.

The Accounting Law was therefore amended in early 1993. The amend-ment was certainly necessary owing to the changes in the economic and business environment. The amendment, however, amounts to piecemeal tinkering. Most of the original provisions in the law were left untouched, although there was a considerable demand for a thorough revamping of the law that was designed for the outmoded centrally planned economy. This may be due to the fact that the market-based economy remains under devel-opment in China and solutions to many emerging accounting issues cannot be fully developed at the moment. Another implicit reason, however, is that the Chinese government is not ready to abandon totally the central planning and control of the national economy. Thus a revamping of the Accounting Law has been deliberately postponed by the government until the market economy becomes healthier some time in the future.

The CPA Law

Following the restoration of public accounting in the earlier 1980s, the central government formulated a series of provisional regulations or rules to exercise control of public accounting practices. *The Regulation on Certified Public Accountants* was issued and enforced by the State Council in July 1986. The regulation played a very important role in promoting the resur-gence and expansion of public accounting in China. However, it was re-placed by a more authoritative legislation when *The Law of Certified Public Accountants of the People's Republic of China* (the CPA Law) was enacted by the Eighth Plenary Session of NPC in October 1993. The CPA Law came into effect on 1 January 1994.

The law contains seven chapters: General provisions, Examination and registration, Scope and rules of business operation, Public accounting (CPA) firms, Association of certified public accountants, Legal obligations and liabilities and Supplementary provisions. The law is designed to be a legal foundation for regulating public accounting practices. This topic will be revisited in Chapter 7, where the development of the public accounting profession in China will be discussed further.

Accounting standards for business enterprises

Traditionally, accounting practices in China were governed by mandatory accounting regulations formulated by the Ministry of Finance and a number of other ministerial authorities of the central government. These regulations, called 'accounting systems' in Chinese, were segregated by business ownership or they were industry-specific. For example, separate accounting regulations were designed for state-owned enterprises, publicly listed corporations and foreign invested enterprises, while variations among them were substantial. In addition, a variety of regulations were set out for different industries such as manufacturing, merchandising, transport, banking, capital construction, and so on.

There were over 50 subsets of industry-specific accounting regulations (accounting systems) in existence before 1993. These regulations specified very detailed procedures or methods for record keeping and financial reporting, including the uniform chart of accounts for general ledgers and sub-ledgers as well as the required format and line items of the financial statements to be prepared and submitted. There were, however, significant discrepancies among the 50-plus accounting regulations segregated by different types of industry and business ownership.[6]

In order to harmonize the various sets of accounting regulations and to facilitate the growth of a partial market economy, the Ministry of Finance decided to develop a new set of national accounting standards applicable to all business entities irrespective of business ownership or industry. Such a move was also motivated by an attempt to adopt the internationally accepted accounting practices in China. Compared with the situation in most western countries, developing accounting standards is a relatively new phenomenon in China. A Steering Committee on Accounting Standards was set up in the late 1980s, followed by the formation of a Working Group on Accounting Standards under the Ministry of Finance in 1988. After several years of preparation, the *Accounting Standards for Business Enterprises* was officially released by the Ministry of Finance in late 1992. The new standards came into effect on 1 July 1993.

The distinct differences between the new accounting standards and the traditional accounting regulations include the following.

1 The accounting standards are enforceable in all business entities instead of specified business ownership and industry, thus the standards will promote the comparability of accounting information across the country.
2 A balance of the information needed by government authorities and other users such as investors, creditors and management of business enterprises is made since leeway is left in the new accounting standards

for business entities to develop their own accounting systems in terms of the information needs of all users.

3   Most of the internationally accepted accounting conventions have been adopted in the new accounting standards as an effort to bridge the gap between Chinese accounting and its counterparts in most other industrialized countries.

Although the newly introduced *Accounting Standards for Business Enterprises* has a very broad coverage of accounting transactions, it specifies the basic principles governing accounting transactions in rather general terms. The standards provide general accounting guidance and are more like a conceptual framework for developing coherent and consistent practical accounting standards. Government authorities have also been working on setting more specific and transaction-based accounting standards since 1993, with financial support from the World Bank and technical support from the 'Big Six' international accounting firms.

According to the original planning, about 30 practical accounting standards will be developed within the framework set out by the *Accounting Standards for Business Enterprises*. The exposure drafts of these transaction-based accounting standards were all issued by the Ministry of Finance to solicit public comments in 1995 and 1996. The first piece of *Accounting Standards on Related Party Transactions* was officially released by the Ministry of Finance in May 1997 and the rest will be issued, piece by piece, in 1997 and thereafter. The standard-setting project is scheduled to be completed by the year 2000. The new set of accounting standards will be applied experimentally to publicly listed corporations first and eventually extended to all business entities across the country.[7]

General rules on financial affairs for business enterprises

Chinese accounting is taxation-oriented. The government has long been rigidly regulating financing transactions or expenditures of individual business enterprises. Business accounting is required to serve as a tool to carry out strictly the government's fiscal and business financing policies in order to facilitate tax assessment and levy by the government.

When the new set of national accounting standards was introduced in 1993, the Ministry of Finance also formulated and enforced a separate set of *General Rules on Financial Affairs for Business Enterprises*, accompanied by several industry-specific financial systems for business enterprises. The financing rules, unique in the Chinese business environment, contain detailed provisions governing the pattern of business financing, the elements of product costs, and the specified spending allowances for business expenses or expenditures. The main justification for these business financing rules is derived from the fact that the majority of business enterprises are state-owned and governments are directly involved in business financing and profit distribution. Business financing activities thus affect governments' tax revenues and redistribution of after-tax profits. The government has to regulate business financing activities directly as its interest is at stake.

In the Chinese business environment, the general financing rules have a predominant influence on accounting transactions. In general, accounting regulations or standards must be in conformity with the specifications laid down in the financing rules even though consistency with a sound accounting conceptual framework may have to be sacrificed.

Industry-specific accounting systems

When the *Accounting Standards for Business Enterprises* (ASBE) was introduced in 1993, the Ministry of Finance released another 13 industry-specific accounting regulations, based on the principles set out in the general accounting standards. These regulations, called 'accounting systems', cover the following: manufacturing enterprises, merchandising enterprises, post and communication enterprises, transport enterprises, banking and non-banking financial institutions, insurance companies, enterprises involved in foreign trade and economic cooperation, property and real estate development enterprises, capital construction and installation enterprises, the railway industry, the civil aviation industry, the tourist and catering industry and the agricultural (grains and foods) industry. The new regulations incorporate industrial characteristics and the requirements of standards to provide technical guidance for enterprises in major industries. All of these industry-specific accounting regulations are mandatory and enforced by the Ministry of Finance.

As discussed earlier, one major goal of Chinese accounting reform in recent years is to replace the varied sets of coexisting accounting regulations segregated by different types of business ownership or industry with a new set of transaction-based accounting standards. Readers may wonder what is the rationale of issuing the new industry-specific accounting regulations in 1993. Does the issuance of the new industrial accounting regulations represent a departure from the designated course of accounting reform currently under way in China? The answer may not be simple. One may have to obtain a better insight of the scheduled reform in setting accounting regulations in China. This topic will be discussed in the last section of this chapter.

Supplementary regulations and rules

Besides the Accounting Law, uniform business accounting and financing standards and industry-specific accounting and financing regulations (systems), there are numbers of accounting-related supplementary regulations, rules, circulars and interpretations issued by various governmental authorities in charge of accounting affairs. Supplementary regulations or rules are an integral part of the accounting regulations in China. They are issued to facilitate the enforcement of national accounting legislation and regulations, or to serve as supplementary guidance for new accounting issues which emerge in practice. Most of the supplementary accounting regulations and rules are industry-specific, aimed at special transactions for which no official accounting regulations or standards are available. The supplementary regulations and rules are usually short-term in nature and will be altered or rescinded frequently, depending upon changes in business and accounting practices.

QUALIFICATIONS AND OBLIGATIONS OF ACCOUNTING PERSONNEL

In a highly regulated accounting environment, accounting personnel are controlled directly by government. Hence the qualification, professional grades or ranks, as well as the rights and obligations of accounting personnel in various business entities and non-business organizations are subject to specific regulations formulated and enforced by governmental authorities in charge of accounting affairs.

Qualifications of accounting personnel

The term 'accountant' was used in a very broad sense before the 1980s, to refer to all persons engaging in accounting work in individual governmental entities, NPOs and business enterprises. Thanks to the immense size of the Chinese economy, the number of accounting personnel is now over 12 million in China. However, a substantial portion of the existing accounting personnel lack formal accounting training because of severe resource constraints in accounting education and training facilities. A large number of accounting personnel, in fact, could not satisfactorily perform duties beyond simple bookkeeping.

The Chinese government introduced a nationwide grading system of accounting qualifications in the mid-1980s.[8] The primary purpose was to enforce a continuing professional education for accounting personnel working for governments, non-profit organizations and state-owned enterprises. Accounting personnel are graded with different professional titles to reflect varied levels of accounting qualification. Accounting staff are therefore required to obtain the certificates of specified professional titles before they can pursue accounting jobs corresponding to their certified qualification. Under the existing rules, no one can hold an accounting post in governments, NPOs and state-owned business enterprises unless he or she has obtained a certificate of accounting qualification issued by governmental authorities in charge of accounting affairs.

The grading system of accounting qualifications is jointly administered by the Ministry of Finance and the Ministry of Labour and Personnel Affairs under the State Council. Four grades of accounting title or rank are designated: accounting clerk, assistant accountant, accountant and senior accountant.

Accounting clerk

This professional title refers to accounting personnel who possess basic accounting knowledge (bookkeeping, in particular) through prevocational schooling and have at least one year of accounting or related job experience. The title of accounting clerk is the minimum qualification grade required for holding an accounting post for governments, non-profit organizations and state-owned enterprises. Accounting clerks will usually be assigned the jobs dealing with cash receiving and disbursement, bookkeeping and other simple accounting functions.

Assistant accountant

This professional title is granted to accounting personnel with a certain level of accounting education and skills, including formal accounting education and training at universities or colleges. They should have at least two to three years of work experience in accounting or financing. Assistant accountant is defined as the junior grade of accounting qualification. Accounting personnel at this level should be able to perform, under a superior's instruction, certain accounting assignments independently.

Accountant

Accounting personnel who possess relatively broad accounting knowledge and substantial work experience in accounting and financing assignments will be graded as 'accountant'. This professional title is an intermediate level of qualification grading for accountants. Accounting personnel with the certificate at this rank should be able to handle most accounting assignments independently and proficiently.

Senior accountant

The title of senior accountant refers to accounting personnel having fairly proficient accounting knowledge and a sufficiently long period of work experience. Senior accountants are usually the persons in charge of accounting or financing departments in large or medium-sized government departments, agencies, non-profit organizations or state-owned enterprises. Senior accountants should have the ability to make policy decisions in relation to accounting and financing affairs.

The professional accounting titles, except for senior accountant, could be obtained by passing the accounting qualification examinations administered by the Ministry of Finance,[9] and by an assessment of performance undertaken by accounting administrative authorities of the central or provincial governments. The national examinations of accounting qualification, with two separate series for 'accounting clerk' and 'accountant', have been held once a year since 1992. Five subjects are usually covered in the examinations, while a few subjects can be replaced by recognized course credits from accounting programmes at colleges or universities. Besides sitting the grading examinations, work experience is another important requisite. The minimum number of years of work experience in accounting, financing and related jobs required for accounting clerks, assistant accountants, accountants and senior accountants are about one, three, five and eight, respectively. Additional requirements such as maintaining personal integrity and obeying related governmental regulations and professional ethics must also be satisfied for the qualification grading.

With the total number of accounting personnel at over 12 million, the accounting qualification examinations have been well received in China. Besides the qualification requirements for accounting jobs,[10] substantial personal benefits such as promotion, increased salaries or wages, housing and other fringe benefits are directly tied to the grades of accounting qualification or the professional ranking received by individual accounting personnel. Thus registration for annual accounting qualification examinations is overwhelming. Many accounting personnel have made great efforts, by taking various vocational education and on-job training programmes, to prepare for the examinations. The qualification examinations, without doubt, have contributed positively to enhancing the professional standard and quality of accounting personnel in China.

Organization of accounting work

The Accounting Law requires all economic entities, whether of governments, social agencies, non-profit organizations or business enterprises, to install accounting set-ups or subunits. Full-time accounting personnel must be employed to keep proper accounts and financial reporting. Although small economic entities may rely upon professional bookkeeping or accounting services offered by public practitioners for cost-effective reasons, they must also designate one or two employees to deal with daily accounting and financing transactions.

The post of chief accountant must be introduced in large and medium-sized governmental organizations, institutions and enterprises, according to the Accounting Law and existing government regulations. Chief accountants are appointed from those qualified as accountants or senior accountants and must be in charge of all activities relating to accounting and financing transactions within an individual entity or organization. Government regulations specify that chief accountants should be members of senior management teams. The chief accountant must exercise economic supervision over the effectiveness and efficiency of operations, as well as the compliance with governments' financing and accounting regulations within individual entities and organizations.

A mechanism of internal control is generally required within accounting set-ups. In particular, division of responsibility amongst accounting staff must be maintained. For example, the *Working Rules for Accounting Personnel*, issued by the Ministry of Finance, specifies that the person handling cash receipts and disbursement be not allowed to deal with record keeping and transaction documentation.

Responsibilities and rights of accounting personnel

In China, the accounting set-ups or accounting personnel within individual entities and organizations are bound to serve the interest of the state and specific government authorities in charge. The Accounting Law specifies the statutory responsibilities and rights for accounting personnel as the following.

1 To exercise accounting supervision over operational activities within individual entities or organizations, in respect of compliance with related legislation and government's financing and accounting regulations.
2 To keep accounts and handle accounting transactions, and to secure the legitimacy, truthfulness and adequacy of books of account and other data.

3 To design accounting systems and procedures suitable to the conditions of corresponding entities or organizations.
4 To participate in the preparation of internal economic plans and operational budgets.
5 To monitor the implementation of operating budgets and analysis of financial performance.
6 To deal with other accounting issues or events, as required by government administrative authorities.

Clearly, accounting personnel have been entrusted with the responsibility for safeguarding the interest of the state in addition to keeping proper books of account. The Accounting Law and related government regulations have also specified the statutory rights for accounting personnel to carry out their statutory responsibilities. Accounting personnel are under the protection of government authorities in charge of accounting affairs. For example, consent of the overseeing authorities is required for the appointment and dismissal of the head of accounting set-ups within the state-owned enterprises and other organizations. Individual entities and organizations have only limited discretion in removing or dismissing accounting personnel. Government authorities in charge will investigate any complaints made by accounting personnel regarding irregularities incurred in individual entities or organizations. Mistreatments of accounting personnel in individual entities or organizations may be prevented or remedied through direct intervention of governmental accounting administrative authorities.

Obligations of accounting personnel

As mentioned earlier, accounting personnel are required to perform accounting supervision over operational activities, and to secure the legitimacy, truthfulness, accuracy and completeness of accounting information generated. Under the umbrella of governmental authorities, accounting personnel in China enjoy a much broader power than their counterparts in other countries. However, Chinese accounting personnel have to shoulder greater obligations in respect of the broader scope of power they can exercise.

The Accounting Law states that accounting personnel be liable for any violations of the required accounting regulations and rules.

1 Accounting personnel are subject to disciplinary actions enforced by various government authorities such as public finance, auditing, taxation and other overseeing authorities, in cases of forging, erasing or altering

books of account and supporting documents, of issuing misleading accounting reports and statements, or of committing tax evasion.

2 Disciplinary procedures will also be launched against accounting personnel for any of the following acts of misconduct:

- preparing accounting records based on illegal or fake transaction documents such as invoices, receipts, transaction orders, and so on;
- failing to submit written reports to top executives about unlawful revenues and expenditures incurred in the entities;
- failure to report to the overseeing authority at a higher level, or governmental authorities in charge of public finance, taxation and auditing, any revenues and expenditures incurred that have caused serious damage to the interest of the state or to the general public.

Besides the disciplinary actions enforced by governmental authorities, serious offenders may also be subject to criminal liabilities.

The dilemma of dual obligation

Within China's accounting administration system, accounting personnel are actually obligated to pursue two major duties, accounting and supervision, simultaneously: *accounting* to perform accounting functions within individual entities or organizations, including keeping records, recognition and measurement, preparing and analysis of financial statements; *supervision* to exercise internal supervision, on behalf of government authorities, over the legitimacy, truthfulness and adequacy of economic transactions or accounting events incurred, and the compliance with government financial and accounting regulations in individual entities and organisations.

This obligation of economic supervision for accounting personnel is unique to China. As discussed at the beginning of this chapter, government authorities intended to exercise overall control of all economic and business activities under a centralized planned economy. Accounting was regulated to serve directly the government's economic planning and control. Thus accounting personnel were treated as the agents of the state within individual economic entities or organizations. They were required to exercise a supervisory function on behalf of the government authorities in charge. The supervision function did work, to a certain extent, in the original highly centralized economy. As the government controlled virtually every aspect of business administration, including the appointment, promotion or sanction, and dismissal of the management and accounting personnel of individual economic entities and organizations, accounting personnel might opt for fulfilling the statutory duty of accounting supervision. However, this obligation has become much more difficult, if not impossible, to perform in the current course of economic reform towards a market-oriented economy. With a diversified business ownership and decentralization in economic administration, the government's direct control over individual entities or organizations has been significantly eroded. Accounting personnel would now encounter much more difficulty in exercising the supervision function, while the management of individual entities and organizations has gained increasing autonomy in decision making (including the power of control of their accounting set-ups). Accounting personnel are caught in the middle whenever there is a conflict of interest between government authorities and individual entities or organizations, since their job security and personal benefits are more directly determined by management of the entities or organizations to which they belong. As a result, accounting personnel are unable to carry out effectively the supervision function, even though they are required to do so.

This dilemma of dual obligation for accounting personnel has been recognized by government authorities as well. This may be a contributing factor to the central government's decision to restore the system of state audit supervision in the early 1980s. However, owing to a severe shortage of government auditing resources, accounting personnel in China remain obligated to carry out the statutory duty of supervision at present. The solution to this dilemma may have to rely upon the development of governmental or non-governmental auditing, where the independent external auditors would exercise a much more rigid audit supervision over operating activities of individual entities or organizations. The topics of governmental and non-governmental auditing will be discussed in further detail in Chapters 6 and 7, respectively.

REFORM OF SETTING ACCOUNTING REGULATIONS

There were two schools of thought regarding the reform of setting accounting regulations or standards in China in the late 1980s. Some people promoted a radical approach to completely revamp the traditional process of setting accounting regulations. They contended that the existing practice of setting accounting regulations by industry and business ownership must be terminated as soon as the new national accounting standards are introduced. Their main arguments are as follows.

1   The industry-specific accounting regulations, with specified format and content of accounting procedures, are designed to facilitate the use of accounting information by governments, even at the expense of management needs of individual business entities and other external users.

2 Those accounting regulations were too detailed and too rigid in regulating accounting procedures to be applied in practice. Overemphasis of uniformity makes it very difficult for business accounting to adapt to a changing environment in a market-oriented economy.

3 The accounting standards containing guidelines for processing individual accounting transactions such as asset valuation, revenue recognition and income determination, following the internationally accepted practices, should be adopted to promote the internationalization of Chinese accounting.

On the other hand, some people, in particular governmental accounting administrative agencies, argued that the industry-specific accounting regulations should not be terminated for at least the foreseeable future, even though the new set of national accounting standards based on individual transactions will be implemented as well. Their major contentions include the following.

1 The traditional pattern of setting accounting regulations has been in place for over 40 years. Government administrative agencies and accounting personnel in individual enterprises and other organizations have become used to it. Changes need to be implemented over time.

2 The transaction-based accounting standards alone may not be in the best interest of governments. In particular, governments remain the major owner of business enterprises and the primary users of accounting information even in a partially developed market economy. A great volume of accounting and related data useful for governments' economic planning and control could be easily obtained through the detailed accounting regulations segregated by business ownership and industry.

3 A significant portion of accounting personnel in business enterprises and other organizations are short of regular accounting education and training. They are unable to deal with accounting transactions stemming from a market economy and cannot make adequate professional judgment in processing accounting transactions. The detailed and industry-specific regulations or rules are much more practicable for the majority of accounting personnel.

4 The transaction-based accounting standards are guidelines for accounting processes. Individual business entities may be short of the capacity to design appropriate internal accounting systems to implement adequately the national accounting standards.

The debates between the two schools of reform strategy were keen and enduring. Government authorities in charge of accounting administration have, however, endorsed the latter view of accounting reforms. A major concern underlying this decision is that various government authorities are reluctant to relinquish their administrative power over accounting affairs. Through formulating and enforcing industry-specific accounting regulations or rules, government authorities may exercise significant influence over the operations of business entities and organizations under their jurisdictions. As a result, the reform of setting accounting regulations has to be a two-phase process, although a new set of national accounting standards are poised to replace the industry-specific accounting regulations.

Phase I: a dual system of accounting regulations (since 1993)

The enforcement of the ASBE and the *General Rules on Financial Affairs for Business Enterprises* in 1993 represents a significant first step towards the goals of the scheduled accounting reform. Most of the internationally accepted accounting principles that are incorporated in the new accounting standards will be applied universally to all business entities across the country. However, 13 industry-specific accounting and financing regulations reformulated by the Ministry of Finance were enforced simultaneously. Thus accounting standards and industry-specific accounting regulations (systems) will be coexistent over a transitional period. Figure 2.2 demonstrates the relationship between the accounting standards and the industry-specific accounting regulations.

Although the industry-specific accounting regulations are maintained during the transitional period, several notable differences can be identified in comparison with the traditional pattern of accounting regulations existing before 1993. First, the total number of the industry-specific accounting regulations has been reduced from over 50 to 13 – a considerable reduction. The reduced number of compulsory industry-specific accounting regulations are much easier to administer.

Second, all of the new industry-specific accounting regulations were exclusively developed by the Ministry of Finance in terms of the ASBE and the *General Rules on Financial Affairs for Business Enterprises*. Thus the accounting principles or the format of financial statements adopted in the 13 sets of industry-specific accounting systems are derived from the same sources. The discrepancies which existed in previous accounting regulations developed by the various governmental authorities (including the Ministry of Finance and other ministerial authorities of the central government) have been reduced significantly.

Third, new industrial accounting regulations have incorporated internationally accepted accounting principles to a great extent, and will lead to an

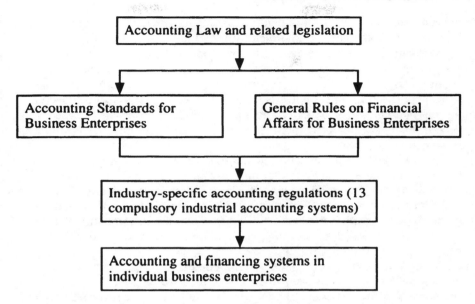

Figure 2.2   Reform of setting accounting regulations (phase I)

enhanced compatibility of Chinese accounting with its counterparts in most other industrialized countries. Finally, the new accounting standards and industry-specific accounting regulations have taken into account, to a certain extent, the accounting information needs of management at a micro level and of other non-governmental users. Individual business entities are actually allowed to make certain adaptations in terms of their own business conditions or management needs.

Phase II: domination of transaction-based accounting standards

It is not difficult to identify the deficiencies under the dual system of accounting regulations installed in 1993, although the system has made significant improvements in comparison with its prior counterparts. For example, conglomerates with operations in various lines of business have increased significantly in the Chinese economy as a result of the growth of a market-based economy and industrial restructuring in recent years. Demarcation between different lines of business is blurred for many business enterprises. In addition, business ownership has become much more intricate. Various sources of funding are available for many enterprises, and non-government sources of capital in particular have expanded considerably. The pattern of accounting administration by industry is now out of fashion. Accountants in many business entities will have difficulty in deciding which set of the industry-specific accounting regulations to apply. Worst of all, business entities may have to prepare multiple sets of accounting statements in respect of compliance with these compulsory industry-specific accounting regulations. This may cause, not only redundancy or waste in processing accounting data, but also inconsistency or incomparability of accounting information generated.

Furthermore, so long as the industry-specific accounting regulations continue in existence, many accounting personnel may opt for following the compulsory and detailed accounting procedures mechanically. This will definitely prevent accounting personnel from exercising professional judgment upon accounting transactions, and so make the full implementation of the transaction-based accounting standards much more difficult, if not impossible, in the future.

The current dual-system model, without doubt, is only an expedient measure adopted in the transitional period because the new set of accounting standards will be developed and enforced, piece by piece, over time. The industry-specific accounting regulations could therefore fill the gap. However, the compulsory industry-specific accounting regulations will be abandoned in phase II of the scheduled reform of setting accounting regulations, although it is premature to predict when the transitional period will end.

The blueprint for phase II of the accounting reform is highlighted in Figure 2.3. The transaction-based accounting standards will prevail in the second stage of the scheduled reform. In contrast to Figure 2.2, some notable differences can be identified in Figure 2.3. First, two tiers of accounting standards will be in place: general standards and practical standards. General standards are the foundation for setting practical standards, while development of detailed practical standards should be based on the basic principles or guidelines specified in the general standards. The practical accounting standards to be developed can be grouped into four categories as follows:

1   Practical standards applicable to accounting transactions irrespective of the types of industry or business ownership, such as standards on accounting for depreciation, inventory valuation, revenue recognition, and so on.
2   Practical standards applicable to special industries, for example, accounting standards for agricultural operations or capital construction projects that have a relatively long business cycle, so that monthly income determination is usually unfeasible.[11]
3   Practical accounting standards for specialized business operations or

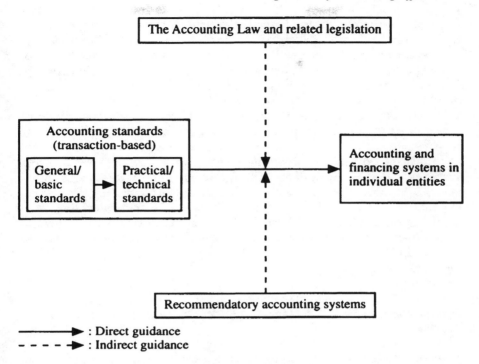

Figure 2.3　Reform of setting accounting regulations (phase II)

transactions such as foreign exchange, leasing, joint ventures, business combination and consolidation of financial statements, and so on.
4　Practical standards governing the format and content of the required financial statements and related disclosure.

Secondly, individual business entities will be allowed to set out their own accounting systems. The design of accounting systems by individual business entities must be in accordance with the national accounting standards and related business legislation or regulations, for instance, the Enterprises Law, Company Law, Taxation Law, Rules on Securities Exchanges and Detailed Rules on Information Disclosure of Publicly Listed Corporations, and so on. Business entities may hire public accountants or business consultants to design accounting systems, so long as the accounting standards and related regulations are applied.

The government authorities may continue to formulate a few industry-specific accounting systems for the purpose of facilitating accounting administration at the macro level. However, a substantial change will be made from the former pattern of accounting regulations. The industry-specific accounting systems will be very limited in numbers and no longer be compulsory regulations. They will merely be recommendations. Adoption or adaptation of these recommendations will be at the discretion of individual business entities or other organizations.

Thirdly, the general financing rules and industry-specific financing systems will be rescinded. Business enterprises will gain autonomy in setting their own financial management systems. This change, however, does not mean that the government would no longer exercise control over business financing activities. How, then, will government authorities be able to ensure that business financing activities are consistent with the state's fiscal and taxation policies? The fundamental issue is actually deciding what should be the guidelines for business financial management when governmental financing rules cease operation. To answer this question, we have to analyse the influence of the compulsory financing rules on Chinese accounting in further detail.

The relationship between general financing rules and accounting standards

Readers outside China may well be puzzled about the incorporation of the general financing rules in the current framework of Chinese accounting regulations. Although accounting standards are common to most countries, almost no counterparts of the compulsory business financing standards can be found in other countries. Thus the rationale behind the general financing rules in the Chinese environment is worthy of further exploration.

Business financing activities should follow certain statutory requirements. In most western countries, the requirements governing business financing activities are usually laid down indirectly through a framework of business legislation. For example, quite specific provisions governing business financial activities such as the sources, means, terms and settlement of business financing or borrowing are incorporated in commerce law, company acts, securities laws, tax legislation, and so on. Business entities are bound to comply with those requirements. In addition, private ownership is dominant in free-market economies. Most business financing and investing decisions are made directly by individual enterprises. A separate set of compulsory governmental financing rules is therefore deemed unnecessary.

The situation is rather different in China. Most business entities are currently government-funded as private ownership accounts for only a very small fraction of the Chinese economy. Financing activities incurred in individual business enterprises have had to be strictly regulated to protect the interest of government. In addition, the business legal framework is still under development in China. A few main elements of business legislation such as securities law and company law have not been enacted or fully implemented. Thus a separate set of compulsory general rules for business financing has been enforced by the central government at present. This determines the coexistence of accounting standards and business financing rules during the first phase of the accounting reform.

The relationship between accounting standards and business financing rules is, however, rather complicated. Under the traditional system of business administration, accounting practices had long been heavily influenced by governments' fiscal and taxation policies. Thus the general rules on business financing may not only dominate but also override the provisions in accounting standards.

The general rules on business financing will, however, lose their relevance when China's business legal system is in full operation. Up to the end of 1996, the Chinese government had enacted or redrawn a series of business legislation, including the company law and new taxation laws. The legislative processing of the security law is now near completion.[12] Once the new legal framework is in place, business entities will eventually be allowed to set up their own financing policies and financial management systems in light of the related business legislation. Then the compulsory set of general rules on business financing will become redundant and will be phased out accordingly.

In summary, a set of transaction-based accounting standards, very similar to the practice in most industrialized countries, will dominate in Chinese accounting as a result of accounting reform. The current situation, with the coexistence of accounting standards, industry-specific accounting and business financing rules, will be ended once the transaction-based accounting standards are in full operation. However, it may take time to reach that stage.

NOTES

1 In China accounting is not only regulated by the government, but is also subject to direct administration by governmental authorities. Organization of accounting work, and appointment and discipline of accounting personnel working in various entities or organizations across the country, are under the administration of governmental authorities.

2 According to the related government regulations, the national accounting associations such as the Accounting Society of China (ASC) and industry-specific accounting associations are subject to the DAA's regulation or supervision.

3　One of the reasons allowing certain industry-specific administrative authorities in the central government to take the lead in accounting administration within their own jurisdictions is due to the regulatory pattern inherited from the practice before the founding of the People's Republic of China in 1949. Certain governmental authorities have historically been involved in the formulation of industry-specific accounting systems in China.

4　A delegation of authority from the Ministry of Finance should be obtained in these cases.

5　Under the old education system in China, post-secondary education is a privilege rather than a right for Chinese people. Only a very small proportion of high school graduates could be enrolled to study at institutions of higher learning free of charge. In addition, the government guarantees and assigns jobs for college graduates. A great majority of government employees joined their work units through a process of 'graduation assignments' and stayed in the same jobs until their retirement.

6　Various requirements were incorporated in individual accounting regulations to serve the specific administration needs of government authorities. Thus inconsistency among these segregated accounting regulations is substantial.

7　See the speech by Zhang Youcai, deputy minister, the Ministry of Finance, at the International Conference on Chinese Economic Reforms and Liberalization of Chinese Accounting Services, 25 April 1997, in Beijing.

8　This professional qualification programme is run independently from the certification programme for certified public accountants (CPA) which will be discussed in Chapter 7.

9　The accounting qualification examinations are different from the national qualification examinations for certified public accountants. Higher standards are required for the latter qualification examinations.

10　A grading system of qualification was introduced by government authorities in charge of accounting affairs. A Certificate of Accounting Qualification, specifying varied ranks or professional titles, will be issued to accounting personnel who have satisfied the qualification requirements. Certificates of accounting qualification are the prerequisite for holding accounting posts in individual business enterprises and other organizations in China.

11　In China, most financial reports are required by government authorities on a monthly basis, although a yearly accounting period is set in the general accounting standards.

12　Several drafts of the securities law have been issued for public comments in the last couple of years. It is widely expected that the securities law will soon be enacted and enforced in China.

3   Accounting Standards

To a great extent, the accounting system in any country is determined by its own economy. In the past 20 years, China has shifted dramatically from a centrally planned economy to a partial market economy. Stock markets were re-established in Shanghai and Shenzhen; commercial banking was revitalized; foreign direct investment was encouraged, and so on. Reform was, however, hobbled by an obsolete and inappropriate accounting system inherited from the Russians. Consequently, the Ministry of Finance responded by proposing an accounting reform. This accounting reform is a historic and significant milestone in Chinese accounting development. The reform changes the Chinese accounting model dramatically in order to accommodate the demands for accounting work suitable to the growth of a market-based economy, or the so called 'socialist market economy'. As a result, the present accounting system centred upon a set of accounting standards adopted since 1993 in China is completely new compared to the one used in the past.

ACCOUNTING STANDARDS AND THE ACCOUNTING REGULATION SYSTEM

In China, the term 'accounting system' has long been used to represent government regulations on accounting work, or a set of regulatory rules governing accounting recognition, measurement, recording and reporting. As mentioned in Chapter 2, the Chinese accounting system consisted of many industry-specific accounting regulations formulated by the administrative authorities of the central government, which served as a major tool to implement the government's specific economic policies and financial control over economic activities. These accounting regulations were set by type of industry and business ownership. They were very detailed and mandatory accounting rules, with emphasis upon the government's needs for accounting information for a great variety of administrative purposes. Accordingly, accounting regulations were heavily influenced by government policies and administrative concerns.

In the mid-1980s, a piece of state legislation was added to the accounting regulation system. *The Accounting Law of The People's Republic of China* (the Accounting Law, hereafter) was enacted on 21 January 1985 at the Ninth Session of the Standing Committee of the Sixth National People's Congress and was promulgated for implementation on 1 May 1985. The Accounting Law, amended in 1993, comprises six chapters and 31 articles and has become a legal foundation of governmental regulations on accounting work in China. In the late 1980s, proposals appeared in Chinese accounting communities that another form of accounting regulation, that is, accounting standards should be developed. The rationale in support of accounting standards includes the following points.

1   A uniform set of accounting standards would promote the comparability of accounting information as the standards can be universally applicable within China irrespective of industry and business ownership, and thus enhance the comparability of accounting information generated in all entities.
2   Accounting standards developed from fundamental theories and principles of accounting will make it possible to set coherent guidelines for accounting transactions and to overcome the problem of greatly diversified rules in the accounting regulations set by different ministerial authorities in terms of varied administrative concerns.
3   Setting accounting standards, instead of accounting regulations, is a common practice in most countries. Establishing Chinese accounting standards will help to promote international harmonization of accounting.
4   Application of accounting standards that are consistent with internationally accepted practice would facilitate foreign investors' understanding of Chinese accounting, and thus could boost the inflows of foreign capital and domestic economic growth.

In response, the Ministry of Finance decided to develop Chinese accounting standards in the late 1980s. A special study group on accounting standards was formed, and a considerable input of resources was made, including financial support from the World Bank and technical support from international accounting firms. By the end of 1992, the *Accounting Standards for Business Enterprises* (ASBE) were officially promulgated by the Ministry of Finance and became effective on 1 July 1993. The implementation of ASBE earmarked a thorough reform of accounting system in China. The traditional accounting model rooted in the centrally planned economy has been replaced by accounting practices compatible with the development of a market-based economy in China and of international accounting harmonization.

All the industry-specific accounting regulations established before 1992 ceased to be operational when the ASBE was implemented. However, the Ministry of Finance formulated a new set of industry-oriented accounting systems at the same time that the ASBE was pronounced. According to the requirements of ASBE, coupled with different characteristics and management needs of business, various enterprises are grouped into several individual lines of business. In all, 13 national industrial accounting systems were also enforced on 1 January 1993 (see p. 35). Thus the current system of accounting regulations in China is mainly composed of three parts: the Accounting Law, accounting standards and industrial accounting systems. The structure of the existing Chinese accounting system is shown in Figure 3.1.

The Accounting Law provides principal guidance on all accounting work performed within China, including the accounting administrative system, organization of accounting work, basic accounting functions and principles, responsibilities and obligations of accounting personnel, and so on. The law has the highest level of authority in the hierarchical structure of Chinese

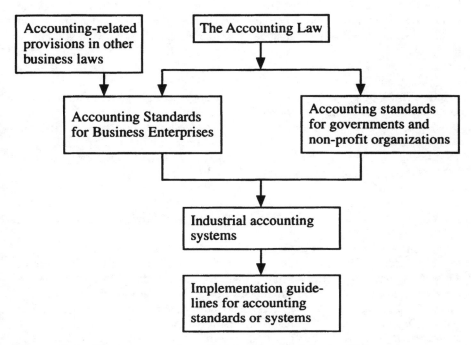

Figure 3.1   The system of accounting regulations in China

accounting regulations and represents the overriding regulatory authority for accounting. All other accounting regulations and standards must meet the requirements of the Accounting Law.

Accounting standards provide general guidance for accounting practice. They are the basic guidelines or standards for accounting and financial reporting. In general, accounting standards comprise the basic principles of accounting and specific guidelines on accounting transactions such as recognition, measurement, recording and reporting. In China, the development of accounting standards must follow the principal guidance laid down in the Accounting Law. In addition, accounting standards are divided into two separate subsystems: one for business accounting and another for accounting for governments and non-profit organizations. At the moment, basic accounting principles or standards for business enterprises have been formulated and enforced and more of the practical accounting standards for business enterprises will soon be promulgated. The establishment of accounting standards for governments and non-profit organizations is also under way in China, which will replace the existing governmental regulations on budgetary accounting (see Chapter 9 for the details).

The new set of 13 industrial accounting systems released in 1993 provide more specific practical guidance for accounting recording and reporting in terms of individual lines of industry. Compared to the accounting standards, the industrial accounting systems are more concrete and operational and they are easy to apply in the real life of accounting work. In particular, the majority of Chinese accountants have been used to complying mechanically with the detailed rules or procedures in the compulsory accounting regulations over the last 40 years. They may not be able effectively to apply accounting standards, which requires the exercise of professional judgment, during the current transitional period. However, as discussed in Chapter 2, the industrial accounting systems are expedient measures. They will cease operation as soon as the complete set of accounting standards have been established.

DEVELOPMENT OF ACCOUNTING STANDARDS IN CHINA

In a country with centralized economic administration system, the development of accounting standards is under direct control of the government. This is contrary to the experience in most industrialized countries where 'self-regulation by the profession' is a norm. According to the Accounting Law, the Ministry of Finance has been authorized to design the national accounting regulations or rules. Thus establishment of Chinese accounting standards is under the auspices of the Ministry of Finance, or the Department of Accounting Affairs (DAA) in particular. The DAA set up a Study

Group on Accounting Standards at the beginning of 1988 to draft the Chinese accounting standards.

Structure of Chinese accounting standards

According to the recommendations presented by the Study Group on Accounting Standards, Chinese accounting standards will have two major components: general accounting standards and practical accounting standards. The general accounting standards specify the fundamental accounting assumptions underlying accounting practice: the basic concepts of accounting elements such as assets, liabilities, owners' equity, revenues and expenses; the general principles or standards governing accounting processes of recognition, measurements, recording and reporting. Thus the general accounting standards provide a basis for more detailed accounting standards or procedures to be developed.

Practical accounting standards are the second tier of Chinese accounting standards specifying practical guidelines or procedures for particular accounting transactions or events. Practical standards apply the general standards to more operational aspects of the accounting process. Thus practical accounting standards are transaction-oriented and they are more detailed and numerous than general accounting standards. These detailed accounting standards can be divided into three areas: general transaction standards, special transaction standards and financial statement standards.

General transaction standards

These standards can be applied to accounting transactions common to all types of business enterprise. In other words, these standards regulate the major accounts of accounting records and reports, for example, account receivable, inventories, investments, fixed assets, depreciation, intangibles, account payable, owners' equity, revenue recognition, and so on.

Special transaction standards

These provide practical guidance for particular types of accounting transactions or events, as well as for the application of specific accounting techniques, for example, foreign exchange, business mergers or combinations, leases, business liquidation, futures contracts, employees' benefits, long-term construction contracts, research and development (R & D), income tax allocation, basic banking business, borrowing costs, donations and government grants, and bad debt restructuring.

Financial statement standards

These practical standards focus mainly on financial reporting and disclosures. They provide the operational guidelines on the preparation of the required financial statements and supplementary disclosures. These standards, for example, specify basic types and content of financial statements required, disclosures of contingencies and commitments, related party transactions and subsequent events, disclosure of accounting policies, format of financial statements, and so on.

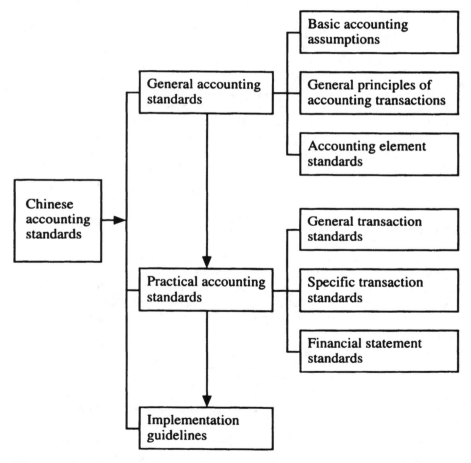

Figure 3.2   Structural interrelation of Chinese accounting standards

Figure 3.2 illustrates the conceptual framework of accounting standards in China.

The process of standard setting

After several rounds of drafting and revisions, the general accounting standards, that is, ASBE, were promulgated by the Ministry of Finance on November 1992, with the approval of the State Council, and enforced on 1 July 1993. Simultaneously, the DAA initiated a five-year project to draft the practical standards in the early 1990s. This project has received financial support from the World Bank, and Deloitte Touche Tohmatsu International acted as technical consultant. Following the implementation of the ASBE in 1993, the process of establishing practical accounting standards has been speeded up. After three years' efforts, the exposure drafts of 29 pieces of practical accounting standards were completed by the Study Group on Accounting Standards in early 1996 and officially released for public comments.

In order to ensure the quality of these accounting standards, the Ministry of Finance sponsored six international accounting seminars in Beijing from November 1995 to March 1996 to review and discuss the drafts of the proposed practical accounting standards. Many accounting regulators, public accountants and scholars from Australia, Canada, Germany, the United Kingdom, the United States, Hong Kong, Taiwan and China participated in these meetings and provided suggestions. These practical accounting standards were originally scheduled to be finalized in one batch and implemented in 1997. The Ministry of Finance, however, decided in early 1997 to release the standards in a piece-by-piece manner. The first piece of these standards, *Accounting Standards on Related Party Transactions*, was officially anounced by the Ministry of Finance in May 1997 and went into effect on 1 July 1997. More pieces of the practical standards are expected to be released soon. According to the government's planning, the new transaction-based practical accounting standards will be first implemented in some selected enterprises, mostly listed companies, selected by the government. After a short period of experimentation, the practical accounting standards will be extended to all business entities in China.

Establishment of accounting standards is a new practice in Chinese accounting. In order to ensure a smooth implementation of accounting standards, the Ministry of Finance will issue implementation guidelines for each practical standard being enforced. The first implementation guidelines were issued in June 1997, in association with the *Accounting Standard on Related Party Transactions*. The implementation guidelines provide specific recommendations on operational procedures to apply accounting standards; they are, therefore, an integrated part of Chinese accounting standards.

As mentioned earlier, the Ministry of Finance has also issued and enforced 13 uniform industrial accounting systems at the same time that the ASBE was introduced. These industrial accounting systems are all designed in terms of the requirements specified by the ASBE. They are very detailed and operational in nature and have been currently adopted as the practical guidelines for accounting and financial reporting. They will be effective at least until all the practical accounting standards have been completed and enforced universally in China. These industrial accounting systems could be treated as a provisional substitute for the practical accounting standards during the current transitional period.

In contrast to business accounting, accounting for governments and non-profit organizations, called 'budgetary accounting' in China, is another major branch of Chinese accounting, Following the reform of business accounting in 1993, budgetary accounting reform has also been initiated by the Chinese government in recent years. The reform of budgetary accounting will adopt the same line of strategy as business accounting reform, although its process is relatively slow. In the meantime, the establishment of accounting standards for budgetary accounting is under way. A separate study group on budgetary accounting standards, formed by the Department of Budgetary Administration under the Ministry of Finance, is currently working on the drafts of uniform national accounting standards and new budgetary accounting systems for governments and non-profit organizations. It is reported that the new set of budgetary accounting regulations, including 'The Accounting System for Aggregated Accounts by Government', 'The Accounting System for Governmental Entities', 'Accounting Systems for Non-profit Organizations' and, later, the 'Accounting Standards for Non-profit Organizations' will be gradually established in the near future. The topic of budgetary accounting will be discussed in detail in Chapter 9.

ANALYSIS OF CHINESE ACCOUNTING STANDARDS FOR BUSINESS ENTERPRISES (ASBE)

The official implementation of ASBE is a cornerstone in Chinese accounting reform because ASBE lays the foundation for the conformation of Chinese accounting and financial reporting to world standards.

Conceptual structure of ASBE

ASBE comprises 66 articles, organized into ten chapters: General Provisions, General Principles, Assets, Liabilities, Owners' Equity, Revenues, Expenses, Profit and Loss, Financial Reports and Supplementary Provisions. The objectives of ASBE are the following:

- to promote fair competition among enterprises,
- to require enterprises to take responsibility for their own operation results,
- to continually extend China's economy and to harmonize its accounting with international practices, and
- to promote the interest of financial statement users other than the government (that is, investors and management).

The main concepts and accounting element standards of ASBE are summarized as Figure 3.3. Judging from Figure 3.3, the conceptual structure of Chinese accounting standards is now fairly similar to its counterparts in most western countries, but some basic accounting concepts or general standards are interpreted with a Chinese flavour to a certain extent. This can be demonstrated in further detailed discussion of the Chinese ASBE, presented below.

Accounting assumptions

On the accounting entity assumption, ASBE stipulates that separate statements be prepared for each separate business entity, and that consolidated statements be prepared whenever an enterprise owns over 50 per cent in equity interest of another enterprise. With respect to the continuity (going concern) assumption, ASBE requires that financial reports be prepared on the basis that an enterprise is a continuing entity and will remain in operation into the foreseeable future. There is, however, no specification on accounting treatment whenever the continuity assumption cannot be held. This may be due to the political doctrine prevailing in China that bankruptcy of state-owned enterprises is restricted and rare in current economic life in China.

Regarding the measurement unit of accounting and reporting, the monetary unit assumption is adopted in ASBE. However, ASBE has clearly specified that the bookkeeping base currency within China is *Renminbi* (the Chinese currency), although enterprises are allowed to apply another foreign currency as a supplementary recording unit so long as it is used for a separate set of internal books of account and reports. In addition, transactions are assumed to

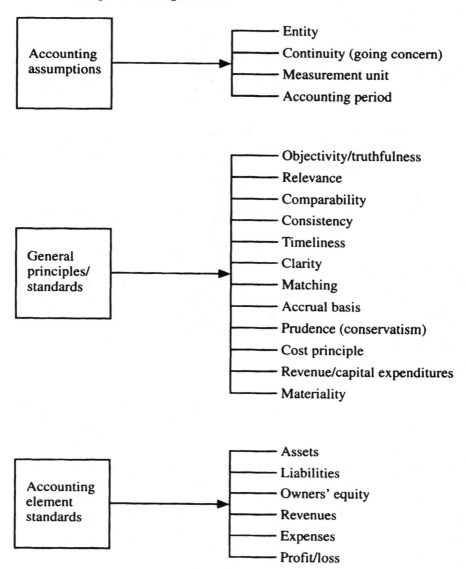

Figure 3.3   Conceptual structure of Chinese ASBE

be measured in stable monetary units and changes in purchasing power of currency are to be ignored. This assumption, however, has been challenged by some Chinese accountants and academicians, who believe such an assumption is a limitation of ASBE because of rising inflation in China. They suggested strongly that the issue of price-level adjustments should be addressed in subsequent revisions of the accounting standards.

Both the concepts of accounting period and accrual basis are recognized in ASBE. However, it is explicitly required in China that annual financial reports usually be prepared on a calendar year basis, which ends on 31 December of each year.

Basic accounting principles

A series of basic accounting principles or general standards have been highlighted in Chapter 2 of ASBE, most are consistent with those prevailing in the western countries. Some of the most important accounting principles specified in ASBE, such as relevance principle, cost principle, realization principle, matching principle, and full disclosure principle are elaborated in further detail below.

Relevance principle　The core of the relevance principle is usefulness of information. As in western countries, financial accounting is structured mainly to provide information to help current and potential investors, creditors and management to make proper decisions. The situation in China, however, is different, since the government, instead of investors and creditors, is the primary user of accounting information. ASBE, therefore, states explicitly in Article 11 that an enterprise must produce accounting information to meet the needs for macroeconomic control by the government. A difference from the accounting regulations in force before 1993 is that the information needs of management and 'other external users' are also addressed in ASBE. Relevance to the decisions of non-government users is, however, only a secondary requirement if it conflicts with the government's information needs.

Cost principle　The historical cost (actual cost) principle is adopted in ASBE. Properties, plants and equipment must be recorded initially at cost. This has long been a standard practice in Chinese accounting since revaluation was not permitted in the past. Nonetheless, one improvement made in ASBE is to allow the use of revaluation of fixed assets for limited purposes such as business reorganization, joint ventures or combination. Approval from government authorities in charge is required, however.

Realization principle　The general guideline of the realization principle in ASBE is that revenues are recognized only when goods or services are rendered and economic benefits can be measured reliably. This represents, nevertheless, an improvement compared to previous accounting practice in China, with the emphasis of revenue recognition being placed more or less upon cash-based revenues before 1993.

Matching principle   The matching principle, closely linking to accrual accounting and revenue recognition, is incorporated in ASBE. However, ASBE is inconsistent with the application of the matching principle. For example, estimating an allowance for doubtful accounts is optional rather than a required accounting practice in China.

Full disclosure principle   Although the term 'full disclosure principle' is not used directly, the application of the full disclosure principle, by and large, is implicitly outlined in ASBE. This requirement is consistent with western standards. Financial reporting is made up of accounting statements and relevant supplementary schedules. ASBE requires that financial statements of business enterprises generally consist of an income statement, a balance sheet, a statement of changes in financial position or a statement of cash flows, an explanatory statement of financial conditions and additional disclosures.

Implementation constraints

In the conceptual framework of accounting and reporting in western countries, a series of constraints relating to accounting and financial reporting is clearly identified. For example, the Financial Accounting Standards Board (FASB) in the United States has set out three constraints in its Statement on Financial Accounting Concepts No. 2: cost effectiveness, materiality and conservatism. [1] In comparison, these implementation constraints have only been partially stated in ASBE.

Materiality   Materiality is explicitly addressed as a general standard in ASBE. For example, Article 21 states that transactions relating to major economic activities are to be identified, appropriately classified and accounted for, and separately reported in financial statements. There are, however, no specific guidelines on the criteria of materiality in the current version of ASBE.

Cost effectiveness   This constraint implies that the accounting and reporting process must be the subject of a cost–benefit analysis. Detailed or new information will be provided only when the benefit derived from the accounting and reporting process is greater than the cost associated with it.

Thus a trade-off between cost and benefit should be made in accounting practice. At present this criterion is not explicitly stated in ASBE, even though it is widely accepted in the West.

Conservatism   This concept is also called the 'prudence convention'. The conservatism concept allows accountants to adopt a less optimistic view of the potential revenues and gains while recognizing all possible expenses or losses. Although this convention is a common practice in most parts of the world, it has long been rejected in Chinese accounting. But ASBE, issued in 1993, has partially incorporated the conservatism convention. For example, enterprises in China are now allowed to use the completed method, besides percentage-of-completion method, to account for long-term construction contracts under some circumstances, but estimating an allowance for doubtful accounts is not a compulsory accounting practice. It is obvious that conservatism does not apply well in this case.

In addition, conservatism is not prescribed with respect to inventory valuation. Under ASBE, inventories are recorded at their actual acquisition costs in financial statements; and the 'lower of cost or market' valuation method, which is generally accepted in the West, has not been permitted in China.

As discussed in Chapter 1, the rejection of conservatism was due to an ideological influence on accounting, since the conservatism convention had been condemned as a tool for capitalists to manipulate income and create business secrets, thus it was accused of being incompatible with a socialist economy. Another more important factor contributing to the rejection of the conservatism, however, is linked to the government's worry about declining fiscal revenues. Some Chinese government officials have argued that conservatism may lead enterprises to write off large amounts of potential losses which will significantly reduce the total profits reported by enterprises, thus costing governments a fortune in tax revenues. This contention, however, was short of concrete evidence and was criticized by many Chinese accounting scholars and practitioners. The demand for the incorporation of conservatism in Chinese accounting standards has continued to rise in recent years.

Overall, the findings about the way the selected accounting items are treated in ASBE can be demonstrated as in Table 3.1.

Accounting element standards

ASBE has defined a series of accounting elements, including assets, liabilities, owners' equity, revenues, expenses and income. The general standards governing these accounting elements are discussed in turn below.

Table 3.1   Treatment of selected items in Chinese ASBE

	Explicitly listed	Presumably recognized	Partially applied
Accounting Assumptions			
Accounting entity	x		
Continuity		x	
Monetary unit	x		
Accounting period		x	
Accrual basis	x		
Basic Principles			
Cost principle	x		
Realization principle		x	
Matching principle	x		x
Full disclosure principle	x		x
Implementation Constraints			
Cost–benefit analysis		x	
Materiality		x	
Conservatism		x	x

Assets

Assets are customarily grouped in the order of their liquidity into several categories such as current assets, long-term investments, fixed assets, intangible assets, deferred charges and other assets. Some observations emerging from the examination of ASBE follow.

Accounts receivable   Enterprises in China can currently select the allowance approach or the direct write-off approach to deal with doubtful accounts. When the allowance method is used, the estimated percentage of bad debt provision should be approved by the government's finance or taxation authorities in advance. In current practice, some enterprises estimate, as a rule of thumb, that 3 to 5 per cent of accounts receivable are uncollectable. Another case in point is the Chinese use of 'reserve for bad debts'. The use of the term 'reserve' has traditionally been rejected by authoritative committees and is gradually disappearing in western societies.

Inventories   ASBE adopts many different cost allocation methods for inventory valuation, which include first in-first out, last in-first out, weighted average, moving average, and specific identification. This approach is consistent with the practice prevailing in the West. However, the western accounting convention of 'lower of cost or market' (LCM) is not permitted in China. Inventories are valued at historical costs: that is, the actual acquisition costs. In addition, no separate contra-account such as 'allowance for write-down of inventory to market', is allowed for losses on inventories. Again, conservatism was considered incompatible with the socialist economy. Thus conservative treatment with regard to valuation of currency receivable and inventories is not allowed in China in accordance with ASBE.

Land   In accordance with Marxist theory, land in itself is not viewed as an asset of any business entity in China. Ownership of land belongs to the state, but the transfer of the right to use land is permitted. In addition, a leasehold is capitalized and amortized over the term of the lease. Accordingly, this approach implies the impossibility of an operating lease. It is, however, plausible that the land lease agreement with the same conditions may be categorized as an operating lease in other countries.

Other fixed assets   In some countries, enterprises should distinguish fixed assets' ordinary repairs from extraordinary repairs. The general guideline is that the costs of ordinary repairs are charged to expense accounts in the period in which they incur, whereas the costs of extraordinary repairs should be capitalized. The most obvious problem is the lack of objective criteria for determining whether and how long the benefit will last in the future. In China, according to Article 19 of the *General Rules on Financial Affairs for Business Enterprises*, enterprises are required to charge repair costs to current profit or loss accounts regardless of their categorization as ordinary repairs or extraordinary repairs. However, the repairs costs, when being not regular or being relatively large, may be capitalized and should be reported to the government's finance departments in charge for record-keeping purposes. The implication of Article 19 is that capital expenditures and revenue expenditures are not clearly divided. Such an accounting treatment apparently violates the materiality principle.

Intangible assets   Enterprises in China are currently permitted to amortize the costs of intangible assets over such period as management consider appropriate, so long as the amortization period is not less than ten years. ASBE further stipulates that research and development costs (R & D) be capitalized. Such a regulation is similar to the practice found in International Accounting Standards No. 9. It is, however, different from the US practice, where the R & D costs must be expensed immediately. ASBE also requires the business organization costs categorized under the heading of deferred assets in the balance sheet to be amortized over a period of not less than five years once the designated business activities become fully established.

Liabilities

Liabilities are generally classified as either current liabilities or long-term liabilities. The distinction is based on a time-frame of one year or an operating cycle, whichever is longer. Under the requirements of ASBE, current liabilities are generally recorded when they are incurred. However, when an obligation clearly exists but the amount ultimately to be paid cannot be definitely determined, contingent liabilities may be made immediately after the amount is reasonably estimated.

Owners' equity

Owners' equity is the difference between assets and liabilities. It is divided into capital stock, capital reserve (that is, additional paid-in capital), surplus reserve (that is, earned surplus) and undistributed profit retained in the businesses which is required to be disclosed separately. Unlike the western case, earned surplus in Chinese accounting is the portion of retained earnings that an enterprise designates exclusively to fulfil legal requirements (for example, reinvestment funds) mandated by the government. Capital reserve consists of premium on capital stock issued, reserve for appreciation of assets, and donations of assets, and so on. This is much in line with the western standards.

Income determination

ASBE states that enterprises should generally recognize revenues when merchandises are shipped, when services are provided or when rights to collect money have been obtained. In addition, ASBE makes it essential to distinguish primary business revenues from other business revenues.

Expenses are divided into cost of goods sold and operating expenses. Prior to the issuance of ASBE, selling and administrative expenses were classified as product costs rather than period costs. According to ASBE, selling and administration expenses are treated as period costs. They are excluded from inventory costs. The reclassification of these two categories of expenses symbolizes a turning point for cost accounting and cost management in China.

In addition, enterprises are required to state inventories of finished goods at actual costs; that is, whenever a standard cost system is used, adjustments from standard costs to actual costs are required for the purpose of valuation on the balance sheet. Enterprises using standard costs and budgeted costs are required to adjust to actual costs of goods manufactured in order to meet the requirements of Article 52 in ASBE.

ASBE provides the foundation upon which accounting transactions and financial statements are constructed. The requirements incorporated in ASBE have brought Chinese accounting much more in line with accounting practices in the western industrialized world. For purposes of comparison, Table 3.2 illustrates, in parallel, the accounting elements incorporated in the Generally Accepted Accounting Principles (GAAP) in the United States and in Chinese ASBE. As is shown, ASBE does not clearly define 'gains', 'losses', 'investments by owners', 'distributions to owners' and 'comprehensive income', as does the US GAAP.

Table 3.2   Comparison of accounting elements of financial statements

Elements	US GAAP	China's ASBE
Assets	Yes	Yes
Liabilities	Yes	Yes
Owners' equity	Yes	Yes
Revenues	Yes	Yes
Expenses	Yes	Yes
Gains	Yes	N/A
Losses	Yes	N/A
Income	N/A	Yes
Investments by owners	Yes	N/A
Distributions to owners	Yes	N/A
Comprehensive income	Yes	N/A

Note: Yes: definition is available; N/A: definition is unavailable.

Financial reporting and disclosures

ASBE's main requirements on financial reporting and disclosure for business enterprises are discussed below.

Components of financial reporting

For financial reporting to be effective, all relevant information should be presented in an unbiased, understandable and timely manner. Accounting information is usually conveyed through a set of designated financial statements. Although Chinese financial reporting differed substantially from its western counterparts in the types and contents of financial statements before 1993, significant changes have been made through the implementation of ASBE. At present, ASBE requires inclusion of a balance sheet, an income statement, a statement of changes in financial position, an explanatory statement on financial conditions and related supplementary schedules in the financial reports of business enterprises. A statement of cash flows may be applied as a substitute for the statement of changes in financial position. The statement of changes in owners' equity, however, is not required at present.

Format of financial statements

In China, the format of accounts is usually prescribed in government-formulated accounting regulations or industry-specific accounting systems, particularly for the format of balance sheet and profit and loss account. While ASBE has prescribed general standards governing the types and content of financial statements being required, no specifications on the statement format are addressed. It is expected that the specific requirements on the formats of financial statements will be incorporated in the practical accounting standards that are developed in terms of the general standards in ASBE.

Two observations can be made with respect to the financial reporting and disclosures standards in ASBE, compared to the generally accepted practice in the West. First, the Chinese practice reflects only income from continuing operations in respect of the content and format of business income to be reported. No detailed requirements are available for the presentation of discontinued segments, extraordinary items and cumulative effects of changes in accounting principles. These items are therefore not required to be disclosed. Second, the classification of selling and administrative expenses symbolizes the change in the traditional cost management method used in China: conversion to the western manufacturing method from the traditional completion method. This reformatting of income statements will increase the comparability of financial statements between China and the rest of the world.

As for the statement of changes in financial position (SCFP), two general types of elements are prescribed for the preparation of SCFP in Chinese ASBE: sources of working capital and uses of working capital. Within sources of working capital, there are two subsources: earnings sources and other sources. In addition, uses of working capital are classified as either earning distribution or other uses. The difference between sources of working capital and uses of working capital represents net increase (or decrease) in working capital in current period. Moreover, an enterprise can also prepare the statement of cash flows instead of SCFP to fulfil the requirement of ASBE.

Supplementary information and disclosures

Financial statements are usually accompanied by lengthy notes and supportive schedules in North America and other western countries.[2] The situation in Chinese financial reporting is quite different. The emphasis is placed on the texts of financial statements focusing on presentation of quite detailed and specific line items. Notes to financial statements are in general short and condensed in Chinese practice. ASBE, however, requires certain items of supplementary information or additional events to be disclosed in reasonable detail, particularly in the Explanatory Statement on Financial Condition, such as follows:

● summary of significant accounting policies adopted;
● rationale for accounting changes and their impacts on financial statements;
● explanation of unusual items or events;
● additional information to support summary totals (not disclosed in the financial statements); and
● other events that may either prevent financial statement users' misunderstandings or that facilitate fair presentation of financial statements.

IMPLICATIONS OF ACCOUNTING STANDARDS FOR BUSINESS ENTERPRISES (ASBE)

In summary, the implementation of ASBE is a milestone in the development of Chinese accounting. This event not only indicates the end of the old accounting model derived from the centrally planned economy, but also heralds a new era of Chinese accounting moving towards the business environment in a partial market economy and the internationally accepted accounting standards. Thus ASBE should have profound influences on the further growth of Chinese accounting in the future. The significance of ASBE cannot be denied. In particular, the major merits of ASBE can be summarised as follows.

1 The release of ASBE has led to great strides in the establishment of Chinese accounting standards. With the new set of accounting standards

being formulated, accounting will promote the progress of a market-based economy in China.

2   ASBE has codified the expanded objectives of accounting and reporting in China. Differing from the practices before 1993, accounting in Chinese enterprises will no longer aim only at the information needs of government. Interests of other, non-government, users will also be taken into account in enterprise accounting.

3   Transformation from the former Soviet-styled three-part fund balance statement, that is, *Zi-Jin-Ping-Heng-Biao* in Chinese, to the western format of balance sheet and other financial statements is dramatic evidence of China's desire to make its accounting standards conform to those of the rest of the world.

4   The ASBE provides a sound foundation from which accounting assumptions, basic principles, accounting elements and implementation constraints may be reassessed, and casts light on the direction of accounting growth in China.

5   ASBE represents a framework upon which more practical accounting standards can be developed coherently in China. In addition, ASBE has established a basis for effective enforcement of new accounting standards in the near future.

Another remarkable and most important feature of ABSE is that it shows that the Chinese government and business community have realized the need for transparency in capital markets. It demonstrates that political and business leaders in China have recognized that a clear and complete set of accounting standards or accounting systems that meet international standards is a necessary condition for enduring economic development. China is growing rapidly, and its accountants are playing an important role in that development.

Nonetheless, this is not meant to suggest that ASBE is perfect in its current form. Growth of a market-based economy in China is an evolutionary process; so too are Chinese accounting reforms. Accounting evolves in terms of the changes in the specific economic environment. Thus ASBE, like any other accounting standards in the world, will be continuously reviewed, modified or updated in order to adapt to the changing demands and needs resulting from China's economic growth in the future.

NOTES

1   See US Financial Accounting Standards Board (1980), Statement of Financial Accounting Concepts No. 2, p. 15.

2   For example, the Financial Accounting Standards Board in the USA has specified that
    notes to financial statements are an integrated part of financial statements and are also
    subject to the requirements of GAAP. It is quite common for the length of the notes to
    financial statements to surpass the text of financial statements in a much greater propor-
    tion in North America and other western countries. But notes to financial statements are
    usually short and condensed in the financial reports released by Chinese enterprises.

4   Securities Markets and Information Disclosure

In most western countries, accounting, financial accounting in particular, aims mainly at providing relevant information for the participants in the capital market, or to assist investors and creditors making investment decisions. The situation is somewhat different in China, since the government is the primary user of accounting information. The functions of Chinese accounting, however, have been expanded as a result of the recent development of securities markets in the country. Accounting information has now played a role in facilitating the smooth growth of securities markets. Thus this chapter illustrates the emergence and expansion of Chinese securities markets and the accounting information or disclosure that is required for securities listing and trading in China.

RESURGENCE AND EXPANSION OF SECURITIES MARKETS IN CHINA

Securities investments and stock markets disappeared in China shortly after the Communists assumed power in 1949. But securities transactions resurfaced in the Chinese economy in the early 1980s, although they had still been rejected by the orthodox ideologies. The formation of the first share-capital (stock) company, Beijing Tianchiao Department Store, in July 1984 heralded the resurgence of the stock company and the capital market in China. The main purpose of experimenting with the share-capital companies, however, was initially related to reforming the business administration system rather than raising funds from the public. For instance, all stocks or shares of those early stock companies were issued only to internal employees. It was intended that the adoption of the share-capital system would serve as a means of raising productivity since the performance of a stock company was tied into the personal interests of employees or staff through the participating shares and dividend scheme being applied.

Thus this kind of share-capital system was quite different from the publicly traded stock company system. The shares issued were more like a hybrid of preferred stocks and bonds since fixed-rate dividends and profit sharing features were evident. However, the experiment was expanded in many industrial centres around the country, such as Shenyang, Tianjing, Shanghai, Guangzhou, Chongqi, and so on. The need to raise capital from outside (through issuing stocks and bonds) were gradually recognized by some stock companies seeking to finance expansion in their operations. This led to the establishment of securities trading centres to facilitate public issuing and trading of securities in a few major business centres. These securities trading centres, however, were different from securities markets, because the securities trading centres were organized and administered directly by the government authority in charge, that is, the People's Bank of China. In addition, trading of securities in these centres was rather limited, for example, geographical and transferability restrictions were imposed on the securities listed in individual securities trading centres.

In the late 1980s, the function of raising funds from the public was emphasized in further expansion of the share-capital system. In particular, the government had realized that the share-capital system might be a measure to alleviate the mounting inflation pressure in the Chinese economy since the mid-1980s. Free transferability of securities became crucial for the growth of the share-capital system. Thus national securities markets were formally established to direct huge amounts of private savings of households into the purchase of stocks and bonds issued by companies and the government. Following a short period of over-the-counter trading (OTC), the first stock exchange was opened in Shanghai in December 1990 after a suspension of almost 40 years in China. Another stock exchange, the Shenzhen Stock Exchange, was inaugurated in July 1991 in the Shenzhen Special Economic Zone neighbouring Hong Kong. The establishment of these two stock exchanges is a milestone in the expansion of securities markets in China, indicating that securities transactions have grown from OTC fragmented trading into centralized trading in the exchanges. More stock companies were set up in the early 1990s. The numbers of publicly listed companies increased from 14 in 1991 to 570 in March 1997, with a multifold increase in total trading volume. The securities markets have thus become an increasingly important source of financing for Chinese enterprises and government. Table 4.1 illustrates the rapid growth of stock companies from 1991 to March 1997 in China.

Table 4.1   Overview of national stock trading, 1991–7 (March)

	1991	1992	1993	1994	1995	1996	1997*
No. of listed companies	14	53	183	291	323	530	570
No. of listed shares	14	72	3 218	345	381	599	604
Total capital (in 100 million RMB ¥)	6	73	328	640	765	1 110	N/A
Market capitalization (in 100 million RMB ¥)	109	1 048	3 531	3 691	3 474	9 842	13 279
Annual turnover (in 100 million RMB ¥)	43	681	3 667	8 127	4 035	21 332	N/A
Annual trading volume (in 100 million shares)	3	38	234	1 013	703	2 533	N/A

Note: * the data for 1997 are for the first quarter, ending on 31 March 1997.

Characteristics of the stock market in China

In general, the main characteristics of Chinese securities markets are as follows.

Stringent governmental regulation

The experiment with the share-capital system was conducted under stringent government control. Formation of stock companies must be approved by several governmental administrative authorities, such as the State Economic Commission, the China Securities Regulatory Committee, the State Commission on Economic Restructuring, the Administration of State-owned Properties and the industrial ministries overseeing those companies. Approval from the central bank and security regulatory authorities must be obtained for public issuing of stocks and bonds.

Coexistence of segregated stock markets

Different types of stock exist concurrently. Shares listed in China comprise (1) shares held by government entities, (2) shares held by Chinese corporations, (3) shares held by Chinese individuals and (4) shares held by foreign investors. The first three groups are called 'A shares', the fourth group is called 'B shares'. They are listed and traded separately. At present, 'A shares' are available to investors, both institutional and individual, within China. The 'A shares' are quoted and traded in Chinese currency

(*Renminbi* ¥). The 'B shares' are designed exclusively for investors outside mainland China. They are denominated in *Renminbi* ¥, but quoted and
traded in Hong Kong dollars on the Shenzhen Stock Exchange or in US
dollars on the Shanghai Stock Exchange. Listed companies wishing to
issue 'B shares' must apply to the securities regulatory authorities for
special permission. As demonstrated in Table 4.2, up to March 1997, a
total of 87 Chinese companies had issued 'B shares', with the listed
amount totalling RMB ¥7.96 billion.

Table 4.2   B share issuing and trading in China by March 1997

	Shanghai Exchange	Shenzhen Exchange	Total
No. of listed companies	43	44	87
Volume of shares issued (in 100 million shares)	46.23	43.62	89.85
Market capitalization of total shares issued (in 100 million RMB ¥)	178.82	266.84	445.66

In addition, a small number of the state-owned companies have been
listed on overseas stock exchanges since 1993. In all, 29 Chinese companies
had been successfully listed and traded in Hong Kong, New York and
London by the end of March 1997. Of these, 22 were listed in Hong Kong
(H shares); six on the New York Stock Exchange (N shares), one on the
London Stock Exchange (L shares); a few more will be listed in Australia
and Singapore soon.

High volatility in stock markets

The stock markets in China are very volatile, for several reasons. First, the
stock markets in China have only been in operation for a short period, and
their activity was far less than normal. Second, the public reaction to stock
markets was overheated since the supply of issued securities fell behind the
demands from an immense pool of potential investors. Third, the concept of
market risks has not been properly realized by most Chinese investors.
Panic reactions were common whenever there was a market correction or
adjustment.

REGULATION OF SECURITIES MARKETS

The Chinese government has exercised fairly rigid control of securities markets, simply because the share-capital system had not been legitimated under the orthodox socialist doctrines and the government could not afford the failure of such capitalist-styled experimentation at the moment.

The regulation of securities transactions was initially under the administration of the central bank, the People's Bank of China (PBC) prior to 1993. Establishing securities trading centres and public offering and trading of securities must be approved by the PBC or its branches at each province. However, many local branches of the PBC could not exercise their regulatory duties free from the influence or intervention of local governments. This resulted in varied standards being applied in regulating securities transactions across the country in the early days of the growth of securities markets in China.

In order to strengthen supervision of securities markets, China's State Council decided, in the early 1990s, to set up more authoritative and specialized regulatory bodies to oversee the securities transactions nationwide. This led to the establishment of the State Council Securities Commission (SCSC) in 1992 and the China Securities Regulatory Committee (CSRC) in 1993, which have taken over the regulatory authority of securities transactions from the PBC.

Securities regulatory authorities

Both the SCSC and the CSRC were the product of China's development of a socialist market economy and securities market. On an Executive Order issued by the State Council on 17 December 1992, the establishment of the SCSC was announced. The Commission is a high-profile policy-making body directly under the State Council, with members coming from the heads of several ministerial authorities of the central government, such as the State Economic Commission, the State Commission on Reform of Economic Structure, the PBC, the Ministry of Finance, the State Taxation Bureau, the Administration of State-owned Properties, and so on. The main responsibilities of the SCSC are as follows:

- to promulgate uniform policies, on behalf of the State Council, governing the development of securities markets and securities transactions;
- to review the drafts of state laws or regulations governing stock companies and securities transactions;

- to oversee the growth of securities markets in China, and
- to formulate necessary regulations or rules to promote standardization of securities transactions nationwide.

The CSRC, officially formed in April 1993, has acted as an executive branch of the SCSC, or has been mandated to exercise concrete regulatory duties under the direction of the SCSC. According to existing regulations, the regulatory power and functions over securities transactions have therefore been transferred from the PBC to the CSRC, although the PBC maintains the authority to grant approval for the aggregated volume of securities (both stocks and corporate bonds) to be offered in each year. The responsibilities of the CSRC include the following:

- drafting and implementing regulations governing securities transitions nationwide;
- regulating public offering, listing and trading of securities;
- administering and supervising activities of brokerage firms, and transactions of securities, such as trading and settlement of securities;
- establishing qualification standards and issuing licences for securities professionals;
- regulating the overseas issuance of securities by China-based enterprises;
- exercising supervision over the operation of listed companies and their compliance with relevant legislation and government regulations;
- overseeing the performance of securities markets;
- investigating illegal acts involved in securities transactions and disciplining the violators in accordance with relevant securities regulations;
- administering information disclosure of publicly listed companies;
- preparing statistics and market analysis of securities transactions, and submitting policy recommendations, on a timely basis, to the SCSC and other government authorities; and
- developing international cooperation with securities regulatory bodies in other countries.

There are several functional divisions under the CSRC which fulfil a broad range of duties as listed above. Among these divisions are the Division of Public Offering, the Division of Regulation and Enforcement, the Division of Trading and Market Supervision, the Division of Securities Institutions, the Office of Chief Accountant, the Division of Overseas Listing, the Division of Compliance and Discipline, the Division of Statistics and Research, and so on. In addition, the stock exchanges have the power, under delegation of authority from the CSRC, to exercise supervision of the issuing and trading activities in the exchanges. Stock exchanges are allowed to establish detailed rules, in terms of the regulations formulated by the CSRC and other government authorities, governing listing and trading of securities.

The current structure of securities regulation in China is shown in Figure 4.1.

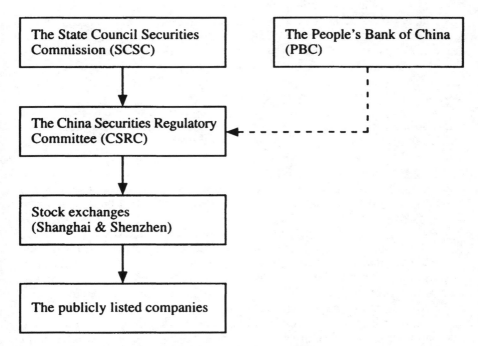

Figure 4.1   Securities regulatory bodies in China

The regulatory framework of disclosure for publicly listed companies

Modern stock markets are established on the basis of disclosure. Information and disclosure released by companies will help investors make accurate decisions and protect the interests of investors, as well as promoting smooth economic growth in a society. Disclosure of publicly listed companies is crucial to normal functioning of securities markets. Therefore the practice of information disclosure is regulated worldwide. China is no exception.

Government authorities in charge of securities markets have made great efforts to draw up regulations or rules governing information disclosure of publicly listed companies since the early 1990s.

Currently, a preliminary regulatory framework of information disclosure has been established. This framework consists of four levels of regulatory requirements. The first level is the state law or regulations governing securities transactions. Substantial efforts have been made by the Chinese government to enact the Securities Law in the last couple of years. To date seven drafts of the law have been prepared and reviewed by Chinese lawmakers and it is widely expected that the law will soon be completed and enforced. In the meantime, the most authoritative national regulation is the *Provisional Regulations on Issuance and Trading of Securities*, formulated and enforced by the State Council on 22 April 1993. There are nine chapters and 84 articles in the regulation. In particular, Chapter 6, Information and Disclosure, states general disclosure requirements for publicly listed companies.

The second level is the detailed regulations on implementation of the state law and regulations. For example, the CSRC issued the *Detailed Rules on the Information Disclosure of Publicly Listed Companies*, on 12 June 1993, as guidance for implementing the *Provisional Regulations* promulgated by the State Council. There are eight chapters and 31 articles in the rules, specifying detailed requirements on the obligations, responsibilities, main content, methods and timing of disclosures that must be presented by publicly listed companies.

The third level is the disclosure guidelines formulated by the CSRC. These guidelines have been developed to provide operational guidance for the listed companies to comply with related securities laws or regulations. In particular, they specify the detailed content and format of information disclosures required for public listed companies. The CSRC had issued seven disclosure guidelines, up to mid 1997.

The fourth level is the interpretation of regulations or supplementary rules on information disclosure, aiming at providing the official interpretation of the related securities laws and regulations. For example, the CSRC issued the *Supplementary Notices on the Policy on Issuing New Shares* in 1994. In addition, supplementary rules on how to implement the new national accounting systems by publicly listed companies were issued by the CSRC on 30 August 1993.

To date, the CSRC has formulated a series of rules or guidelines on the contents and format of information disclosures to be prepared by publicly listed companies, covering the compilation and presentation of the prospectus, the annual report, the interim report, the report on stock dividends and legal opinions. The present information disclosure system is illustrated in Figure 4.2.

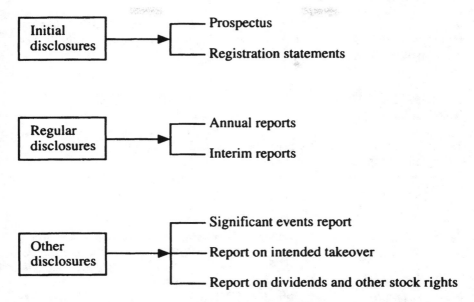

Figure 4.2   Required disclosures for publicly listed companies

Characteristics of Chinese disclosure requirements

When formulating these regulations and rules, the CSRC consulted the S-K and S-X regulations formulated by the US Securities and Exchange Commission (SEC), the regulations on trading of securities of the Hong Kong Exchange Commission, the relevant rules in Taiwan and the detailed rules set out by the two major stock exchanges inside China. Consequently, foreign investors will not be unfamiliar with the disclosure requirements for publicly listed companies in China.

China's disclosure requirements are, however, more detailed than those established in most other countries. For example, 27 articles are specified in Chinese standards for the disclosure of significant events. Chinese requirements on disclosure of performance variance, a difference between actual operation results and projected profits, are somewhat different from the practice in other countries. Publicly listed companies in China are required to provide a fairly detailed explanation for the variances which have occurred during a fiscal year.

In addition, the disclosure requirements for publicly traded companies in China are in general broader than their counterparts in other countries. This can be attributed to the fact that the Chinese government has exercised a highly centralized control over the growth of securities markets. Heavy regulation will better serve the government's interest in protecting the newly developed stock markets from potential failure.

REQUIREMENTS ON PROSPECTUSES AND REGULAR REPORTS

The main requirements on information disclosure for publicly listed companies can be summarized as below.

Prospectus disclosure

Among all of the CSRC's regulations or guidelines governing information disclosure, the rules on the presentation of prospectuses for public offering of securities are relatively more important and more complicated than others. Under the regulations, companies seeking to issue new securities must file registration statements with the CSRC. Both financial and non-financial information, as specified below, must be included in the prospectus statements.

Accounting and financial information

Under current regulations, the following accounting-related information must be incorporated in a prospectus statement:

- the audited financial statements issued over the previous three years or from the date of operation;
- shares owned by organizers/sponsors, ownership of the company, and verification of the contributed capital;
- earnings forecast for the following year;
- financial planning of capital investments and income, and an analysis of any associated investment and operating risks;
- a valuation report on assets;
- the explanatory statement on operating results for the previous three years or from the date of operation;
- the number and monetary amount of shares held by the company, and the type, total amount, par value and selling price of the securities to be offered; the net asset value per share before *and* after the issuance of new securities; the formula for determining the issuing costs and commissions, and so on.

Non-accounting information

Non-financial information required in the registration statements includes the following:

- the name and location of the issuing company;
- a brief history or basic operating background of the issuer;
- the purpose of the proposed issuance of new securities and the intended use of the proceeding from the public offering;
- the names of designated underwriters, and the underwriting process;
- the target market, timing, location of issuing, and the subscription methods of securities being offered;
- any important business contracts;
- major pending litigation, if any;
- the personal profile and brief history of the board of directors and trustees; and
- the management explanation of significant operating activities.

When the prospectus statement has been prepared, an issuing company must submit the statement together with other relevant documents for the required approval. Issuing companies must apply for an approval of public offering from the CSRC and the PBC. All documents relevant to public offering must be passed to the CSRC for review. The CSRC will issue a review report within 20 business days and file a report to the SCSC. After obtaining approval to issue securities, issuer and underwriter must publish a summary of the prospectus (in under 10 000 words) in the national newspapers or magazines which are recognized by the CSRC two to five business days prior to public trading of the securities. Moreover, the prospectus and related summary information must be made available for public review. An issuing company must lodge ten copies of such documents with the CSRC and the listing stock exchange(s) for the purpose of public reference or inspection.

Regular disclosure

Under current regulations, all listed companies are required to submit regularly their financial statements and other accounting-related disclosures to the securities regulatory authorities and to make the statements available to the public. Two types of statements, annual reports and internal reports, must be filed in accordance with the requirements laid down by the securities regulatory authorities.

Annual reports

Financial disclosure in an annual report should include the following:

- a set of audited financial statements, including the balance sheet, income statement and statement of changes in financial position (or cash flow statement) and notes to the statements, which must be presented with two-year comparative numbers;
- a set of consolidated financial statements presented with comparative numbers for the last two periods if a listed company is a parent company;
- a summary of financial disclosure over the last three years or from the initial date of the company's operation;
- the performance of outstanding shares, including any changes in the number and market prices of the shares;
- a brief summary of important factories, mines and real estate properties;
- the description of transactions among related parties and the financial effects.

Annual reports should also disclose the following non-financial information;

- a brief background of the company;
- a message from the Chairman of the board of directors;
- the major line of business/products or services provided by the company;
- comparative analysis in terms of industrial standards;
- the trading performance of outstanding shares, numbers of total shareholders, a list of shareholders owning 50 per cent or more voting shares and the top ten largest shareholders;
- a profile of the board of directors, trustees and senior management, and their respective remuneration and percentage of shares owned;
- management's explanation for the company's financial condition and operating results;
- major pending litigation, if any.

Publicly listed companies are required to prepare and file ten copies of annual reports to the CSRC within four months of the end of each fiscal year. They are required to publish a summary of the annual report in a recognized national newspaper or magazine in 20 working days before the annual shareholders' meeting. Companies must make annual reports available for public review and inspection. Annual report must be audited by Chinese certified public accountants. Since the disclosure of publicly listed companies covers transactions and events involving financing, accounting, laws and valuation of assets, a higher degree of audit assurance is required. The CSRC requires that the annual reports of publicly listed companies be audited or verified exclusively by a very small number of Chinese CPA firms or law firms which have been approved and authorized by the CSRC.

Interim reports

Apart from annual reports and the statement on performance of outstanding shares, interim reporting is required for publicly listed companies. Interim reports must disclose the following information:

- interim financial statements on a semi-annual basis;
- a review of the operational forecast;
- an analysis of the company's financial condition and operating results made by management;
- proxy statements sent to shareholders by the company;
- major litigation, if any.

Publicly listed companies must prepare and file ten copies of interim reports to the CSRC six months before the end of each fiscal year or 60 business days after the fiscal year end. Companies are also required to publish the summary of interim reports in national newspapers or magazines. Interim reports do not need to be audited by CPAs except in unusual circumstances.

Reports of significant events

Companies with securities traded publicly are required to submit reports to the securities regulatory authorities regarding any unexpected and unusual events that may affect the prices of securities traded in the markets. According to existing regulations, any of the following events must be reported within one day of its occurrence:

- intended business combination, takeover and reorganization;
- change of a significant portion of the board of directors, and change of the chairman of the board in particular;
- default of large debt repayment, or plan of debt reconstruction;
- new litigation that may have a significant impact on a listed company;
- resignation and replacement of existing auditors;

- potential liquidation and insolvency.

In the case of a potential takeover bid, a listed company is required to report to the securities regulatory authorities, the stock exchanges and the public, within three business days of obtaining direct and indirect holdings of 3 per cent of the outstanding voting shares of a target company. A subsequent increase in holdings of an additional 2 per cent of the target company's voting shares must also be reported.

COMMENTS ON DISCLOSURE TO SECURITIES MARKETS IN CHINA

Remaining problems

Currently, a preliminary framework for regulating securities markets and publicly listed companies has been established in China. A number of regulations or rules have been formulated by securities regulatory bodies and stock exchanges to provide guidance for information disclosure by publicly listed companies. This is a sign of progress in standardizing securities transactions in terms of the prevailing practice in the rest of the world. The information disclosure system in China is, however, less than perfect at the present moment. Some problems still exist.

First, the disclosure system is not uniform. Besides the detailed regulations or rules on implementation of the national securities regulations issued by the CSRC, each stock exchange has imposed its own rules for required disclosure on publicly listed companies. Even though the Ministry of Finance has formulated a uniform national accounting and financing system, publicly listed companies are currently allowed to adopt another set of *Accounting Regulations for Enterprises Adopting the Share-capital System* jointly promulgated by the Ministry of Finance and the State Commission on Reform of Economic Structure in 1992. In addition, local authorities, in particular local governments in the so-called 'Special Economic Zone', such as Shenzhen, would continue formulating their own regulations or rules (including accounting and disclosure requirements for listed companies) with certain local flavour. Concurrent existence of many different sets of regulations has made publicly listed companies confused and resulted in inconsistent practice of disclosure.

Secondly, information provided by many publicly traded companies fell short of the required quality standard. The quality of information disclosure is generally low. The main reason for this problem lies in a weak mechanism for enforcing the disclosure regulations or rules. The CSRC is short of resources to exercise necessary supervision over the performance of securities markets. In addition, the quality of securities professionals is also problematic. For example, their understanding of some technical terms was inaccurate; the calculations of certain indicators contained some technical errors; the report on major business decisions was not fully disclosed. Also, there is far more positive news than negative news in many companies' disclosures, which signals the problem of withholding negative news from disclosure to the public.

Thirdly, China lacks self-regulated professional organizations which can form a basis for reliability of information disclosure. In China, accounting firms are mostly under the direction of sponsoring organizations such as governmental entities, universities or enterprises. Thus most accounting firms lack independence. Furthermore, the number of certified public accountants is small, and most public practitioners lack proper training. In addition, the disciplining of non-compliance with professional ethics and auditing standards has been weak so far. All these factors have therefore cast a negative light on the objectivity of auditing over disclosures made by publicly listed companies.

Lastly, there are few independent companies specializing in analysis of financial statements and other disclosures presented by listed companies. Investment consulting agencies offering general investment analysis to the public are rarely available at the moment. A system of standard rating of companies has not yet been established. The use of information disclosed by companies in securities transactions is therefore far from effective.

Possible solutions

To develop solutions to the existing problems in information disclosure in China, a uniform disclosure system must be established. The regulatory authorities and various professional bodies should work together to design a set of meaningful financial indicators, the elements of annual reports and supplementary disclosures, basic securities trading concepts, and technical terminology, to ensure the quality and usefulness of information disclosed by publicly listed companies.

In the meantime, training of financial officers and accountants of publicly traded companies should be increased, aimed at improving the relevance and accuracy of accounting information disclosed. In addition, it is important to enhance the independence or self-regulation of professional organizations. Promoting accounting firms in a form of partnership so as to be independent of government sponsors could enhance auditors' responsibilities and obligations in public practice. This will also provide a good environment for training young accountants who understand both Chinese and western practices of finance, accounting and securities trading, and who will be able to ensure the objectivity and fairness of auditing for publicly listed companies.

The above-mentioned measures are certainly essential to the establishment of a properly functioning disclosure system that can meet the information needs of investors in Chinese securities markets.

5 Cost Accounting and Managerial Accounting

Contrary to financial accounting, managerial accounting focuses on providing accounting information for the purposes of cost management and of assisting management to make adequate operating decisions. In China's accounting field, cost accounting and managerial accounting are usually treated as two separate accounting systems. This is because cost accounting has been in use in Chinese accounting practice for several decades, while managerial accounting was not recognized and accepted until the 1980s. Thus this chapter will discuss separately the basic principles and practices relating to Chinese cost accounting and managerial accounting.

PRINCIPLES OF CHINESE COST ACCOUNTING

Cost information is needed for all kinds of business entities for a variety of purposes. Decisions regarding profit determination, product pricing and performance evaluation must be based on cost information. Cost accounting or cost management is therefore an integral component of business management. There are some unique principles and procedures of cost accounting in the business environment in China.

Regulation of cost management

Since the founding of the People's Republic of China in 1949, cost accounting and cost management have been highly regulated by the central government. The main rationale for this governmental regulation lies in the fact that product costs in business enterprises will directly affect the government's fiscal revenues under a system of state ownership of business enterprises and a centralized business administration.

In 1984, the State Council issued the *Regulations on Cost Management for State-owned Enterprises*. This cost management regulation was the first component of national accounting regulations issued by such a high level of authority in China. Before issuance of this cost management regulation by the State Council, the governmental regulations on cost management included the *Unified Procedures on Product Costing Chart of Accounts for State-owned Industrial Enterprises*, formulated by the Ministry of Finance in 1953, and its successor, the *Procedures on Product Costing for State-owned Industrial Enterprises*, promulgated in 1973.

Significant changes in business administration have taken place in step with the progress of economic reforms initiated in the late 1970s. Management in enterprises have gained certain autonomy in making operating decisions and the sources of capital for enterprises have expanded. Business financial management has become much more complex than before. This has resulted in the issuance of the cost management regulation by the State Council, with an emphasis on strengthening cost management in the changing business environment. Accordingly, the Ministry of Finance has issued a revised version of *Procedures on Product Costing for State-owned Industrial Enterprises*. In addition, the Ministry of Finance formulated a set of similar cost management rules for other specific industries. For example, the *Rules of Cost Management for State-owned Merchandising Enterprises* was formulated in 1991,[1] aimed at regulating cost accounting and cost management for the state-owned enterprises engaging in operations in non-manufacturing industries such as wholesaling and retailing, food and beverages, servicing, repairing, shipping and transport. The content of these cost management regulations is fairly standardized, including principles of cost measurement, scope of cost and expenditures, procedures on cost accounting, responsibility accounting, cost budgeting and evaluation, and so on.

Along with the introduction of the new business accounting system in 1993, cost accounting has also undergone fairly substantial changes. With the government's decision to speed up the process towards a market-based economy, decentralized business administration patterns have been adopted. The changes in business environment made the old rules and regulations on cost accounting and cost management previously issued out of date. Thus new provisions on 'costs and expenditures' have been incorporated in the *Accounting Standards for Business Enterprises* (ASBEs) and the *General Rules on Financial Affairs for Business Enterprises*, both incorporating the general framework of the new business accounting systems implemented in 1993. In addition, the Ministry of Finance has formulated a set of 13 industry-specific business financing systems in order to provide more detailed and operational guidance on business cost management. In the current accounting practice, the *General Rules on Financial Affairs for Business*

Enterprises and the 13 industry-specific business financial systems have served as the main sources of governmental regulations on cost accounting and cost management for all business entities.

Cost classification and measurement

Classification of costs is a fundamental element in the Chinese cost accounting system. Cost classifications are decisive and important in forming and applying the concept of cost. Prior to 1993, 'factory costs' was the most important cost concept employed in Chinese cost accounting, for manufacturing enterprises in particular, in terms of the requirements on cost management specified by the government authorities in charge. Factory costs were defined as the total monetary value of the production elements consumed by a manufacturing enterprise in producing goods and services over a period of time. Factory costs consisted of monetary values of the following components: raw materials, fuel and power, salaries and fringe benefits, spoilage loss, transport costs, manufacturing overheads and administration expenses. Thus factory costs included not only costs incurred in the direct manufacturing process (product costs) but also expenses related to the organization and administration of production at the level of the entire enterprise (period costs). This cost concept was different from the general pattern of cost classification in the West, where a distinction between product (manufacturing) costs and period (non-manufacturing) costs is clearly defined.

Following the accounting reform of 1993, the concepts of manufacturing costs and period costs have been adopted in Chinese cost accounting, in an effort to incorporate internationally accepted accounting practice and to enhance the comparability of cost information in terms of the norms prevailing in the rest of the world. As a result of this reform, the original concept of factory costs has been discarded, while the new definition of factory costs is similar to that of manufacturing costs in the West, no longer including period costs. Under the new accounting system, cost of goods manufactured includes direct materials, direct labour and factory overheads.

Principles and requirements of product costing

A set of principles of financial accounting basically are also applicable to cost accounting. These include the relevance principle, the objectivity principle, the historical cost principle, the matching principle, the consistency principle, the materiality principle, accrual accounting, and so on.

The ASBE and the related industry-specific accounting and financing systems have laid down more specific provisions on accounting for product costs and expenses.

1   Direct labour, direct material, purchase expenses and other direct costs which are directly associated with manufacturing products or providing services must be directly charged to the costs of goods manufactured or production costs. All indirect costs incurred should, however, be allocated to the costs of goods manufactured based on appropriate allocation criteria.

2   Administrative expenses and finance expenses incurred by administrative departments for organizing and managing activities, and marketing and purchasing expenses associated with selling of products or services, should be classified as period costs to be charged to income accounts in the current period.

3   Prepaid expenses must be allocated, based on matching principle, over the accounting periods to which the benefits of these expenses are associated, on a proper allocation basis. Accruals should be applied for the expenses associated with the production activities in the current accounting period even though the actual payments of these expenses have not yet been made.

4   Product costing should be conducted generally on a monthly basis.

5   Enterprises may select the methods of product costing most suitable to their own operational conditions in light of the nature of production, types of operation and applicable cost management requirements. However, once the costing method is selected, it should not be changed too frequently.

6   All expenses and costs should be accounted for in terms of the amounts actually incurred for the purpose of product costing. Enterprises employing a fixed-quota (standard) costing system[2] or a budgetary costing system should determine the cost variances reasonably and make necessary adjustments so as to report the actual costs, when preparing accounting statements at the end of each month.

7   Enterprises should accurately and punctually calculate the costs for all products or services sold in each period and transfer the costs of goods sold, along with the period expenses, to income accounts for the determination of period profit or loss.

8   Enterprises cannot use budgetary costs, estimated costs or fixed-quota costs as substitute for actual costs.[3]

9   The following expenditures should not be included in costs and expenses:

- expenses incurred for acquisition and construction of fixed assets, intangible assets and other assets;
- investments in external entities;
- loss from assets foreclosed by government authorities;
- fines or penalties for delayed payments, breach of contract and other compensations or remedies associated with them;
- donations and sponsorship expenditures, and
- the expenses or expenditures that are excluded from product costs by other government regulations.

As a more specific interpretation of the requirements of cost management mentioned above, differentiation for four categories of expenses or expenditures has been particularly emphasized in the practice of cost accounting in China: (1) the distinction between manufacturing costs and period costs, (2) the cut-off effect of monthly determination of manufacturing costs, (3) the allocation of manufacturing costs among various products, and (4) the allocation of manufacturing costs between finished goods and work-in-progress (unfinished goods). It is obvious that the proper distinction of these four categories of expenses or expenditures will determine the accuracy of product costing. More detailed and specific guidelines have therefore been provided in the cost management regulations or rules formulated by government.

Practices of product costing

Under China's cost management system, the basic procedures of cost accounting mainly consist of setting product costing accounts and selecting of costing methods, measures or applicable rules in the light of the circumstances relating to particular business enterprises.

Designing product costing accounts

In an environment of direct governmental regulation over accounting and business financing, cost accounting in business enterprises must follow the specific rules or procedures required by government authorities. In particular, the product costing accounts employed by individual enterprises must be designed in terms of the uniform chart of account highlighted in the 13 industry-specific accounting and financing systems. However, as a result of the accounting reform of 1993, a certain leeway has been left in the uniform chart of product costing accounts for individual enterprises to design their own cost accounting systems. The uniformity and flexibility in the setting up of these costing accounts is briefly illustrated in Table 5.1. Within the

Table 5.1   Illustration of chart of product costing accounts

	Level 1 accounts	Level 2 accounts	Level 3 accounts	Supplemental accounts
Chart of Accounts (Categories)	Operating/production expenses	Production costs and manufacturing costs	Basic production Supplemental Manufacturing exp.	Material variance Work-in-progress Product cost variance
Applicability	Small enterprises with complex cost accounting	Between level 1 and level 3	Large enterprises with complex cost measurement	Costs of raw materials can be accounted for on the basis of the standard/budgetary costing system Costs of work-in-progress can be accounted for separately Fixed-quota or standard costing system can be employed for internal use

framework of the uniform requirements specified in the industry-specific accounting and financing systems, individual enterprises are currently allowed to design their own product, to a certain extent, in terms of their own operating conditions and cost management needs.

Methods of product costing

Product costing is, in general, a two-stage process: cost accumulation and cost allocation (assignment), aiming at determining the total costs and unit cost of the manufactured goods. Different procedures can be applied to the process of cost accumulation and cost assignment, thus constituting various methods for product costing. In Chinese cost accounting, five methods of product costing are allowed from which individual enterprises can choose in accordance with the nature of their operations and the needs of cost management. The first three methods below are regarded as the basic methods of product costing in China; in addition, there are two supplementary methods in practice.

Process costing   Product costs are determined by allocating costs to masses of like units that usually proceed in continuous fashion through a series of uniform production stages.

Job-order costing   Product costs are obtained by allocating costs to a specific unit or to a small batch of products or services that proceeds through the production stages as a distinct, identifiable job lot.

Product-based costing   Product costs are calculated by each type of product manufactured. This method is usually applicable to enterprises producing few types of product but in large volumes.

Operation costing   When categories and specifications of products are numerous, application of process costing or product-based costing may be too time-consuming. In order to simplify the process of cost accounting, products can be categorized into certain groups to calculate product costs. This method is actually a two-stage product costing. First, costs are calculated for different categories of product and then the costs are allocated to individual products within each category according to product specifications.

Fixed-quota costing   Fixed-quota costing is similar to the standard costing system applied in western countries. Quota or standards are predetermined costs for each element of the product. Actual costs incurred in production are divided into standard costs and cost variances. Only the predetermined cost quota or standards will be accounted for during each period. This method simplifies the daily work of cost accounting. Cost variances are then processed separately to calculate the actual production costs at the end of each period.

The five product costing methods possess their own characteristics in respect of cost object, cost elements, costing period, pricing of work-in-progess, and so on. The application of specific cost accounting methods is usually determined by an enterprise's operational conditions, but filing the cost accounting methods employed with the overseeing government authorities is required. An enterprise can either utilize one method for product costing or employ more than one method even for the purpose of cost accounting for one product. Multiple costing methods are usually applied when the production process or operating activities are complex.

Procedures of cost accounting

Procedures of cost accounting include necessary steps to be taken by cost accountants to determine product costs, from recognition of production expenses to the calculation of the total and unit costs of goods manufactured. Five major steps are usually employed in the practice of Chinese cost accounting.

Step 1 Identifying cost objects and cost categories, and establishing product costing accounts or cost subsidiary ledgers in accordance with the nature of an enterprise's production, and the needs of cost management.

Step 2 Verifying transaction vouchers in respect of the validity and relevance of the expenditures in accordance with the cost management requirements specified in governmental regulations. The procedure of voucher verification not only helps recognition and classification of expenses with varied nature, but also serves as an effective tool of cost control.

Step 3 Dividing the recognized production expenses into direct costs and indirect costs, and recording such costs in proper product costing accounts.

Step 4 Assigning all indirect costs or expenses at the end of each month and posting such costs in the general ledger and subsidiary ledgers under 'production expenses'.

Step 5   Allocating the total costs accumulated in the account of production expenses between finished products and unfinished products (work-in-progress) at the end of each month. Computing unit cost of finished products in accordance with the total costs of goods manufactured and the total output of finished products in each period.

Cost accounting systems

Cost accounting systems are established to perform product costing in a systematic way. Therefore standard procedures on product costing are an important component of business accounting systems which has been formulated by government authorities. The *Standard Procedures on Product Costing*, as a tool of governmental regulation of cost accounting and cost management, consists of specific requirements on the work of product costing to be adopted in individual enterprises.

As mentioned earlier, the cost accounting system and the standard procedures on product costing, before 1993, were uniformly formulated by the Ministry of Finance and/or the industrial administrative authorities of the central government. However, since the business accounting reform of 1993, enterprises' management have been granted autonomy to a great extent in the design of cost accounting systems. Enterprises can now determine their own cost accounting systems and design the costing procedures most applicable to their operating conditions, so long as they can meet the general requirements laid down in the *ASBE* and the *General Rules on Financial Affairs for Business Enterprises*, as well as the industry-specific accounting and financing systems formulated by the Ministry of Finance. This is a substantial improvement in cost accounting, compared to the practice in the past, since cost information generated in product costing may now better serve the management's operating decisions.

PRACTICES OF COST MANAGEMENT

In China, cost management is an integrated component of operational management in all business entities. Some practices of cost management have been widely accepted by enterprises over time, and have proved effective in the Chinese business environment. These cost management systems with Chinese characteristics include the 'responsibility system of cost control' and 'enterprise economic accounting' for cost management.

The responsibility system of cost control

Cost management is a process of forecasting, planning, measurement, control, analysis and evaluation of costs incurred in the process of manufacturing or operating activities. The basic goal of cost management is to achieve desirable production results (output of goods manufactured) with minimum input of production elements (resources), which is consistent with the overall goal of a business enterprise.

In line with this management philosophy, cost control has been treated as a comprehensive task in the Chinese practice of cost management, which requires participation of all functional departments and producing units within an enterprise. Thus the responsibility system of cost control has been installed in many Chinese enterprises in order to mobilize overall internal efforts to achieve the specified targets of cost management within individual enterprises.

The system is a combination of responsibility accounting and budgetary control in cost management. Cost budgeting will first be performed for the entire enterprise. The cost quotas or standard costs will then be broken down by operating departments within an enterprise, with the head of each department being responsible for the control and fulfilment of the cost targets or standards assigned. As a result, cost control becomes a process involving the participation of various functional departments at multiple levels. An important procedure of the responsibility system of cost control is deciding how to decompose the cost quotas or standards within an enterprise appropriately. In practice the costs in question are usually decomposed and assigned using two approaches, the lateral and the vertical.

Decomposition of costs with a lateral direction emphasizes the performance of the firm as a whole. This means that cost control is not restricted to producing departments, although most of the product costs or expenses will be incurred in producing departments. The task of cost control will thus be extended to other functional units engaging in product design and development, equipment and facilities acquisition and maintenance, human resource management, product storage and marketing, general administration, and so on. Common efforts made by all functional units will contribute to a significant reduction of production costs and to enhanced production output and efficiency.

Decomposition of costs with a vertical direction divides an enterprise into multiple levels of cost control: factory, workshop, division and team. Target costs are decomposed and assigned in a top-down manner through the hierarchical chain, with the managers at lower levels being held responsible for the fulfilment of the assigned cost targets by the next higher level. The vertical decomposition of costs will assist the supervision of cost control, cost analysis and performance evaluation, and thus may improve the efficiency and effectiveness of cost management.

Enterprise economic accounting

In China, economic accounting has two perspectives: macroeconomics and microeconomics. Here discussion is centred on microeconomics accounting. Thus enterprise economic accounting refers to the comprehensive business management system, with emphasis placed upon the element of cost management.

Enterprise economic accounting system

Enterprise economic accounting is a type of management system initiated by some manufacturing enterprises in Northern China around the early 1980s. This system has been endorsed by government and expanded to most state-owned enterprises since then. In general, the economic accounting system includes the following five functions.

1 Analysing operational goals and decomposing operating targets by the organizational chain within an enterprise.
2 Examining and setting the fixed quota or standard for the consumption of production elements (that is raw materials, parts, fuel and energy, labour hours, fixed assets and other facilities) for all producing and functional units at various levels.
3 Determining gains (profits) and expenses of individual internal operating units.
4 Establishing an internal transfer pricing system for inter-departmental flows of production elements and measuring transaction income by department.
5 Evaluating the performance of operating departments at various levels and implementing rewards and penalties based on the evaluation results.

Cost management of an enterprise is thus implemented via the enterprise economic accounting system. To carry out the enterprise economic accounting, it needs to measure, record and analyse expenses incurred in production processes; to forecast or estimate the costs that will incur in each manufacturing stage; to measure production costs; to assess operating efficiency and economic effectiveness of operating activities; and to implement rewards and penalties in relation to the actual operating results achieved by individual producing departments or functional units. An important aspect of economic accounting is therefore to apply comprehensive cost accounting or cost control over all aspects of operating activities.

Varied approaches of enterprise economic accounting

In practice, two approaches are available for the implementation of the enterprise economic accounting: the centralized approach and the decentralized approach.

The centralized approach   If the task of enterprise economic accounting is implemented mostly by the accounting department at the overall firm level, this model is called centralized enterprise economic accounting. Under the centralized approach, not all internal producing units and functioning departments are treated as separate cost centres. Each internal unit will only examine the supportive evidence for the consumption of production elements or other expenditures relating to its operations, and then classify them on the basis of a predetermined chart of product costs. These expenditures are then reported to the accounting department at firm level, which will uniformly analyse, calculate and record them in ledgers to determine product costs, along with generating performance reports for the purposes of evaluating the contributions made by individual producing units or administrative departments towards the fulfilment of the firm's costs targets and operating goals.

The centralized approach has certain distinctive characteristics. The advantages of this approach include fewer levels (or stages) of the costing process and more efficient accounting work. As the work of product costing has been centralized at the firm/enterprise level, it will help the accounting department to exercise supervision over production expenses and expenditures throughout the firm and to implement cost control within a top-down structure.

There are, however, some disadvantages associated with the centralized approach. For example, the information provided by producing units and administrative departments is usually incomplete. The work of cost analysis and performance may become inefficient owing to a lack of pressure for operating departments to participate in cost control. As a result, the concept of responsibility accounting may be difficult to apply. Therefore the centralized approach is generally adopted only by small business enterprises with a simple production process and organizational structure.

The decentralized approach   Decentralized enterprise economic accounting is just the opposite of the centralized approach in performing cost accounting and cost management. Under decentralized economic accounting, a hierarchical approach of cost accounting is implemented. Individual producing units and administrative departments are responsible for the measuring and control of their own costs. An accounting set-up is installed in every operating department to account for the total costs or expenses incurred within the department. At the end of each accounting period (usually every month), accounting staff in each operating department submit its cost reports to the accounting department at the firm level, with the accounting department determining the production costs of the entire enterprise.

The characteristics of the decentralized approach are the opposite of those of the centralized enterprise economic accounting. Decentralized economic accounting enables relatively independent measurement of costs by department and it enables the implementation of responsibility accounting in cost management. The disadvantage of this approach is that more accounting work is necessary since all operating departments are directly involved in the cost accounting process. The procedure of decentralized economic accounting is also more complex in nature. Thus the decentralized approach is usually applied in large enterprises or enterprises with a complex production process and organizational structure.

Decentralized economic accounting has also been applied through a vertical structure. For example, some enterprises have implemented the economic accounting with a multi-level structure via the production chains. The current practices vary where cost accounting has been applied at two, three or four levels within enterprises. Under the two-level approach to cost accounting, an enterprise is divided into two cost centres with vertical linkage: company headquarters (enterprise level) and branches (department level). Cost accounting at the first level addresses product costing on a company-wide scale while the focus of second-level cost accounting is placed upon the production expenses incurred at individual branches (departments) or the costs of work-in-process by individual departments.

When three-level cost accounting is implemented, the additional level of product costing will be conducted by divisions under operating departments. Similarly, subdivisions or working teams (or groups) can also be treated as the further lower level unit of cost accounting. The installation of decentralized economic accounting obviously tends to facilitate the implementation of the responsibility system of cost control.

In summary, centralized and decentralized cost accounting are two different forms of the enterprise economic accounting system. It is possible for the two approaches to be applied simultaneously within one enterprise. For example, the centralized approach can be employed at the company level while the decentralized approach is utilized at the level of operating departments and further lower-level units of divisions or producing teams. The actual form of internal economic accounting to be adopted is subject to the decision of management in individual enterprises in the light of the unique features of their production process and the availability of resources to operate effectively the economic accounting system.

THE RISE OF MANAGERIAL ACCOUNTING IN CHINA

The current status of managerial accounting

With a close relationship to financial accounting, cost accounting has existed and been practised in Chinese enterprises over a long period. Managerial accounting, on the contrary, is still at an early stage of development in China. Although the concepts and practices of managerial accounting, with their roots in western countries, have been widely introduced into China since the beginning of the 1980s, the development of managerial accounting in China has mainly been evident in education and academic circles. At present the application of managerial accounting is relatively weak in practice.

Educational development of managerial accounting

The introduction of managerial accounting in China commenced in the early 1980s, thanks to a small number of Chinese scholars, who intended to use the western managerial accounting textbooks as supplements to their teaching material immediately after the government began to encourage an opening attitude towards the West in the late 1970s. The topic was certainly new and attractive to Chinese students. Seminars on managerial accounting were then well received at universities and colleges. More translations of western textbooks and research papers on managerial accounting became available. Thus the subject of managerial accounting was added to the curriculum at many Chinese universities and colleges, evolving from an elective course to a required core course for accounting students, and later from the accounting curriculum to a professional course for all management students. The volume of teaching classes on this subject is increasing, as is the importance of managerial accounting courses. This development results in numerous managerial accounting textbooks prepared by Chinese professors. The research interest of managerial accounting has expanded accordingly. At present, a significant number of Chinese scholars have devoted great efforts in pursuing in-depth studies and academic research on managerial accounting.

Managerial accounting courses currently offered at Chinese universities and colleges, however, are relatively shallow, for the following reasons.

First, the content of the textbooks has not been updated for nearly ten years and the structure of the textbooks remains the same as those which prevailed in the West in the early 1980s. The textbooks have not been updated with the new developments of managerial accounting theories and practices in North America and other industrialized countries, nor have they systematically summarized and incorporated the managerial accounting practices in China. Secondly, only technical methods of managerial accounting were introduced and no studies have been done on the application and theory of managerial accounting. Thirdly, there is a gap between academic teaching and real life practice. This restricts the application of managerial accounting in China.

Practical aspects of managerial accounting

As a part of the enterprise accounting system, managerial accounting plays a very significant role in assisting management decision making and in promoting the efficiency and effectiveness of operations in business organizations. Although this has been confirmed by the experience of most industrialized countries, the acceptance of managerial accounting in business management in China is less satisfactory at the moment. Only limited applications of certain basic managerial accounting methods can be found in the real world.

The low acceptance of managerial accounting in practice, in comparison with the status of financial accounting and cost accounting, is not an isolated phenomenon. Without doubt, the current accounting education system in China has fallen behind the demands for qualified management accountants. Simple introduction or duplication of managerial accounting from western textbooks may not be sufficient to train Chinese accounting students to apply managerial accounting techniques most effectively in the business environment in China. The poor quality of Chinese business accountants has also made the application of managerial accounting difficult, if not impossible, to expand. Among the 12 million accounting personnel in China, only a very small faction has received regular school training. The majority of Chinese enterprise accountants lack knowledge of business management, or even general accounting knowledge and skills. They are unable to apply managerial accounting effectively in the real life of business management.

However, the unpopularity of managerial accounting was caused by other factors. In particular, the existing economic administrative system and business management practice may also prevent the expansion of managerial accounting in practice. Most of China's enterprises are state-owned and run by the government. Under such circumstances, the issues of how to finance and invest are, generally speaking, not the concern of management of the state-owned enterprises. As a result, there was no (or little) motivation to utilize managerial accounting, although things have been changing in the last few years. In addition, since accounting and financing staff have not been in a position to make important business decisions in enterprises, the application of managerial accounting in practice is very limited.

Functions and organizations

Managerial accounting has not yet been exercised as a complete and organized function in the Chinese enterprise accounting system. This situation can be seen in the existing structure of accounting departments within enterprises. In most Chinese enterprises, there usually are separate accounting departments (or financial accounting divisions), but no separate financial management (controller) divisions. Thus managerial accounting has been treated as subordinate to the financial accounting function, instead of a very active supporting function for an enterprise's management in making various operational and financial decisions, as is experienced in most western countries.

Changes have only taken place in recent years. Resulting from the restructuring of state-owned enterprises, many new forms of business organization appeared. Diversity in business ownership, such as joint ventures and foreign-affiliated entities, increased significantly. During the process of moving from a planned economy towards a partial market economy, management in individual enterprises have gained increasing autonomy in making operating and financial decisions. In addition, enterprises have been increasingly exposed to competition and market risks. Enterprises' management will have to pay more attention to business financing, cost control and profits. Thus enterprise accounting, both financial and managerial, will play a greater role in business management. In particular, managerial accounting will become a much more important player in providing relevant information for management decision making. The function of managerial accounting in individual enterprises will be well received as a supportive tool for analysing and controlling: analysing the uses of capital, providing relevant and reliable information for financial decisions and proposing solutions to control costs.

THE PRACTICES OF CHINESE MANAGERIAL ACCOUNTING

As a relatively independent stream of the accounting system, managerial accounting has only been recognized and accepted in China's accounting industry for a little more than ten years. Certain practices of integrating the accounting system with the business management system, however, did exist in China even before the 1980s. In addition, some important techniques of western managerial accounting, such as flexible budgeting and responsibility accounting, have also been practised in China for years, although their applications are somewhat different from the western practice. All of these practices can be recognized as the Chinese version of management accounting, even though they remain in a rather simple or basic form.

Economic responsibility and responsibility costing

Starting in the 1960s, the economic responsibility system has been introduced as a part of the production management system in Chinese enterprises. The core of the economic responsibility system lies in the interrelation of responsibility, rights and benefits within any enterprise with which the integrated mechanisms of incentive and reward or penalty are established to stimulate the efficiency and effectiveness of production activities.

Emerging at the same time as the economic responsibility system, enterprise economic accounting developed. As mentioned earlier, enterprise economic accounting focuses on accounting for responsibility costs, that is, assigning and measuring responsibility based on costs. The system matches cost management with economic responsibility, and employs cost accounting to monitor and evaluate the fulfilment of economic responsibility by operating units and employees within an enterprise. The cost targets or quotas are broken down in line with operational responsibility to set standard costs for individual departments, divisions and employees. Implementation of responsibility accounting follows the principle of cost controllability. Operating units have control over the incurring of costs and operating expenses will be the responsibility of accounting centres. Thus responsibility costs are controllable: each responsibility unit has the ability to adjust and control the responsibility costs assigned to it.

Thus the responsibility of departments, teams or individual employees becomes measurable on the basis of cost targets. The output of cost accounting in connection with responsibility measurement becomes the primary input for performance evaluation. In addition, a hierarchical structure has been incorporated in responsibility accounting, in parallel with enterprises' organizational chart. For example, under three-level responsibility accounting, target costs are clearly divided, measured and evaluated in relation to the responsibilities associated with the entire enterprise, operating departments and divisions (teams) respectively.

Although the economic responsibility system was initiated before the 1980s, its application in the early stages was very simple. Following the progress of market-based economic reforms, as well as the influence of accounting practice in foreign-affiliated business entities operating in China, the business management system (including the accounting system) for the state-owned enterprises has also undergone a rapid reform. Currently the system of responsibility cost accounting has been significantly improved, both in its measurements and in its functions.

Economic responsibility and responsibility budgeting

In Chinese management accounting practice, budgeting techniques have been widely utilized. In particular, the responsibility budgeting system has been developed to accommodate the implementation of the responsibility cost accounting system. The two systems are closely interrelated. Budgeting for responsibility costs is usually prepared first in order to measure and evaluate responsibility centres. Techniques of budgeting are not foreign to most Chinese accountants, since budget preparation in China has long been an important tool of economic management, at both the macro and micro levels. There have been problems, however, in the area of accuracy of forecasting and in the efficiency of budgetary control.

The core of responsibility budgeting in business management is to set budgeted costs for each responsibility unit. The total budgeted costs of an enterprise are then decomposed and assigned to operating units. Under the previous centrally planned economy, the responsibility budgets of enterprises had only been utilized for implementing responsibility costs accounting. This is because the other two types of responsibility centre, the profit centre and investment centre, were not functioning, since the majority of enterprises were directly administered by the government. With business profits having to be remitted to the government at 100 per cent, and because all business financing and investment decisions were made by government authorities in charge, concepts of profit centre and investment centre were hardly applicable to business management in the planned economy. However, responsibility budgeting for the control and evaluation of the performance of profit centres and investment centres has been developed in recent years as the management of state-owned enterprises have gained increasing autonomy in making operating and financing decisions in the partial market economy currently evolving in China.

Comprehensive cost control

The comprehensive cost control system, as a component of managerial accounting, was installed in some Chinese enterprises in the 1980s. Three components, or subsystems, are usually incorporated in a comprehensive cost control system: cost control by all staff, cost control over the entire production process, and cost control for all production elements.[4]

The cost control by all employees emphasizes the participation of all employees in an enterprise's cost control and management. Thus management should make every employee, from top managers to individual workers, aware of the importance of cost control. All employees are required to build up the sense of responsibility for cost control and to participate actively in the process of cost management. In order to achieve this goal, rewarding (or disciplinary) mechanisms have also been developed to tie the fulfilment of responsibility for cost control to each employee's performance.

The essence of cost control over the entire production process is continuing control of costs or expenses over the entire production or operating cycle. Thus cost control starts from the purchase of raw materials, followed by manufacturing of the product, the inventory of finished goods, sales of products and warranty services for the product sold. Measures of cost control are implemented through the entire production chain, aimed at achieving a high degree of production efficiency and effectiveness of cost management.

The cost control for all production elements places an emphasis upon the control of consumption of all production elements such as raw materials and parts, fuel and power, plants and facilities, labour (both direct and indirect), supportive services and other administrative facilities. The goal of this subsystem of cost control is to minimize the production expenses or spending (input) in relation to the target level of production output.

Cost planning

Cost planning is a strategic process in implementing the economic accounting system. It requires drawing up plans or forecasts for total quantity of production elements and the necessary costs to produce the given quantity of product during a specified period in the future. Although cost planning is similar to cost budgeting in the sense that both need forecasting or estimation of production expenses, there is a remarkable distinction between the two measures of cost management. While cost budgeting is short-term in nature, with a time horizon of one year, cost planning involves strategic plans for cost control or cost management over a longer time spectrum. The preparation of cost plans must incorporate the forecasts of overall operating activities such as acquisition of production elements from suppliers, maintenance of production facilities and marketing of finished products to customers. Both internal and external economic conditions must be taken into account. In addition, cost planning includes setting particular targets of cost reduction for individual responsibility centres or for particular cost items based on an analysis of costs incurred in the previous periods.

In practice, cost plans are prepared for the total products to be produced over a planned period (including total costs and unit cost) or for the products to be sold over the planned period. Generally, the content of cost plans must include the following items.

1 The target costs for each product in a planned period and the cost components of those products. Spending quota or cost standards must be set for the use of primary raw materials and labour.
2 The proposal for cost reduction in the production process, including specific policies and methods to be implemented to achieve the cost reduction targets.
3 The analysis and explanation of cost planning. Items to be specified include the execution and evaluation of previous cost plans; the assumptions underlying cost planning and any possible changes of economic or market conditions in the planned period; the feasibility analysis of the cost targets; the effects of specific policies or methods to be adopted to reach cost targets; any uncertainty or potential impact of unforeseeable future events, and so on.
4 The spreadsheets or working papers describing the cost plans. Various tables or diagrams, such as the 'Direct Labour Plan', the 'Planned Cost Assignment of Supplementary Production Expenses' or the 'Predetermined Rate of Manufacturing Overheads', must be attached.

It is important to note that both financial accounting and managerial accounting are heavily regulated by the government in China. Accounting information is therefore government-oriented. Cost planning in individual enterprises must be in line with the requirements in specific governmental regulations or rules governing business financing and product costing. In particular, enterprises are not allowed to set cost plans which deviate from the required scope of cost expenditures and spending criteria of production elements. This is unique to the Chinese practice of managerial accounting, because ensuring the interest of the state is an overwhelming obligation for Chinese accountants.

PROSPECTS OF MANAGERIAL ACCOUNTING IN CHINA

In summary, modern managerial accounting has been introduced into China for more than ten years now. Great efforts have been made by Chinese accounting scholars to disseminate the knowledge of managerial accounting. The subject has been incorporated in the curriculum of management education programmes in China and have been well received by students. The practical development of managerial accounting in China is, however, less satisfactory at present, but changes have taken place in recent years. Many managerial accounting techniques which originated in the West have been implemented by increasing numbers of Chinese enterprises and some managerial accounting practices with Chinese characteristics have been experimented with and popularized. It appears likely that managerial accounting will expand at a greater pace in the near future. The motive forces behind a faster development of managerial accounting in China include the following.

First, the demands for managerial accounting have increased. Chinese economic reforms have gained momentum in recent years. Reform of the state-owned enterprises is under way. Enterprises have currently been increasingly exposed to the markets, while direct government involvement in business administration is retreating. With a diversification of business ownership and emergence of a capital market in China, sources and means of business financing have also expanded. All of these developments will lead the management of Chinese enterprises to bear more responsibility for their enterprises' survival and expansion in the market-based economy. Management will have more incentives to improve internal management. Managerial accounting with techniques to assist management in strategic planning and control of operations will certainly have a much greater role to play in business management.

Secondly, the general quality of business managers and accountants in China has improved remarkably. Increasing numbers of a new generation of business managers and accountants have been trained in modern management. They have a better understanding of the importance of scientific business management. The new generation of enterprise managers or entrepreneurs are willing, and will be able, to apply effective management theories and methods (including managerial accounting) in the process of decision making. In fact, business managers in China are paying increasing attention to the application of accounting information, both financial and managerial, in decision making. The status of accountants in business management has risen. Thus managerial accountants can be more actively involved in the business management process.

Finally, the positive role of managerial accounting in promoting production efficiency and effectiveness has also been recognized and emphasized by the Chinese government. Strengthening accounting work (managerial accounting in particular) has been adopted as an integral part of the new enterprise system introduced by the government authorities during the current process of economic reform. In step with the progress of enterprise reform, managerial accounting has gained greater popularity. For example, some large enterprises have invited external consultants or college professors specializing in managerial accounting to participate in the designs of their business management systems. This trend will continue, perhaps to a heightened degree in the near future.

NOTES

1 In China, the focus of accounting regulations was traditionally placed upon accounting activities in manufacturing enterprises. Thus the core pieces of governmental regulations on accounting and cost management have always been related to manufacturing enterprises, which served as a benchmark for other industry-specific regulations or rules.
2 The fixed-quota costing system is fairly similar to the standard costing system applied in western countries. A few differences do exist, however, between the fixed-quota costing in China and the standard costing system in the West. In particular, the fixed quotas of cost components are mainly imposed by government authorities outside of enterprises.
3 Therefore when a budgetary costing system or a fixed-quota (standard) costing system is employed, timely adjustment will be made to report the actual costs for each accounting period specified in governmental regulations.
4 In Chinese, the comprehensive cost control system is also called 'three-overall cost control'. This means that all staff, the entire production process and all production elements will use the Chinese character of *Quan-Bu*, which means 'overall'.

6   Auditing

Auditing is closely related to accounting. The nature of an audit is to examine accounting books and related transactions in order to render the auditor's opinions on the quality of financial statements released by economic entities, or on individual auditees' compliance with the specified statutory requirements. Auditing enhances the reliability of accounting information and promotes auditees' accountability and operating efficiency, and thus plays a significant role in any given society. This chapter elaborates the development of Chinese auditing. The statutory requirements on auditing, the system of state audit supervision, the structure of state audit organs, the responsibilities and rights of auditors, and the standardized procedures of governmental audits will be delineated in turn.

OVERVIEW OF THE CHINESE AUDITING SYSTEM

Generally speaking, auditing comprises governmental auditing and non-governmental auditing. The former is performed by government auditing agencies over the operations and financial results of governments and other economic entities in the public sector, whereas non-governmental auditing is mainly performed by public practitioners over the operation or financial transactions of industrial and commercial entities. Although non-governmental auditing or public accounting has a predominant influence in auditing practices in the West, the situation is reversed in China. In an economy with an immense proportion of state ownership of means of production, and with centralized state economic planning, governmental auditing, or 'state audit', is naturally a dominant force in Chinese auditing practice, while non-governmental auditing, or 'social auditing', or independent auditing, is only a secondary player, especially at this early stage of the market-based economy currently evolving in the country.

Auditing in China is under rigid governmental control irrespective of governmental audits or public accounting practices. We will start this chapter by examining China's state audit system. The emphasis is therefore

111

placed upon the development of governmental auditing. Non-governmental auditing will only be referred to as necessary to elaborate the statutory components of the state audit supervision. Non-governmental auditing or public accounting practices in China will be elaborated more specifically in the next chapter.

Establishment of state audit supervision

Auditing practices, both governmental and non-governmental, existed in China before the founding of the People's Republic of China in 1949.[1] For example, a state audit organ, the Bureau of Auditing, was set up by the government of the Nationalist Party (*Guomindang*), in the early 1920s. However, the audit system in place then only played a very limited role in social life, corresponding to the relatively underdeveloped national economy in the country.

After the communists assumed power in China on 1 October 1949, a formal Soviet-style, centralized planned economy with public ownership of means of production was installed. The central government exercised very rigid planning and control over the national economy. All economic entities, including government bodies, business enterprises, social institutions and non-profit organizations (NPOs), were directly funded through the state's budgetary appropriations and all revenues or business profits realized by economic entities had to be handed over to the state treasury. Under such a fiscal administrative system, the auditing function, both governmental and non-governmental auditing, became incompatible with public ownership in an economy where the state had directly exercised entire control of economic activities. For this reason, the system of auditing was outlawed in China in the early 1950s. All auditing set-ups in governmental auditing and public practices were entirely dismantled.

Thereafter, governments at different levels relied mainly upon the 'financial checking' performed by varied governmental authorities in charge of public finance, taxation and banking institutions,[2] to exercise supervision over the operation and financial transactions in individual economic entities. In addition, the so-called campaigns of 'financial and taxation examination' were launched irregularly by the state's finance or taxation authorities to pursue limited economic supervision over the legitimacy and appropriateness of financial transactions incurred by individual economic entities.

Changes have taken place since 1978 when comprehensive economic reforms were initiated in the country. A new policy of 'opening to the outside world and energizing the domestic economy' was adopted. The central government intended to save the ailing planned economy by decentralizing certain functions of economic planning and control. Limited autonomy of decision making and economic benefits were granted to lower authorities and to the state-owned enterprises. In addition, government authorities made substantial efforts to attract badly needed foreign investments to enable economic reconstruction. Economic reforms generated a much diversified economy with multiple ownership in business and non-business sectors. The state monopoly on commercial banking was gradually replaced by competition among an increasing number of commercial banks. As a result, the government's direct control of economic activities was considerably eroded. The need for a more effective mechanism to carry out the state's economic supervision under changing economic and business environment became apparent.

The central government therefore decided to restore the system of state audit supervision in China. A new provision on state audit supervision was incorporated into the Constitution of 1982, followed by the appointment of the State Auditor General at the First Plenary Section of the Sixth National People's Congress in June 1983. The National Auditing Administration of the People's Republic of China (NAA) was officially established on 15 September 1983 and mandated to take the lead in rebuilding the state audit supervision throughout the country.

Concurrently, the Chinese government decided to resume non-governmental auditing or public accounting as a response to increasing demands of foreign investors for the services of independent auditing. In the early 1980s, accounting or auditing firms formed by public practitioners reappeared, under the auspices of government finance and auditing authorities, in a few coastal commercial centres such as Shanghai and Guangzhou, where most of the early foreign investments flowing into China were located.

Both governmental and non-governmental auditing have grown rapidly since the early 1980s.

The system structure of state audit supervision

The Constitution of 1982 requires that the state audit supervision be installed across the country. The Chinese system of state audit supervision comprises three elements: governmental auditing, institutional internal auditing and non-governmental auditing (or 'social auditing' as it is officially named by the government authority in charge).

Governmental auditing involves the audit supervision of governments and government-related entities. Government audits are exercised by the state audit offices such as the NAA and the bureaux of auditing at lower levels of government.

Institutional internal auditing is the audit supervision performed by internal auditing set-ups or personnel within individual government departments, state-owned financial institutions, business enterprises and NPOs. Internal auditors are responsible for supervision of operating activities and financial performance of the institutions and organizations in which they serve, and of the subordinate entities associated with them.

Non-governmental (social) auditing refers to the independent auditing services provided, on the basis of client engagement, by public practitioners who are certified and registered with government authorities. Currently, the non-governmental or social auditing is performed mainly by Chinese certified public accountants (CPAs).[3]

Distinctions and linkages exist among the three components within China's auditing system. In fact, they are integrated into a complete system of state audit supervision while governmental auditing has played a dominant role until now. The structural framework of China's state audit supervision system is illustrated in Figure 6.1.

THE REGULATORY ENVIRONMENT OF STATE AUDIT SUPERVISION

Regulatory authority over auditing

Auditing in China is subject to strict governmental regulation or administration. The Auditing Law states that the NAA is the supreme authority in charge of audit supervision nationwide. The NAA, located in Beijing, is a ministerial authority under the State Council. Under authorization of the Auditing Law, the NAA's major mandates include the following:

- studying and drafting national auditing legislation and regulations, formulating measures to enforce audit legislation or regulations, and developing national standards or operational guidance for auditing practices;
- being in charge of audit supervision throughout the country, and investigating or handling emerging auditing issues of great significance;
- exercising supervision through audit over the execution of the state's fiscal budgets and submitting the audit results to the Premier of the State Council;
- performing financial audits of the central bank, state-owned financial institutions, key state-owned enterprises, NPOs and social programmes;

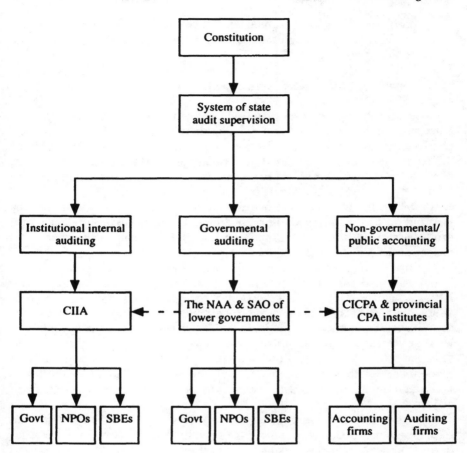

Notes:

CIIA = Chinese Institute of Internal Auditing.

NAA = National Auditing Administration.

CICPA = Chinese Institute of Certified Public Accountants (restructured after 1995 and now subject to joint administration of the NAA and the Ministry of Finance).

Govt = governments and government-related entities.

SAO = state auditing offices.

NPOs = Non-profit organizations.

SBEs = State-owned enterprises.

Figure 6.1 Structural framework of state audit supervision in China

- participating in professional exchanges with government audit authorities in other countries or international bodies of governmental auditing; and
- planning and supervising the education and training of auditing personnel for state auditing offices across the country.

Governmental audits at lower levels of government are carried out by the bureaux of auditing at individual jurisdictions (including provinces, municipalities and counties). Local offices of state audit, under dual leadership of the administrators in corresponding jurisdictions and the state audit offices of higher leading authorities, exercise audit supervision over the implementation of the state fiscal budgets by each government and the revenues and expenses incurred by the state-owned enterprises or other entities under the jurisdiction of the corresponding governments. Local audit bureaux report to the administration at corresponding jurisdictions, and to the state audit offices at the higher level of authority.

The institutional internal auditing is carried out by internal auditors within individual governmental departments, state-owned enterprises and other NPOs, to perform internal supervision of the operations of the entities with which they are associated. Institutional internal auditing is, however, a compulsory component of the state audit supervision in China. Under related government legislation and regulations, internal auditors within individual entities or organizations must comply with the working rules or guidelines stipulated by the NAA, and the work of internal auditing in individual organizations must be subject to the supervision of the state audit offices.[4]

Non-governmental auditing, or public accounting, is directly monitored by national professional associations of public practitioners, under delegation of authority from government authorities. Before 1996, there existed two major national professional bodies in public accounting practice, the Chinese Institute of Certified Public Accountants (CICPA) and the Chinese Association of Certified Public Auditors (CACAuP). Both bodies are semi-governmental agencies; CICPA is subordinate to the Ministry of Finance and CACAuP is administered by the NAA.

Division existed over business scope for the members of the two professional associations. The CPAs concentrated on offering auditing and accounting services to publicly listed corporations and businesses with foreign capital, while the CAuPs provided auditing services mainly to the state-owned enterprises which were a dominant force in the national economy. The split over business scope between the two professional bodies of public practitioners, however, was motivated by a rivalry of jurisdictional authority over public accounting between the Ministry of Finance and the NAA.

There were continuous quarrels or wrangles between the two professional associations competing for business transactions and service revenues. The turf war generated a negative impact on the quality of public accounting or auditing services and tarnished the reputation of public practitioners.

Responding to mounting criticisms from both domestic and foreign investors, the Chinese government decided to consolidate the two professional associations. CICPA and CACAuP were officially merged in late 1995, with CICPA as the surviving body in charge of public accounting across the country. Members of the former CACAuP were converted to CPAs. The newly restructured CICPA is now subject to joint supervision by the Ministry of Finance and the NAA.[5]

Auditing legislation and regulations

Auditing legislation and regulations did not exist in China until the system of state audit supervision was rebuilt in the mid 1980s. Relatively rapid progress in the development of auditing regulations has been evident since then, with the legal framework for audit supervision having been built. The statutory auditing requirements in China are currently derived from the following four sources.

State laws enacted through legislative procedures

Within the Chinese legal system, the most important auditing requirements are in the form of the state laws, which must be enacted by the National People's Congress or its Standing Committee and enforced through state presidential decrees across the country.

The Audit Law of the People's Republic of China (the Audit Law) was enacted by the Standing Committee of the Eighth National People's Congress on 31 August 1994. It came into effect on 1 January 1995. The Audit Law, with seven chapters and 51 articles, specifies basic requirements for the regulatory or administrative system of state audit supervision, formation of state audit offices and staffing, and for the rights, responsibilities, practising procedures and legal obligations of the state audit offices, and so on. The law lays down a legal foundation for state audit supervision in China.

Regulations stipulated by the State Council

Under authorization of the constitution, the State Council (Chinese Cabinet) may stipulate national auditing regulations in the form of the State Council's Administrative Rules and Decrees whenever deemed necessary. For instance, the State Council issued the *Auditing Regulation of the People's Republic of China* in 1988.[6]

Regulations formulated by the NAA

The NAA stipulates practical guidelines or working rules governing audit work within its mandates that are empowered by legal authority. For instance, the NAA issued the *Rules on Field Audit Work Performed by State Audit Offices, Guidelines for Non-governmental (Social) Auditing* and *Working Rules on Institutional Internal Auditing* during the 1980s. More recently, in late 1996, the NAA redrafted and enforced a package of regulations and rules for state audit supervision. This package of state audit regulations and rules, which includes 38 pieces of basic auditing standards, ethical rules and detailed practical standards or operational guidance, became effective on 1 January 1997.

These auditing regulations or rules aim mainly at a standardization of state audit supervision, and at assurance of the quality of audit work performed by government auditors. They are supplementary to the related state audit legislation and regulations. In addition, the NAA may issue, on an irregular basis, various circulars or interpretations governing significant audit issues or emerging new audit problems. These circulars or interpretations issued by the NAA are, in effect, a component of the auditing regulations in China.

Auditing standards and guidelines formulated by professional bodies

The professional bodies of public practitioners such as the CICPA and the CACAuP, under delegation of authority of government authorities in charge, could formulate a series of practical standards or rules on professional ethics governing public accounting ('social auditing'). The Chinese Independent Auditing Standards formulated by the CICPA is one example falling within this category. The auditing standards or practical guidelines formulated by professional bodies are a part of the auditing regulations in China. In particular, all public practitioners, under the bylaws of their professional associations, are bound to comply with these professional auditing standards and ethical rules.

GOVERNMENTAL AUDITING

Governmental audits are carried out by government auditors at state audit offices, such as the NAA and the auditing bureaux of local authorities.

Organizational structure

The Audit Law requires that state auditing offices be installed in all jurisdictions at county level and above,[7] and that each government appropriate sufficient funds for the operations of the state audit office within its jurisdiction.

In the central government, the NAA is the agency in charge of regulating and administering audit supervision nationwide. The Auditor-General, the head of the NAA, is responsible, under the leadership of the Premier of the State Council, for all kinds of audit work performed within China. He or she must report to the Premier, and present annually the audit reports regarding the execution of the state fiscal budgets to the National People's Congress. The Auditor-General is a cabinet member, should be nominated by the Premier of the State Council and appointed by the President of China after confirmation by the National People's Congress. A number of Deputy Auditor-Generals will be appointed by the Premier of the State Council to help the Auditor-General in running the NAA.

The NAA has been empowered with a very broad range of mandates, including policy formulating and analysis, exercising audit supervision over ministerial authorities in the central government and over key state-owned financial institutions and business enterprises, training of audit personnel and auditing research. Several functional departments or institutes are formed within the NAA accordingly: the department of auditing administration, the department of audits of the state fiscal budgets, the department of financial institution auditing, the department of audits over projects with foreign aids or loans, the research institute of auditing, the education and training centre, and so on. Several professional associations, such as the China Society of Auditing, the Chinese Institute of Internal Auditing (CIIA) and the formal Chinese Association of Certified Public Auditors (CACAuP), are semi-governmental agencies directly under the control of the NAA. The total staff numbers of the NAA was about 900 at the end of 1996.

In addition, the NAA has dispatched a number of resident auditors to ministerial authorities in the central government and some local governments. The resident auditors will, as representatives of the NAA, exercise in-house audit supervision over the implementation of state fiscal budgets, and over the budgetary management of local governments or the financial performance of the state-owned financial institutions and key business enterprises directly administered by ministerial authorities in the central government. Up to the end of 1996, the NAA had appointed resident auditors to 41 ministries in the central government, 16 major municipalities and large state-owned enterprises throughout the country. Figure 6.2 illustrates the organizational structure of the NAA.

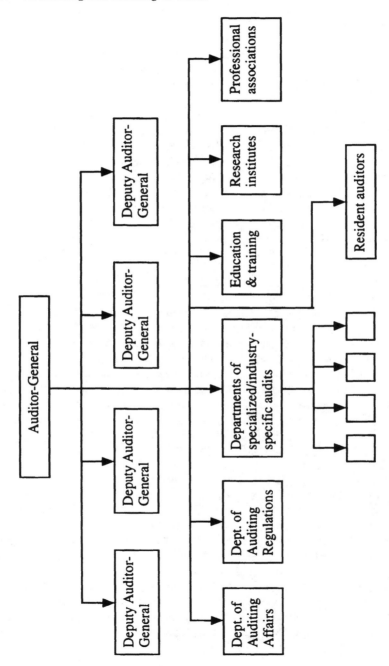

Figure 6.2   Organizational structure of the NAA

The Audit Law requires local governments of individual provinces, municipalities and counties to install state audit offices to carry out audit supervision within their own jurisdictions. Up to the end of 1996, local state audit offices (that is, local auditing bureaux) had been set up in over 95 per cent of governments at county level and above in China. The auditing bureaux of local authorities are subject to the dual leadership of the administrators of corresponding jurisdictions and the state audit offices of the next higher authority. Within the frame of dual administration, local auditing bureaux should also serve as agents for the NAA and protect the interest of the central government. In order to strengthen the control of the NAA over local auditing bureaux, the Audit Law states that any decisions regarding the appointment, reward or discipline and removal of the heads of local audit bureaux be conducted in consultation with the state audit authorities at the next higher level of government. Such a mechanism may, nonetheless, enhance the relative independence and authoritativeness of the state audit offices of local governments. Furthermore, this arrangement will encourage local audit bureaux to exercise audit supervision on behalf of the state's interest.

State audit offices of local governments are also able to appoint or dispatch resident auditors to governmental departments, key state-owned enterprises and NPOs within their jurisdictions. The resident auditors, with delegated authority from the state audit offices in charge, will perform audit supervision inside the residing entities on a year-round basis, in accordance with the statutory responsibilities and rights specified in related auditing legislation and regulations.

Responsibilities of state audit offices

In a centralized economy, the state has direct control over all economic and social programmes. Thus the state audit offices are empowered with fairly broad mandates to exercise supervision through audit over almost every dimension of economic activities in China. As specified by the Audit Law, the state audit offices are particularly responsible for performing audit supervision over the following areas.

1   The formation, revision and implementation of the fiscal budgets and the preparation of the final accounts of government in individual jurisdictions, as well as the government's control and use of the off-budget funds.[8]
2   The levy, collection and remittance of the state's fiscal revenues by governmental authorities in charge of public finance, taxation and

customs tariff; the issuance, management and settlement of the treasury bills and government bonds, and the budgetary appropriations made by the finance departments of governments at different levels.

3 The revenues and expenditures incurred by the central bank, and the assets, liabilities and profits or losses of other state-owned financial institutions.

4 The revenues and expenditures of governmental institutions and non-profit organizations, as well as the off-budget funds being utilized.

5 The operation results and financial position of the state-owned enterprises that are vital to the national economy and people's livelihood, or that depend heavily upon government subsidies, or that have incurred a large amount of losses.

6 The operations of the enterprises with a significant portion of equity interest owned by the state or the enterprises over whom the state has exercised a significant control.

7 The budget implementation and the final accounts of capital construction projects directly funded by the state.

8 The revenue and expenditures of social security funds, public donations and other funds managed by governmental departments and agencies.

9 The revenues and expenditures of projects with aid or loans provided by international organizations such as the World Bank, International Monetary Fund (IMF), the Asia Development Bank, and so on, or by governments of other countries.

In addition, state audit offices are empowered to supervise non-governmental or social auditing and institutional internal auditing, as well as to administer the certification process of government auditing personnel, and so on. The state audit offices or government auditors may contract out certain audit work (mainly the audits of the state-owned enterprises and some NPOs) to non-government auditors or public practitioners, for example the CPA firms or auditing firms registered with government authorities.

Rights of state audit offices

The Audit Law vested the state audit offices with a very broad range of rights in exercising the state audit supervision. Accordingly, the state audit offices have the following rights.

1 To request auditees to submit the budgets or financial plans of budgeted revenues and expenditures, the summaries of budget implementation, the final accounts or other financial reports, the audit reports, if any,

issued by practising professionals, that is, the CPA firms or auditing firms, as well as other related statistical data and supportive documents and explanations.

2 To investigate the authenticity and appropriateness of auditees' accounts, books, minutes, financial statements and related properties.

3 To engage in investigation of auditees' related parties or persons to obtain evidence deemed necessary for the audit work being performed.

4 To prevent or stop auditees' transactions or operations that violate the state's fiscal policies or financial regulations.

5 To request, with the approval of the head of the state audit offices at county level or above, governments' finance departments or other authorities to suspend appropriations or monetary transfers to auditees who are violating the state's fiscal policies or financial regulations, or to freeze the appropriations received by the auditees in question.

6 To recommend to auditees' oversight authorities to revise any internal rules or procedures that are in conflict with the state's legislation or regulations. State audit offices can report to appropriate authorities that have the legal right to take the necessary remedial actions, if the auditees' oversight authorities have refused to do so.

7 To report the audit results to government authorities, or to the public, conditional on maintaining the confidentiality of the state's policies or commercial secrets of the auditees.

The state auditing authorities or government auditors in China, apparently, are empowered with much broader range of rights to carry out audit supervision than their counterparts in most other countries. In particular, Chinese government auditors have the right to suspend or freeze, directly or indirectly, funding for auditees who are allegedly violating the state's fiscal policies or financial regulations. This unique characteristic of Chinese governmental audits can be explained by the fact that the central government has direct control of operations in all governmental agencies and state-owned enterprises. Departures from the government's planning and control are not permitted. The state audit offices are thereby designated to play an active role of economic policing for the central government against any violations of the state's fiscal budgets and financial regulations.

Forms of governmental auditing

A significant portion of governmental audits in China consists of financial audits with respect to the implementation of the state fiscal budgets. The scope of governmental auditing is, however, much broader. For example, audits of the operations of individual governmental departments, agencies and key NPOs are another major component of Chinese governmental auditing, while audits of performance effectiveness have also gained popularity in recent years.

In addition, compliance audits, that is, examining auditees' compliance with specific government legislation and regulations, are always emphasized in Chinese governmental audits in order to ensure proper enforcement of the government's fiscal planning and control over all revenues and expenditures incurred in individual governmental authorities, agencies, state-owned enterprises and NPOs.

Technically speaking, the audits performed by government auditors can be classified into three major categories: routine audits, rotative audits and special-case audits.

Routine audits

These are audits performed on an annual basis, or the audits of auditees' financial budgets or revenues and expenditure accounts in every fiscal year. Audits of the implementation of fiscal budgets and the final accounts of government at different levels are typically routine audits. In addition, routine audits are usually required for the central bank, the state-owned financial institutions, the state-owned enterprises having a significant impact upon people's livelihood, those enterprises receiving a large amount of government funding or subsidies, the key state capital construction projects and the projects with international aid or loans from governments in other countries. Both financial and operational audits may be performed on a routine basis.

Rotative audit

The audit work performed by government auditors on a selective basis, for individual government departments, agencies, state-owned enterprises and NPOs, are rotative audits. Owing to a shortage of manpower in state audit offices, it is impossible for government auditors to perform routine audits over all of these entities. Except for a small number of key government departments, agencies and state-owned financial institutions or business enterprises, most governmental entities, NPOs and state-owned enterprises are currently audited on a selective or rotative basis, determined by operating capacity and availability of government auditors in the state audit offices in charge.

Special-case audits

Special-case audits, also called 'special investigations', are the audits of particular transactions or events incurred by individual governmental agencies, NPOs or state-owned enterprises that are allegedly in violation of the state's fiscal budgets or financial regulations. The investigation results must be reported to the administrations in the corresponding governments and the state audit offices at the higher level of authority. Special-case audits are conducted whenever they are warranted or when demanded by the Disciplinary Committees of the Communist Party or governmental judicial authorities.[9]

Procedures of governmental auditing

The practices of governmental auditing in China have been standardized after experimentation over one and a half decades since the early 1980s. The following standardized procedures formulated by the NAA must be adopted in all governmental auditing.[10]

Preparation of audit planning

Each office of state auditing should determine a list of auditees and make proper planning to specify the types of audit to be performed every year. The audit objectives and the necessary audit programmes in terms of specific circumstances relating to potential auditees would be specifically set out at the planning stage.

Formation of audit teams

Appropriate audit teams for the selected auditees will be formed by individual state audit offices, with respect to the audit objectives and operational specifications determined at the audit planning stage. Each audit team will be staffed with qualified and competent audit personnel for different job assignments. The head of each audit team is responsible for the audit work performed by his or her team members.

Delivery of audit notice

State audit offices must deliver a written letter of audit notice to potential auditees at least three days before the scheduled audit work. The purposes of the audit, a list of audit team members, and the requisite documents or assistance to be provided by auditees must be specified explicitly in the notice.

Performance of field audit work

Each audit team will, in accordance with the specifications highlighted in the audit notice, start field work at the offices of individual auditees

- to examine accounting documents, books and financial statements;
- to review minutes, legal documents and other data related to operations or transactions incurred in the period to be audited;
- to perform a physical examination of cash, properties and marketable securities owned by the auditees; and
- to obtain confirmations or relevant audit evidence from other entities or individuals related to the auditees.

Submission of field audit reports

Each audit team must submit a field audit report to the state audit office in charge, within 15 days of the completion of field audit work unless special circumstances warrant otherwise. According to the NAA's working rules for government auditors, each audit team must discuss with the auditee's management before submitting its field audit report to the state audit office in charge. Auditees are allowed to submit their responses to audit teams or the state audit offices in charge within ten days of being so consulted.

Issuance of audit opinions

The state audit offices in charge review the report of field audit submitted by each audit team and make an overall evaluation of all audit issues involved, and the adequacy of audit evidence collected during field audits. An official statement of audit opinion will be issued by the state audit offices in charge, followed by notifying auditees of the audit conclusions that have been reached.

Delivery of audit decisions on illegal acts

State audit offices, within their statutory rights and responsibilities granted by the Audit Law and other government regulations, will make necessary decisions regarding auditees' illegal acts or activities that violate the state's fiscal policies and regulations on budgetary revenues and expenditures. The state audit offices will, through the auditing decisions, demand that the auditees in question take specified courses of remedy for the alleged illegal acts or irregularities incurred, such as:

- making payment for any fiscal revenues in arrears;
- refunding the revenues and gains realized through illegal acts;
- returning the assets or property obtained through illegal acts, or
- making any necessary adjustments to the books of account.

Government auditors may also recommend that appropriate authorities take specified remedial measures, such as fines or disciplinary actions against the auditees in question.

According to the NAA's working rules, state audit offices must, within 30 days from the date of receiving field audit reports, serve audit opinions and/ or audit decisions on the irregularities or illegal acts discovered during the field audits. The audit opinions and decisions come into effect from the date when they are duly served. Follow-up review will be conducted by state audit offices in respect of the implementation of the audit decisions within three months of the date when auditor's opinions and decisions are served.[11]

Figure 6.3 demonstrates the standardized procedures for governmental auditing in China.

INSTITUTIONAL INTERNAL AUDITING

Internal auditing is a subsystem of state audit supervision in China. The Audit Law requires that permanent set-ups of internal auditing be installed in the following entities:

- individual ministries at the central government, and other authorities that are directly administered by the State Council;
- governmental departments of local authorities;
- the central bank and other state-owned financial institutions; and
- large and medium-size state-owned enterprises, governmental agencies, and NPOs funded by governments.

Small state-owned enterprises or NPOs are not required to establish separate set-ups of internal auditing, but a certain number of full- or part-time internal auditors should be staffed within those organizations as well.

An internal auditing department or division is generally independent of other operating departments within the same organization. Internal auditors report to the chief executive officers of the organization. However, Chinese internal auditors, as required by the Audit Law and the NAA's *Rules on*

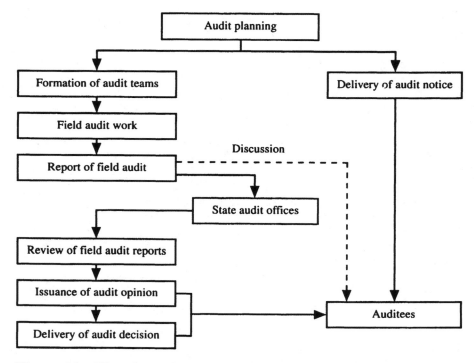

Figure 6.3   Flowchart of procedures for governmental auditing

Supervision over Internal Auditing by State Audit Offices, are subject to the regulatory control of state audit offices. Contrary to practice in most western countries, internal auditors in China must directly shoulder the responsibility for safeguarding the interest of the state, even above their obligations to the organizations to which they belong.

According to Chinese government statistics, up to the end of 1996 there were about 9000 internal auditing set-ups in various governmental entities or state-owned businesses throughout the country, with 15 000 full-time internal auditors and another 14 000 on a part-time basis. However, a significant number of Chinese internal auditors are less than competent at this moment, owing to a lack of sufficient and adequate auditing experience and training.[12]

Responsibilities of internal auditors

As required by the *Working Rules on Institutional Internal Auditing* issued by the NAA in 1985, internal auditing set-ups or internal auditors will, under the leadership of the chief executives of the organizations, independently exercise supervision over operations of the corresponding organizations and their subordinates. In particular, Chinese internal auditors are required to bear the legal responsibilities for the following:

- securing the safety and completeness of all properties entrusted by the state to the organizations in question;
- examining the financial plans or expenditure budgets, cash receipts and disbursement, financing or borrowing and foreign exchange transactions, as well as the effectiveness of all economic contracts executed by the organizations;
- reviewing the justification, efficiency and effectiveness of internal control systems being installed within individual organizations, including monitoring the functioning of internal controls in respect of compliance with the state's financing and accounting regulations;
- confirming that the financial statements or final accounts prepared by the organizations are true, adequate or reasonable, and in conformity with the government's fiscal policies and accounting regulations;
- conducting special investigations of illegal acts or other irregularities that severely violate the state's fiscal policies and accounting regulations; and
- helping state audit offices or external auditors to conduct statutory audits as required.

Apparently, Chinese internal auditors have to bear greater responsibilities than their counterparts in most western countries. One of the significant differences derives from the fact that the institutional internal auditing is a component of state audit supervision in China, so internal auditors are obliged to exercise audit supervision, on behalf of the state's interest, over operations of the organizations with which they are associated. Ensuring compliance with the state's fiscal budgets or accounting regulations is one of the primary duties they have to fulfil. Internal auditors are therefore required to report their work to the state audit offices regularly.

Rights of internal auditors

Corresponding to the broad range of responsibilities or duties mandated, internal auditors in China also enjoy certain statutory rights granted by government regulations, such as the right

- to participate in the design of internal control systems;
- to prevent or suspend transactions that violate the state's fiscal policies, accounting regulations or economic contracts;
- to recommend to the senior executives of the organization necessary remedial actions to be taken against irregularities discovered in internal audits;
- to take compulsory remedial measures warranted under specific circumstances, such as suspending appropriations to subordinates which had committed illegal acts or other irregularities;
- to report to the internal auditing bodies at the higher leading authorities or the state audit offices any significant illegal acts or irregularities discovered during internal audits, and
- to perform follow-up review to ensure that the implementation of internal auditing decisions had been completed.

It is not difficult to understand why Chinese internal auditors are empowered with statutory rights from legal sources. Since internal auditors are required to protect the state's interest, these statutory rights enable internal auditors to exercise supervision on behalf of the state over the operations and financial performance of individual organizations they are associated with.

Procedures of internal auditing

Internal auditing may be organized at regular or irregular intervals, depending upon specific needs and availability of internal auditing resources within individual organizations. Unlike the case of governmental auditing, no standardized procedures for internal auditing have been developed at present, except for the general guidelines laid down in the NAA's working rules on internal auditing. The procedures of internal auditing vary significantly among different organizations with greatly diversified operations.

The relative independence of internal auditors with respect to the executives of corresponding organizations is emphasized, however, as a condition to secure the internal auditors' role in safeguarding the state's interest whenever conflicts between the state and individual organizations arise. Thus government regulations specify that the appointment, promotion and removal of the heads of internal auditing set-ups in individual organizations be discussed with the internal auditing bodies at the overseeing authorities in advance.

Internal auditors should submit reports of internal audit to the top executives of the relevant organization when an internal audit is completed. They should also report to the internal auditing bodies at the overseeing authorities and the state audit offices whenever significant violations of the state's fiscal budgets and financial regulations have been discovered during the internal auditing.

NON-GOVERNMENTAL (SOCIAL) AUDITING

Non-governmental auditing, called *Shehui Shenji* in Chinese, or social auditing, represents another statutory component of China's state audit supervision. Non-governmental audit is performed by public practitioners registered with the Chinese government, including certified public accountants (CPAs) and certified public auditors (CAuPs) before 1995. Under the Audit Law, regulation of non-governmental auditing is also within the mandates of the NAA.[13] Thus the state audit offices have been actively involved in public practices through a control of CAuPs and auditing firms organized by CAuPs since the restoration of public accounting in the early 1980s. There were, by the end of 1995, about 3600 auditing firms operating in almost all parts of the country, with total numbers of CAuPs at over 42 000.

Certification procedures for CAuPs and formation of auditing firms were directly administered by the CACAuP, the national professional body of CAuPs. The CACAuP, founded in November 1992, is a semi-governmental agency under the jurisdiction of the NAA.[14] Under the original framework of non-governmental auditing or public accounting in China before 1995, CPAs and their accounting firms, subject to the administration of CICPA and the Ministry of Finance, provided independent auditing services to publicly listed corporations and business entities affiliated with foreign investments. CAuPs and their auditing firms, subject to the administration of CACAuP and the NAA, would offer auditing services to other business entities, in particular the financial audits for state-owned enterprises, governmental entities and non-profit organizations.

Rivalry between the two players in public practising has, however, always been keen, owing to a turf war for potential market shares as well as for the regulatory control of public accounting at the ministerial level. In particular, the NAA insisted on its regulatory authority over all kinds of audit supervision performed in the country. The NAA permitted CAuPs and their auditing firms sponsored by the auditing bureaux at local authorities to compete with CPAs or CPA firms for clients and business services. This turf war resulted in 'dual audit' for many business entities, that is, the publicly listed companies and business entities with foreign investments must hire CPAs or CPA firms to perform annual financial statement audits in accordance with the requirements of the security trading regulations and legislation on foreign funded businesses, while the auditing firms or CAuPs perform audits again in terms of supervision over the state-owned properties in those business entities. Rivalry became so fierce in many local markets that the quality and reputation of public accounting were seriously tarnished owing to inappropriate solicitation of clients and a price war for service revenues between the two groups of public practitioners. In particular, some CAuPs and local auditing firms had considerably lowered practising standards to expand their client base.[15] This resulted in many deficiencies or even scandals associated with opinion shopping or falsification of attestation documents, which generated negative impact on non-governmental auditing or public accounting practices.[16]

This situation of 'dual audits' and the price war for public accounting or auditing services (associated with lower quality) was continuously criticized by both domestic and foreign investors. Demands for a unified system of public accounting ran high, but little progress was made in resolving these problems owing to the rivalry for regulatory control of non-governmental auditing or public accounting between the NAA and the Ministry of Finance. The NAA was very reluctant to relinquish its overseeing authority over public accounting simply because it had to provide patronage for the CACAuP and auditing firms that were under its jurisdiction.

When the Chinese government introduced a new set of national accounting standards in 1993, these being uniformly applicable to all business sectors and entities, the importance of financial statement audits was re-emphasized. In order to smoothly implement the newly introduced national accounting standards, the need for unified and high-quality public accounting or auditing practices was realized by the central government. With the intervention of the State Council, the Ministry of Finance and the NAA eventually reached an agreement upon the merger of the CICPA and the CACAuP in late 1995. According to this agreement, the CACAuP was merged into the CICPA with all practising CAuPs being converted into CPAs through a review process, while the existing auditing firms could select either to change the name to accounting firms or retain the original name of auditing firms.[17] The NAA officially delivered its endorsement of the restructured CICPA in early 1996.

The NAA, however, has not given up its regulatory authority over non-governmental auditing or public accounting in the country. The NAA issued the *Rules on Regulation of Social Auditing* in 1996, which require state audit offices in the central and local governments to exercise supervisory control of non-governmental auditing, such as the following:

- setting regulations and standards on public accounting and auditing practices, jointly with the government's finance departments;
- conducting financial audits of entities performing social auditing, such as accounting firms or auditing firms; and
- making necessary correction of the reports issued by public practitioners if they are, in the opinion of state audit offices, inappropriate or inconsistent with government legislation or regulations.

It must be pointed out that all auditing firms and their staff (the original CAuPs), irrespective of changes in their professional designations or firm's name, remain subordinate, in terms of their jurisdictional links, to the NAA or state audit offices in lower governments. In particular, the formation of auditing firms is mainly controlled by the NAA and state audit offices of corresponding governments. Thus the turf war between the two original rivals may not completely disappear in public practice so long as public practitioners have not severed their ties with governmental sponsors.

Currently, non-governmental auditing or public accounting is directly administered by the restructured CICPA, under the joint leadership of the Ministry of Finance and the NAA. The CICPA is responsible for the certification of all public practitioners as well as annual review and licensing control of practising CPAs and accounting or auditing firms through the enforcement of professional standards and disciplinary process. This subject will be discussed in further detail in the next chapter.

NOTES

1 According to some accounting historians, China has the longest history and the most sophisticated governmental auditing system of ancient civilizations in the world, dating back to the *Zhao* dynasty, about 2000 BC. See Michael Chatfield (1977), *A History of Accounting Thought*, Huntington, New York: Robert E. Krieger Publishing Co. Inc.; and W. Shuo and S.C. Yam (1987), 'Audit Profile: People's Republic of China', *International Journal of Government Auditing*, **14**,(4): 11–12.
2 There was only one commercial bank in China before 1978, the People's Bank of China. All economic entities had to deal exclusively with the bank for their domestic financial services. The bank could, on behalf of the state, exercise a very broad range of supervision over the operations and financial transactions of individual economic entities.
3 There were two groups of professional practitioners, the certified public accountants (CPAs) and the certified public auditors (CAuPs) in China before 1995. The two

professional bodies were merged in late 1995, with existing CAuPs being converted into CPAs.

4 See NAA (1985), *Rules on the Work of Internal Auditing*; and NAA (1996), *Rules on Supervision over Internal Auditing by State Audit Offices*.

5 See Chapter 7 for a more detailed discussion of the Chinese accounting profession and public accounting practices.

6 As a standard procedure in the Chinese legislative system, governmental regulations for emerging new issues would be formulated and enforced over an experimental period before the official laws were enacted through legislative process. Thus this auditing regulation was stipulated and enforced by the State Council in 1988. It was replaced by the Audit Law in 1994.

7 Within China's jurisdictional system, a county is the level of government below a municipality, while a municipality is subordinate to a province.

8 In China, governmental funds are separated into two major categories: on-budget funds and off-budget funds. All funds incorporated in the state fiscal budget are called 'on-budget funds' and they are subject to the stringent control of the central government. The off-budget funds include the revenues and expenditures not directly administered by the central government. In other words, the collection and use of off-budget funds are at the discretion of local authorities. The central government, however, will also exercise supervision over the sources and uses of the off-budget funds incurred in lower authorities.

9 In China, alleged violations of government fiscal policies or regulations, along with other illegal acts, may be handled by the Ministry of State Supervision or the Disciplinary Committee of the Communist Party at each level of government. Government auditors will be requested to participate in investigation of the cases involving violations or irregularities with respect to government fiscal policies and regulations.

10 See NAA (1996), *The Basic Standards for Performing State Audits in the People's Republic of China*.

11 NAA (1996), *Rules on Compulsory Remedial Measures Imposed by the State Audit Offices*.

12 Most Chinese internal auditors are retired or near-retired accounting staff in individual organizations. Owing to a serious shortage of accounting and auditing personnel in China, many accounting staff work beyond the statutory retirement age. These retired or near retired accountants or internal auditors, however, were trained under the old systems of business administration and they have little knowledge and experience of accounting and auditing practices in a market-based economy. Shortage of qualified personnel or staff has a negative impact on the growth of auditing, including internal auditing, in China.

13 *The Certified Public Accountants Law of the People's Republic of China* empowers the Ministry of Finance with jurisdictional authority over public accounting or independent auditing in the country. Because the term 'non-governmental/social auditing' is less clearly defined in related legislation, state audit authorities were very aggressively involved in the regulatory process of public accounting in the country, which fuelled continuous rivalry between the NAA and the Ministry of Finance.

14 Local associations of CAuPs were established at provincial level throughout the country.

15 Generally speaking, the members of CACAuP had a lower quality standard than CICPA's members, because the qualification requirements and certification procedures for CAuPs were less stringent than those for CPAs. For instance, there was no mandatory entrance examinations for CAuPs. In addition, the guidelines for professional conduct issued by the CACAuP fell short of those issued by the CICPA.

16 See Jinghua Li (1994), 'Some Problems in the Audits of Business Enterprises', *Auditing in China* (in Chinese), January: 6–7; also Jun Kang (1995), 'Current Problems and Solutions to Chinese Public Accounting', *Finance and Accounting* (in Chinese), (3): 50–51.

17 In fact many auditing firms opt for maintaining their original name simply because they do not intend, or are unable, to cut ties with their sponsoring bodies, that is, the state audit offices at different levels of government.

7   Public Accounting and the Profession

The accounting profession consists of accounting practitioners providing professional accounting or independent auditing services to the public. The accounting profession in China is still in its infancy but significant developments have become evident in recent years. This chapter examines the evolution of public accounting in China. The qualification process of public accountants, the formation and administration of CPA firms, the obligations of CPAs, the development of professional ethics and auditing standards, and the professional associations of CPAs will be discussed in turn.

HISTORICAL EVOLUTION OF PUBLIC ACCOUNTING IN CHINA

The earliest practices of public accounting in China date back to the beginning of the 20th century. The entrance of western colonialists and the emergence of domestic industry and commerce brought about a demand for new techniques in bookkeeping and industrial or commercial auditing. The public accounting practices prevailing in the West were thus introduced into China through foreign businesses operating in the country, and by the dissemination of some Chinese scholars who completed their education in western countries.

In June 1918, Xie Ling, who completed his education in Japan, submitted a petition to the then central government for the adoption of a public accounting system in China. The government approved his petition in the same month and granted Xie the first Certificate of Public Accountants to set up his accounting firm in Beijing. The *Tentative Rules for Public Accountants* were also issued by the government in 1919. Later, more Chinese scholars returning from Europe and North America, along with other local practitioners, obtained the government's certification to offer public accounting services. In 1930, the government revised and reissued the *Regulation on Public Accountants* in an attempt to set up a legal framework for the accounting profession.

However, the early development of the Chinese accounting profession went at a very slow pace, owing to the relatively poor status of nationalist industry and commerce. The number of public practitioners was small, while the business volume of public accounting was insignificant. In fact, with the exception of a very limited number of major business and trade centres such as Shanghai, Beijing, Tianjing, Wuhan, Chongqing and Guangzhou, public accounting was almost non-existent in most parts of the country.

After the change of political and economic systems in China in 1949, the communist government adopted public (state) ownership of means of production and highly centralized economic planning and control. Public accounting rooted in the private sector became incompatible with the centrally planned economy. In particular, government authorities employed direct and comprehensive control over the national economy and left no room for independent public accounting services. Thus public accounting was abolished by the Chinese government in the early 1950s. As a result, public accounting in China disappeared for almost the next 30 years.

The Chinese government decided to restore public accounting in the early 1980s, in conjunction with the restoration of the state audit supervision. One of the major concerns behind this decision was the need to satisfy the demands of foreign investors, who poured badly needed capital into China, for independent (or non-governmental) auditing and accounting services. The first accounting firm, although it was under the sponsorship of government authorities, reappeared in Shanghai in 1981. Since then, public accounting has undergone a rapid growth in China, with the professional designation of 'certified public accountants' (CPAs) introduced and new accounting firms organized. In 1988, the State Council issued *The Regulation on Certified Public Accountants* in order to standardize the regulation of public accounting practices. Later, the central government passed a legislation, *The Certified Public Accountant Law of the People's Republic of China* (the CPA Law) on 31 October 1993. The CPA Law came into effect on 1 January 1994, laying down a legal foundation for the development of public accounting in China.

The CPA Law contains seven chapters and 46 articles. It sets out explicit requirements on eligibility, social status, the qualification examination, the certification process, the responsibilities and legal obligations of certified public accountants, on the permitted business scope and working rules of accounting (CPA) firms, and on the administration of professional associations. In addition, the CPA Law authorizes the Ministry of Finance to regulate and govern public accounting practices across the country. Both the certification of CPA candidates and the formation of CPA firms must be reviewed and approved by the Ministry of Finance, or by the national professional association – the Chinese Institute of Certified Public Accountants (CICPA) – under delegation of authority from the Ministry of Finance.[1]

The Chinese CPAs play an increasingly important role in the Chinese economy. In particular, they have provided a great variety of public accounting services to the listed companies and all business entities affiliated with foreign capital and have facilitated the growth of a market-based economy in China. Corresponding to a huge demand for public accounting services, the Chinese accounting profession has also grown rapidly. There were only 500 CPAs and 80 CPA firms in China prior to 1986, but the total numbers of Chinese CPAs exceeded 120 000 by March 1997. Among them, 58 000 are practising CPAs and 66 000 are non-practising CPAs. The total number of CPA firms has gone up to 7000.[2] Despite this significant increase, the shortage of qualified public practitioners remains severe. Thus the Chinese government has decided to further expand public accounting practices as a means of promoting the growth of the market-based economy in China, with an ambitious target to raise the total number of CPAs to 300 000 by the year 2000.

QUALIFICATION OF CERTIFIED PUBLIC ACCOUNTANTS

Under the CPA Law, the qualification requirements for a Chinese CPA include the following three components.

Education

A CPA candidate must complete an undergraduate education at an accredited college or university, or pass the accounting qualification examinations and obtain a professional title of 'accountant' (a rank which stands at the intermediate grading level of accounting qualification)[3] or an equivalent rank in other related disciplines such as financial management, economics, auditing or statistics. Currently, the great majority of CPA candidates in China have completed tertiary education.

Qualification examination

Candidates must write a nationwide Uniform CPA Examination. The examination is administered by the National CPA Examination Committee appointed by the Ministry of Finance. The Committee's mandate includes (1) reviewing and approving the Guidelines on CPA Examinations and the study materials, (2) approving examination questions and passing grades for each examination, and (3) supervising the CPA Examination Committees under the provincial authorities. The CPA examinations, however, are organized and monitored by the CICPA, or its National CPA Examination Office, under delegation of authority from the National CPA Examination Committee of the Ministry of Finance.

The first national CPA examination was held in 1991, the second in October 1993. It has become a regular event which takes place once a year, usually in September, since 1994. The examinations are in written form and currently consist of five subject papers: Accounting, Auditing, Financial Management, Economic/Business Law and Taxation. The length of each paper is three hours. Sitting for all five subjects at the same time is optional rather than compulsory. A candidate may write all five papers in one attempt or write individual papers cumulatively, but he or she must pass all of the five papers to be eligible for certification application. A maximum period of three consecutive sittings is allowed for any candidate to pass the examination if he or she chooses the cumulative approach to write the five papers required. Under current regulations, however, those people who have obtained a professional accounting title at the senior level of qualification grading (that is, senior accountants), or an equivalent rank in other related disciplines, or a senior-level professorship of accounting or auditing at tertiary educational institutions, may be partially exempted from the CPA examination, with one of the five papers being waived. The statistics of CPA examinations over a period of five years are compiled in Table 7.1. It is interesting to note that the overall pass rates in 1995 and 1996 were lower than those in prior examinations, while the total numbers of candidates increased significantly.

Originally, only Chinese citizens could sit the CPA examination, but overseas candidates have been allowed to sit the CPA examinations since 1994. Over 1000 overseas candidates, mainly from Hong Kong, Macao, Taiwan and South Asian countries, wrote the examination papers in 1994. The number of candidates from outside China has increased sharply and continuously since then. Ironically, the performance of overseas candidates, on average, was better than that of domestic candidates. Table 7.2 lists the statistics of the overseas candidates sitting the national CPA examinations in 1994–6.

Owing to a severe shortage of qualified public accountants, an expedient approach of CPA certification was introduced before 1994 by the Chinese government in order to expand public accounting practices. The CPA certificate was granted through an evaluation process administered by the

Table 7.1 Statistics of national CPA examinations, 1991, 1993–6

Year	Item breakdown	Accounting	Auditing	Financial management	Economic laws	Taxation*	Five papers	Overall
1991	attended	—	—	—	—	—	—	—
	passed	2 351	912	1 703	2 123	—	473	7 089
	pass rate (%)	—	—	—	—	—	—	—
1993	attended	27 060	18 443	19 642	21 717	—	—	86 862
	passed	12 705	7 147	10 267	13 495	—	3 754	43 608
	pass rate (%)	46.95	38.72	52.27	62.14	—	—	50.2
1994	attended	62 057	48 060	49 828	48 520	—	—	208 465
	passed	22 018	26 723	22 446	11 375	—	4 642	82 562
	pass rate (%)	35.48	55.60	45.05	23.44	—	—	39.60
1995	attended	104 599	64 758	83 238	76 206	92 081	—	420 882
	passed	12 626	6 843	9 693	13 624	12 929	769	55 715
	pass rate (%)	12.07	10.57	11.64	17.88	14.04	—	13.24
1996	attended	82 186	42 830	53 046	61 339	67 143	—	306 544
	passed	14 577	6 857	9 072	12 462	11 221	309	54 189
	pass rate (%)	17.74	16.01	17.10	20.32	16.71	—	17.68
	Total passed	64 277	48 476	53 181	53 079	24 150	9 947	243 163

Note: * The subject of taxation was not required in the examinations prior to 1995.

Table 7.2 Statistics of overseas candidates in national CPA examinations, 1994–6

Year	Item breakdown	Accounting	Auditing	Financial management	Economic laws	Taxation*	Five papers	Overall
1994	attended	336	330	321	354	—	—	1 341
	passed	172	156	196	159	—	88	683
	pass rate (%)	51.19	47.27	61.06	44.92	—	—	50.93
1995	attended	1 224	1 119	1 140	1 031	1 192	—	5 706
	passed	334	172	271	83	118	41	978
	pass rate (%)	27.29	15.37	23.77	8.05	9.90	—	17.14
1996	attended	1 054	907	877	865	1 088	—	4 791
	passed	137	56	97	76	60	2	426
	pass rate (%)	13.00	6.17	11.06	8.79	5.51	—	8.89
	Total passed	643	384	564	318	178	131	2 087

Note: * The subject of taxation was not required in the examinations prior to 1995.

governmental authorities in charge. In particular, those persons with sufficiently long experience in accounting, auditing practices or teaching could
obtain the CPA certificates without taking the qualification examinations.
A considerable proportion of the existing Chinese CPAs was, in fact, certified through this kind of evaluation process. However, the certification
process was not consistently applied throughout different provinces owing to
a lack of standardized evaluation criteria. Actually, the evaluation approach
could hardly guarantee the high standards of CPA certification and was
severely criticized by many interest groups. As a result, this kind of expedient
measure was terminated in 1995. The CICPA has specified that, with effect
from 1 January 1995, all candidates must pass the uniform CPA examinations prior to their application for professional certification.

Work experience

A CPA candidate must have at least two years' work experience in public
accounting or auditing. Usually, such experience should be obtained through
working in accounting or auditing firms. Failure to meet the requirement of
public practising within five years of passing the uniform examinations will
result in avoidance of a candidate's eligibility for CPA certification.

When a candidate has fulfilled all three components of the qualification
requirements, as well as maintaining professional integrity and an honest
character, he or she can apply to the government authority in charge of
public accounting at the provincial level or above, or to the national or
provincial CPA institutes authorized by government authorities, for CPA
certification. Successful candidates will receive an official CPA certificate
issued by the CICPA.

There are two categories of CPA in China at present; one is the practising
CPAs, that is to say the CPAs who are working in accounting or auditing
firms; the other is the non-practising CPAs, or the CPAs who have obtained
the professional certificate but do not engage in public practice; instead,
they serve in industry, government or educational institutions. According to
the regulations, a practising CPA who has not performed public accounting
over one year must be registered as a non-practising CPA. In other words, a
CPA's practising certificate will be relinquished upon his or her departure
from a CPA firm, but it can be reinstated at a later date when his or her
affiliation with a CPA firm is resumed. So far, the numbers of practising and
non-practising members of the CICPA are roughly half and half among a
total of 120 000. The CPA qualification and certification must be reviewed
and reconfirmed by the CICPA or by the provincial-level professional institutes on a yearly basis.

Continuing professional education (CPE)

According to the *General Standard on Continuing Professional Education* issued by the CICPA in 1996,[4] a CPA must pursue continuing professional education to update his or her professional knowledge and skills. In addition to the subjects of accounting, auditing, financial management and business law, a CPA is required to have updated knowledge of new developments in related disciplines such as asset appraisal, EDP systems, public finances, banking, taxation, economic laws, commerce and trade, and business management. It is required by the CICPA that each member take at least two weeks (40 hours) of CPE programmes each year, and that the total CPE programmes to be taken be not less than two months, on a full-time basis, in any three consecutive years.

The CPE may be obtained through various formats or programmes, including special-topic training programmes sponsored by CPA institutes, on-the-job training and inter-firm exchange programmes conducted by a member's own firm or other CPA firms, regular college education operated on a full-time or vocational basis, and/or other related professional seminars and conferences. The fulfilment of CPE is one of the requirements for annual renewal of CPA certification.

FORMATION AND ADMINISTRATION OF CPA FIRMS

According to the CPA Law, a CPA can only practise publicly through an accounting firm or auditing firm, that is to say, Chinese CPAs must join CPA firms to provide public services.[5]

Requirements for formation of CPA firms

A CPA firm may be in the form of a limited-liability entity with the liability being restricted to the total assets of the firm. Under current regulations, a CPA firm with limited liability should meet the following three conditions: (1) to have not less than RMB ¥300 000 of the registered capital; (2) to be staffed by at least five full-time CPAs and an appropriate number of practising staff; and (3) to conduct business, in respect of the ranges and types of operations, in conformity with government regulations or other relevant rules.

A CPA firm may also be a partnership organized by practising CPAs. The partnership should be formed by two or more full-time CPAs and maintain a professional risk reserve of not less than RMB ¥50 000. Each partner is liable for the firm's liability on the basis of his or her proportion of contributed capital or of the partnership agreement. In addition, each partner must be responsible for the firm's liability in the case of any other partner's insolvency.

Currently, the great majority of CPA firms operating in China are limited-liability entities. They have maintained close ties with the sponsoring organizations (governmental or other social institutions) which initially formed the CPA firms. A few CPA partnerships, however, emerged in some coastal business centres with huge foreign investments, such as Shanghai, Shenzhen and Fuzhou, after the CPA Law came into effect in 1994. There were, by March 1997, about 7000 CPA firms operating within China, with about 60 000 practising CPAs plus a significant number of other staff.

Since 1994, foreign CPA firms have been allowed to enter the Chinese markets of public accounting services, but mainly in the form of joint ventures with Chinese CPA firms so far. Applications for the formation of CPA joint ventures should be submitted to authorities of the central government (particularly the Ministry of Foreign Trade and International Cooperation or other authorities designated by the State Council), or to provincial governments. Final approval must be obtained from the Ministry of Finance of the central government. At present, all of the 'Big Six' international accounting firms have set up CPA joint ventures with Chinese partners in major business centres and some coastal cities across the country. In addition, a number of other international or regional accounting firms, including some from Hong Kong and Taiwan, have established their representative offices in some coastal cities, with the approval of the Ministry of Finance, to offer accounting and auditing consulting services. Foreign CPAs may also offer public accounting services for their clients' operations in China, provided they apply for a temporary practising permit from the Ministry of Finance. The permit may be granted on a one-job only basis or for a short period of three to six months.

The Chinese government has recently decided to further liberalize domestic accounting services. For instance, foreign CPA firms, particularly the 'Big Six' international accounting firms, are allowed to establish their member firms in China according to the *Temporary Methods for Administration of the Resident Offices of Overseas Accounting Firms* issued by the Ministry of Finance in 1996. Thus it is quite possible that we will see some Chinese CPA firms officially adopting the names of the 'Big Six' in the near future.

Procedures for setting up CPA firms

Before the formation of a CPA firm, including setting up branches or local offices, its sponsor(s) must submit an application to the Ministry of Finance or the CICPA, or to their counterparts at the provincial level. The following documents must be presented with the application:

- the official letter of application;.
- the name, organizational structure and business location of the proposed CPA firm, or its local branches or offices;
- the by-laws or partnership agreement of the proposed CPA firm;
- the name, rank, personal profile and other relevant information of the managers of the proposed firm;
- the name, personal profile and certification documents of all full-time CPAs who are associated with the firm;
- the verification report of the capital contribution made by all sponsors or partners.

The sponsor(s) of a CPA firm must apply to the local administration bureaux of industry and commerce for the business registration and licence within 30 days of an approval of the CPA firm by government finance departments being received. In addition, a tax registration must be filed with local taxation authorities not later than the required deadline before the firm commences its operation.

Business scope of CPA firms

According to government regulations, a CPA firm is permitted to pursue business activities as follows:

- financial audits of business entities;
- verification of capital contributions to business entities;
- tax services and consultation;
- participation in processing business combination, separation and liquidation;
- appraisals of assets or contributed properties for the purpose of changes in business equity holding, and formation of joint ventures;
- accounting system design, bookkeeping services and training of accounting personnel for business and non-business entities;
- management consulting services;
- investigations and testimony in legal cases; and
- other activities authorized by related legislation and regulations.

A CPA firm may carry out its operations in different industries and jurisdictions. Under the existing business legislation and regulations, all business entities affiliated with foreign capital and all publicly listed companies must hire Chinese CPAs to perform verification of contributed capital and annual financial statement audits. Not all CPA firms are eligible, however, to provide public accounting services to the listed companies at the moment. A special licence is required for CPAs and CPA firms to offer accounting services to the listed companies in China. The major purpose of the government's special licensing programme is to authorize a very selective and small number of high-quality CPAs or CPA firms to engage with the publicly listed companies. CPAs must write additional papers on securities regulations jointly administered by the China Securities Regulatory Committee (CSRC) and the Ministry of Finance, and must meet strict requirements, to apply for the special licences. Up to March 1997, only 1108 CPAs and 105 CPA firms, out of the total of about 60 000 practising CPAs and 7000 CPA firms nationwide, had been granted the special licences by the government authorities in charge.

Financial management of CPA firms

A firm is a business entity with independent financing and its own accounting arrangement. Thus a CPA firm provides public accounting services based on client engagement and financial compensation. A varying range of fees applies, according to the different services offered and will be charged in two ways: (1) flat rates – service fees are charged on the basis of predetermined ratios of a client's total assets or total revenues; or (2) hourly rates – fees are charged according to the actual service hours rendered by practising CPAs with varying levels of hourly rate.

In China, the service rates of CPA firms are controlled or regulated by government authorities. The finance bureaux of each provincial government, or the provincial CPA institutes under delegation of authority by the government, will set the standard rates, as a range of fees for different types of service, for all CPA firms registered in the province. Although individual firms may exercise some flexibility within the range of standard rates, they are not allowed to surpass the ceiling of service charges imposed by government authorities.

A CPA firm must submit 3 per cent of its total operating revenues, as membership dues and administration fees, to a provincial CPA institute and the CICPA, of which each receives 50 per cent. Any net income generated (operating revenues minus operating expenses) is taxable, although a CPA firm is allowed to deduct a reasonable portion of the before-tax profit as a provision for professional risks. Under current regulations, all CPA firms must set up reserves against professional risks.

Staffing of CPA firms

Under the existing regulations, a CPA firm should be staffed by a chief accountant and a director, with the chief accountant in charge of the firm's operations. The director is mainly responsible for internal administration of the firm. Usually, there are several divisions or sections within a CPA firm, each staffed by a number of section heads or project managers to deal with particular areas of operations such as financial audits for listed companies, accounting and auditing services for business entities with foreign investments, verification of capital contribution and asset appraisals, taxation services and management consultations. In addition, a CPA firm is staffed by a certain number of junior professionals and supporting clerks. At present, most Chinese CPA firms, however, are local market-oriented. They are usually small, with staff numbering not more than 50.

All CPA firms are subject to supervision or operational monitoring by the government authority in charge of public accounting or the CPA institutes at either central or local level. Thus a CPA firm must report to the overseeing authorities if it has encountered any of the following events:

- revision of the firm's by-laws;
- change of the firm's chief accountant or director;
- implementation or revision of the main internal control systems for job assignment and coordination, financing, accounting and personal training;
- preparation of annual business planning, operational summary and financial reporting; and
- any significant violation of professional ethics or practising standards.

The CPA Law specifies that all CPA firms be subject to an annual review of the CPA qualification and operating performance organized by the government authorities in charge, that is, the government's departments of finance or the CPA institutes. The review process includes an examination of whether a CPA firm has complied with all government regulations and professional standards as required.

CPAs' LEGAL OBLIGATIONS

The legal obligations of a Chinese CPA or a CPA firm are derived mainly from the CPA Law, the Corporation Law and the *Tentative Measures for Prohibition of Deception and Dishonesty in Securities Trading*,[6] as well as other related government regulations. Article 21 of the CPA Law states that a CPA should not issue an audit report if he or she has encountered any of the following events in his or her auditing engagement:

- a client has raised the issue of false or misleading reports;
- a client has deliberately held back necessary accounting data and other relevant documents;
- proper assessment could not be made on significant accounting and reporting transactions owing to any unreasonable restrictions imposed by a client.

The Law specifies that a CPA or a CPA firm, when issuing an audit report, should not commit any of the following acts of misconduct.

1   Failure to disclose the fact that a client's major financial and accounting procedures are in conflict with government legislation and regulations.
2   Intentionally withholding information or issuing a false report when he or she knows that a client's financial and accounting practices are directly damaging to the interests of financial statement users and other interested parties.
3   Failure to disclose the fact that a client's financial and accounting practices will severely mislead the users of financial statements and other related interested parties.
4   Failure to disclose the fact, to his or her knowledge, of other significant misrepresentations in a client's financial statements.

Under the CPA Law, a CPA firm that commits any of the acts of misconduct outlined above must be disciplined by the government authority in charge of public accounting, that is, the Ministry of Finance or the CICPA. The disciplinary actions may include warning, confiscation of income from the misconduct and a fine equivalent to one to five times the income from the misconduct. The CPA firm may be suspended or have its business licence revoked from practising public accounting service if the offences are severe in nature.

The government authority in charge may also issue a warning to a CPA who has committed the misconduct. He or she may be suspended or have his or her practising licence or CPA certificate revoked. In addition, a CPA or a CPA firm might be subject to criminal charges for any false audit reports or certificates of capital contributions intentionally issued.

Under Provision 219 of the Corporation Law of 1993, any individuals or entities involved in the issuance of false certificates and documents of asset appraisals, false verifications of capital contribution, or false audit reports of financial statements, enclosed in corporate registration files, may face the following punishments: (1) confiscation of the income derived from the illegal act, (2) a fine equivalent to one to five times the illegal income, (3) a suspension or revocation of professional licences and certificates by the government authorities in charge; and (4) individuals or organizations who commit fraud are also subject to criminal charges. In addition, individuals or entities who have issued certificates or attestation documents containing significant omission or misrepresentation of information owing to negligence during the performance of asset appraisal, verification of contributed capital, or financial statement audits are responsible for correction of the documents and for paying a fine of one to three times the income received. A suspension or a revocation of their practising licences or professional certificates may follow if the misrepresentation or omission is severe in nature.

Furthermore, the National People's Congress passed a special *Resolution on Discipline of Criminal Acts that Violate the Corporation Law* in 1995, in order to crack down on dishonest acts in corporate formation and registration. Accordingly, any CPA involved in knowingly issuing false attestation documents in the course of asset appraisal, verification of contributed capital or financial statement audits, for the purpose of corporate registration, is subject to a maximum imprisonment of five years and a fine of up to RMB ¥200 000.

In order to regulate the emerging stock market in China, the CSRC issued *Tentative Measures on Preventing Cheating and Swindles in Securities Listing and Trading* in 1993. Any CPA firm that has been involved in false presentation of audit reports, asset appraisals or other attestation documents will face a variety of penalties such as warning, confiscation of income from the illegal act, a fine, suspension or revocation of business licence and so on. Individual CPAs who have direct responsibility for the illegal act will face disciplinary actions of warning, confiscation of income from the illegal act, a fine of RMB ¥30 000 to ¥300 000, and/or revocation of his or her professional certificate. He or she may have also to bear criminal liability if the illegal act is severe in nature.

It appears that Chinese CPAs shoulder broader legal responsibilities than their counterparts in other industrialized countries. The legal system in China, however, is fairly weak at present. Although the Chinese government has enacted a series of business and accounting legislation and regulations in recent years, their enforcement remains highly unsatisfactory. Violations of the legislation and regulations are common but only a handful of offenders have been punished. In a country where most of the economic and social entities are directly controlled by government, even CPA firms have to maintain links with their sponsoring organizations which are tied to various types of governmental authorities. Thus the misconduct or illegal offence committed by CPAs or by CPA firms is fairly difficult for the designated disciplinary agencies (that is, government's finance bureaux and the CICPA) to handle. In fact, only rare cases involving serious criminal offences by CPA firms have been exposed and disciplined thus far,[7] although the State Council Securities Supervision Committee (SCSSC) reported in early 1995 that up to half of the audited financial statements submitted to the stock exchanges are unsatisfactory. The Chinese government must put much more effort into enforcing the legal obligations of the public practitioners.

PROFESSIONAL ETHICS AND AUDITING STANDARDS

Quality of services and ethical conduct by practitioners are crucial to the healthy growth of any profession. The Chinese accounting profession has devoted considerable efforts to developing the ethical rules and practical auditing standards for public practitioners in recent years.

General standards on professional ethics

The CICPA issued *The Rules of Professional Ethics for Chinese Certified Public Accountants* (tentative) in 1992, in an attempt to provide a general guideline for ethical conduct of public practitioners and to raise the quality of CPAs and the societal reputation of the profession. The *Rules of Professional Ethics* set out minimum ethical standards for CPAs, including principles of professional ethics, rules of conduct, disciplinary action, a CPA's responsibilities to clients and colleagues, and so on. The ethical rules were reissued as the *General Standards on Professional Ethics* by the CICPA in December 1996, to be an integrated part of the newly established Chinese Independent Auditing Standards.

Technically speaking, the *General Standards on Professional Ethics* for Chinese CPAs is fairly similar to the *Code of Professional Conduct* issued by the American Institute of Certified Public Accountants (AICPA). Most of the main ethical principles and rules specified by AICPA, such as independence, objectivity and integrity, competence, due care, compliance with laws and regulations, confidentiality of client information, responsibility to colleagues and the profession, contingent fees, proper advertising and solicitations, commissions and referral fees, and so on, are also contained in the CICPA's *General Standards on Professional Ethics*.

Formulation of ethical rules itself, however, may not automatically guarantee a high standard of professional conduct of the CPAs. Enforcement of the ethical rules is much more crucial. The current status of ethical conduct in public accounting in China remains less satisfactory owing to the lack of an effective mechanism in the enforcement process of professional ethics. In particular, the CICPA has been in a fairly weak position in policing the behaviour of its members because the accounting or auditing firms that were affiliated previously to various governmental authorities may find ways to bypass the CICPA's screening. Responding to increasing demands for more reliable public accounting services from domestic and international business communities as well as from the general public, the CICPA has recently decided to tighten the monitoring of its members' conduct by setting up a more authoritative special committee, the Disciplinary Committee. Accordingly, the performance of public accountants will be monitored more closely and the violators of professional ethics will be brought to disciplinary account more quickly by the CICPA. However, it is too soon to judge the real effects of the CICPA's new efforts in promoting ethical standards for its members.

Chinese independent auditing standards

The CICPA formulated a set of practical rules for public accountants in the late 1980s and early 1990s,[8] as an initial attempt to develop a Chinese equivalent of generally accepted auditing standards. The practical rules serve as the recommended guidelines for CPAs or CPA firms in performing and reporting public accounting services. The practical rules lay down fairly detailed procedures but they are voluntary rather than mandatory. Thus compliance with these practical rules was poor and the existing practices remained highly diversified, with significant departures from the recommended practical rules.

The CICPA decided, therefore, to establish a set of much more authoritative auditing standards to replace the previously recommended practical rules. The Task Force on Independent Auditing Standards was set up by the CICPA and authorized to study and draft the *Chinese Independent Auditing Standards* (CIAS). In late 1995, the first batch of nine auditing standards was approved and issued by the Ministry of Finance and the National Auditing Administration (NAA) and came into effect on 1 January 1996. The second batch of a further 14 pieces of auditing standards was promulgated in December 1996 and became effective on 1 January 1997.

According to the *Introduction to Chinese Independent Auditing Standards,* the CIAS is an integral part of the professional regulations for public accounting in China. Three components are included in the CIAS.

General standards for independent auditing

This element of the CIAS provides a summary of the basic principles of independent auditing and general standards on the qualification and professional conduct of CPAs in public practice. The general standards lay down a foundation for setting more specific practical standards and guidelines for independent auditing.

Practical standards for independent auditing (PSIA) and statements on independent auditing practices (SIAP)

The PSIA are applicable to general-purpose auditing engagements, that is, the financial statement audits, while the SIAP are designated for audits in specific industries or for special-purpose attestation acts performed by CPAs.

Practising guidelines (PGs)

These guidelines consist of more specific rules and operational guidance for the application of the PSIA and the SIAP.

The structure of CIAS is illustrated in Figure 7.1. At present, they are drafted by the CICPA, or its Task Force on CIAS, in accordance with the principles laid down in the CPA Law. All standards of the CIAS must,

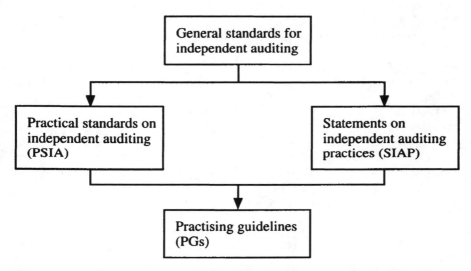

Figure 7.1   Structure of Chinese independent auditing standards

however, be approved and promulgated jointly by the Ministry of Finance and the National Audit Administration (NAA).

According to CICPA's original planning, about 30 PSIA, ten SIAP and ten PGs, in total, will be developed in three to five years. Hence more statements of the CIAS will be promulgated later on. Table 7.3 lists the main auditing standards that have been in effect in China, up to 1 January 1997.

In order to ensure the quality of the CIAS, the Ministry of Finance has set up two advisory groups to review the proposed auditing standards. One is the Advisory Group of Domestic Experts, consisting of Chinese accounting and auditing experts from the CICPA, CPA firms and academics, and the other is the Advisory Group of Foreign Experts, with members coming from overseas professional bodies, international accounting firms and academics abroad. Thus the procedures for setting the CIAS are as follows.

Initiation of standard projects   The Task Force on CIAS of the CICPA identifies a list of proposed standard projects, which must be approved by the state Ministry of Finance after consultation with the two advisory groups.

Preparation of exposure drafts   The Task Force on CIAS studies the proposed standards and prepares exposure drafts (EDs) for each project, with input from the two advisory groups. The exposure drafts will then be submitted by the CICPA to the Ministry of Finance.

Solicitation of comments   The exposure drafts will be released by the Ministry of Finance to solicit comments from related governmental authorities, CPA institutes at provincial level, CPA firms, industries and academics.

Revision of EDs   The Task Force on CIAS revises the exposure drafts based on public comments solicited and submits the revision to the two advisory groups for review. The final version of the standard projects must be approved by the CICPA and the Ministry of Finance.

Pronouncement   Every piece of new auditing standards must be issued jointly by the Ministry of Finance and the NAA. Any amendments to the existing CIAS should be prepared by the CICPA and approved by the Ministry of Finance and the NAA.

The CIAS have incorporated the internationally accepted auditing practices to a great extent and are fairly similar to the 'Generally Accepted Auditing Standards' (GAAS) in most industrialized countries. Under the existing

Table 7.3   List of Chinese independent auditing standards (January 1997)

Chinese Independent Auditing Standards – General Standards for Independent Auditing
Practical Independent Auditing Standard No. 1 – Audits of Financial Statements
Practical Independent Auditing Standard No. 2 – Audit Engagement Letters
Practical Independent Auditing Standard No. 3 – Audit Planning
Practical Independent Auditing Standard No. 4 – Audit Sampling
Practical Independent Auditing Standard No. 5 – Audit Evidence
Practical Independent Auditing Standard No. 6 – Audit Working Papers
Practical Independent Auditing Standard No. 7 – Audit Reports
Practical Independent Auditing Standard No. 8 – Fraud and Error
Practical Independent Auditing Standard No. 9 – Internal Control and Audit Risk
Practical Independent Auditing Standard No. 10 – Audit Materiality
Practical Independent Auditing Standard No. 11 – Analytical Reviews
Practical Independent Auditing Standard No. 12 – Using the Work of Specialists
Practical Independent Auditing Standard No. 13 – Using the Work of Other CPAs
Practical Independent Auditing Standard No. 14 – Opening Balance
Practical Independent Auditing Standard No. 15 – Subsequent Events

Statements on Independent Auditing Practices No. 1 — Verification of Capital Contribution
Statements on Independent Auditing Practices No. 2 – Management Letters
Statements on Independent Auditing Practices No. 3 – Special Consideration for Audits of Small Business
Statements on Independent Auditing Practices No. 4 – Examination of Profit Forecast

Practical Guideline No. 1 – Annual Audits of Financial Statements
Practical Guideline No. 2 – Audit Working Papers
Practical Guideline No. 3 – Verification of Capital Contribution

regulations, the independent auditing standards are applicable to all types of auditing actions. Every CPA is bound to comply with the standards if he or she is involved in an auditing engagement, irrespective of the size, ownership, business or non-profit nature of a client's operation. In addition, the standards may also be applicable to other courses of engagement in public accounting under certain circumstances.

PROFESSIONAL BODIES OF CPAs

The CICPA, with its headquarters located in Beijing, is the national professional body for CPAs in China. The CICPA is a semi-governmental agency acting as a liaison between CPAs and government. According to the CPA Law, the CICPA is under the jurisdiction of the Ministry of Finance.[9] Its president and vice-presidents are selected nominally by its annual general member conference, but candidates must be approved by the Ministry of Finance and the NAA. Usually the president and vice-presidents of the CICPA serve only on a part-time basis. Operational decisions are mainly made by the secretariat of the CICPA, which consists of a secretary-general and his deputies. There are several functional departments under the CICPA, including the Department of Certification and Licensing, the Office of National CPA Examinations, the Department of Professional Education and Training, the Task Force on Independent Auditing Standards, the Disciplinary Committee, the Liaison Office of Overseas Membership, the Department of Financial Management, and so on.

The CICPA is delegated with the authority from the Ministry of Finance to be in charge of all affairs relating to public accounting, such as registration of CPAs, licensing for CPA firms, administration of uniform CPA examinations, monitoring the performance of CPAs and CPA firms, and so on. The main objectives and responsibilities of the CICPA include the following.

1 To review and approve applications for CPA certification, under delegation of authority by the Ministry of Finance.
2 To organize the national CPA examinations and the grading of examination papers.
3 To develop the rules of professional ethics and the auditing standards for public practitioners, in light of related government legislation and regulations.
4 To reflect members' reasonable demands or requests and to protect members' vested interests and benefits.
5 To monitor members' ethical conduct and practising performance, as well as to discipline members who violate ethical rules and auditing standards.
6 To organize exchange of information and work experience among CPA

firms across the country, to sponsor professional training and CPE programmes, and to offer professional consultations to enhance members' professional competence.

7   To establish exchanges and connections with relevant professional bodies in other countries.

8   To fulfil other tasks requested by government authorities in charge.

The CICPA has actively expanded its ties with professional bodies in other countries. It is reported that CICPA has been officially admitted into the Confederation of Asian–Pacific Accountants (CAPA) and the International Federation of Accountants (IFAC), in 1996 and 1997, respectively. It became a member of the International Accounting Standards Committee (IASC) in July 1997. Increasing cooperation between the CICPA and international or regional professional bodies has promoted a rapid growth in the Chinese accounting profession and will also benefit the international business community.

CPA institutes are also established in all provinces, autonomy regions and municipalities directly under the State Council, as the local professional bodies of CPAs in individual jurisdictions. The provincial CPA institutes follow patterns similar to the CICPA with respect to their organizational structure and responsibilities. They are subject to a dual leadership of the provincial government authorities in charge of public accounting (that is, the finance bureaux) and the CICPA.

Individual CPAs must join the provincial institutes in their resident provinces. Since the provincial institutes are institutional members of the CICPA, all members of provincial CPA institutes automatically become members of the CICPA as well. In addition, every CPA firm is an institutional member of the professional CPA institutes. All members, whether individual or institutional, must pay membership dues regularly. They can exercise their rights and obligations as specified in the by-laws of the CPA institutes they belong to.

Under the existing regulations, all CPAs and CPA firms are subject to an annual review of practising performance administered by professional CPA institutes at the central or local levels for annual renewal of the practising licences. Any alleged acts of misconduct will be investigated by provincial CPA institutes or the CICPA. Appropriate disciplinary action, including warning, suspension of practising licence or revocation of the CPA certificate, will be sanctioned, depending upon the nature of the offence. In addition, the CPA Law states that a CPA will have his or her professional certificate revoked by the CPA institute in charge if he or she has (1) lost his or her civil rights or been in imprisonment, or (2) committed serious fraud or negligence in his or her work in the field of accounting, auditing, or business management, and been dismissed from the public post he or she held.[10]

NOTES

1   The CICPA is a semi-governmental body under the jurisdiction of the Ministry of Finance. Further detailed discussion of the CICPA is presented in a later section of this chapter.
2   The numbers include the previous Certified Public Auditors, another professional designation for practitioners in public accounting. The Chinese Association of Certified Public Auditors, administered originally by the National Auditing Administration (NAA), was merged into the CICPA in 1995, and all of the existing certified public auditors have been converted into certified public accountants.
3   As discussed in Chapter 2, the Chinese government implemented a national grading system of accounting qualification with four ranks of accounting titles: accounting clerk, assistant accountant, accountant and senior accountant. The accounting titles refer to the general qualification requirements, as well as the seniority, of accounting personnel. However, this grading system of accounting titles is completely different from the professional designation of CPAs, with the latter being strictly applied to qualified public practitioners.
4   This standard replaced the previous *Education and Training Systems for Certified Public Accountants*, issued by the CICPA in 1992.
5   According to the merger agreement between the CICPA and the CACAuP, the original auditing firms formed by CAuPs can choose either to change to the name of accounting firms or to retain the original name of the auditing firms. Up to March 1997, about 3000 accounting firms and 4000 auditing firms were in operation in China. The term 'CPA firms', however, is used in this chapter to refer to both accounting firms and auditing firms since the original CAuPs have been converted into CPAs following the merger of the CICPA and the CACAuP in late 1995.
6   This legislation was enacted by the National People's Congress in 1994, as one of the government's efforts to develop a legal framework for the emerging stock market and securities trading in China.
7   The disciplinary actions have only been taken with political motivations when serious public outrage arose against the alleged violations. For instance, the accounting/auditing firms that have been sanctioned in the last couple of years were all involved in serious scandals such as forging attestation documents for public offering of the listed corporations, which caused losses to a larger number of investors nationwide.
8   The practical rules issued by the CICPA include the following: *Practical Rules on Financial Statement Audit by Certified Public Accountants (Tentative)*, 1988; *Practical Rules on the Verification of Contributed Capital by Certified Public Accountants (Tentative)*, 1991; *Practical Rules on Auditing Working Papers Prepared by Certified Public Accountants (Tentative)*, 1991; *Practical Rules on Audit and Attestation Reports Prepared by Certified Public Accountants (Tentative)*, 1991; *Practical Rules on the Review of CPA Firm Performance (Tentative)*, 1991; *Practical Rules on Audit Planning by Certified Public Accountants (Tentative)*, 1992; *Guidelines on Management Recommendations Submitted by Certified Public Accountants (Tentative)* 1992; *Education Requirements and Training Systems for Certified Public Accountants (Tentative)*, 1992.
9   As a result of the merger of the CICPA and the CACAuP in late 1995, the newly

restructured CICPA is now subject to the joint supervision of the Ministry of Finance and the National Auditing Administration (NAA) at the central government.

10   Dismissal from a public post is a severe punishment for misconduct committed by any employee in government-run departments, agencies and business enterprises. The employee will become ineligible for a job in all entities funded by, or associated with, governments.

8   Taxation and Tax Returns

Taxation is a major factor affecting accounting and financial reporting. This is particularly true in a country like China where accounting and reporting are directly mandated and regulated to serve the government's fiscal and taxation policies. Accounting and financial reporting in China are tax-based. In particular, accounting measurements are not allowed to depart from tax regulations or rules in order to facilitate tax levy by government. Thus this chapter introduces the tax system, tax policies and the procedures for filing tax returns in China, in the context of the tax reforms implemented in recent years. The existing preferential tax policies applicable to foreign invested enterprises will also be examined.

OVERVIEW OF THE CHINESE TAXATION SYSTEM

The Chinese taxation system was originally established within the framework of a highly centralized planned economy, aimed at achieving the fiscal control of 'collection of all revenues and financing of every programme' by the central government. Although some piecemeal changes in tax policies took place over the period from 1949 to 1993, the taxation system remained highly centralized. Owing to the government's monopoly of business profits produced by the state-owned enterprises and a policy of low personal income, direct taxes on business and personal income were not emphasized. The core of the taxation system in place before 1994 was primarily indirect taxes, essentially taxes on spending, such as product tax and sales tax, where the tax burden can be shifted from producers to customers.

In addition, various tax categories, tax bases and tax rates were designated separately for different business ownership or geographical regions, as a tool to facilitate the central government's fiscal planning and budgetary control. For example, different types of taxes, both direct and indirect, were set out for the state-owned enterprises, collective ownership, individual industrial and commercial households (private businesses) and enterprises with foreign capital respectively, with the tax base and tax rates varying considerably. One of the motivations behind the segregated tax system is the government's intention to have separate administration of the preferential tax policies for entities with foreign capital while curbing private business ownership. Such a tax system has, however, caused a lot of confusion and ineffectiveness in tax management.

Also, in step with the progress of economic reforms started in the late 1970s, the highly centralized planned economy has been gradually dismantled and a partial market economy has emerged with a substantial diversification in business ownership. The state-owned enterprises have gradually lost their significance in respect of the government's fiscal revenues, while private businesses and enterprises with foreign capital have expanded dramatically. Thus the differential tax system for different business ownership have generated more harm than good to the government's tax revenues. It has become outmoded in an emerging partial market economy. Reformation of the taxation system has become an urgent task facing the Chinese government since the late 1980s.

Tax reform of 1994

The central government introduced a wide range of tax reforms in 1993, with financial and technical assistance from the World Bank and other international organizations. A new tax system was implemented on 1 January 1994 in China. Compared to the previous tax systems, the 1994 tax reform has introduced some significant changes. Major features of the new tax system can be summarized as follows.

Emphasis on both direct and indirect taxes

The new tax system has changed the traditional practice of overreliance on indirect taxes and placed an emphasis on both direct and indirect taxes. Increased weight is given to the direct taxes, such as business income tax and personal income tax, as a major source of government revenues.

Harmonization of taxes and tax base

The tax system of 1994 introduced a total of 18 taxes to replace the original tax categories which numbered more than 30. Many old taxes were eliminated while a few new taxes were introduced in the light of the changed economic environment. In addition to simplifying the taxation system, the major objective of the 1994 tax reform was to harmonize the taxes originally designated separately for different business ownership and geographical locations. The taxes introduced in 1994 apply universally in the country, irrespective of differences in business ownership or industry, except that certain business entities with foreign capital are allowed to continue the application of originally designated taxes over a specified transitional period.

Equalization of tax burdens for all taxpayers

Under the tax system of 1994, the principle of equality was introduced and the prior practice of differential tax rates for taxpayers with varied business ownership was terminated. Thus the newly designed standard tax rates are applicable to all taxpayers, regardless of whether they are domestic entities or foreign invested entities.[1] Government authorities claimed that the change is necessary to equalize tax burdens for all taxpayers and to promote fair competition and development of a market-based economy. Another reason for this change, however, is the government's intention to halt a severe decline in tax revenues. As the majority of state-owned enterprises incurred continuous losses, governments could no longer afford to continue the originally designed preferential tax policies for business entities with foreign investments, or for special economic zones in the coastal areas in China.

Implementation of a revenue-sharing system

The 1994 tax reform altered the original highly centralized fiscal and taxation systems with respect to the fiscal relationship between the central government and local authorities. With a decentralization of the economic administrative structure, the central government had become incapable of rigidly controlling, or entirely reimbursing, all programmes and expenditures incurred by local authorities. The central government had therefore to introduce the 'revenue-sharing system' with a separation of tax revenues between the central and local governments based on divided taxes and a preformatted revenue-splitting scheme. As a result, separate taxation systems were installed to administer tax collections for the central authority and local governments respectively. It is the intention of the central government that the revenue-sharing tax system provide incentives for local governments to expand their own tax revenues, and prevent local governments from diverting or retaining the tax revenues that should go to the central government.

Taxation Regulations

Tax regulations in China are derived from various sources, in the forms of state legislation and regulations or the executive rules issued by relevant government administrative authorities. They include the following.

1   The tax laws established through legislative procedures. Usually the essential tax regulations are enacted by the NPC or its Standing Committee and enforced through the State President's decrees. Included in this category of tax legislation are *The Law of Tax Levy and Administration of the People's Republic of China* (1991), *The Law of Personal Income Tax of the People's Republic of China* (1993) and *The Income Tax Law of the People's Republic of China for Enterprises with Foreign Investments and Foreign Enterprises* (1993).
2   The tax regulations formulated by the State Council under delegation of authority from the NPC or its Standing Committee. This group of tax regulations are usually in the form of 'Provisional Regulations' and enforced through the executive order of the State Council. Currently, most of the Chinese tax regulations fall into this category, they include *The Provisional Regulation on Value-added Tax of the People's Republic of China, The Provisional Regulation on Business Income Tax of the People's Republic of China, The Provisional Regulation on Consumption Tax of the People's Republic of China, The Provisional Regulation on Business Tax of the People's Republic of China, The Provisional Regulation on Resources Tax of the People's Republic of China, The Provisional Regulation on Land Appreciation Tax of the People's Republic of China*, and so on. All of these regulations were issued in December 1993 as a package of the new taxes coming into effect on 1 January 1994. In addition, the State Council may, within its jurisdictional authority, formulate specific rules for implementing the essential tax laws, such as the *Detailed Rules for Enforcing The Income Tax Law for Enterprises with Foreign Investments and Foreign Enterprises* (1992).
3   The tax regulations or rules issued by the Ministry of Finance or the State Taxation Bureau, as operational guidance for implementing the tax regulations promulgated by the State Council, such as *Detailed Rules on the Enforcement of The Provisional Regulations on Income Taxes for Business Enterprises* and *Detailed Rules on the Enforcement of The Provisional Regulations on Value-added Taxes*, and so on. In addition, the official interpretations or rulings issued by state tax authorities, that is, the State Taxation Bureau (STB) and the State Administration of Customs (SAC) governing emerging tax issues are a part of this source of tax regulations.

4   The 'Implementation Guidelines' issued by local governments in respect of the levy of taxes and fees administered by local authorities.
5   The specific taxation treaties signed by the Chinese government and governments in other countries. At present, China has established bilateral taxation treaties with about 40 countries of the world.

The legislative authority over taxation, in respect of the central and local taxes, is controlled directly by the central government. Local governments are not allowed to add, suspend or alter the taxes which have been introduced, unless they have obtained delegation of authority by the central government. In addition, local authorities are not allowed to formulate any tax rules or guidelines that are in conflict with the tax legislation and regulations promulgated by the central government.

Tax administrative agencies

State Taxation Bureau

The State Taxation Bureau (STB) is the national authority of tax administration. The STB is a ministerial agency under the State Council. The headquarters of the STB is located in Beijing, with branches and agencies in all provinces, autonomous regions and municipalities directly under the central government, as well as in large and medium-size cities in China. The STB's mandates include:

- levying of taxes designated for the central government;
- collection and remittance of tax revenues to the state treasury;
- drafting of national tax policies and regulations;
- formulation of detailed rules or procedures for tax administration, and of the required accounting and statistics database;
- determination of major tax exemptions or reductions;
- participation in negotiating international tax treaties with foreign counterparts;
- administration of taxes for business entities with foreign investments.

In order to carry out its mandates, the STB maintains a centralized administration over all of its branches and agencies in lower levels of government throughout the country.

Bureaux of Local Taxation

Resulting from the revenue-sharing system introduced by the tax reform of 1994, taxation agencies for local governments, separate from local branches of the STB, emerged at provincial level. The Bureaux of Local Taxation (BLT), as they are called, are subordinate to corresponding provincial governments. The BLT's duties include:

- preparing tax policies of individual provincial governments, in the light of the state taxation legislation and regulations;
- levying local taxes that are under their jurisdiction;
- formulating tax rules or requirements that are applicable within local jurisdictions;
- enforcing or monitoring the execution of local taxation plans.

The BLTs can establish their branches or own agencies at lower authorities under provincial jurisdiction, such as the taxation branches in municipalities, or tax stations and substations in rural areas.

The Taxation Bureau for Marine Petroleum Resources

Segregated administration of the taxes for marine petroleum resources is maintained in China, inherited from the earlier practices before 1949. Thus, a special tax authority, The Taxation Bureau for Marine Petroleum Resources (TBMPR) is established under the STB. The TBMPR has set up its own branches in four coastal cities where major marine petroleum producers are located: Shanghai, Tianjing, Guangzhou and Zhanjiang. The TBMPR is charged with:

- carrying out centralized tax collection and administration over marine petroleum resources;
- formulating tax regulations and detailed rules for marine petroleum products; and
- supervising tax payments made by corporations and other entities involved in the operations of marine petroleum resources.

TYPES OF TAXES

The 1994 tax reform introduced a total of 18 taxes (both direct and indirect), which are classified into five groups.

1 Turnover (indirect) taxes, including value-added tax, consumption tax, operation (business) tax and customs tariff or exercise duties.
2 Income taxes, including income tax for business enterprises, income tax for enterprises with foreign investments and foreign enterprises,[2] personal income tax and agricultural taxes.
3 Resources usage taxes, including resources tax, rural land use tax and urban land use tax.
4 Property taxes, including real estate and property tax, property title tax, land appreciation tax and transportation facilities tax.
5 Behaviour (activity) taxes, including regulating tax for capital investments, stamp tax and tax for urban construction and maintenance.

Among the five groups, the turnover taxes and income taxes are the principal sources of the state's revenues, accounting for 60 per cent and 20 per cent, respectively, of the governments' total tax revenues. The other three categories of taxes have a relatively insignificant impact on governments' fiscal revenues, especially for the central government.

Within the revenue-sharing framework, some of the 18 taxes are designated as tax revenues for the central government: for instance, value-added tax, consumption tax, income tax for enterprises under the central authorities and customs tariffs. Operation tax, income tax for enterprises under local authorities, personal income tax, real estate and property tax, and land appreciation tax are designated as local taxes and subject to administration by corresponding LTBs. In addition, a few taxes such as resources taxes and stamp tax are designated as joint taxes that will be shared by the central and local governments on the basis of predetermined formulae.

Each type of tax may consist of several subgroups. Tax rates may be on either a flat or a progressive basis, varying with specific tax categories and subgroups. In general, most of the taxes are determined on a price basis, while a few taxes may be calculated according to the quantity of taxable items. More detailed discussions of the main taxes currently in existence in China are provided below.

Value-added tax (VAT)

VAT is an indirect tax levied on the value added during manufacturing or merchandising processes. Conceptually, value-added (VA) is the new value generated at each producing stage. For tax purposes, however, VA is practically determined by subtracting all non value-added items (total of external purchases) from total sales (operating revenues) realized during a specified tax period.

Tax base and taxpayers

VAT is applicable to operating activities in manufacturing, merchandising, imports and exports, as well as non-manufacturing processing, repairing and assembling services. Individuals or entities engaging in these operating activities within Chinese territory are payers of the VAT. Here 'entities' includes state-owned enterprises, publicly listed corporations, private proprietorships or partnerships, enterprises with foreign investments, foreign enterprises, governmental or non-profit organizations and military units; 'individuals' includes both Chinese citizens and aliens.

Tax rates

Three tiers of tax rate are designated for the VA; standard rate of 17 per cent, preferential (low) rate of 13 per cent and 'zero' rate (tax exemption).

The low rate is applicable to taxpayers involved in manufacturing and merchandising commodities or goods that are related to household necessities and agricultural uses, and subsidized by the state, such as grains, cooking oil, water, heating, hot water, petrol, petroleum gas, natural gas, coal products for household use, books, newspapers, magazines, forage and feed, pesticides, agricultural equipments, plastic films for agricultural usage, and so on.

The 'zero' rate (tax exemption) is applicable to exported commodities and goods, excluding a small number of export-restricted items.[3] The 'exported' commodities and goods include those being sold abroad and those being transferred to the designated duty-free storehouses or storage districts administered by customs authorities.

The standard rate is applicable to other manufacturing and merchandising commodities and goods that do not fall into the above-mentioned categories, and non-manufacturing assembling and repairing services.

Tax calculation

In practice, VAT is levied according to the subtraction method, supported by official purchase receipts, that is, the standardized VAT sales invoices supplied by the STB. Thus the VAT is determined by the following formulae:

$$\text{VAT payable} = \text{taxable amount of sales items} - \text{taxable amount of purchase items}$$

$$\text{Taxable amount of sales (purchase)} = \text{total amount of items sold (purchased) in the period} \times \text{applicable VAT rate}$$

Under the existing regulations, VAT will only be levied when a taxpayer's operating revenues have met one of the following thresholds:

- minimum monthly sales of commodities or goods about RMB ¥600–2000;
- minimum monthly sales of taxable services about RMB ¥200–800; or
- minimum daily sales (per transaction) of RMB ¥50–80 when the VAT is assessed on a transaction basis.

VAT is directly administered by the STB, except for the levy of VAT for imported and exported goods which is delegated to the SAC. Generally, VAT payable is assessed on the date when a sale transaction is completed. The VAT for imported or exported goods is assessed on the date of customs clearance.

Exemption or deduction

Existing tax regulations grant VAT exemption or deduction for certain specified goods or services, but application for such exemption or deduction is very restricted. Accordingly, only the State Council has the authority to grant the exemption or deduction of VAT.

Consumption tax

Consumption tax is a new tax introduced by the tax reform of 1994. This tax is aimed at production and importing of certain kinds of commodities and goods that are beyond people's daily necessities. Thus consumption tax is another turnover tax on top of the VAT.

Tax base and taxpayers

Consumption tax applies to special consumer goods (such as tobacco, alcohol and fireworks), luxury goods (such as jewellery, perfume and cosmetics), high energy-consuming products (such as cars and motorcycles) and products using non-regenerable resources. All entities and individuals engaging in manufacturing and importing of the taxable goods and commodities within Chinese territory are subject to the consumption tax. Owners of such specified consumer goods under consignment must also pay the consumption tax.

Tax categories and tax rates

Currently consumption tax is designed with 11 categories and 13 subcategories. Varied tax rates, ranging from 3 per cent to 45 per cent, with 14 scales, are applicable. Table 8.1 shows the existing categories and rates of the consumption tax.

Table 8.1   Categories and rates of consumption tax

	Tax categories	Tax rates or amount
I.	Tobaccos and cigars (including all imported tobaccos)	40–45%
	Cut tobacco	30%
II.	Wines and alcohol	10–25%
	Beers	RMB ¥220/tonne
	Ethylalcohol	5%
III.	Cosmetics	30%
IV.	Facial creams and hair gel	17%
V.	Jewellery (made of precious metals or jades)	10%
VI.	Fireworks	15%
VII.	Petrol products	RMB ¥0.20/litre
VIII.	Diesel products	RMB ¥0.10/litre
IX.	Tyres	10%
X.	Motorcycles	10%
XI.	Automobiles	
	Cars (engine capacity > 2200cc)	8%
	(engine capacity 1000–2200cc)	5%
	(engine capacity < 1000cc)	3%
	Four-wheel drive vehicles	
	(engine capacity > 2400cc)	5%
	(engine capacity ≤ 2400cc)	3%
	Mini-vans	
	(engine capacity > 2000cc)	5%
	(engine capacity ≤ 2000cc)	3%

Tax calculation

The consumption tax is calculated on the basis of selling prices for most consumer goods, except for certain alcohol and petrol products, for which the tax is determined on a quantity (standard unit) basis:

$$\begin{matrix} \text{Consumption} \\ \text{tax payable} \end{matrix} = \begin{matrix} \text{total sales (quantity)} \\ \text{of the taxable goods} \end{matrix} \times \begin{matrix} \text{applicable} \\ \text{tax rates} \end{matrix}$$

Here the tax rates are in the form of either a percentage of the selling prices or a flat amount per standard unit of the taxable goods.

Tax assessment and deduction

Consumption tax is assessed whenever a sale of the taxable goods or commodities is completed, or on the date when a taxpayer starts to consume the self-produced taxable goods. The tax is generally not exemptible or deductible except for a fairly limited number of exported goods.

Operation tax

Operation tax is particularly designed for non-manufacturing business activities in servicing and real estate industries.

Tax base and taxpayers

The operation tax is levied on business operations in the fields of transport, construction, banking and insurance, post and communication, culture and sport, entertainment, professional services, as well as sales of intangible assets and real estate. All entities and individuals who engage in these transactions within Chinese territory must pay this turnover tax.

Tax rates

Nine subcategories are designed for the operation tax, with the proportionate tax rates of 3 per cent or 5 per cent, and a progressive range of 5–20 per cent. The rates applicable to taxpayers are assessed or determined by the tax authority on an individual basis. Table 8.2 lists the existing rates of operation tax for various industries.

Table 8.2   Categories and rates of operation tax

	Tax categories	Taxable items	Tax rates (%)
I.	Transport	Surface, sea and air cargo, pipelines, loading and unloading	3
II.	Construction	Building construction, equipment installation, repairs, decorations, etc.	3
III.	Banking and insurance		5
IV.	Post & telecomm.		3
V.	Sport & culture		3
VI.	Recreational		2–20
VII.	Services	All kinds of professional services	5
VIII.	Transfer of intangibles	Royalties, copyright, trademarks, goodwill, etc.	5
IX.	Real estate development		5

Tax calculation

The operation tax is imposed upon sales revenues of the taxable services or transactions. It can be determined as follows:

Tax payable   =   sales amount   ×   applicable tax rates

Operation tax will be levied when a taxpayer's monthly revenues are over RMB ¥200–800 (the rate varies with the size of business) or daily sales are over RMB ¥50. The tax will not be levied if a taxpayer's sales are below these thresholds.

Exemption or deduction

The operation tax is waived for entities or organizations involved in public welfare, charity, health care, education, agricultural services, public sports and cultural services such as libraries, museums and exhibition halls. The tax is not exemptible for business enterprises.

Business income tax

Currently, business income tax is imposed only on domestic business entities, including the state-owned enterprises, private proprietorships or partnerships and publicly listed companies, as well as other organizations that have pursued business-like activities and generated operating income or other income. However, the tax is not applicable to business entities with foreign investments at the moment.[4]

Tax base and Taxpayers

The taxpayers of business income tax include all business entities engaging in manufacturing, excavation, transport, construction, agricultural products, forestry, stock raising, fishery, irrigation, hydro-power, wholesale and retail, banking and insurance, post and telecommunications, professional services, and other business activities. Operating income (profits) and non-business income (such as dividends, interest, rent, property disposal gains, royalties and other non-operating gains) generated inside and outside Chinese territory are combined to determine the income tax payable. Business income earned abroad must be combined with domestic income for income tax purpose. Tax credits may be applied to income tax paid in foreign countries, to offset the domestic tax payable. Income tax credits are, however, limited to the tax payable on foreign income calculated in accordance with Chinese income tax laws. Tax credits are determined separately by country instead of by individual types of business income.

$$\text{Limit of tax credits on foreign income tax paid} = \frac{\text{tax payable on foreign income determined by Chinese tax law} \times \text{income from individual foreign country}}{\text{aggregate domestic and foreign income}}$$

Tax rates

A flat rate is set for business income tax. The statutory rate is 30 per cent plus an additional 3 per cent of local income tax. However, the Business Income Tax Law allows small businesses to be taxed at lower than standard rates. The preferential income tax rates include (1) a 15 per cent income tax rate for business entities with total annual income not more than RMB ¥30 000; (2) a 20 per cent income tax rate for business entities with total annual income greater than RMB ¥30 000, but not more than RMB ¥100 000.

Business income tax payable is calculated as follows:

$$\text{Business income tax payable} = \text{taxable income} \times \text{applicable tax rates}$$

Tax calculation

Business income tax payable is determined by taxable income earned by a taxpayer during a tax period (calendar year), that is, gross revenues minus deductions allowed:

$$\text{Business income tax payable} = \text{gross revenues} - \text{costs, expenses and losses} \pm \text{allowed tax deductions}$$

Determination of gross revenues, costs, expenses and losses must follow the specific provisions in the business income tax law. Any costs, expenses and losses over the standard adjustments are not allowed to be included in the deductions. In addition, income tax payable must be calculated in the light of the tax laws when there is a discrepancy between business income calculated under accounting standards and tax laws.

An accrual basis will generally be employed for the determination of taxable income. Income in the form of non-monetary assets or share equity must be valued on the basis of current market prices or reasonable appraised values that are acceptable to the tax authorities. Related-party transactions must be treated according to the principle of an 'arm's length transaction' between independent entities. The tax authority may make necessary adjustments to determine a taxpayer's taxable income.

Personal income tax

Personal income tax was initially introduced in 1980, targeting a fairly small number of high-income earners, such as wealthy professionals and foreigners who have earned income in China. The vast majority of ordinary Chinese people have a very limited personal income which is far below the threshold for taxable personal income.[5] Unlike practices in most industrialized countries, personal income tax does not play a significant role within China's taxation system and is designated as a tax revenue to local government.

However, the average level of personal income has risen dramatically in recent years, which expanded the number of taxpayers for personal income tax. With an increased fiscal significance, the personal income tax has become one of the major revenue sources for local authorities across the country.

Taxpayers

Personal income tax is imposed on taxable income earned from domestic and foreign sources by a resident in China or the income earned within Chinese territory by a non-resident. The status of 'resident' and 'non-resident' is defined in related tax legislation and regulations.

Resident   Any person who has a permanent residence in China, or who has no residence but has lived in China over one year, is a resident. A resident must report all of his or her domestic and foreign income or other earnings in filing returns for personal income tax. The existing tax regulations, however, grant certain deductions or exemptions for foreign income earned by a resident, in an effort to attract foreign investors and promote economic cooperation with trade partners in other countries. The deduction or exemption would apply as follows. If an alien, without permanent residence in China, has lived in China over one year but not more than five years, only his or her income earned from Chinese sources (from corporations, other economic entities or individuals) is taxable. But approval by the relevant taxation authorities is required to get his or her income from foreign sources exempted from Chinese personal income tax. An alien should pay the personal income tax for all income earned from Chinese and foreign sources starting from the sixth year of his or her stay in China.

Non-resident   Any person who has no residence and does not live in China, or stays in China for less than one year, but has income earned from Chinese sources, is a non-resident. Within the meaning of tax regulations, only the income earned from Chinese sources by a non-resident is taxable, regardless of whether the income is made inside or outside China. Again, tax exemption may be applied for a non-resident under certain circumstances. For example, if a non-resident has lived in China less than 90 days, continuously or cumulatively, the salary income paid by his or her foreign employer is exempted from Chinese personal income tax, conditional upon the salary costs not being charged to the expenses of the employer's operations inside China.

In order to avoid double taxation, Chinese tax laws allow tax credits for a taxpayer's personal income taxes paid abroad. Personal income taxes paid in foreign countries may be applied as tax credits against a taxpayer's liability for taxable income derived from foreign sources. However, the allowable foreign income tax credits are capped with the tax payable calculated according to Chinese personal income tax law for a taxpayer's foreign sources income. Tax credits will be calculated separately by country. The sum of tax payable for all taxable personal income, including wages or salary, interest, dividend, royalties and so on from one country is the maximum tax credit applicable to all a taxpayer's incomes earned from that particular country.

Tax base

According to current tax laws, taxable personal income includes wages or salaries, job-related bonuses and subsidies, profits from private proprietorships or partnerships, distributed profits to persons who are operating state-owned enterprises on a contracting or leasing basis, compensations for professional services (such as engineering design, equipment installation, experimentation, health care, legal consultation, accounting, seminar presentation, business consultation, broadcasting, book reviewing, video recording, art performance, advertisement, specialized technical assistance, brokerage or agency service and so on), copyright, royalties, interest, dividends, disposal gains on rental properties, lottery income and other windfall income.

Taxable personal income may include cash, physical goods or marketable securities received. Income in the form of physical goods or properties must be valued at prices specified in the acquisition documents, or at their fair market values as recognized by the local taxation authorities if acquisition documents are not available. Prices of marketable securities must be determined by the taxation authorities in terms of face value and fair market price of the securities in question.

Tax calculation

Taxable personal income is the balance of gross income minus standard deduction allowance. Tax payable will be determined by individual categories of personal income separately. The standard deduction allowances will also be determined for each category of income separately, with various deduction allowances being applied. If an income is earned jointly by two or more persons, the deduction allowances must be applied proportionately. However, if a taxpayer has the same category of income from two or more sources in China, the income must be combined in filing income tax returns.

Standard deduction allowance for wages or salary income is currently RMB ¥800 per month per person, that is, only the portion of monthly income over RMB ¥800 is taxable. This allowance, however, is applicable only to Chinese citizens who are working inside the country. Foreigners working in China or Chinese citizens who are working overseas may apply for an additional supplementary allowance of RMB ¥3200 per month.

For incomes from professional services, copyright, royalties, rental or leasing, a deduction of RMB ¥800 per person is allowed for total income less than RMB ¥4000 per transaction and a flat-rate 20 per cent deduction will apply to the income amount over the standard deduction allowance. No deduction allowances are applicable to interest, dividend, lottery or other windfall income.

Taxable income for the owners of private proprietorships or partnerships is the balance of total business revenues less total operating expenses or losses incurred during the fiscal year. The taxable income is, however, subject to a review by the taxation authority.

Tax rates

Various tax rates are set for different categories of personal income.

Wages and salaries   A progressive income tax rate with a range of 5–45 per cent is in place. Current tax rates for wage or salary income are shown as Table 8.3.

Table 8.3   Tax rates for personal income (wages and salaries)

Scale	Monthly income (RMB ¥)	Tax rates (%)*
1	less than ¥500 inclusive	5
2	over ¥500 and up to ¥2 000	10
3	over ¥2 000 and up to ¥5 000	15
4	over ¥5 000 and up to ¥20 000	20
5	over ¥20 000 and up to ¥40 000	25
6	over ¥40 000 and up to ¥60 000	30
7	over ¥60 000 and up to ¥80 000	35
8	over ¥80 000 and up to ¥100 000	40
9	over ¥100 000	45

Note: * based on marginal income.

Income from business profits   Progressive tax rates of 5 per cent to 35 per cent, as shown in Table 8.4, apply to business income of the owners of private proprietorships or partnerships, or the distributed profits to those persons operating state-owned enterprises on a contracting and leasing basis.

Other personal income   A flat tax rate of 20 per cent applies to income from copyright, service income, royalties, interest, dividends, rental, gains

Table 8.4   Tax rates for personal income (income from business profits)

Scale	Annual income (RMB ¥)	Tax rates (%)*
1	less than ¥5 000	5
2	over ¥5 000 and up to ¥10 000	10
3	over ¥10 000 and up to ¥30 000	20
4	over ¥30 000 and up to ¥50 000	30
5	over ¥50 000	35

Note: * based on marginal income.

on property disposal, lottery or other windfall income. In addition, a 5–10 per cent surtax may also be levied on high income from professional services.[6]

Tax deduction and exemption

Certain types of personal income are exempted from personal income tax, such as awards granted by governments at provincial level or above, or by international agencies; interest income from treasury bonds, special governmental subsidies, social welfare payments, pensions, insurance payouts and compensation for ex-servicemen. Personnel of diplomatic missions in China or others specified by international treaties are exempted from Chinese personal income tax. In addition, tax deduction may be applied to certain disabled and senior persons, or residents in government-declared disaster areas.

Tariffs and duties

A tariff is a kind of tax imposed on imported and exported commodities and goods. Traditionally, the Chinese government has adopted a policy of protective tariffs and implemented a high-tariff system on imported commodities and goods. The motivation is to protect domestic manufacturers or producers whose products are unable to compete with the imported goods in respect of prices and quality. Also a tariff on certain types of exported products or goods, usually the raw materials or semi-products, was imposed to restrict the outflow of those goods facing severe shortage in domestic markets.

Currently, tariffs are administered by the State Administration of Customs (SAC), under delegation of authority from the STB. The existing tariff consists of 'customs duties on imported goods' and 'customs duties on exported goods'.

Import duties

All imported commodities and goods must pay import duties. Two-tier tariff rates, a preferential rate and a standard rate, are designed for each of the main categories of imported commodities and goods. The preferential rates apply to commodities and goods imported from those countries which have signed bilateral treaties on trades and tariffs with China. The standard rates apply to commodities and goods imported from countries without the bilateral trade and tariff treaties. Import duties are levied according to the prices of imported commodities and goods. At present, there are 17 scales in the import duties, with a range of 3 per cent to 150 per cent for the preferential rates and a range of 8 per cent to 180 per cent for the standard rates. Import duties are calculated as follows:

Duties payable = clearance prices × applicable tariff rates

The clearance price is the full cost of the imported commodities or goods arriving at a Chinese port (FOB destination), including reasonable invoice prices in the exporting countries, export duties paid abroad, freights paid to transport the commodities or goods to Chinese ports, packaging expenses, insurance and other related commissions or fees.

According to statistics issued by the Chinese government, the average level of tariffs for all imported commodities or goods stood at 35.9 per cent before 1995. This level of tariff is relatively high compared to the standards in most industrial countries. The Chinese government, however, has made promises to lower its import duties in recent years, as a concession for its bid for membership of the World Trade Organization (WTO). For example, Chinese President, Jiang Zeming, announced in the APEC Summits in Osaka, Japan in November 1995, that China would implement an overall cut of import duties for about 4000 commodities and goods starting in 1996, with a reduction margin of not less than 30 per cent from the existing level. A second round of tariff cuts was announced at the APEC Summits in Manila, Philippines in 1996, with a target of lowering the overall level of import duties to about 25 per cent. China's moves to bring down its tariff barrier have been positively received by its regional and worldwide trade partners.

Export duties

In recent years, the Chinese government has repeatedly reduced export duties to encourage domestic producers to export their products to world markets. Except for a very small number of 'goods restricted from export', the majority of products are now exempted from export duties. In fact, only eight types of exported goods, such as slag wool, chestnuts, tungsten ore, antimony, goat skins, raw silk, prawns, and eel fry, have been subject to export duties since 1987. Currently, the export duties consist of four scales of flat rates at 10 per cent, 20 per cent, 30 per cent and 60 per cent. Export duties are calculated as follows:

$$\text{Duties payable} = \text{clearance prices} \times \text{applicable tariff rates}$$

The clearance price is the selling prices (FOB), subject to approval of the Chinese customs authority, of exported commodities or goods minus the export duties applied:

$$\frac{\text{Clearance prices}}{\text{of exported goods}} = \frac{\text{selling prices (FOB)}}{1 + \text{export duties applied}(\%)}$$

Resources tax

Resources tax is designed to level out the differential revenues (income) from mining operations and salt production within Chinese territory. This tax currently applies to all mineral products and salt products, including solid, gas and liquid products. Entities or individuals engaging in production of the taxable mineral and salt products, including the joint ventures with Chinese and foreign capital and foreign enterprises, pay the resources tax. Since 1994, the resources tax has been extended to those foreign enterprises and joint ventures with Chinese and foreign capital involved in onshore and offshore petroleum exploitation, although they were originally exempted from this tax on the condition that they paid the utilization fees for mining facilities to local authorities.

Resources tax is levied on the basis of output quantity of the taxable products. The basic principle underlying this tax is 'broad levy and differential treatment'. Thus all entities and individuals engaging in production of the taxable products must be taxed, while the tax rates are varied according to the differences in production and marketing conditions, such as volume and grades of the mineral reserves, mining or producing facilities, geographical locations, and so on. The varied rates of resources tax are shown in Table 8.5.

Table 8.5   Categories and rates of resource tax

Categories	Tax rates (RMB ¥)
1. Crude oils	8–30/tonne
2. Natural gas	2–15/m³ (000s)*
3. Coal	0.30–5/tonne
4. Ore (non-metal)	0.50–20/tonne
5. Ferrous ore	2–30/tonne
6. Nonferrous ore	0.40–30/tonne
7. Salts	
Solid	10–60/tonne
Liquid	2–10/tonne

Note: * thousand cubic metres.

A variable range of unit rate is designed for each category of taxable products. The actual rate applicable to each taxpayer is determined by the tax authorities on an individual basis. The tax liability is calculated according to output quantity of the taxable products and the specified tax rates:

$$\text{Tax payable} = \text{output levels of taxable products} \times \text{applicable tax rates}$$

Urban and rural land use tax

The urban and rural land use tax ('land use tax') is imposed on entities and individuals who occupy the lands owned by the state or local authorities in municipalities, towns and industrial or mining areas, based on the acreage of lands being used. The land use tax is a revenue source for local governments. However, foreign enterprises and joint ventures with Chinese and foreign capital are currently exempted from this tax. In addition, governmental entities, government-sponsored non-profit organizations, military units and public utility agencies are also exempted from the land use tax.

Land use tax is determined on the basis of actual acreage of lands being occupied by a taxpayer. The actual acreage of lands occupied must be certified by a surveyor officially recognized by government authorities at provincial level or above. The rates for land use tax (flat rates with a progressive scale) are set by local governments, varying according to the location and sizes of municipalities or towns.

Land appreciation tax

Land appreciation tax is a new tax introduced in the tax reform of 1994. It is designed to regulate the heavy profits derived from the emerging speculative real estate markets in recent years. The tax is imposed on commercial trading or disposal of the use right of the state-owned lands and of the properties on the lands. All entities and individuals, both domestic and foreign, engaging in real-estate or property transactions are payers of this tax. Under the existing regulations, governmental land registration agencies will not accept any application for title transfer for lands or properties unless the land appreciation tax has been paid.

The taxable base of land appreciation tax is the appreciated value of the lands and/or properties realized in a transaction. The realized appreciation value is the balance of sales of the lands and/or properties minus the statutory deductibles. A taxpayer's revenues must include all cash, physical properties and other equivalent valuables received in the transaction. The statutory deductibles consist of the original purchase costs, the development costs and other expenses and taxes paid for the lands and/or properties which have been sold. The land appreciation tax is calculated as follows:

$$\text{Tax payable} = \text{appreciated values of land and/or property} \times \text{applicable tax rates}$$

$$\text{Appreciated value of land and/or property} = \text{gross revenues of land/property disposal} - \text{statutory deductibles}$$

Four-scale progressive rates are currently designed for this tax:

1   a tax rate of 30 per cent is applied if the appreciated values realized are less than 50 per cent of the total amount of the deductibles allowed,
2   a tax rate of 40 per cent is applied if the appreciated values realized are more than 50 per cent but less than 100 per cent of the total amount of the deductibles allowed,
3   a tax rate of 50 per cent is applied if the appreciated values realized are more than 100 per cent but less than 200 per cent of the total amount of the deductibles allowed, and
4   a tax rate of 60 per cent is applied if the appreciated values realized are more than 200 per cent of the total amount of the deductibles allowed.

THE TAX SYSTEM FOR BUSINESS ENTITIES WITH FOREIGN INVESTMENTS

Initially, the China government set out segregated tax systems for each type of business entity with foreign capital in the early 1980s. Thus separate taxes were introduced, respectively, for equity joint ventures with Chinese and foreign capital, cooperative associations (that is, contractual joint ventures) with Chinese and foreign investments, and foreign-owned enterprises operating in China. An effort was made to harmonize the income taxes for all types of business entities with foreign investments by the introduction of the new *Tax Law for Business Enterprises with Foreign Investments and Foreign Enterprises* ('Tax Law for Foreign Invested Enterprises' hereafter) on 1 July 1991. Segregated tax systems remained in place, however, for domestic and foreign invested enterprises. Contrary to tax systems for domestic counterparts, the tax systems for business entities with foreign investments maintain certain preferential tax treatments, including (1) different types and lower rates of direct and indirect taxes, (2) tax exemption, especially from import duties for foreign invested enterprises, and (3) a broad range of income tax deductions.

As mentioned earlier in this chapter, one of the main objectives of the 1994 tax reform was to harmonize taxation systems nationwide. Thus the new tax system implemented in 1994 would apply universally to all entities and individuals, domestic and foreign, within the country. However, the Chinese government decided to postpone the enforcement of the new tax system on foreign invested enterprises. In particular, a transitional period was granted to those foreign invested enterprises that had been in existence or were approved before 1 April 1996. The originally designed preferential tax systems for those foreign invested enterprises will continue to apply over their remaining contract life. In addition, a grace period was granted to foreign invested enterprises established after 1995.

Foreign invested enterprises are currently allowed to follow the previously designed tax system or they can claim tax refunds for the marginal taxes they have paid as a result of the differences between the old and new tax systems. This policy is designed to maintain the foreign investors' confidence and to prevent a mass pull-out of foreign investments.

Most of the preferential tax policies for foreign invested enterprises will therefore be phased out gradually. The originally designed segregated and preferential tax system will remain in effect during a specified transitional period, at least for those foreign invested entities which have been in existence or approved up to the end of 1995.

Uniform industry and commerce tax

Under the existing tax regulations, two major taxes are exclusively applicable to foreign invested enterprises. One is the uniform industry and commerce tax, the other is business income tax for foreign invested enterprises and foreign companies.

The uniform industry and commerce tax (UICT) is an indirect tax. It is imposed on the turnover of goods and services through manufacturing and merchandising processes. This tax was originally introduced to the state-owned enterprises in 1958, but it was replaced by other turnover taxes for all domestic entities after a tax reform of 1973. The UICT became a tax which applies exclusively to foreign invested enterprises. At present, the qualified foreign-invested enterprises will pay this tax, at least during the transitional period specified by the government, instead of other turnover taxes such as value-added tax, consumption taxes or operation tax, as introduced in the 1994 tax reform.

Tax bases

The UICT is imposed on goods or services generated from manufacturing, merchandising, importing, wholesaling or retailing, transport, banking, insurance, entertainment and other servicing activities. Entities with foreign investments engaging in these operations, whether equity and contract joint ventures or wholly foreign-funded enterprises, are subject to this tax,

Tax rates

Tax rates of the UICT vary according to the industry a taxpayer is involved in. Individual rates are set on the basis of the types of products for manufacturing and agricultural industries, while different flat rates are set for wholesaling and retailing, transport, banking, insurance, entertainment and other service industries. The tax rates are formulated and enforced by the STB.

The UICT is levied upon total sales or revenues realized by a taxpayer, but it is determined by the payments when purchases of agricultural products are involved, and by the taxable prices for all imported goods.

Income tax for foreign invested enterprises and foreign companies

This tax, also called income tax for foreign invested enterprises (ITFIE) is the business income tax specially designed for foreign invested enterprises and foreign companies. According to Chinese tax laws, 'foreign invested enterprises' refers to business entities with foreign investments, that is, the equity or contractual joint ventures among Chinese and foreign partners, while 'foreign companies' refers to business entities or branches established and operated within Chinese territory by foreign companies, or foreign companies having income from Chinese sources even though they have not set up or operated a branch within Chinese territory.

Tax bases and tax rates

The ITFIE is levied on business income and other income generated from Chinese sources by foreign invested enterprises or foreign companies. Business income refers to profits from producing operations, while other income includes dividends, interest, rental, disposal gains of capital assets, patent rights, copyright, royalties and franchise fees for transfer of technological know-how.

If a taxpayer's headquarters are inside China, all of the income generated from Chinese territory and abroad is taxable. Income generated by subsidiaries or branches in China or overseas can be consolidated, with the tax returns filed by the headquarters. A standard rate of 30 per cent is set for the ITFIE, with an additional 3 per cent of local income tax. This tax rate is applicable to both business profits and other income generated.

Tax calculation

The ITFIE is levied directly on taxable income, which is the balance of total revenues less allowable costs or other expenses. Determination of taxable income and allowable costs or other expenses is subject to the provisions in tax laws and related regulations. The taxation authority in charge may make adjustments for any tax return that is inconsistent with the tax regulations.

Income taxes paid outside China for business income generated abroad can be treated as either income tax credits or deductibles. However, tax credits or deductibles are limited to the tax payable determined under the ITFIE. If a loss is incurred by a foreign invested enterprise, the loss can be carried forward within a period of not longer than five years.[7]

TAX REGISTRATION AND TAX RETURNS

Tax registration

According to Chinese tax laws, all taxpayers engaging in producing operations, including domestic businesses, foreign invested enterprises, other entities and individuals, must file tax registrations with local taxation authorities within 30 days of receiving a business licence. Tax registrations should contain information on the taxpayer's business name, location, ownership, organizational structure, types of operation and business scope. Any changes incurred after the initial tax registration, such as business restructuring, relocation, combination, split or termination of operation, must be refiled with tax authorities within 30 days of the changes or events having been approved by related administrative authorities, or having been announced publicly.

A taxpayer must maintain proper books of account in terms of the specifications required by taxation authorities. Every taxpayer must file the detail of his or her accounting and financing systems with the local tax authority in charge. If the accounting or financing policies adopted by a taxpayer are inconsistent with the specifications formulated by government finance and taxation authorities, the taxable income must be determined in terms of the related government regulations.

Tax returns

The procedures for filing tax returns vary with respect to different types of taxes. Usually, tax returns will be filed with local taxation authorities. If a taxpayer's headquarters and branches are not located in the same city, separate tax returns should be filed with local tax authorities individually. The taxable income for branches or subsidiaries, however, can be consolidated and reported in the tax returns of the headquarters, if approved by the tax authorities in advance.

Varied deadlines are set for different types of taxes. Turnover taxes, resources taxes and property taxes are due whenever the underlying transactions are complete. Tax authorities usually set a specified tax period for individual taxpayers to file the returns, such as one day, three days, five days, ten days, 15 days or 30 days. Advance tax payments must be made within five days of the end of the specified tax period and tax returns must be filed within the first ten days in the following month. Tax returns on imported goods should be filed within seven days of clearance from customs.

Business income taxes are assessed annually on the basis of the calendar year, with tax returns to be filed not later than four months after the year end. But monthly or quarterly advance payment, determined by tax authorities in light of the size of taxable income, is required within 15 days of the end of each month or quarter. Interim tax payments must be equal to the actual amount of the tax payable in each payment period, unless it is agreed upon by the tax authorities for the taxpayer to make advance payments based on the tax payable in a prior year. A taxpayer must file tax returns and financial statements with tax authorities, regardless of whether profit or loss has incurred in a tax year.

Personal income tax is levied according to source deduction and self-assessment. Tax payable on wages and salaries is withheld monthly by individual employers or institutes from which taxpayers receive the income. Tax payable must be remitted to the state treasury by employers or taxpayers, accompanied by personal income tax returns, within the first week in the following month. Tax payable for personal income from private proprietorships or partnerships is assessed annually, but monthly advance payment is required. Annual tax returns must be filed within three months of the year end.

Taxpayers who receive personal income outside China should file tax returns with payment within thirty days of the end of each calendar year.

Tax penalties

Tax authorities conduct tax audits regularly. Tax penalties will be enforced over alleged irregularities committed by taxpayers in the process of tax registrations and filing tax returns. The main tax penalties include the following:

- a fine as specified by the tax laws;
- daily overdue penalty interest for tax payable in arrears;
- freezing a taxpayer's bank deposits equivalent to unpaid taxes or confiscating the taxpayer's other physical properties if tax authorities believe that the taxpayer intends to transfer out assets illegally for the purpose of tax evasion, and
- criminal charges against taxpayers who have refused to pay taxes, committed serious tax evasion or other violations of tax regulations.

According to Chinese tax laws, taxpayers must first make full payment of tax penalties even if they disagree with the tax bureaux over the penalty imposed. Taxpayers are, however, allowed to appeal to tax authorities at a higher level within 60 days of payment of the penalty being made. The higher tax authorities must review the appeal and reply officially within 60 days. Taxpayers can file a lawsuit in court within 15 days of receiving the reply, if they disagree with the review decisions made by the higher-level tax authorities.

PREFERENTIAL TAX POLICIES FOR REGIONAL DEVELOPMENT

The Chinese government stipulated a series of preferential tax policies in the 1980s, aiming at attracting foreign investment and advanced technology, as well as speeding up economic growth in coastal areas. In general, the preferential tax policies are mainly applicable to the designated special economic zones (SEZs), coastal opening cities and economic developing areas, high-tech development districts and a number of industries on the government's list of investment priority.[8]

Preferential tax policies for special economic zones

Five SEZs were set up by the Chinese government in the early 1980s – Shenzhen, Zhuhai, Santou, Xiamen and Hainan – all of them geographically close to Hong Kong and Taiwan. One of the purposes of setting up the SEZs is to provide limited experimental sites for capitalist-style reforms and to stimulate economic development in those areas for the political motive of competing with Hong Kong and Taiwan. Thus many special economic policies and tax incentives are granted to the SEZs.[9] In particular, foreign invested enterprises located in the SEZs benefit from the following preferential tax policies.

Exemption from turnover tax

1　The turnover tax applicable to foreign invested enterprises, that is, the UICT, is waived for imported materials, parts, production equipment and management facilities used by foreign invested enterprises located in the SEZs. However, the tax must be paid if those materials and parts are used to produce products that are sold in domestic markets.

2　Personal tools and transport vehicles brought in by foreign investors for self-use are exempted from the UICT.

3　Manufactured products are exempted from the UICT when they are exported, except for a very small number of products whose export is restricted by the government.

As mentioned earlier, the Chinese government decided to phase out the preferential tax policies for foreign invested enterprises, following a significant reduction of tariffs for imported goods in 1996. However, a grace period has been granted, initially up to the end of 1997, and is now being extended indefinitely as one of the government's recent efforts to retain and attract foreign investors after the Asian financial crisis occurred in late 1997. In addition, foreign invested enterprises established or approved before 1

April 1996 are allowed to follow the original tax policies over their remaining contract life.

Reduction of business income tax

1 Business income tax for foreign invested enterprises located in the SEZs is reduced to 15 per cent instead of the standard rate of 30 per cent.
2 Foreign invested enterprises involved in manufacturing, and with a contract life longer than ten years, receive a tax holiday for the first two profitable years and an additional 50 per cent reduction of business income tax (that is, 7.5 per cent effective income tax rate) for another three years.
3 Non-business income such as dividends, interest, rental and royalty fees received from the SEZs by foreign companies who do not have residential branches inside China will be taxed at a rate of 10 per cent.
4 After-tax profits received by foreign investors are exempted from personal income tax.
5 Local income surtax for foreign invested enterprises may be waived or reduced by local governments.

Tax refund for reinvested after-tax profits

If the after-tax profits distributed to foreign investors are reinvested inside China for new projects with more than five years of contract life, the investors are eligible for a partial refund of business income tax, up to 40 per cent of the amount that had been originally paid. The refunded tax, however, must be repaid if the new investment is withdrawn in less than five years.

Preferential tax policies for coastal economic developing areas

The Chinese government set up 14 coastal economic developing areas (CEDAs), also called coastal opening cities, in the 1980s. Certain preferential policies were granted to speed up economic development of these areas. The designated CEDAs are Dalian, Qinghuangdao, Tianjing, Yantai, Qingdao, Lianyungang, Nantong, Shanghai, Ningbo, Wenzhou, Fuzhou, Guangzhou, Zhanjiang and Beihai, all located in coastal port cities with relatively sound industrial infrastructures. Preferential tax policies for foreign invested enterprises located in the CEDAs include the following:

Exemption from turnover taxes

The same policies are applied as for investments in the SEZs.

Reduction of business income tax

The tax rate for business income is reduced to 24 per cent. The rate may be reduced to 15 per cent for technology-intensive business entities, or investment projects with foreign capital over US$30 million or a long payback period, such as investment in energy, transport or harbour infrastructure projects, if approved by the Ministry of Finance and the state tax authority. The length of the tax reduction period is subject to negotiation of initial or renewal contracts.[10]

Exemption or reduction of local income surtax

Individual local governments may grant this preferential treatment upon negotiation.

Preferential tax policies for state high-tech industrial districts (SHTIDs)

The Chinese government established 21 SHTIDs across the country in the late 1980s, in order to promote the growth of high-tech industry. Foreign invested enterprises located in the SHTIDs, and with a contract life longer than ten years, are eligible for the following preferential tax benefits: (1) exemption from turnover tax (that is, the UICT) and (2) reduction of business income tax. Business income tax will be levied at a reduced rate of 15 per cent. The tax may be further reduced to 10 per cent if an enterprise's exported products account for more than 70 per cent of its total output. In addition, a tax holiday for the first two profitable years is applicable. A longer period of tax reduction may be granted to technology-intensive enterprises, subject to an assessment by government authorities.

The preferential tax policies mentioned above remain in effect for the existing foreign invested enterprises during the transitional period, even though they are set to be phased out by the tax reform of 1994. The Chinese government has postponed the enforcement of new tax systems on foreign invested enterprises and foreign companies. However, certain preferential tax policies, the exemption of turnover taxes in particular (for example, the UICT), may no longer apply to new foreign invested enterprises established after 1996.

It is worth mentioning that the Chinese government, in the meantime, intends to redesign the preferential tax policies instead of eliminating them altogether. According to the government's plan, the preferential tax incentives will be used to encourage or stimulate investments flowing into less developed inner regions or industries where large amounts of investment and longer payback periods are required. Currently, restrictions have been imposed upon investments in coastal areas and manufacturing and service industries, but most of the existing preferential tax policies are available for foreign investors pouring capital into the less developed north-west regions or other inner regions of China, and into the specified industries on the government's investment priority lists, such as projects in the fields of energy, transport, harbour and railway infrastructures, post and telecommunications, forestry, fisheries, animal husbandry, hydro-power and irrigation, and agricultural facilities.

NOTES

1   Before the 1994 tax reforms, the Chinese government established a separate tax system for business entities with foreign capital. Many preferential tax policies were introduced in an effort to attract foreign investors. The tax burdens for business entities with foreign capital or taxpayers located in certain special economic zones were substantially lower than for their domestic counterparts.

2   Under the old tax system before 1994, taxes for enterprises with foreign investments and foreign enterprises were levied separately from those for domestic enterprises. Although the tax reform of 1994 has harmonized taxes for both domestic enterprises and enterprises with foreign investments and foreign enterprises, the existing segregated taxes for enterprises with foreign investment and foreign enterprises will be phased out gradually, or they will remain in effect during the transitional period. See the next section of this chapter for further discussion.

3   Although export is generally encouraged, a very small number of commodities or goods that are in extremely short supply in domestic markets are restricted from export by the Chinese government.

4   Currently, a segregated business income tax system is in place, at least for the specified transitional period, for business entities with foreign investments. This topic is discussed further in the next section of this chapter.

5   The Chinese government maintained a low personal income policy before the 1980s. The general level of personal income was deliberately set at a minimum and personal income tax was not in existence in the country prior to 1980.

6   The surtax is imposed on income over RMB ¥20 000 per transaction from professional services.

7   Carryback of losses is generally not allowed under Chinese taxation rules.

8   Some of the preferential tax policies have been phased out since the enforcement of new tax systems in 1994.

9   Domestic enterprises located in the SEZs also enjoyed the preferential tax treatments before the 1994 tax reforms. But the preferential treatments were terminated for domestic business entities thereafter.

10 Some local governments may grant more favourable tax incentives to attract or retain foreign investments within their jurisdictions. There is generally leeway for bargaining during the negotiation process.

9 Accounting for Governments and Non-profit Organizations

In China, unlike the practices in most western countries, there is at present no explicit classification of 'governmental accounting' and 'accounting for non-profit organizations'. Rather, these two areas of accounting are blended into the so called 'budgetary accounting', which refers to accounting and reporting for all transactions and operating results of the state's centrally budgeted funds. Budgetary accounting, in contrast to business accounting, represents one of the two main accounting systems operating within China. Thus the term 'budgetary accounting' is employed in this chapter as a synonym of Chinese accounting for governments and non-profit organizations.

In a country like China where public (state) ownership and centralized economic planning and control have been installed, spending in the public sector accounts for an immense proportion of the national economy. The government's budgetary control dominates all expenditures and programmes in nationwide economic and social developments. Budgetary accounting has, therefore, played a significant role in the economy through measuring and reporting the efficiency and effectiveness of public spending and the accountability of government at all levels. Budgetary accounting is certainly an important area that should not be ignored when examining accounting developments in China. Thus this chapter delineates the unique characteristics of Chinese budgetary accounting and the prospect of its reform that is currently under way.

THE ADMINISTRATIVE STRUCTURE OF BUDGETARY ACCOUNTING

A formal Soviet-style centralized planned economy was installed in China immediately after the founding of the People's Republic of China in 1949.

The state directly maintained the ownership of means of production, the authority over national economic controls and the right to distribute funds for social development programmes. The central government therefore exercised simultaneously a dual function of 'regulator' and 'administrator' in the national economy. All economic entities, irrespective of government bodies, social institutions and non-profit organizations (NPOs), or even industrial and commercial enterprises, were fully owned by the state. Their operations had to be financed by the government's fiscal or budgetary appropriations. All government units, NPOs and other organizations have been, in effect, the composing units within the central government's state economic plans and fiscal budgets. Economic entities in the public sector were designed as the 'budgetary units' to facilitate the government's budgetary planning and control.

Under a centralized fiscal system of 'collecting all revenues and financing every programme', all governmental institutions and non-profit organizations were directly funded by annual budgetary appropriations from the central government. The budgetary units were mandated to carry out various governmental and societal functions, as well as other non-profit undertakings in line with the state's social development policies. The main accounting task in the budgetary units was simply to perform bookkeeping and to report the execution of the state budgetary plans and the operating results of the budgetary funds. In this regard, 'budgetary accounting' is a quite explicit terminology which reflects the nature and basic characteristics of Chinese accounting for governments and non-profit organizations.

System of governmental budgetary administration

Comprehension of budgetary accounting cannot be achieved without an understanding of the Chinese system of budgetary administration. The fiscal or budgetary system in China is organized in terms of the jurisdictional structures and administrative responsibilities of governments at various levels. Within a framework of centralized economic planning and control, a top-down structure of budgetary administration has been adopted. The central government prepares and enforces the state fiscal budgets that encompass sub-budgets for government and other budgetary organizations. Governments at all levels (including the central, provincial, municipal, county and township) must prepare the fiscal budgets of the respective jurisdictions in accordance with the centrally budgeted revenues and expenditures imposed in the state fiscal budgets.

Corresponding to the responsibilities for administration of budgetary funds, Chinese governmental fiscal budgets are classified in two major categories:

master fiscal budgets and institutional budgets. These two types of fiscal budget must be prepared at each level of government. The master fiscal budgets (or aggregate budgets) incorporate all budgetary revenues and expenditures that will be incurred within individual jurisdiction. Usually, the master fiscal budgets are prepared by the finance departments at corresponding levels of government, such as the Ministry of Finance at national level and the finance bureaux at various local authorities (including provinces, municipalities, counties and townships). The institutional budgets refer to the budgets prepared by individual budgetary institutions such as governmental administrative departments and NPOs. Institutional budgets are the components of master fiscal budgets administered by government at corresponding jurisdictions. The relationship among the various budgets is as follows:

1   The master fiscal budgets govern the institutional budgets, with the former setting out the budgetary revenues and expenditures for the latter.
2   The fiscal budgets at the lower level of government are subordinate to the fiscal budgets at the higher level of authority. Accordingly, the state fiscal budgets, which are the highest level of the budgetary hierarchy, govern the fiscal budgets prepared in all governments and other budgetary institutions down through the hierarchical system of budgetary administration.

Figure 9.1 illustrates the system of budgetary administration in China. The state fiscal budgets are prepared by the Ministry of Finance on behalf of the State Council and enforced after approval and authorization by the People's Congress at the national level. Similar procedures are adopted for master fiscal budgets at the lower levels of government. Interim reporting is required for all budgetary units to submit data regarding the execution of the state fiscal budgets at various intervals of every ten days, each month and each quarter. The main purpose of interim reporting is to allow the central government to monitor or modify the execution of the state fiscal budgets. At the end of each fiscal year (currently the calendar year), final accounts must be prepared by each aggregate budgetary unit, that is, the finance bureaux of local governments and the Ministry of Finance, to report the operating results of the master fiscal budgets. Then the 'state final accounts' will be prepared by the Ministry of Finance, based on a bottom-up consolidation of the final accounts of all jurisdictions through the chains of budgetary hierarchy. The state final accounts must be presented to the National People's Congress for approval in conjunction with the submission of new state fiscal budgets for the next fiscal year.

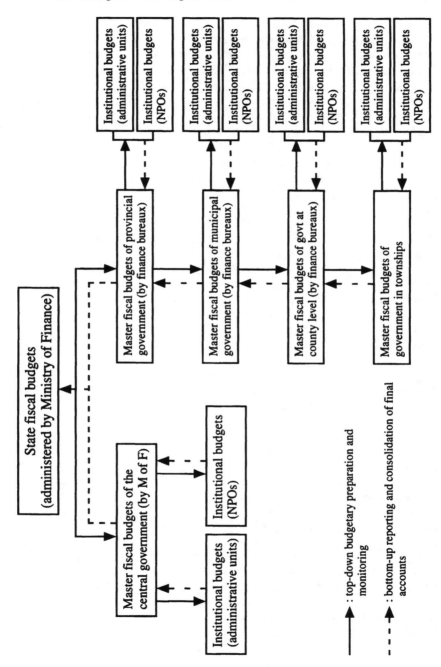

Figure 9.1 The system of state budgetary administration in China

Components of budgetary accounting

Budgetary accounting plays an important role in the central government's budgetary administration. For example, budgetary accounting is required to supply data for the purposes of budget preparation, execution and monitoring, and for the preparation of final accounts to summarize the results of budget execution. Corresponding to the classification of governmental budgets, the budgetary accounting comprises accounting for master fiscal budgets and institutional budgetary accounting, respectively.

Accounting for master fiscal budgets

Accounting for master fiscal budgets refers to accounting procedures for recording and reporting the execution of the fiscal budgets and the operating results of the budgetary revenues and expenditures directly administered by each level of government, that is, the central or local governments, also called the aggregate budgetary units. Accounting for master fiscal budgets actually comprises accounting for the collection and remittance of tax revenues (organized by the state taxation authority), accounting for the state treasury (kept by the central bank) and accounting for the state appropriations for capital constructions (administered by the designated state-owned specialized banks). The main aims of accounting for master fiscal budgets are threefold:

- to record and report the collection and remittance of budgetary revenues, the allocation and disbursement of budgetary appropriations, and the final balance of budgetary funds in each fiscal year;
- to prepare the combined budgetary financial statements, that is, the final accounts for each government;
- to supply data necessary for governments to conduct overall fiscal budgeting and to monitor the execution of budgetary controls.

Institutional budgetary accounting

Within the Chinese budgetary administrative system, all governmental bodies, agencies and NPOs are grouped together as institutional budgetary units, in contrast to the aggregate budgetary units designed for government at various levels, that is the central, provincial, municipal, county and township. Thus institutional budgetary accounting refers to the accounting and reporting work performed by administrative departments, social programmes (such as education, health care, culture and sport, science and research, social welfare and public work), political parties and other non-profit organizations. These institutions, although widely diversified in their functions and operations, must rely upon annual appropriations from governments' budgetary funds and must comply with the specific guidelines for designated programmes, spending authorizations and expenditure criteria codified in the state's budgetary plans.

Because of the great variety in jurisdictional structures, programme functions and administrative responsibilities, the connections between governmental and non-profit organizations (institutional budgetary units) and the state's budgetary revenues and expenditures vary. These institutional units are therefore further grouped into three subcategories in terms of their dependency upon the state's budgetary appropriations and the patterns of budgetary administration imposed by government. The three subcategories are as follows.

Full-amount budgetary units   Those institutions that depend directly and entirely upon appropriations from the state's fiscal budgets for their operating revenues are classified as 'full-amount budgetary units' (FABUs). Entities that fall into this category include governmental administrative departments and many of the social programmes or non-profit organizations that could not generate their own revenues through their operations.

Marginal budgetary units   Marginal budgetary units (MBUs) are the entities for which only the margin or difference (deficit) between their operating revenues and expenditures is supported by the state's budgetary appropriations. For instance, hospitals and educational institutions may generate certain revenues from their daily operations (service fees or tuition income), but the revenues generated are usually insufficient to cover their total operating costs. The MBUs must rely upon governments' appropriations to make up the shortfall in their operating funds.

Self-financed budgetary units   The non-profit organizations that could generate sufficient operating revenues to cover their own operating costs are labelled 'self-financed budgetary units' (SFBUs) for the purpose of budgetary administration. The components of the SFBUs include research institutes of applied sciences, publishing houses, theatres, gymnasiums or recreational clubs, and so on. The SFBUs generally do not depend upon the state's budgetary appropriations for operating revenues, but they differ in nature, and are separated from profit-seeking business enterprises. Thus the SFBUs are treated as self-financed operating units within the state's budgetary administration system.

The institutional budgetary accounting is therefore composed of accounting for FABUs, accounting for MBUs and accounting for SFBUs. Although they must fulfil a common task of recording and reporting the execution of the state's budgets within individual institutions, varied emphases are placed upon these three subsets of institutional budgetary accounting. As an analogy, the FABUs are more or less like cost centres, with the expenditure side as the focus of accounting. The MBUs are similar to revenue centres where the maximization of revenues (service fees) is emphasized for the purpose of accounting. The SFBUs are virtually in line with profit centres. Accounting for the SFBUs must focus on measuring and reporting of profit-making activities, and on assisting management to maximize the surplus of funds from operations. Accordingly, certain unique accounting and reporting procedures are required with respect to each of the three subsets of the institutional budgetary units. Figure 9.2 depicts the overall structure of budgetary accounting in China.

REGULATIONS FOR BUDGETARY ACCOUNTING

Government bodies and non-profit organizations in China must strictly comply with rigorous accounting regulations, the so called 'budgetary accounting systems' (BAS), which are formulated by the Department of Budgetary Administration under the Ministry of Finance in the central government.[1] This is to ensure that budgetary accounting will directly serve the government's needs for state budgetary administration.

The BAS specify guidance for the basic accounting principles, for the uniform charting of ledger accounts and the format of financial statements, as well as for the recording and reporting procedures to be adopted by all budgetary accounting units across the country. Thus the BAS represent nationwide mandatory accounting regulations for all governmental and non-profit organizations.

The BAS, in fact, consist of a few subsets of accounting and reporting regulations in correspondence with the pattern of budgetary administration. One of the subsets promulgated by the Ministry of Finance is the *Accounting System for Master Fiscal Budgets*. This set of regulations applies to the aggregated budgetary units (that is, the Ministry of Finance, or the finance bureaux at lower levels of government) for the preparation of final accounts by each government. Another important subset of the BAS is called the *Budgetary Accounting System for Administrative and Institutional Organizations* (BASFAIO), which is applicable to all governmental departments and government-like social institutions and organizations adopting the pattern of 'full-amount budgetary administration' (that is, the FABUs).

Different budgetary administration patterns are in place for other social institutions and non-profit organizations such as hospitals, universities and

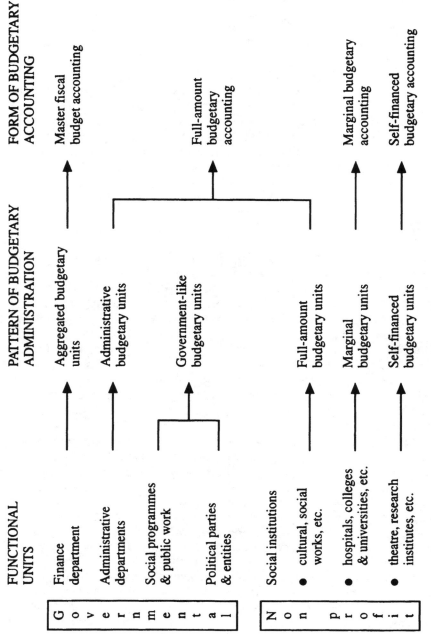

Figure 9.2   The structure of budgetary accounting in China

colleges, applied science research institutes, and cultural and recreational facilities. The underlying rationale to justify such varied treatments is that those institutions may generate certain revenues from their operations and depend only partially (or not at all) upon the state's budgetary appropriations. Thus industry-specific accounting regulations, such as the *Budgetary Accounting System for Health Care Institutions*, the *Budgetary Accounting System for Universities and Colleges* and the *Budgetary Accounting System for Scientific Research Institutes*, have been promulgated to accommodate the specific accounting and reporting needs of those budgetary institutions with significantly diversified operations. Such supplementary sets of budgetary accounting regulations are formulated by related ministerial authorities in the central government, for example, the Ministry of Public Health, the State Education Commission and the Chinese Academy of Sciences, with delegation of authority from the Ministry of Finance. To ensure consistency with the BASFAIO, the industry-specific budgetary accounting regulations must be approved by the Ministry of Finance before their issuance and enforcement.

Although several subsets of accounting regulations for various components of budgetary accounting coexist, their contents are fairly standardized. Usually, each set of the accounting regulations contains two major parts: (1) the uniform chart of accounts to be adopted, including the specification for general and sub-ledger accounts; and (2) the types and format of the financial statements to be presented, including the specification on main line items of each statement. In addition, the regulations set out fairly detailed requirements on the recording and reporting procedures to be followed in carrying out budgetary accounting work. All requirements are mandatory and must be implemented rigorously.

Governments' fiscal or budgetary policies have predominant influences upon budgetary accounting. The central government has stipulated regulations on state fiscal budgetary administration from time to time. For instance, the central government enacted the *Budget Law of the People's Republic of China* in 1994 which became effective on 1 January 1995. The new law codifies most of the existing practices in budgetary administration and some changes resulting from the fiscal and taxation reforms introduced in 1994. Accordingly, the Ministry of Finance stipulated a new set of *General Rules on Financing for Administrative and Institutional Units* at the end of 1996 which came into force on 1 January 1997. As budgetary accounting is required to perform supportive functions to enhance the state's fiscal planning and budgetary control, the formulation of BAS must be in line with the general principles and requirements laid down by the Budget Law and the general financing rules.

BASIC CHARACTERISTICS OF BUDGETARY ACCOUNTING

Chinese budgetary accounting differs considerably not only from business accounting in China, but also from its counterpart systems in western countries. Some fundamental characteristics of Chinese budgetary accounting, within the framework of the current BAS, can be demonstrated in what follows.

Objectives

The primary objective of budgetary accounting is to serve the state's budgetary administration and to facilitate the preparation of fiscal budgets and the supervision of budget execution. The designation of the chart of accounts and the format of financial statements for all governments and non-profit organizations must, therefore, be in conformity with the classification of budgetary revenues and expenditures specified in the state fiscal budgets. To record and report the implementation of fiscal budgets and the operating results of fiscally budgeted funds in the budgetary units is the main task of budgetary accounting. In addition, budgetary accounting is required to prevent spending in individual budgetary units in excess of the budgetary appropriations.

The system of accounts

Segregated accounting is required for on-budget funds and off-budget funds, and each should be self-balanced. Under the current system of centralized budgetary administration, governmental funds are divided into two categories: 'on-budget funds', that is, the revenues and expenditures included directly in the state fiscal budgets, and the so-called 'off-budget funds', the revenues and expenditures that are at the discretion of local governments or other budgetary organizations. Relatively speaking, the focus of budgetary accounting is upon 'on-budget funds' because the off-budget funds are not subject to the same degree of scrutiny and control by the central government.

Why are the off-budget funds allowed? The initial motivation for having the distinction of on-budget and off-budget funds was mainly to exclude certain trivial or miscellaneous items in the state fiscal budgets for the sake of simplifying the preparation and execution of state fiscal budgets. The 'off-budget funds' have, however, been utilized by the central government as a tool to implement the decentralization-oriented reforms of the state's fiscal administration system over the last ten years. Besides the on-budget funds, the central government had deliberately set aside certain fragmentary revenues as the sources of funds for local authorities or other budgetary organizations, aiming at stimulating their efforts to generate additional revenues and develop local programmes without relying totally upon the state's fiscal appropriations. The logic behind this distinction of the two categories of funds is to provide certain incentives to lower authorities while maintaining a highly centralized budgetary administration.

Such a two-tier system of budgetary administration requires a stringent separation, as well as self-balancing, amongst the on-budget and off-budget funds. Thus separate sets of accounts or books must be maintained for the two types of funds in all governments and non-profit organizations, accompanied by segregated recording and reporting procedures. Transactions involving fund flows between the on-budget and off-budget funds should be clearly distinguished and appropriately accounted for. Adjustment entries must be made to prevent any interflows between the two types of funds at the end of each fiscal period.

Fund accounting

The concept of 'fund accounting' is adopted in Chinese budgetary accounting and reporting. Instead of employing the classifications based on assets, liabilities and net assets, a framework of 'three-category budgetary fund flows', that is, sources of funds, uses of funds and stocks of funds (the final balances of fund assets), is utilized to develop and group ledger accounts for the purposes of recording and reporting. The basic equation, as well as the financial statements structure, of the budgetary accounting is the following:

sources of funds – uses of funds = stocks of funds (fund balances)

The focus of budgetary accounting is thus placed on 'stock of funds', or the balances of funds over fund flows incurred during each accounting period. Every transaction is interpreted and recorded in respect of its effect on 'stocks of funds'. Recording of 'sources of funds' (long-term liabilities in particular) and 'uses of funds' may be simplified or net-off in accounting processing if they have no effect on fund balances. Although this system may be adequate for the purposes of budgetary control, it has led to inaccurate deficit measurement and neglect of long-lived assets and long-term liabilities.

Cash-based accounting

Unlike the practice of governmental accounting in many western countries, Chinese budgetary accounting adheres strictly to a cash basis in the recognition of revenues and expenditures for accounting and reporting purposes. Thus the cut-off treatment of periodic revenues and expenditures of governmental entities and those non-profit organizations with government-like budgetary management (that is, the FABUs) is based on actual bank deposits or disbursements incurred at the closing date of each fiscal period (such as the calendar year).[2] However, those non-profit organizations not following a government-like budgetary administration pattern, that is, the MBUs and the SFBUs, have switched to the accrual or modified accrual basis in their accounting and reporting since the late 1980s.

Generally cost accounting is not required in accounting and reporting for governments and non-profit organizations (except for certain SFBUs), because the collections, appropriations and uses of the state's fiscally budgeted funds are free of charge and the operations of most budgetary institutions are non-profit in nature. Even for the SFBUs that operate on a cost-recovery basis, the costing system in place is relatively simple or incomplete, in comparison with business accounting.

In addition, for governmental entities and most of the non-profit organizations, fixed assets are directly supplied through the state's budgetary appropriations and there is no need to accumulate replacement funds. Hence depreciation accounting for fixed assets, in general, does not exist in Chinese budgetary accounting.

Bookkeeping method

Various bookkeeping methods are currently applied in terms of the basic characteristics of particular types of budgetary funds. Although the double-entry bookkeeping method with *debit* and *credit* entries is used in western governmental and non-profit accounting, its application in Chinese budgetary accounting is rare. Instead, the so called 'fund receipt–disbursement bookkeeping method' is, at present, predominant in Chinese accounting for governments and non-profit organizations.

It was contended by governmental administrative authorities that the 'fund receipt–disbursement' method, with a tripartite classifications of ledger accounts in terms of sources of funds, uses of funds and stocks of funds, embody more explicitly the essential features of budgetary fund flows. In other words, the method could better serve the designated accounting and reporting purposes of budgetary accounting, because accounting and reporting for budgetary funds must focus directly on the receipts, disbursements

and balances (surplus or deficit) of particular fund flows in individual entities or organizations. However, the 'debit–credit' method has been adopted,
as a reform measure, in certain non-profit organizations not subject to the
government-like budgetary administration (that is, the MBUs and the SFBUs)
in the late 1980s.[3]

Features of the fund receipt–disbursement bookkeeping method

The 'fund receipt–disbursement method', in theory, is a special form of
double-entry bookkeeping. It requires each ledger account to have two sides
of entry, recording receipt and disbursement, and each transaction to be
recorded in two (or more) related ledger accounts. However, its emphasis is
placed on the changes and final balances (surplus or deficit) of ledger
accounts under the category of 'stocks of funds'. The recording rules under
this bookkeeping method are as follows.

First, transactions that represent inflows of funds to an entity and which
would have increased its fund balances (either monetary or non-monetary
fund assets), for example, receiving the state's budgetary appropriations,
must be recorded as entries of 'receipt' in ledger accounts under both
categories of 'stocks of funds' and 'sources of funds', simultaneously.

Second, transactions that represent outflows of funds from an entity and
which would have decreased its balances of funds (for example, incurrence
(payment) of operating expenditures) must be recorded as entries of 'disbursement' in ledger accounts under both categories of 'stocks of funds' and
'uses of funds', simultaneously.

Third, transactions involving movements between different ledger accounts within only the category of 'stocks of funds', which would not cause
changes in an entity's total fund balances (for example, withdrawal of cash
from bank deposits or purchase of inventories or office supplies) must be
recorded as one entry of 'receipt' and another of 'disbursement' in the
accounts involved, respectively.

Fourth, transactions not involving ledger accounts in the category of
'stocks of funds', and which would not cause changes in an entity's total
balances of funds, for example, alterations in the types of appropriations or
expenditures, must be simultaneously recorded as one entry of 'receipt' and
another of 'disbursement' in ledger accounts under the category either of
'sources of funds' or of 'uses of funds'.

In other words, journal entries under the 'fund receipt and disbursement
method' should follow the following recording rules:

1   Transactions causing an increase or a decrease in fund balances should
    be recorded as both 'receipt' entries, or both 'disbursement' entries, with

one entry in the 'stocks of funds' category and another in either the category of 'sources of funds' or 'uses of funds'; the total entry amount in the two categories of accounts being recorded must be equal.

2　Transactions that would not change the fund balances should be recorded as one entry of 'receipt' and another of 'disbursement' within the 'stocks of funds' category, or in either the category of 'sources of funds' or 'uses of funds' simultaneously, with the total 'receipt' amount being equal to the total 'disbursement' amount.

Figure 9.3 illustrates the interrelation of the journal entries to be recorded under the 'fund receipt–disbursement method'.

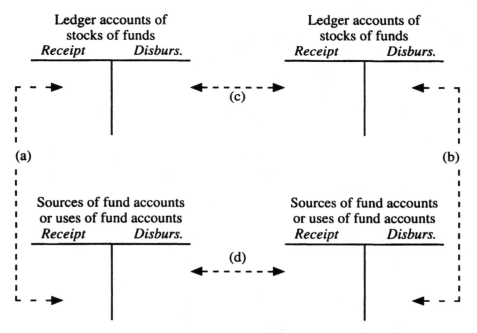

Figure 9.3　Interrelation of journal entries under the fund receipt–disbursement bookkeeping method

When applying the 'fund receipt–disbursement method', trial balancing of the books is conducted on the basis of one of the following equations.

●　Trial balancing by ending balances of funds:

Total balances of 'receipt' entries of the ledger accounts in 'sources of funds' category	total balances of 'disbursement' entries − of the ledger accounts in 'uses of funds', category	total balances of 'receipt' entries of = the ledger accounts in 'stocks of funds' category

- trial balancing by differential amounts between the entries of receipt and disbursement:

Differential amount between entries of 'receipt' and 'disbursement' in the accounts of 'sources of funds' category	Differential amount between entries of 'receipt' and − 'disbursement' in the accounts of 'uses of funds' category	Differential amount between entries of 'receipt' and = 'disbursement' in the accounts of 'stocks of funds' category

Some Chinese governmental accountants have claimed that the receipt–disbursement method was easier to comprehend than the debit–credit method, in addition to being a better reflection of the nature of fund flows in governments and non-profit organizations. This may be partially true, since the notion of debt–credit was relatively remote to many Chinese accountants under a centrally planned economy. However, as discussed in Chapter 1, another reason for the rejection of the 'debit–credit bookkeeping method' in Chinese accounting was ideologically motivated: that is, the debit–credit method originated in the capitalist world should not be applied in a socialist economy. The alleged superiority of the 'receipt–disbursement method', nonetheless, becomes less tenable when China is moving from a centrally planned economy towards a partial market economy. This has led to increasing demands for the adoption of the 'debit–credit method' in budgetary accounting in recent years.

FINANCIAL REPORTING FOR GOVERNMENTS AND NON-PROFIT ORGANIZATIONS

Within the current framework of budgetary accounting, financial reporting practices vary to a certain extent for governments and non-profit organizations in view of the different administrative patterns of budgetary funds in use.

Financial reporting for aggregate budgetary units

Financial statements of the aggregate budgetary units at each level of government (equivalent to the annual financial reports or final accounts of governments in western countries) are required to report the executive results of the government's fiscal budgets. The finance department at each level of government must prepare and submit the required financial statements to the administrative branch and legislature at the respective jurisdiction, as well as to the finance department at the next higher level of government. The Ministry of Finance is responsible for preparing the aggregated state fiscal budgets and the consolidated state final accounts based on a bottom-up consolidation of the financial statements through a hierarchical system of budgetary administration. The state final accounts must then be presented to the National People's Congress by the minister of finance on behalf of the State Council after the end of each fiscal year.

In order to ensure comparability of financial statements prepared by all levels of government, and to facilitate the central government's budgetary administration, the Ministry of Finance will routinely stipulate specific requirements regarding the types, formats, line items and submission dates of the aggregated financial statements that should be prepared by local governments. The annual financial statements currently prepared by the aggregate budgetary units include 'final accounts of fiscal revenues and expenditures', 'statement of revenues and expenditures of off-budget funds', 'statement of funds status at the end of the fiscal year' (with separate reporting of the on-budget and off-budget funds) and a 'combined statement of revenues and expenditures of local authorities'. A series of schedules, a summary of sub-ledger accounts, supplementary statistics and 'explanations to the final accounts' should also be presented.

In addition to the annual reports, local governments must prepare and submit interim reports to the administration at the higher levels of authority. The interim reports, comprising ten-day highlights or monthly and quarterly statements, focus mainly on the execution of state fiscal budgets and the actual progress of budgetary revenues and expenditures under administration in each interim period. Interim reporting is a major tool for the central government to monitor and modify the process of budget execution. All aggregate budgetary units must prepare and submit the interim reports strictly in terms of the specific requirement laid down by the central government.

Financial reporting for the FABUs

For other governmental departments and social institutions following the pattern of government-like budgetary administration (that is, the FABUs), both annual reports and interim reports are required. The annual reports comprised a 'statement of funds activities', a 'statement of appropriation revenues and expenditures', a 'statement of specially designated funds', a 'statement of revenues and expenditures of off-budget funds' and a 'statement of changes in appropriations received', as well as supplementary schedules, basic statistics and explanatory statements.

The annual financial statements must be prepared in terms of the specifications laid down by the BASFAIO and must be submitted to governing authorities at the higher levels on the date required. The interim reports consist of monthly and quarterly statements, containing fewer types of statements than the annual reports. Interim reports of the FABUs mainly serve the purpose of internal budgetary planning and control, but they are submitted simultaneously to the executive branches at the respective level as well as to the overseeing authorities at a higher level. The format of the interim reports is similar to that of the annual reports which are specified by the mandatory requirements of the BASFAIO.

Financial reporting for the MBUs

Financial reporting for MBUs differs somewhat from that of governmental bodies and the FABUs. This is justified by the fact that the MBUs have to follow different accounting principles or procedures (accrual accounting, for example) in their accounting and reporting processing. Currently, the MBUs must submit to their governing authorities the annual reports of 'statement of fund activities', 'summary of operating revenues and expenditures' and 'statement of revenues and expenditures of specially designated funds'. The financial statements must be prepared in accordance with the specified provisions in the accounting regulations established by industrial administrative authorities of the central government.

Financial reporting for the SFBUs

Owing to the nature of self-financing, the accounting and reporting practices for the SFBUs are much more like those of their business counterparts, and may involve a use of accrual accounting, absence of distinction between on-budget and off-budget funds, income determination and establishment of operating reserves. The financial statements by the SFBUs, therefore, consist of a 'statement of fund activities', an 'income statement' and a 'statement of operating reserves'. The contents and formats of these statements are fairly similar to those prepared by business entities. The SFBUs have been encouraged to adopt business-like accounting systems since the late 1980s. At present, all SFBUs must submit their financial statements to their governmental overseeing authorities quarterly and annually. Financial reports of the SFBUs have been increasingly used by internal management for the purpose of making operational decisions.

Irrespective of the differences in the types of financial statements prepared by the varied types of governmental and non-profit organizations, basic information contained in those statements mainly relates to the implementation of the state's fiscal administration and reports the operating results of the state's budgetary funds. The information needs of users other than governmental authorities have not, however, been adequately addressed in the existing practice of budgetary accounting in China.

PROSPECTS OF BUDGETARY ACCOUNTING REFORM

Need for reform

Changes in Chinese accounting have taken place continuously in step with the progress of economic reforms in the country. In particular, the Chinese government introduced a completely new business accounting system in 1993, aimed at adopting internationally prevailing accounting practices for business accounting.[4] By contrast, there is little significant change in China's accounting and reporting for governments and non-profit organizations thus far. But the success of business accounting reforms in the early 1990s has prompted the government authorities in charge, and the practitioners of governmental and non-profit accounting, to explore the possibility of reforming the existing budgetary accounting system.

The fiscal reform launched by the central government since the early 1990s has brought about significant changes in the system of budgetary administration. For example, a revenue-sharing system was introduced as a result of the tax reform of 1994, aimed at lightening the fiscal burden on the state by encouraging certain degrees of financial autonomy for local governments and other budgetary institutions. As a result, the off-budget funds proliferated dramatically, while the portion of on-budget funds shrank substantially. The Budget Law of 1994 reaffirmed the need for the adjustment of the relationship between the central and local governments. In addition, the *General Rules on Financial Affairs for Administrative and Institutional*

Units were stipulated and implemented by the Ministry of Finance at the end of 1996. These changes in the system of state budgetary administration made reform of budgetary accounting inevitable.

After several rounds of public discussions, consensus on the need for a thorough overhaul of budgetary accounting emerged. Most practitioners agree that the existing regulatory system of budgetary accounting, derived from the needs for highly centralized state fiscal planning and control under the old economic system, has become much more difficult to operate in the partially developed market economy currently evolving in China. As local authorities and other social or non-profit organizations gain considerable autonomy in their operational decision making, and as their sources of funds have expanded in a diversified economy, a new form of accounting and reporting system for governments and non-profit organizations must be developed to serve the information needs of the state's fiscal administration and of the financial management of individual entities involved. A new governmental accounting and reporting system is badly needed to enhance efficiency, effectiveness and economy in the use of public funds, and to ensure the accountability of all governments and non-profit institutions.[5]

Proposed changes

Many proposals for the reform of budgetary accounting have emerged since the early 1990s. Some of them have received wide exposure and even the endorsement of government authorities in charge. At the National Conference on Accounting Affairs, sponsored by the Ministry of Finance, held in Beijing in late 1995, the proposed reform of budgetary accounting has highlighted the following potential changes.

Redefinition of 'budgetary accounting'

It is argued by some Chinese governmental accountants and academics that the terminology 'budgetary accounting' itself seems quite confusing and is hard to fit into the reality of today's partial-market economy. As a result of the reform of the fiscal and taxation systems in recent years, the centrally budgeted funds are shrinking in terms of their significance in total spending in the public sector, while off-budgeted funds are increasing at a remarkable rate. Budgetary accounting may no longer be able to account for the overall revenues and expenditures incurred in governments and non-profit institutions. Thus budgetary accounting should be renamed to reflect the changes in accounting in the public sector. A possible alternative is to replace 'budgetary accounting' with 'governmental accounting' and 'accounting for non-profit organizations', which prevail in most other countries. In addition, a thorough overhaul of the existing budgetary accounting and reporting procedures should be undertaken in light of the progress in the reforms of the state's fiscal or budgetary administration.

Development of uniform accounting standards for governments and NPOs

As mentioned earlier, various sets of rigorous accounting regulations currently coexist, corresponding to the different patterns of budgetary administration. But such a regulatory system has become outmoded in the changing economic environment in China and has caused problems of inconsistency and inadaptability of accounting and reporting practices for governments and non-profit organizations. New accounting standards for the public sector should be developed to replace the existing BAS.

Separate sets of accounting standards for governments and for non-profit organizations are likely to be needed, however, in order to take into account the considerable diversities of operations among governmental units and non-profit institutions.[6] With respect to the great diversity in the operations of non-profit institutions, a set of more general accounting standards will also need to be formulated to serve as a guide for setting up more industry-specific accounting systems for various types of non-profit organizations. At present, setting the national accounting standards for all non-profit institutions is a high priority on the reform agenda. The Ministry of Finance set up a Study Group on Accounting Standards for Non-profit Institutions in late 1994. The study group has been working on drafting the new accounting standards since then. The preliminary drafts of the proposed accounting standards were released to solicit public comments in 1996, while the new accounting standards were scheduled to be officially released by the end of 1997.

Centralization of the standard-setting process

Any proposed new accounting regulations and standards for governments and non-profit institutions will be set by the Ministry of Finance of the central government. Other ministerial authorities will generally no longer be allowed to set industry-specific accounting regulations except for the practical rules that are needed to implement effectively the national accounting standards or regulations. Issuance of the supplementary rules by local governments or the overseeing authorities of the central government must, however, be approved by the Ministry of Finance.

Redesigning of the structure of financial statements

Since the existing framework of financial statements, with the tripartite classification of 'sources of funds', 'uses of funds' and 'stocks of funds', based on the old-fashioned administrative pattern for the state's budgetary funds, has become outmoded, the basic classification of transactions underlying accounting for governments and non-profit organizations will be replaced by the elements of assets, liabilities, net assets (that is, balances of funds), revenues and expenditures, in an effort to reshape the content and format of the financial statements for governments and non-profit organizations. Thus the demarcation between on-budget and off-budget funds will be abolished in governmental accounting and reporting practices. In addition, a uniform system of accounts will be designed for all budgetary units instead of the segregated account systems adopted currently for FABUs, MBUS and SFBUs.

Introduction of modified accrual accounting

Although cash-based accounting dominates in the current practice of budgetary accounting, a switch will be made towards a modified accrual basis for governmental accounting and reporting, especially for non-profit institutions. The modified accrual basis, as experienced in many western countries, will provide better measurements of the operations of governments and non-profit organizations, in respect of the total financial resources entrusted and the assessment of the trustees' accountability. The long-term liabilities and assets could therefore be accounted for in a more accurate and complete manner. In addition, the basic principles of cost accounting associated with accrual accounting would also be adopted in some governmental and non-profit organizations pursuing fee-seeking activities.

Alteration of the bookkeeping method

The 'fund receipt–disbursement' bookkeeping method will be replaced by the 'debit–credit' bookkeeping method, similar to the prevailing practices in other countries. Such a change had been codified in the exposure draft of the recently proposed new accounting standards for non-profit institutions. It is expected that the debit–credit method will be officially adopted in accounting for governments and non-profit organizations in China when the new accounting standards are issued and enforced in the near future. This change will promote international understandability and comparability of Chinese accounting for governments and non-profit organizations.

Although there has been a consensus upon the needs and goals for reforming accounting and reporting for governments and non-profit organizations
in China in recent years, it must be pointed out that the specific reform
measures have yet to be finalized. With regard to the schedule of budgetary
accounting reform, a resolution was adopted at the National Conference on
Accounting Affairs held in late 1995 to commence a five-year period of
experimentation in 1997. Thus it may take some time to see any significant
changes in Chinese accounting and reporting for governments and non-
profit organizations.

NOTES

1 By contrast, the national accounting regulations for business accounting are formulated
   by the Department of Accounting Affairs, under the Ministry of Finance.
2 In practice, the cut-off date for expenditure recognition is usually 25 December, while
   that for revenue recognition is 31 December, of each calendar year.
3 One explanation behind the change is the need to close the gap between business
   accounting and accounting for these business-like budgetary units.
4 See Jiashu Ge and Z. Jun Lin (1993), 'Economic Reforms and Accounting Internationalization in The People's Republic of China', *Journal of International Accounting,
   Auditing and Taxation* (USA), **2**, (2): 129–43.
5 See W.G. Zhang and J.Y. Zhao (1994), 'Some Main Issues in Developing Accounting
   Standards for Institutional Units', *Journal of Accounting Research*, (in Chinese), Beijing,
   (6): 5–11.
6 It is reported by Chinese sources that three sets of uniform national accounting regulations, that is, the *Accounting System for the Final Accounts of Governments*, the *Accounting System for Governmental Administrative Units* and the *Accounting System for
   Non-profit Institutions*, will be established in the near future.

10 Computerization of Accounting

At present, manual data processing remains the norm in accounting work in China. The application of computer technology in accounting is, however, under development and has gained momentum in recent years. This chapter discusses briefly the current status of the computerization of accounting in China and the prospects of its development in the near future.

EVOLUTION OF COMPUTERIZATION OF ACCOUNTING

Unlike the experience of most industrialized countries, utilization of computer technology in accounting is a fairly new phenomenon in China. Although a pilot experiment was initiated on a small scale in the end of the 1970s, meaningful progress of accounting computerization did not start in China until the mid-1980s. The experimental process has speeded up since then, accompanying the popularization of computer technology in business management.

The computerization of accounting in China has gone through four distinct development stages since the late 1970s.

Stage I Pilot experimentation (before 1983)

This is the period when a pilot experiment of applying computer technology in accounting was initiated. Computer technology or facilities were only available in a very small number of large, state-owned enterprises before 1980. The Ministry of Finance sponsored the experimentation of computerized accounting data processing in 1979. The First Automobile Manufacturing Plant located in Changcun City, Jiling Province in north-eastern China, one of the ten largest state-owned enterprises in the country, was selected for the experiment. Funding support for the experiment was granted directly by the Ministry of Finance. Two years later, a special Symposium on the Application of Computers in Financial Management, Accounting and Product Costing, jointly sponsored by the Ministry of Finance, the Ministry of Machinery (the oversight authority of the First Automobile Manufacturing Plant) and the China Society of Accountants, was held to appraise the outcome of the experimental project. Fairly positive responses were generated. It was at this symposium that the term 'application of computers in accounting', or simply 'accounting computerization', was officially adopted by government authorities in charge of accounting affairs.

Stage II   Extended experimentation (1984–86)

A rapid expansion of the experimentation of accounting computerization was the main feature in this developing stage. Following the Chinese government's policy of 'opening to the outside world', advanced technology and management experience in the West had been introduced into China. Application of computer technology in business management has become a fashion since 1983. In particular, the experimentation of accounting computerization was extended to some government administrative bodies and business enterprises in manufacturing industries. The utilization of computer technology in accounting processes developed from simple transactions such as payroll processing to the more complicated tasks of recording general ledgers, inventory, fixed assets, and financial statements and analysis. Following the emergence of Chinese word processing systems in the mid-1980s, accounting computerization became much more accessible to accounting personnel who had little knowledge of English language.

A few research institutions specializing in developing computerized accounting programs or software appeared during this period. Training programmes for operating computerized accounting processing were initiated by some universities and research institutions. The subject of accounting computerization was added to the accounting curriculum in many universities and colleges. Postgraduate studies on the computerization of accounting were also offered, aimed at producing specialists with advanced knowledge and skills in both accounting and computer technology.

Stage III   Development of commercialized accounting software (1987–93)

Development of commercialized software for accounting applications could be identified as the main element in progress of accounting computerization during this period. Business entities had to design their own computerized accounting programs and application software individually in the earlier experimental period. Two deficiencies, however, became apparent. One is the waste of resources in the process of system design and software development. When each entity involved in the experiment had to spend significant amount of resources separately, substantial work overlap or waste had resulted. Another major problem lies in the difficulty for a great number of medium or small-size business enterprises and other entities of adopting computerized accounting programs owing to shortage of the resources needed to pursue in-house development.

Responding to emerging demands for commercialized accounting software in the mid-1980s, the Accounting Society of China (ASC) organized a Task Force on Developing Accounting Software in 1987. The task force was mandated to take a lead in developing computer software for a variety of accounting applications. In addition, a number of other research groups or institutes were formed by some ministerial authorities of the central government to develop industry-specific accounting software that could serve the accounting administration and fit the information needs of those governmental authorities in this regard.

Within the framework of governmental accounting administration, the computerization of accounting is directly regulated by governments. Even the development and utilization of computer software for accounting applications must be subject to strict governmental control. In December 1989, the Ministry of Finance formulated the *Tentative Procedures for Administration of Accounting Software*. This regulation specifies that all accounting software be evaluated or approved by the Ministry of Finance or the finance bureaux of governments at provincial level.

General-purpose computer software appeared during this period, resulting from expanded utilization of computer technology in business management. About 20 types of accounting software had been approved by government authorities by 1993. With the availability of this commercialized accounting software, an increasing number of business entities and other organizations have adopted computerized accounting programs, although many of them adopted only a single function application, such as payroll or inventory accounting.

Stage IV   Standardization of accounting computerization (since 1994)

Standardization of computerized accounting systems has become a major trend in recent years. As governments are primary users of accounting information, uniformity is always emphasized in Chinese accounting. The accounting software developed before 1993, was mainly targeted at individual industries or enterprises and lacked general applicability. Although demands for standardized accounting software rose continuously, in practice a great variety of accounting software remained, owing to the fact that over 50 pieces of industry-specific accounting regulations were in place, segregated by different business ownership and types of industry. Lack of standardized or general-purpose software, in fact, had deterred many organizations from adopting computerized accounting programs.

The introduction of new national accounting systems in 1993 provided a good opportunity for the standardization of accounting software. Since the new set of national accounting standards for business enterprises was implemented in 1993, the diversity in accounting practices for various business ownership and industry has been reduced significantly. Development of standardized accounting software has gained momentum accordingly.

At the same time, the Ministry of Finance stepped up its efforts to promote the standardization of accounting computerization and the application of commercialized accounting software. Three regulations, *The Administration of Computerization of Accounting, The Procedures for Appraisal of Commercialized Accounting Software* and *The Requirements for Basic Functions of Accounting Software*, were released by the Ministry of Finance in June 1994, all of them coming into effect on 1 July 1994. This development indicates a move towards a standardization of the computerization of accounting in China.

CHARACTERISTICS OF COMPUTERIZED ACCOUNTING

Current status

According to government statistics, about 20 per cent of Chinese business enterprises and non-business organizations had installed computerized accounting systems up to the end of 1996.[1] Although this level of accounting computerization is not impressive when compared with the existing standard in most industrialized countries, it does indicate a fairly rapid growth in the current business environment in China. The development of computer technology, particularly the application of computers in business management in China, has only a fairly short history, owing to its relatively under-developed and huge economy. The growth of accounting computerization in China is, however, gaining momentum. The computerization of accounting is currently a very popular subject in the accounting curriculum at college level and in vocational or part-time training programmes. Numerous text-books or learning materials on the computerization of accounting are available at present. Several hundred accounting software dealerships are in operation across the country. The computerization of accounting in China will grow at a much faster pace from here on.[2]

Application of computerized accounting systems has progressed from the simple to the sophisticated level over the last ten years. Preparation of payroll lists was the only application during the initial experimentation before the mid-1980s, but many business entities have now installed compu-terized systems to perform data processing and analysis for multiple accounting functions. The most popular applications of accounting computerization are currently in areas such as payroll, recording of general ledgers, sales, inventory control, product costing, preparation of financial statements and financial analysis.

The process of accounting computerization is under direct control by government. Approval of government authorities is required in advance for the installation of computerized accounting programs in any business entities or other organizations. The general requirements for the installation of computerized accounting programs include the following:

- possession of accounting software that has been appraised or approved by the government authorities in charge;
- presence of adequate hardware facilities, including computer terminals or workstation, and full or part-time operators of computer systems;
- satisfactory test run parallel to the manual processing system over a period of not less than three months, where the computerized output is consistent with that of the manual accounting processing;
- establishment of internal control of the computerized accounting system, including the division of duties among system operators and security devices of hardware and software; and
- formulation of adequate documentation procedures for the operation of the computerized accounting program.

An appraisal of the adequacy of the computerized accounting system to be adopted is generally required by the government authorities in charge. The appraisal can be conducted by a CPA firm or other independent appraisers recognized by the government authorities. The appraisal reports issued by CPA firms or independent appraisers are subject to reviews by the government authorities in charge.

Major characteristics

Some distinct characteristics of the computerization of accounting in China can be summarized as follows.

1 Emphasis is placed on separate application programs such as payroll system, inventory management and so on, in the initial experiment period. Efforts have been shifted to standardize the procedures for system analysis, design and control, following the adoption of the experience gained in other countries.
2 Most of the commercialized accounting software is industry-specific applications. This has resulted from the existence of different sets of industry-specific accounting regulations at present. Thus accounting software and application programs available so far have relatively limited applicability within the specified industries. They can hardly be called general-purpose software or application programs. This situation will only be changed when the industry-specific accounting regulations have been phased out in the future.[3]
3 In-house design of computerized accounting programs by individual enterprises or other organizations was the norm in the initial period of experimentation. Redundant work or waste of resources in computerized system design and software development was common. This situation changed only in recent years when the commercialized accounting software developed by specialized computer manufacturers or dealers became available.
4 Application of computerized accounting data processing is more popular in governmental administrative bodies and manufacturing enterprises, especially the large enterprises equipped with better technological and financial resources. Accounting computerization is less developed in non-manufacturing industries at present.
5 The move from simple to advanced applications has been evidenced in recent years, and system support for accounting software had been upgraded continuously. More advanced programming technologies are widely adopted in the design of application software.
6 Most accounting software was based on the MS-DOS operating system. Although MS-Windows systems have gained popularity in recent years, various supportive systems for accounting software will coexist for a

while, thanks to an uneven development of accounting computerization across the country.

7 Accounting software and application programs developed in Hong Kong, Taiwan and other foreign countries have entered Chinese markets. They were mainly adopted by business entities with foreign investments, but have been increasingly extended to domestic enterprises or other organizations in recent years.

8 Computerized programs for auditing purposes appeared in the early 1990s, indicating an expansion of the application of computerized programs from accounting to auditing fields.

Some constraints

Nonetheless, computerization of accounting remains underdeveloped in China. The existing level of application of computer technology in accounting lags behind the practices of western countries. A number of major difficulties can be observed in the current process of accounting computerization in China. First, manual accounting systems still remain dominant in a majority of business enterprises and non-business organizations. One of the main reasons is related to shortage of specialized personnel who are capable of running the computerized accounting systems. The majority of accounting personnel lack knowledge in computer technology and computerized accounting systems. Education and on-job training programmes on computerization of accounting lag behind demand. The shortage of specialized personnel for computer system design, programming, analysis, control and maintenance is severe. Many enterprises, in fact, are hesitant to install computerized accounting systems owing to a lack of confidence in their ability to operate the computerized systems effectively.

Second, utilization of accounting software or computerized programs is limited to a fairly narrow range of accounting processing. For a large portion of business enterprises or other organizations that have adopted computerized programs, only a very small part of accounting functions, mainly bookkeeping, is processed by computerized systems. Underuse of accounting software or computerized accounting programs is a common problem.

Third, application of computerized programs for management accounting and business financial management is rare. Computerized accounting programs have yet to be widely utilized for generating data to assist managers in making daily operating decisions. Integrated application of a computerized accounting information system and a management decision support system has not yet been explored. Thus the effectiveness of accounting computerization is not in full play.[4]

Fourth, computerization accounting systems have been adopted mainly by large business enterprises and other entities located in the regions with relatively fast economic growth. Little progress of accounting computerization can be seen in economically less developed inland regions. In addition, application of computerized accounting programs is seldom to be found in most medium and small business enterprises or other organizations, mainly for reasons of resource constraints such as lack of funding and specialized personnel.[5]

Fifth, piracy is currently a fairly serious problem in China as software can be copied easily by others. This has dramatically reduced the incentives for the development of accounting software. Lack of protection for the copyright and royalty of accounting software has hindered the healthy growth of software markets, and of accounting computerization, in China. The Chinese government has enacted a piece of piracy legislation in 1996, in order to stop illegal piracy of accounting software, but it may take time for an effective enforcement of this law to be achieved.

The above-mentioned deficiencies or constraints on promoting accounting computerization are directly associated with the relatively underdeveloped nature of the Chinese economy at the moment. The government authorities in charge have, however, paid increasing attention to the existing problems. Measures to overcome these deficiencies in the process of accounting computerization are under study. The computerization of accounting will be expanded at a much faster pace, so long as Chinese economic growth maintains its momentum.

REGULATION OF ACCOUNTING SOFTWARE

The development of computer software for accounting applications is currently under direct and rigid governmental regulation, in particular, it is subject to the control of the Ministry of Finance and other agencies authorized by the Ministry of Finance.

Regulatory requirements

Accounting software, in general, can be classified into two major categories: (1) user-specific software that is designed for applications in a specified entity, and (2) general-purpose software that can be applied to a great variety of user entities. Both types of accounting software are subject to the specifications laid down in the *Requirements for Basic Functions of Accounting Software* formulated by the Ministry of Finance in 1994.

Accounting software to be adopted by business entities or other organizations in China should satisfy the following basic requirements.

1   Program design and software development must be in accordance with the related laws and regulations enforced by the Chinese government.
2   Application of accounting software should secure the legitimacy, truthfulness and completeness of accounting data processing, and enhance the efficiency of accounting work.
3   Programming on the chart of accounts, format of financial statements and cut-off treatment of accounting transactions in any software must be in accordance with the national uniform accounting regulations or standards, although another set of internal processing programs based on users' operational specifications is allowed.
4   Chinese word processing must be adopted as a standard system for data input and output, while word-processing systems based on other languages can be maintained as secondary devices in the computerized accounting programs.
5   Built-in devices should be in place to safeguard software and application programs against data loss or abnormal breakdown of data processing.

In addition, the *Requirements for Basic Functions of Accounting Software* laid down quite specific provisions on the mechanical functioning of accounting software. Requirements on programming for data input, processing, output, data security, protective devices, and system control and maintenance are among the statutory provisions. Accounting software not meeting the specified requirements is not allowed for use in China.

Appraisal of accounting software

Under current regulations, any accounting software to be installed by business entities or other organizations must be approved by governments' finance or taxation departments in advance. Specification of the accounting software to be adopted must also be filed with the government authorities.

According to the *Procedures for Appraisal of Commercialized Accounting Software* stipulated by the Ministry of Finance, all accounting software developed for commercial purposes must be appraised by government authorities before entering markets. The process of appraisal is as follows:

● evaluating whether the basic functions and programming of the software are consistent with the related business laws, government regulations and accounting principles;

- reviewing the technical specifications being designed or programmed in the software;
- testing the application programs in respect of their capacity for accounting data processing and financial analysis;
- examining the adequacy and effectiveness of the protective devices built into the programming; and
- evaluating the quality standard of the authorized dealers and their arrangement to provide product warranty services.

A two-tier system of appraisal

Appraisal of commercial-purpose accounting software can be conducted through two different channels: central appraisal and local appraisal. Local appraisal is organized by the finance departments of governments at provincial level, while the central appraisal is directly administered by the Ministry of Finance in the central government.

Central appraisal maintains a higher level of authoritative recognition and product reputation. Usually, the newly developed accounting software should be appraised by local authorities first. Application for the central appraisal should not be made until at least one year after a successful local appraisal. The application must be supported by the recommendations initiated by the accounting administrative authorities of local governments. More stringent standards or requirements are applied to evaluating the software's technical functions and application programming in the process of central appraisal.

All packages of accounting software are allowed to go into markets within Chinese territory without geographical restriction so long as they have successfully passed either local or central appraisal. However, accounting software obtaining the certificate of approval from the central appraisal will have a higher reputation and a greater marketing potential.

Appraisal procedures

Individual software developers must apply to governments' accounting administrative authorities for an appraisal when development of a new piece of accounting software is complete. The application should be addressed to the Appraisal Committee for Commercialized Accounting Software organized by the finance departments of either the central or local government. The committee usually consists of three to seven specialists in computerization of accounting. Several technical assisting groups may be formed under the committee.

Applicants should submit the following documents to the Appraisal Committee in the appropriate government authorities:

- an introduction to the new accounting software, including a description of software development, basic functions or designed application programs, and records of test runs of the software;
- specifications of software programming, and other relevant technical data;
- a copy of the user's manual;
- comments from a specified number of users during the pilot-run process;[6]
- samples of print-out for accounting vouchers, ledgers and financial statements, including comparison with the outcome from a parallel run of manual processing system; and
- particulars of the designated dealers and their capacity to offer user services.

The programming specifications and user's manual must be prepared in standardized format as recommended by the Ministry of Finance.

Government authorities in charge decide whether an appraisal will be proceeded with and inform the applicants officially within two months of the applications having been received. The appraisal process may be conducted initially by a technical assisting group under the Appraisal Committee.[7] The technical assisting group should (1) check all materials and data presented by applicants; (2) investigate the results of the software's pilot-run; a survey based on sampling questionnaires or on-site observation will be conducted; (3) test the functions of programming and the uses of designated application devices; and (4) prepare and submit the testing reports to the Appraisal Committee in charge.

The mandates of the Appraisal Committee formed by governments' finance departments include the following:

- to examine the materials and data submitted by applicants;
- to supervise the testing procedures performed by technical assisting groups or independent appraisers;
- to review the testing reports submitted by technical assisting groups or independent appraisers;
- to ensure that the software meets the requirements specified in government accounting regulations or standards;
- to issue appraisal reports with opinions on technical specifications of:
  - (a) the particulars of the developers or manufacturers of the accounting software which has been appraised;

(b)　the title of the software that has been appraised, including detailed records of the application programs that have passed, or failed to pass, the appraisal process;

(c)　the applicability of the software which has successfully passed the appraisal;

(d)　the requirements governing product warranty services; and

(e)　the documentation process for any further revision or modification of the software.

The Appraisal Committee's reports will be reviewed by the governments' finance departments which authorized the appraisal process. A confirmation will be made if the appraisal reports are approved. The applicants will receive final official confirmation in writing, accompanied by an official certificate applicable to the software approved. No commercial-purpose accounting software will be allowed to enter the market unless a certificate of approval issued by government authorities has been obtained.

Software developers are obligated to report, in writing, to governments' finance departments which issued the original certificate of approval whenever there is significant modification or alternation to the software which has been appraised. Reappraisal of the modified software may be required, upon the decision of the finance departments at appropriate levels of government.

Governments' finance departments maintain the power to disqualify certain accounting software by revoking the certificate of approval originally granted. This may happen particularly when the developers or dealers of accounting software have committed unlawful marketing and sales of their products, or when serious complaints against the product qualities are launched by a substantial number of users of the accounting software in question.

Appraisal of accounting software developed abroad

All accounting software developed outside China, including that from Taiwan, Hong Kong and Macao, must be appraised under the supervision of the Ministry of Finance. Thus a central appraisal is required if foreign developers or dealers intend to market their software in China. Besides compliance with the standards for domestically developed accounting software, additional requirements such as the following must be met for software developers or dealers from abroad:

●　a representative office or official dealership must have been lawfully established inside China;

- the display or output devices of the software and all application programs should be based on Chinese word processing, or on a bilingual display system in Chinese and another foreign language;
- legal documents or an official certificate regarding the copyright of the software should be obtained;
- the application forms, the programming specifications, and other materials so attached, must be prepared in the Chinese language or in bilingual text with Chinese and another foreign language.

It should be pointed out that the commercialized accounting software developed within Chinese territory by foreign invested enterprises (including equity or contractual joint ventures and foreign owned companies) will be treated as a domestic product and subject to the appraisal procedures applicable to domestic developers or dealers.

COMMERCIALIZED CHINESE ACCOUNTING SOFTWARE

To date, many kinds of commercialized accounting software are available in Chinese markets, growing at a remarkable pace. For example, over a hundred software developers or dealers participated in the National Fair of Accounting Software and Application Programs that was held in Beijing in September 1994 under the joint sponsorship of the Ministry of Finance, the Chinese Association of Science and Technology and the Accounting Society of China. Among the participants were some well-known international computer software manufacturers, such as the DacEasy Company (USA), the Oracle Company (USA) and United Systems Ltd (UK). This software fair was well received and has generated a profound impact on the speedy expansion of accounting computerization in China.

Although foreign developers or dealers have been allowed to enter Chinese software markets, they are in a relatively disadvantageous position in respect of the existing requirements of Chinese word processing for all application programs and the local network of warranty services. Domestic developers are currently a dominant force in the accounting software markets. Some of the most popular accounting software packages in the Chinese markets are summarized below.

Anyi-Tongyong (easypack) finance and accounting software

This software package was developed by the Research and Development Centre for Computerization of Accounting, later renamed Beijing AnYi

Computer Company, in September 1991, under the Research Institute of Finance Sciences of the Ministry of Finance in the early 1990s. The software package passed a central appraisal organized by the Ministry of Finance in February 1991, and became the first accounting software to receive the certificate of approval from the central government.

A new version of the accounting software has been developed following the introduction of the new national accounting system in 1993. Eight application programs (subsystems) are available with the updated software: bookkeeping, financial statements, payroll, control of fixed assets, inventory accounting, sales, account receivable and account payable. Two separate series of this software package are developed: one for the accounting system of the state-owned enterprises, the other for the accounting system for foreign invested enterprises (including equity and contractual joint ventures and foreign owned companies). Both a personal computer (PC) version and a networking version are available for each series of the product. The revised software package has successfully passed the official appraisal organized by the Ministry of Finance in April 1994. This software package currently maintains a dominant market share in China's accounting software markets.

Wangneng (general-purpose) financial accounting software

This software package was developed by the China Centre for Sciences and Technology Consultation Services, a subordinate of the Chinese Association of Science and Technology. Version 2.1 of this software was appraised by the Ministry of Finance in 1992. Six application programs or subsystems are included in the software package: bookkeeping, payroll, accounting for fixed assets, product costing, general ledgers and preparation of financial statements. This package is particularly applicable to manufacturing enterprises adopting the Accounting System for Manufacturing Enterprises regulated by the Ministry of Finance.

Version 2.3 of this software package, reappraised by the Ministry of Finance in 1993, was made available to accommodate the changes in new accounting standards and industry-specific accounting regulations introduced in 1993.

Yongyou (users' friends) financial accounting software

Yongyou EDP Financial Technology Company is one of the major accounting software developers in China. The company has developed a series of commercialized accounting software, including both networking and PC versions. Among the Yongyou series of software, a general-purpose accounting information system, a financial statement system and a payroll management system passed the appraisal organized by the Ministry of Finance in 1991, while the financial management networking system and general-purpose financial statement system were appraised in 1992. Version 5.1 of the Yongyou package, designed to meet the new national accounting standards and regulations, is now available on the market.

Xiangfeng (pioneers) accounting software

Xiangfeng accounting software was originally developed in 1989. The manufacturer, Xiangfeng Accounting Computerization Company, introduced its updated Version 9307 and obtained the certificate of approval through a central appraisal in 1993. Seven application programs are included in the updated software package: bookkeeping, product costing, sales, payroll, fixed assets, financial reporting and inventory management.

Top financial software

Top financial software, developed by Beijing Engineering and Construction Company, is mainly applicable to accounting for construction enterprises. The package includes four application programs: bookkeeping, financial statements, fixed assets and financial analysis. The updated version of the Top 4.0 package passed a central appraisal in 1993.

Stone finance and accounting software package

Stone Computer Company is one of the main Chinese manufacturers of office automation equipment. The company has developed a package of Stone Series General-Purpose Accounting Software. Application programs included in this software package are bookkeeping, financial statements, inventory management, and supply and tools. The software package was appraised by the finance bureau of the Beijing municipal government in the early 1990s.

Chuangjian (creation) 123 accounting software

Chuangjian 123 software was developed by the Chuangjian Electronic Technology Research Institute located in the high-tech development district in Beijing. Five subsystems of application, general ledgers, payroll, fixed assets, sales and financial statements are available. The software was appraised by the finance bureau of the Beijing municipal government in 1993.

Yuanjian (vision) finance and accounting software

Yuanjian software was developed by Shenzhen Yuanjian Science and Technology Development Company, located in the Shenzhen Special Economic Zone neighbouring Hong Kong. The software was originally appraised by the finance bureau of the Shenzhen government in 1992, with its updated version reappraised in 1993. This package is relatively comprehensive and contains 11 application programs: general ledgers, financial statements, payroll, fixed assets, account receivable, account payable, cost management, inventory, sales, consolidation of financial statements and financial analysis.

This list of Chinese accounting software is certainly not exclusive. Many other commercialized accounting software packages (including some imported from abroad) are also available on the market, but they are not as popular as the eight packages mentioned above. It can be seen, however, that most accounting software currently available in Chinese markets contains application programs in a piecemeal fashion. Commercialized software for an integrated accounting information system has not yet been developed.[8]

EDUCATION AND TRAINING IN ACCOUNTING COMPUTERIZATION

As mentioned earlier, the shortage of competent specialists equipped with adequate knowledge in computer technology and accounting skill is one of the major constraints hampering the progress of accounting computerization in China. The Chinese government has realized the importance and urgency of training a large number of accounting personnel who are able to operate the computerized accounting systems. Substantial efforts have been made to promote education and training for the computerization of accounting. The subject of accounting computerization has been a mandatory component of accounting curricula at colleges and universities since the late 1980s.

On the other hand, attention has to be paid to training a great number of accounting personnel through professional or continuing education. Governments, businesses and other organizations have contributed a considerable amount of resources to sponsor a variety of training programmes on a part-time basis, aimed at disseminating the knowledge and skill of accounting computerization to accounting personnel working in business and non-business organizations.

The Ministry of Finance issued *Tentative Procedures for Administration of Training Programmes on Knowledge of Accounting Computerization* in early 1995. The document intends to set out guidelines and standards for both full-time and vocational training programmes, so as to meet the increasing demands for accounting personnel to be equipped with the knowledge and skills of computerized accounting. A three-tier training system with varied objectives or standards has been introduced by the responsible government authorities.

Introductory training programmes

The main objective of training programmes at introductory level is to make the majority of accounting personnel familiar with the basic functions of the computerized accounting system, and able to operate some basic applications.

Intermediate training programmes

The intermediate level of training programmes is intended to train a number of accounting personnel who are provided with the necessary knowledge and skills to run a variety of application programs, as well as to perform certain work on system maintenance.

Advanced training programmes

The training programmes at an advanced level seek to produce a small number of specialists who possess well-developed computer and accounting knowledge and skills. These specialists should be able to perform comprehensive functions of accounting computerization, such as system analysis, system design, system maintenance, software programming, and so on.

Accordingly, many concrete efforts have been made by governments, accounting professional bodies and individual business entities. The training programmes at advanced and intermediate level are currently being offered at colleges or research institutes where sufficient resources and facilities are available. In addition, a great variety of vocational or on-job training programmes on computer knowledge and electronic data processing (EDP) accounting applications, providing an introductory level of training, are available across the country. The implementation of the specified education and training programmes has, in fact, contributed to a quite rapid growth of accounting computerization in China in recent years.

PROSPECTS FOR COMPUTERIZATION OF ACCOUNTING IN CHINA

Although the current status of computerized accounting in China is relatively underdeveloped, greater progress will be made in the near future in step with rapid economic growth in China. The Chinese government has set a long-term target for speeding up the process of accounting computerization. A strategic plan for the development of accounting computerization was adopted at the Fourth National Conference on Accounting Work held in Beijing in October 1995. The government authorities in charge decided to

> gradually promote and expand the computerization of accounting across the country, in order to have computerized accounting systems installed in about 40–60 per cent of the large and medium-size enterprises and some key industries by the year 2000. ... The growth of accounting computerization should be in an evolutionary process, moving from simple-function and separate applications of computerized data processing towards the operations of an integrated computerized accounting system.

It was also stated in the development plan endorsed by the government that

> The application of computerized data processing shall be extended to managerial accounting, in order to install integrated management information systems combining computerized accounting data processing and other management data processing within individual business enterprises and other organizations.

Such strategic planning for the development of accounting computerization in China is realistic. When business enterprises were funded and directly controlled by government authorities, business managements lacked motivation for the installation of a computerized accounting system. However, business managements have now gained increasing autonomy in making operating decisions as a result of the market-based economic reforms. Managements' demands for more accurate and speedy information in decision making are increasing, as is their need for the computerized accounting systems. Expansion of computerized accounting will lead to a dramatic improvement in accounting and business management. The computerization of accounting in China will have a bright future, although the goal will be reached via an evolutionary process owing to the inherent constraints on computer technology and human resources in the Chinese economy.

NOTES

1   While most government departments and large state-owned enterprises have adopted computerized accounting programs, a much greater number of medium and small entities have not so far considered the use of computer technology in accounting. Thus the overall level of accounting computerization in China is relatively low at present.

2   Although the experiment of computerized accounting was initiated by government authorities at the end of the 1970s, its meaningful expansion did not start until the mid-1980s, owing to unavailability of computer facilities in a majority of business entities and general lack of computer knowledge among accounting personnel.

3   As discussed in Chapter 2, the industry-specific accounting regulations will eventually be replaced by a set of transaction-based accounting standards in China in the near future.

4   This may be due to the underdevelopment of management accounting in China. Although the concepts of management accounting have been widely introduced, the actual application of management accounting in the real world is less satisfactory so far.

5   For example, the prices of the existing commercialized software are, in general, too high for most medium or small users, compared to the low labour costs for running manual accounting systems in China at present. Thus the adoption of commercialized accounting software is less attractive to many medium and small business entities.

6   According to the existing regulations, every piece of accounting software developed for commercial purposes must take a pilot-run to a small number of users prior to application for appraisal. Comments from users during experimental run should be included in the application documents.

7   The initial testing may be performed by external specialists, such as CPA firms or business consultants recognized by the Appraisal Committee under appropriate government authorities in charge.

8   One of the reasons for this lies in a relatively weak demand for an integrated computerized accounting system at present. Many business enterprises or other organizations lack resources and confidence to effectively install and run an integrated computerized accounting system. Thus most packages of the commercialized accounting software in China are currently utilized below capacity.

11 Accounting Education

Accounting education in China consists of two major areas: regular education programmes and continuing professional education programmes. There have been dramatic changes in the content of these educational programmes since the implementation of the new Chinese accounting system in 1993. This chapter describes the development of accounting education in China. Three interrelated areas are examined: China's administration system of accounting education, the representative curricula of accounting programmes at college level and the continuing education programmes for professional accountants and auditors.

THE ACCOUNTING EDUCATION SYSTEM

The system of accounting education in China is immense in size, since the demand for training of potential accountants is enormous in China where the total number of accounting personnel is currently over 12 million. Basically, the Chinese education system comprises three components: institutional education, continuing professional education and vocational education programmes.

Institutional education

Institutional education is defined as academic programmes offered by recognized post-secondary educational institutions. This is the traditional approach for delivering the accounting education programme in China.

Components of institutional education

At present, educational institutions that offer regular or full-time accounting programmes include universities, independent colleges specializing in business management programmes and polytechnic schools (with advanced and intermediate levels). The structure of academic programmes offered at various educational institutions are more or less in line with the educational pattern in North America: that is, doctorate programme (three years), master degree programme (two and a half to three years), bachelor degree programme (four years), diploma programmes (three years) and specialized programmes for senior high school graduates, of two to three years' duration. The hierarchical structure of post-secondary education in China and the relationship between academic institutions and students are illustrated in Figure 11.1.

There were about 1100 universities and specialized independent colleges in China by the end of 1996.[1] The total enrolment of students at universities and colleges is about 600 000 per year, but the numbers of students enrolled in accounting programmes are much smaller. In a country with almost 1.3 billion people, the total number of places in institutes of higher education is insufficient. Only a small proportion of high school graduates can be en-

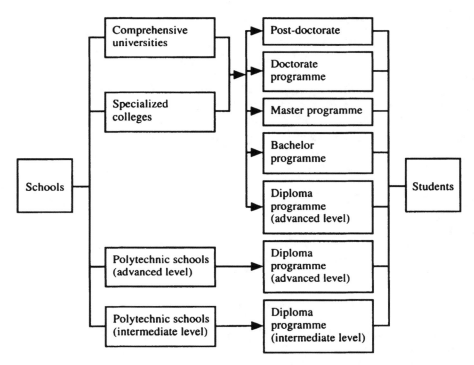

Figure 11.1   The structure of the post-secondary education system in China

rolled to study at colleges and universities. Thus students must pass a fairly stringent national entrance examination to pursue college studies.

Accounting programmes at college level

In China, quite a number of universities and colleges have established academic departments of accountancy (otherwise called departments of finance and accounting or departments of accounting and auditing) to offer training in accounting to provide for accounting students at different levels.

Although accounting programmes were offered in many of the oldest universities before the People's Republic was founded in 1949, the accounting programmes, indeed the entire business administration programmes, were removed from these comprehensive universities and transferred to independent colleges specializing in a particular discipline (such as the colleges of finance and economics) as a result of a restructuring of the higher education system by the Chinese government in 1952. Thus accounting programmes have been, with few exceptions, mainly offered at independent colleges since then. This situation, however, started to change in the early 1980s. Driven by mounting demands for accounting students, most Chinese universities and colleges have offered or started to offer training in accounting (including finance and auditing training). This development reached its peak in the early 1990s.

In the light of increasing popularity, the numbers of academic programmes of accounting grew steadily. However, qualified professors and instructors, as well as other educational resources, are still scarce, and there exists a wide range of differences in respect to the quality of accounting programmes offered. At present, the Chinese educational institutes offering accounting programmes can be classified into five distinct groups. The first group consists of a small number of universities and independent colleges in which accounting programmes have been offered for a relatively long period. Among this group are Xiamen University,[2] Renmin (People's) University of China, Shanghai University of Finance and Economics (SUFE), Zhongnan University of Finance and Economics, the Northeastern University of Finance and Economics and the Tianjin Institute of Finance and Economics. The special features of these universities are that they have relatively advanced facilities and resources for accounting education and have produced many graduates over the years. The professors are experienced and maintain a good relationship with government authorities in charge of accounting affairs and industries or business sectors, as well as with overseas universities. Currently, these universities are recognized as the leaders in accounting education in China.

The second group comprises a conglomeration of better-known independent colleges such as the Central Institute of Finance and Banking, the Beijing Institute of Business Administration, the Beijing Institute of Economics (renamed Capital University of Economics and Trades in 1995), and the Southwestern University of Finance and Economics. The special features of these colleges are the same as those of the first group except that their resources are relatively limited and they have fewer contacts with overseas institutions.

The third group includes some of the most famous universities in China, such as Beijing University, Tsinghua University, Nanking University, Fudan University, Wuhan University, Nankai University, Xi'an Jiaotong University, Sichuan United University, Shanghai Jiaotong University, Zhongshang University, the University of International Business and Economics, Jilin University and Harbin Industry University. The distinctive features of these universities are that accounting programmes have only been offered for a short period of time (commencing in the early 1990s). Although these universities have a fairly long history and high academic standards, they offered no accounting or business programmes before 1993 owing to the government's restructuring of the higher education system in 1952. Thus the numbers of experienced professors are limited and most of the business faculty members are relatively young in these universities. However, the quality of their students is high, as the favourable reputation of these universities can attract top graduates from high schools across the country. The international academic exchange, especially with the top-ranked universities in the West, is well developed thanks to these universities' long history and high reputation. In addition, the relationship between accounting faculty members and governmental authorities or industries has gradually been built up.

The fourth group consists mainly of universities or colleges specializing in engineering or applied sciences, such as the Central China Institute of Engineering and the Northern University of Communication and Transportation. The reason for these engineering colleges setting up accounting programmes derived directly from the need to supply accounting students for the enterprises under the jurisdiction of the industrial administrative authorities to whom these engineering colleges are subordinate. Most accounting courses at these colleges were designed to train potential accountants using a less theoretical approach. Most courses are distinguishable from those in other universities in terms of content and emphasis. Students are required to take a few engineering courses in addition to accounting subjects. Thus the graduates of these accounting programmes are required to be able to handle accounting transactions associated with the day-to-day operations of factories in the specified industries.

The fifth group consists of all other universities and colleges offering accounting programmes at bachelor level and above. They account for the largest portion of higher educational institutes with accounting programmes but are of relatively lower-quality in comparison with their counterparts.

Accounting programmes offered by polytechnic schools

Accounting programmes have also been offered at polytechnic schools. Although the accounting education provided by these schools is not a degree-offering programme, its features of shorter school terms and flexible curriculum design enable it to train large numbers of accounting graduates who are prepared for junior or clerical accounting assignments.

There is further division in the system of polytechnic schools. One class is advanced level and another is intermediate level. Polytechnic schools at advanced level offer three years, of training in accounting. Compared with universities and colleges, the duration of their curriculum is shorter and the courses offered are limited in numbers and content, with the emphasis being placed more on day-to-day operations and the practical aspect of accounting. Polytechnic schools at intermediate level accept senior and junior high school graduates. Their accounting programmes last for two to three years, with limited subjects and classes. The content of the accounting curriculum employed in polytechnic schools at intermediate level is of an introductory nature, with special focus on bookkeeping and routine accounting assignments.

Graduates from polytechnic schools receive diplomas instead of degrees. More students, however, are enrolled in polytechnic schools than in universities and colleges every year. At present, polytechnic schools play a significant role in providing graduates with basic accounting training.

Full-time v. part-time accounting curricula

At universities, independent colleges and polytechnic schools, the academic programmes are offered either on a part-time basis or a full-time basis. While full-time students spend all their time studying during school terms, part-time students study and work concurrently, and the courses last longer than those for full-time students: that is, diploma programmes four years, bachelor degree programmes six years, master degree programmes four to five years and doctorate programmes at least five years.

According to the current accounting education curriculum, most students who have been enrolled in the usual programme must study on a full-time basis, although the ratio of part-time students has risen recently. In particular, increasing numbers of students who graduated in a different discipline

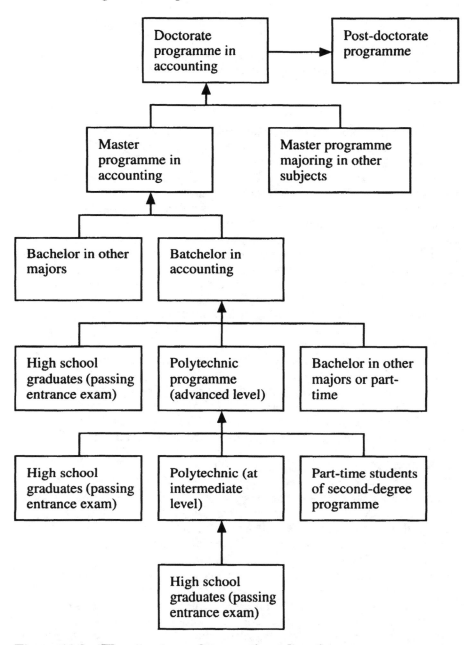

Figure 11.2   The structure of accounting education programmes

seek accounting as a second degree since the job markets for accounting graduates have become much brighter in China in recent years. Many of these students pursuing a second degree in accounting take part-time studies. Figure 11.2 illustrates the structure of accounting education offered by different programmes.

Continuing professional education

Continuing education in accounting is defined as educational training aimed at professional accountants and auditors. In China, continuing education is carried out by both government agencies and professional associations. Three subsystems of continuing education programmes are currently offered, for general accountants, government auditors and certified public accountants (independent auditors), respectively.

Continuing education for general accountants

According to information released by the Ministry of Finance, there were over 12 million accounting personnel working in China by the end of 1996 (compared with nine million in 1988). Among the accounting personnel working in business and commerce, a substantial proportion have not received formal education or training in accounting. In order to train accounting personnel to achieve a desirable level of competence, the Ministry of Finance adopted a continuing education programme for general accountants nationwide in 1992 and set a target that 50–60 per cent of accounting personnel working in state enterprises and government agencies should reach the standard of accounting training of polytechnic schooling at intermediate level. According to a more recent government document, *Accounting Reform and Development Outlook (1995)*, 80 per cent of all accountants should have received accounting training to the standard of polytechnic schooling (intermediate level) or above by the year 2000, and 40 per cent of accounting personnel working in township businesses and other non-state-owned entities should reach that level. In addition, all accounting personnel are required to receive 12 days of continuing education annually to update their knowledge in areas such as general accounting, business ethics and professional conduct.

Implementation of the continuing education programme interrelates with the professional accounting qualification examinations. In March 1990, the Ministry of Finance formulated the *Administrative Rules on Accounting Certificates*, which require that all accountants sit the uniform qualification examination to earn the appropriate professional rank. Procedures on post-examination review and certificate renewal have also been established, based on the achievement in the qualification examinations. In March 1993, the Ministry of Finance and the Ministry of Labour and Human Resources jointly formulated *Temporary Rules on the Administration of Accountant Qualification Examinations* and the related *Implementation Guidelines and Procedures*. Accordingly, all accounting personnel working in governmental entities and state-owned enterprises must take the qualification examination. The first national accounting qualification examination was conducted in November 1992.

At the same time, the professional grading system was installed. Professional titles with different ranks, such as accounting clerk, assistant accountant and accountant, have been granted according to candidates' performance in qualification examinations and their job experience. Through the process of the qualification examination, continuing accounting education has become a commonly accepted practice, with its content and procedures becoming standardized.

Continuing education for government auditors

In China, government auditors are under the jurisdiction of the National Auditing Administration (NAA). In March 1992, the NAA and the Ministry of Labour and Human Resources jointly promulgated the *Temporary Regulation on Auditing Qualification Examinations* and the *Implementation Procedures* pertaining to this set of examinations. Commencing on 1 August 1992, the qualification examination system for government auditors has been fully implemented for all auditing personnel working in the state audit offices and other governmental agencies.

Continuing education for certified public accountants (CPAs)

CPAs in China are monitored by the Chinese Institute of Certified Public Accountants (CICPA) under delegation of authority from the Ministry of Finance. According to the CPA Law enacted by the Chinese government in 1993, candidates who apply for the CPA examination must meet the minimum education requirement of college schooling, or hold a professional grade at the intermediate rank or above, such as accountant, actuary, economist, statistician, engineer or lecturer in related business management fields. In general, the educational level of CPAs is higher than that of other accounting designations.

According to the *Requirements on CPA Education and Training System*, formulated by the CICPA, candidates who have passed the CPA exam but have not fulfilled the experience requirements are required to take at least one month of continuing education annually in the areas relating to specific accounting knowledge and business ethics. After receiving the certificate, CPAs must pursue at least two weeks of continuing education annually, and not less than two months cumulatively within three years.

Vocational accounting programmes

Vocational programmes, called 'social accounting education' in Chinese, refer to all kinds of accounting programmes offered through various channels other than regular schooling and professional continuing training. These vocational programmes are provided by organizations other than traditional educational institutes. Currently, the vocational accounting programmes are offered by open (TV) universities, distance-learning institutions, correspondence schools, evening schools and various learning centres. Students who opt for vocational programmes are from different backgrounds; they include accounting personnel taking part-time studies, people working in different professions, unemployed workers pursuing retraining, new high school graduates, and so on. The purpose of attending vocational accounting programmes is to gain knowledge in accounting in order to be prepared for job promotion or for seeking new jobs. In general, vocational programmes aim at the teaching of accounting knowledge at junior or intermediate level and will accommodate students' diversified needs and flexible time schedules. In particular, many people have attended the vocational programmes to prepare for national accounting qualification examinations. The significance of vocational accounting education must not be underestimated since it provides a supplementary channel to offer training in accounting for a vast number of accounting personnel who lack formal accounting training. In particular, the development of traditional accounting education lags far behind the demand for qualified accounting personnel owing to the resource constraints facing most traditional educational institutes at present. Thus vocational accounting programmes present a valuable alternative to China's accounting education.

THE CURRICULUM OF FORMAL ACCOUNTING EDUCATION

This section illustrates the structure of the accounting curriculum at Chinese universities and independent colleges specializing in business management programmes.

The functional curriculum of undergraduate programmes

The accounting curriculum for undergraduate programmes is the most important indicator of accounting education at universities and colleges. Since 1949, there have been numerous changes in the content of the curriculum. Between 1950 and the early 1980s, the accounting curriculum in most Chinese universities and colleges was fairly similar to that in the former Soviet Union. From the mid-1980s to 1992, auditing courses based on teaching materials in western countries were introduced. However, the entire curriculum has undergone a thorough revamping since the accounting reform in 1993.

Accounting core courses before the mid-1980s

During this period (lasting approximately 30 years), the accounting curriculum was a replica of the former Soviet system with slight modifications to accommodate the Chinese economic environment. The basic structure consisted of 'four essential cores', that is, principles of accounting, industry sector accounting, financial management and analysis of economic activities. To be more specific, the 'four essential cores' were not simply four independent functional courses, but four major areas of accounting courses, as illustrated in Figure 11.3.

The figure illustrates two features of this set of the accounting curriculum. First, not every university or college provided all the courses outlined under the 'four essentials cores'. The courses actually offered by each university depended on the school's jurisdictional link to the oversight government authorities. For example, more accounting courses relating to merchandising transactions were offered in those universities which were subject to administration of the ministerial authorities in charge of merchandising or service industries. In addition, their 'four essential cores' would be structured to place more emphasis on commerce. Secondly, apart from the 'four essentials' many universities have also offered some additional electives such as abacus and accounting examination (accounting checking).

The core courses offered during this period were structured to accommodate the needs of the government to exercise highly centralized economic planning and control. For instance, all the core courses emphasized the importance of government regulation of accounting work and the interpretation of the government's uniform accounting and financing regulations.

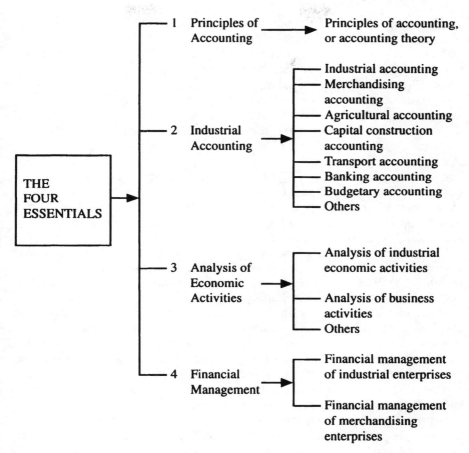

Figure 11.3   Functional cores of the accounting curriculum (before mid-1980s)

The dual-core curriculum, mid-1980s to 1992

The Chinese economy was a closed economy with limited trade with foreign countries before 1979. Consequently, Chinese accounting was also a 'closed' system, focusing only on domestic accounting issues. This situation started to change when the Chinese government adopted the 'open door' policy in the late 1970s. In particular, *The Law of the People's Republic of China on Joint Ventures With Chinese and Foreign Capital*, which was enacted and enforced by the Second Session of the Fifth National People's

Congress on 1 July 1979 (amended on 4 April 1990), provided a legal foundation for increasing trade and economic ties with the rest of the world.

As a result of this opening policy, foreign capital flowed into China. Joint ventures between Chinese and foreign partners mushroomed. The traditional Chinese accounting system, which was designed for the state-owned enterprises operating in a centrally planned economy, was no longer operable in the new economic environment. The system was therefore modified in 1983, when the Ministry of Finance formulated *The Accounting Regulations on Joint Ventures Using Chinese and Foreign Investment (Interim Provisions)*. The accounting regulations for joint ventures became official and were implemented in 1985. The western accounting system was introduced into China through the proliferation of the joint ventures. Under such circumstances, the traditional 'four essential cores' became obsolete. Many new accounting courses were therefore introduced at leading schools offering accounting programmes.

Thus the reform of accounting education was pursued. The 'new four essential cores', based on the western accounting system, was developed, which comprised principles of accounting, financial accounting, cost accounting and managerial accounting. The 'new cores' challenged the 'old cores' and a dual system of accounting curriculum appeared. In terms of courses being offered, more choices became available. For example, accounting for joint ventures, responsibility accounting, auditing, and computerization of accounting were a few of the new courses adopted from the western accounting teaching materials.

The accounting curriculum during this period was classified as 'dual system' because of the following phenomena. First, the 'old cores' dominated the accounting curriculum at most Chinese universities and colleges in this early period of accounting reform because the traditional accounting patterns rooted in the former Soviet model were still functioning. The necessity of the new cores could only be justified by the joint ventures. Second, the new core courses derived from the western accounting system had not been well developed and accepted because of the lack of understanding of essential theories among Chinese accounting faculty members and the difficulty of applying new accounting concepts and methods under the traditional business administrative system.

The accounting curriculum after 1993

Since the beginning of 1992, the Chinese government has adopted a new economic strategy to switch the centrally planned economy to a partial market economy, called a 'socialist market economy' in China. A series of economic reforms have been implemented. In the accounting field, a new national accounting system has been installed with the implementation of the *Accounting Standards for Business Enterprises* in July 1993. Developments in accounting practice led to a new round of accounting education reform in China, which brought about a revolution in accounting curriculum designs at universities and colleges.

In the third research seminar organized by the Accounting Education Reform Committee under the Accounting Society of China in August 1993, representatives from most educational institutions agreed that the old accounting curriculum, with its too detailed industry-specific emphasis, would no longer be applicable in the new economic environment and a thorough revamping of accounting curriculum was inevitable. As a result, many reform measures have been experimented with, aimed at redesigning the accounting curriculum at universities and colleges since 1993. Substantial progress has been made, and the main features of accounting curriculum reforms can be summarized as follows.

First, the curriculum based on the 'old cores' was discredited and abolished. However, owing to the evolving nature of a market economy in China, the direction of the accounting curriculum reform has not been clearly set, at least during the current economic transitional period. In accounting practice, a uniform set of accounting standards for enterprise is still in the process of fine-tuning, and accounting standards for governments and non-profit organizations have not been established. In such an accounting environment, the core courses of the accounting programme keep changing and a great diversity exists in the accounting curriculum among different universities and colleges.

Second, even though the accounting curriculum has many deviations in terms of course content, a small number of core accounting courses have emerged, resulting from the recommendation by the Ministry of Finance. This set of core courses is illustrated in Figure 11.4. Here, the courses listed have generally been accepted by universities and colleges at present, although the number of credit hours and specific descriptions of the courses remain slightly different.

Third, although the accounting core courses offered are fairly similar among most education institutions, the elective courses are remarkably different, in respect of the quantity (how many) and the nature (restrictive or flexible) of the electives to be offered. In general, courses such as accounting system design, international accounting, taxation accounting, accounting theory, accounting history, financial statement analysis and budgetary accounting are among the most popular electives to be offered.

Fourth, there is no consensus regarding standard textbook materials. A few leading universities, which have good internal resources to prepare the complete set of textbooks for the accounting curriculum, have therefore

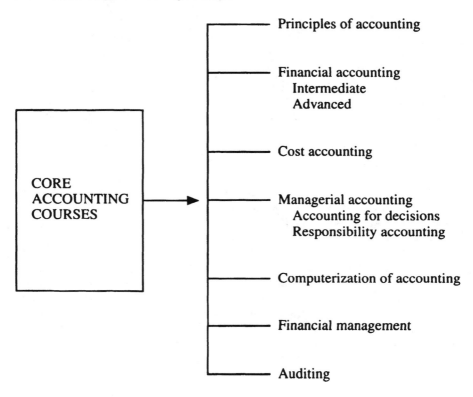

Figure 11.4   Subjects of core accounting courses

adopted the textbook materials complied by their own staffs in accounting programmes. However, each university would make its teaching materials somewhat distinct from the others', since the ability to compile the complete set of textbooks helps to boost the reputation of a university's accounting programme. Table 11.1 lists, in a comparison format, the textbooks prepared and adopted in the four top accounting universities in China.

Fifth, thanks to increasing interaction with overseas universities, a few top universities in China have started using English accounting textbooks (mostly US publications) in order to enhance students' competency in English communication and to avoid misinterpretation due to translation errors. Since 1995, a few leading universities, such as Xiamen University, Shanghai University of Finance and Economics (SUFE) , Renmin University of China, Beijing University, Tsinghua University, Fudan University, the Northeastern University of Finance and Economics, the Southwestern University of Fi-

Table 11.1 Accounting core textbooks adopted in top accounting schools

Xiamen University series	SUFE series	Renmin University series	Beijing University series
Principles of accounting	Fundamental accounting	Junior accounting	Fundamental accounting
Intermediate accounting	Intermediate accounting	Financial accounting	Financial accounting
Advanced accounting	Advanced financial accounting	Financial management	Cost accounting
Managerial accounting	Cost accounting	Cost accounting	Managerial accounting
Cost accounting	Management accounting	Auditing	Financial management
Business finance	Auditing	Decision accounting	Accounting info. system
Computerization of accounting	Computerized accounting	Responsibility accounting	Auditing
Auditing	Financial management	Advanced accounting	

nance and Economics, the Central University of Finance and Banking and the Tianjin Institute of Finance and Economics have used English-version accounting textbooks in their accounting classes. Nevertheless, only the old textbooks donated by overseas universities were available to students because the prices of current edition textbooks are too high for the majority of Chinese students. Fortunately, professors had the luxury of using new editions of the texts for teaching purposes. Adoption of English texts in class, in general, remains a small-scale experiment because of resource constraints: the original versions of foreign textbooks have been adopted for only a couple of accounting courses, even for these leading universities in China.

Sixth, it was a traditional practice to separate auditing from accounting in the Chinese educational system, for instance, there was even an institution specializing in auditing alone (the Nanjing Institute of Auditing under the administration of the NAA). Since the accounting reforms of 1993, many accounting educators have realized that accounting and auditing were inseparable. However, consolidation of accounting and auditing into a single major was still a gradual but slow process because of the restrictions on the college administration system and the concern regarding the demands from job markets.

Accounting curriculum for graduate programmes

Graduate schools in China offer both master and doctorate programmes. Master programmes were structured around the three major areas of lecturing, discussion and practical training. The doctorate curriculum was based mainly on seminars and research.

Master programmes

There are quite a few institutions that offer master programmes. However, the programmes are diversified among institutions, for two reasons. First, the curriculum is established by professors and graduate students independently at each institution. As a result, the course content and research directions are not uniform. Second, there are no textbooks for master programmes. English textbooks and research papers have been adopted in the top universities, but the less fortunate schools with limited resources can only rely on teaching materials written by their own professors. There is, therefore, a distinct difference in quality among schools.

Doctorate programmes

In China, the doctorate programme is highly regulated by the governmental authority in charge of higher learning, aiming at a strict control of programme quality. The doctorate tutorship must therefore be reviewed and granted by a high-ranking National Committee on Academic Accreditation under the State Council. In other words, only those well-recognized senior professors approved by the National Committee on Academic Accreditation can admit doctorate students.

At present, only a very small number of leading universities in China can offer a PhD programme in accounting. They are Xiamen University, Shanghai University of Finance and Economics (SUFE), Renmin University of China, Zhongnan University of Finance and Economics, the Northeastern University of Finance and Economics, the Tianjin Institute of Finance and Economics, the Southwestern University of Finance and Economics and the Research Institute of Finance Sciences under the Ministry of Finance.[3] The doctorate programmes focus usually on training in academic research, while the coursework or seminars are optional and vary in content from school to school.

The CPA specialization programme

There is a new undergraduate accounting programme in Chinese educational institutes, called the 'CPA specialization programme', which was initiated in 1994 and is unique when compared with the accounting education system in North America and other industrialized countries.

Establishment of the CPA specialization programme

As discussed in Chapter 7, there is a severe shortage of qualified public accountants in China. In order to speed up the formation of a competent team of CPAs, the Chinese government set up a special group in April 1994 to oversee the training of CPAs. The members of this leading group consisted of senior administrators from several ministries under the State Council, including the Ministry of Finance, the State Planning Commission, the State Education Commission, the NAA, and so on, and the office of this leading group is located at the CICPA. The leading group decided to set up a CPA specialization programme at some top universities as a measure to speed up the supply of CPA candidates. Although responses from most universities and educators were not positive, this specialization programme has been implemented at some universities since 1994 as a result of strong initiative efforts and financial support provided by the government.

Institutions offering the CPA specialization programme

In 1994, the first batch of seven leading universities were selected to establish the CPA specialization programme. They were Xiamen University, Renmin University of China, Shanghai University of Finance and Economics (SUFE), Zhongnan University of Finance and Economics, the Northeastern University of Finance and Economics, the Tianjin Institute of Finance and Economics and the Southwestern University of Finance and Economics.

In 1995, the second batch of 16 more universities were allowed to offer the programme. They included Tsinghua University, Fudan University, Wuhan University, Jilin University, Xi'an Jiaotong University, Zhongshan University, the Central Institute of Finance and Economics, the Anhui Institute of Finance and Trade, the Shenxi Institute of Finance and Trade, the Capital University of Economics and Trade, the Jiangxi Institute of Finance and Economics, Jinan University, the Changchun Institute of Taxation, the Hunan Institute of Finance and Economics, the Beijing Institute of Business and Liaoning University. The third batch of universities that wish to implement this programme are currently awaiting approval from the government.

The goals of the CPA specialization programme

The primary objective of the CPA specialization programme, as mandated by the government authorities in charge, is to train professionals who are capable of performing public accounting and financial consulting at CPA firms, or work at financial institute and securities agencies, the publicly listed companies and government or other organizations requiring accounting personnel equipped with market-oriented accounting knowledge and skills. Furthermore, professors and graduate students are also the target of this programme.

The CPA specialization programme, currently concentrates on nine core courses: intermediate and advanced financial accounting, financial management, managerial accounting, auditing, management consulting, taxation, business law and computerization of accounting. In addition, this programme focuses more on the training of English communication skills and the international dimension of accounting and auditing practice. Compared with the counterpart accounting programmes offered in Chinese universities and colleges, the CPA specialization programme is much more attractive to both students and potential employers since students will get more specialized training and be better prepared to sit for national CPA qualification examinations. The first batch of students on this programme is expected to graduate in the summer of 1998.

PROFESSIONAL QUALIFICATION EXAMINATIONS AND CONTINUING EDUCATION

As introduced in the first section of this chapter, China's continuing accounting education comprises three subsystems designated for the varied groups of accounting professionals: general accountants, government auditors, and certified public accountants. The content and requirements of these three subsystems of continuing professional education are not identical, but they still share one common characteristic: there is a close link between continuing accounting training and professional qualification examinations.

Accounting qualification examinations

China has established a system of professional grading of accounting personnel, based on nationwide qualification examinations. Corresponding to different ranks and responsibilities of the designated accounting grades, there are three separate series of qualification examinations: examination for accounting clerks, examination for assistant accountants and examination for accountants.

Regulations before 1996

In 1992, the Ministry of Finance and the Ministry of Labour and Human Resources jointly regulated the requirements on accounting qualification examinations, as shown in Table 11.2. According to the regulations, candidates intending to sit accounting qualification examinations must obtain an accounting certificate. In addition, they need to fulfil the specified education requirements. First, candidates registering to sit the qualification examination for accountant clerk were required to have a graduate diploma from a high school and have at least one year of work experience in the field of accounting.

Second, candidates registering to sit the Type A examination for assistant accountant were required:

- to be high school graduates, to have worked as an accounting clerk for over four years, and to have passed the Type B examination; or
- to be graduates from polytechnic schools (intermediate level) and to have had at least three years of work experience as an accounting clerk; or

Table 11.2   Content of accounting qualification examinations

Professional grades (ranks)	Types of examination	Content of examination	Eligibility requirements
Assistant accountant Accountant	Type A	Proficiency in professional knowledge and skills	To have met the necessary education requirement, or have passed the Type B examination
	Type B	Fundamental concepts of financial accounting	Not to have met the necessary education requirement
Accounting clerk		Basic professional knowledge and skills	

- to be graduates from polytechnic schools (advanced level) and to have had more than two years of work experience as an accounting clerk; or
- to be bachelor degree holders and to have had at least one year of work experience as an accounting clerk.

Third, for candidates registering for the Type A qualification examination for the grade of accountant, the eligibility requirements include the following:

- to be graduates from polytechnic schools (intermediate level) and to have had over four years of work experience in the rank of assistant accountant; or
- to be graduates from polytechnic schools (advanced level) or bachelor degree holders from recognized universities, and to have had at least three years of work experience in the rank of assistant accountant; or
- to be graduates of master degree programmes, and to have worked in the rank of assistant accountant for over three years; or
- to be graduates from accounting doctorate programmes.

Table 11.3 demonstrates the content of the accounting qualification examinations under the regulations of 1992.

From 1992 to 1994, the national accounting qualification examinations were held in the fourth quarter of each year. A very large number of accounting personnel have sat the examinations in order to obtain or upgrade their professional grades or ranks.

Amended regulations effective from 1996

The accounting qualification examination of 1995 was postponed owing to a pending review by the government authorities. In June 1996, the Ministry of Finance and the Ministry of Labour and Human Resources issued the amended *Temporary Rules on the Administration of Accountant Qualification Examinations* and the related *Implementation Procedures*. The amendments related to the requirements for the two series of qualification examinations for assistant accountant and accountant, with the requirements for the series of accounting clerk examinations remaining unchanged. The major changes in the amended regulation are as follows.

1   The examinations for assistant accountant and accountant are no longer divided into Type A and Type B, respectively; instead, the examinations are divided into Type A and Type B independently. In addition, it is not necessary for candidates to pass the Type B examination before taking the Type A examination.

Table 11.3 Subjects of the national accounting qualification examination (before 1996)

Professional grades (ranks) (Types of examination)	Subjects of examination
Accounting Clerk	1. Fundamentals of accounting and accounting regulations 2. Basic accounting practice
Assistant accountant (Type A)	1. Comprehensive knowledge and skills in accounting and related disciplines 2. Accounting practices for assistant accountants
Assistant accountant (Type B)	1. Writing of business thesis 2. Political economics 3. Accounting (level 1) 4. Cost accounting 5. Basic concepts of economic laws 6. Finance and banking
Accountant (Type A)	1. Comprehensive knowledge and skills in accounting and related disciplines 2. Accounting practices for accountants
Accountant (Type B)	1. Mathematics for business applications 2. Accounting (level 2) 3. Managerial accounting 4. Auditing 5. Financial management 6. Statistical management

2 The subjects to be tested are prepared in accordance with the classification of Type A and Type B examinations.
3 The practical requirements for candidates have been changed to specify accounting-related work experience.

There are no substantial changes in the subject content of the examinations. The date of the annual examinations, however, has been changed from the fourth quarter to May since 1996.

The qualification examination for government auditors

The professional grading system for government auditors is under the joint administration of the NAA and the Ministry of Labour and Human Resources. Four ranks of professional grades for government auditors, parallel to those for general accountants, are in place: auditing clerk, assistant auditor, auditor and senior auditor. National auditing qualification examinations have also been organized to assess and award professional grades for government auditors. However, the qualification examination aims only at the grades of assistant auditor and auditor, while there is no national qualification examination for auditing clerks. This is different from the professional grades for general accountants. Because of a severe shortage of auditing personnel in China at the moment, the qualification requirements for government auditors are, in general, less stringent.

According to the *Temporary Regulation on the Administration of Auditing Qualification Examinations* and the related *Implementation Procedures* issued in May 1992, the national auditing qualification examinations are divided into two types. The Type A examination, which aims at testing professional knowledge and skills, requires candidates to meet the standards on necessary educational and practical competence. The Type B examination is offered for those candidates who are non-degree holders. Applicants without a former educational background must sit the Type B examination prior to taking the Type A examination.

Educational background and related work experience

It is worth noting that formal education or schooling is a more important factor in the professional grading system for auditors. For instance, government auditors who have received education in business administration programmes from the recognized colleges and have sufficient experience of auditing-related jobs are exempted from the auditing qualification examination. Again, this is different from the requirements for accounting personnel. This can be illustrated by the requirements on professional auditing grades, listed in Table 11.4. Candidates who do not fulfil these requirements must sit the uniform national auditing qualification examination in order to gain the professional ranks.

Examination requirements

According to existing government regulations, candidates applying for a Type A qualification examination at assistant auditor level must meet one of the following specifications.

Table 11.4 Professional grading for government auditors

Professional ranks	Eligibility
Auditor	Doctorates in accounting or finance majors Master in accounting or finance and engaging in auditing work over three years
Assistant auditor	Bachelor degree holders, and having completed the probationary term in auditing work Graduates of accounting or management programmes at polytechnic school (advanced level), having completed the probationary job assignment and worked in the auditing field over two years
Auditing clerk	Graduates of accounting or management programmes at polytechnic school (intermediate level), having completed the probationary job assignment

1   Graduates of polytechnic schools (advanced level) with an emphasis in auditing and having two years' work experience in the auditing field, or university graduates with a specialization in accounting and auditing and having at least one year's work experience in auditing.
2   Graduates of polytechnic schools (intermediate level) with an emphasis in auditing and having three years' work experience in the rank of audit clerk.
3   High school graduates with four years' work experience in the rank of audit clerk and having passed the Type B qualification examination for assistant auditor.

Candidates applying for the Type A qualification examination at the level of auditor must satisfy one of the following requirements:

1   Master degree holders who have two years of work experience in the auditing field, or who have received a doctorate degree.
2   University graduates whose degrees have an emphasis in auditing and who possess three years' work experience in the rank of assistant auditor.
3   Graduates of polytechnic schools (intermediate level) who have had over four years of work experience in the rank of assistant auditor and

have passed the Type B qualification examination for the professional grade of auditor.

Table 11.5 lists the subject requirements of the national auditing qualification examination.

Table 11.5   Content of the national auditing qualification examination

Professional grades (ranks) (Types of examination)	Subjects of examination
Assistant auditor (Type A)	1. Auditing knowledge and skills 2. Basic theory and practice of auditing
Assistant auditor (Type B)	1. Political economics 2. Public finance, economics and trade 3. Fundamental auditing 4. Principles of accounting 5. Economic and business laws (level 1)
Auditor (Type A)	1. Comprehensive auditing and related knowledge and skills 2. Auditing theory and practice
Auditor (Type B)	1. Economic and business laws (level 2) 2. Enterprise management 3. Analysis of economic activities in enterprises 4. Acounting 5. Financial auditing 6. Audits of economic effectiveness (operating audits)

Qualification examination for certified public accountants

A separate system of qualification examination for certified public accountants (CPAs) has been established in China since 1991. The national CPA qualification examinations were administered by the Chinese Institute of Certified Public Accountants (CICPA) under delegation of authority from the National Committee on CPA Examinations under the Ministry of Finance. According to *The CPA Law of the People's Republic of China*, candidates for the CPA profession must satisfy the specified requirements in three areas: education, qualification examination and practical experience. Currently, CPA candidates must have obtained a formal accounting education at college level or above. From 1995, every candidate has had to sit the national CPA qualification examination and to obtain two years' work experience in public accounting and auditing. It should be pointed out that the CPA designation is very rigidly regulated by the Chinese government, as CPAs are professionals offering independent accounting and auditing services to the public. Thus higher standards, as compared to the qualification requirements for general accountants and government auditors, have been applied to the CPA qualification examination and certification process. This topic has been discussed in detail in Chapter 7.

Training for professional qualification examinations

Education and training are always vital to the implementation of the various types of professional qualification examinations. In China, the three sets of national professional qualification examinations are associated with preparatory training on a grand scale. Government authorities, the accounting profession, educational institutions and business communities have all made substantial efforts to provide training programmes for potential candidates to prepare for the examinations. In general, the training programmes associated with professional qualification examinations include, first, preparation and releasing of examination outlines by organizers of the examination, after which the supplementary reviewing materials are written, compiled and printed under the supervision of governmental or professional bodies in charge of the qualification examinations; and second, organization of national training programmes for instructors sponsored by the administrative bodies of the qualification examinations, followed by more specific or supplementary training classes for potential candidates in all parts of the country. This training process will serve, not only the purpose of examination preparation, but also the educational campaign to upgrade the knowledge and skills of accounting and auditing personnel, since a majority of them will take part in the training process.

Obviously, the quality of accountants cannot depend upon supplementary training courses accompanied by the qualification examinations alone, owing to the immense size of the accounting and auditing profession in China. Other types of on-job training, including a great number of special training courses sponsored by professional bodies, enterprises and other organizations, are also available. However, much more will have to be done to enhance the quality and professional competence of Chinese accounting and auditing personnel.

NOTES

1   This number is for the regular institutes of higher education offering programmes at the bachelor degree level and above. A greater number of polytechnic and vocational schools are not included in this statistic.
2   Xiamen University is one of the oldest and best-known universities in China. The accounting programme has been offered at the university without disruption since its accounting programme, exceptionally, was not removed during the restructuring of the higher education system in 1952. With the longest history of non-disrupted availability, the accounting programme of Xiamen University is generally recognized as the strongest in China at present.
3   When the system of graduate studies was officially adopted in China in 1980, only two accounting professors, one in Xiamen University and the other in Shanghai University of Finance and Economics, were granted the doctorate tutorship in the entire country. The number of accounting doctorate tutors increased to four in 1986 and expanded further after 1993.

12   Accounting Associations

In step with rapid economic growth in the last 15 years, accounting in China, both practical and academic, has witnessed a remarkable expansion. As a result, the accounting profession has emerged and the social status of accountants has risen. Various accounting associations have mushroomed in China. These professional associations have played a visible role in promoting accounting education and research, standardization of accounting practice and professional self-discipline or professionalism in recent years. This chapter introduces the major accounting associations in China, with emphasis being placed upon an elaboration of their organizational structure, functions and responsibilities. In addition, a brief discussion of accounting research and accounting publications in China is presented at the end of the chapter.

THE NATURE OF ACCOUNTING ASSOCIATIONS

By definition, accounting associations are professional bodies of distinct groups of professionals. At present a quite large number of accounting associations exist in China. Some, such as the Accounting Society of China, the Chinese Society of Auditing, the Chinese Institute of Certified Public Accountants, the Chinese Institute of Internal Auditors, and so on, are national associations. Others are accounting associations within a specific industry: the Chinese Budgetary Accountants Association, the Chinese Association of Accountants in the Electronic Industry, the Chinese Association of Accountants in the Grains and Foods Industry, the Chinese Association of Asset Appraisers, the Chinese Association of Cost Accounting Research, the Middle-Young-Aged Society of Finance and Cost Research of China, and so on. In addition, accounting associations corresponding to the national associations have also been established at provincial levels and lower authorities.

As defined by government regulations, accounting associations are societal entities consisting of groups of professionals. They are non-governmental organizations and non-profit-making in nature. The purposes of professional associations are to promote the interests of their members, to exchange experience among members and to enhance the self-discipline of the specified groups of professionals. To form accounting associations, like other non-profit organizations, it is necessary to apply to the Ministry of Civil Affairs and Social Welfare at the central government or its designates at provincial level for registration. In addition, the formation of accounting associations must be approved by the government authorities in charge of accounting affairs. For example, the national accounting or auditing associations must get the consent of the Ministry of Finance or the National Administration of Auditing (NAA), respectively. Formation of industry-specific accounting associations should be approved by the ministerial authorities in charge of the specific industry.

Within a framework of governmental accounting control, all accounting associations in China are subject to supervision by the government. A significant number of the senior executive officers of most accounting associations, such as the president, vice-presidents and secretary-general, are nominated by government authorities, even though they are nominally selected by general member meetings of the individual associations. It is worthy of mention that most associations are funded, or partially funded in some circumstances, through the government's budgetary appropriations. Some national accounting associations have even been delegated with certain duties of governmental accounting administration. For example, the Chinese Institute of Certified Public Accountants has been authorized by the Ministry of Finance to administer the certification and licensing for public accountants and CPA firms in China. In this sense, many accounting associations in Chinese are, in fact, semi-governmental bodies in nature.

Four of the most influential accounting associations in China, that is, the Accounting Society of China, the Chinese Institute of Certified Public Accountants, the China Society of Auditing and the Chinese Accounting Professors' Association, are discussed in further detail below.

THE ACCOUNTING SOCIETY OF CHINA

The Accounting Society of China (ASC) is the first, and the largest, accounting association in China. Immediately after the ten-year chaotic 'Cultural Revolution' in the late 1970s, the Chinese government launched a campaign of 'economic consolidation' in order to restore order and regulation in economic life. Accounting was emphasized as an important tool to carry out the task of economic consolidation. Thus accounting work was expanded in the country, with the numbers of accounting posts and personnel increasing dramatically nationwide. Demand for an enhancement of the standards of accounting practice arose as well. This resulted in a proposal to form a national accounting association to promote professionalism and to lead studies on accounting issues and develop solutions to emerging accounting problems in practice. A steering committee was formed under the auspices of the Department of Accounting Affairs under the Ministry of Finance in 1980 to prepare for organizing a national accounting association. From 26 December 1979 to 7 January 1980, the steering committee held meetings in Guangdong province, and in January 1980 formally announced the establishment of the ASC.

Objectives and structure of the ASC

The ASC consists of members from government, education and practice in China. There are two types of membership: institutional and individual. It is structured in such a way that all other national or industrial accounting associations or societies, including those in different provinces, municipalities and autonomous regions, ministries of the central government and large enterprises are institutional members of the ASC. For example, the Chinese Institute of Certified Public Accountants (CICPA), and the Chinese Accounting Professors' Association (CAPA) are also the institutional members of the ASC. Individual members include accounting personnel in various organizations and accounting educators and researchers. The president of the ASC is currently nominated by the Ministry of Finance, with a number of vice-presidents selected from former senior government officials in charge of accounting affairs and prominent accounting scholars in China.

The main office of the ASC is located in Beijing. According to the ASC's by-laws, a general meeting or conference of members should be held once a year. Most important issues, such as election or change of executive officers of the society and strategic planning for accounting development, must be presented, reviewed and approved by the annual general meeting. Besides the society's president and vice presidents, the members of the council of the ASC must be elected at the general member conference. The executive body of the ASC is its secretariat, which consists of a secretary-general and his/her deputies. Usually, the post of secretary-general is held concurrently by the director of the Department of Accounting Affairs under the Ministry of Finance, on a part-time basis.

According to the revised by-laws of the ASC adopted in April 1992, the nature of the ASC is an accounting academic association whose purpose is to carry out studies on accounting and to promote the advance of accounting practice. The primary mandates of the society are as follows:

- to organize and encourage members to participate actively in accounting studies;
- to promote the implementation of accounting standards and regulations and to provide government policy makers with input and suggestions;
- to report and investigate new accounting issues or problems, and to develop practical solutions;
- to promote accounting education reform and to design educational and training programmes that can satisfy the needs of accounting development;
- to protect the legal rights and interests of members, and to provide services for members;
- to organize exchange of work experience among members and to introduce and disseminate advanced accounting theories and practices of foreign countries;
- to promote accounting professionalism and enhance the quality of accounting personnel;
- to publish accounting journals and data, and to organize accounting research seminars;
- to coordinate input, suggestions and enquiries of members; and
- to carry out other tasks assigned by the government.

Member conferences of the ASC

In order to accommodate the needs of accounting reform, the ASC holds annual conferences to discuss and analyse emerging accounting issues derived from the changing environments in the process of rapid economic growth in China. Annual conferences are also held to discuss solutions to practical accounting problems and to solicit opinions and suggestions made by members regarding China's accounting development. Some of the major themes discussed in the ASC's previous annual conferences, for example, included: (1) generalization of accounting experience in the past, (2) enhancement of the status and function of accounting in business management, (3) reform of the accounting administrative system, (4) utilization of accounting experience from other countries, (5) redesign of the double-bookkeeping system, (6) curriculum reform in accounting education, (7) responsibilities and obligations of accounting personnel, (8) establishment of the auditing system and (9) compliance with business laws. The keynote theme of the ASC annual conference held in Beijing on 5–7 October 1996 was on the improvement of accounting regulations and accounting standards.

The ASC's planning of accounting research

As a leading accounting association, the ASC has played an active role in promoting accounting research and studies in China. Following the accounting reform of 1993, the ASC has decided to encourage its members to participate actively in the studies of emerging accounting issues and to deliver recommendations for continuing accounting reforms. Two areas of study interest are particularly advocated by the ASC: to study accounting issues or problems being encountered during the current transitional period of economic reform and accounting reform, and to analyse the accounting theories and practices in the industrialized western countries, in order to adopt and adapt successful western experience for China's socialist market economy. Substantial efforts, including research grants and a best accounting research paper awards, have been introduced. In addition, the society has been actively promoting the dissemination of the study results which have been achieved.

In order to strengthen the research aspect of the society's performance, the ASC has continuously initiated research projects that are pertinent to the government's policy making in respect of accounting issues with significance on a nationwide scale. Many special study groups or task forces have been formed or financially supported by the ASC. Major study projects that have been supported by the ASC over the last ten years include the following:

- research on basic principles of accounting;
- research on the increasing importance of accounting in managing large and medium-sized state-owned enterprises;
- research on strengthening the function of accounting in macroeconomic management;
- research on directions for China's accounting reforms;
- research on accounting education reform and expanding knowledge and skills for accounting students and trainees;
- research on the establishment of accounting standards compatible with a socialist market economy;
- research on the reform of the national accounting administration system;
- a national survey of the quality of accounting personnel;
- research on the popularization of the computerization of accounting in China;
- joint research with academic and professional bodies abroad (Hong Kong, Macao and Taiwan, in particular).

Most of the research projects initiated by the ASC were closely related to the hot topics in China's accounting reforms. The society's intention is to influence the government's accounting policy making through the study results generated by research task forces. The ASC set up a five-year plan on accounting research at the fourth national accounting conference held in Beijing in 1996. The following study topics were adopted in the research plan:

- the economic theory which explains the role of accounting in a changing society;
- the conceptual framework of Chinese accounting standards;
- the procedures for transition of enterprise accounting systems;
- the accounting problems relating to budgetary administration;
- the mechanism to enhance the economic supervision function of accounting systems;
- the issues relating to accounting education and training;
- the studies of accounting history and of the development of accounting standards in other countries; and
- the emerging practical accounting issues in the Chinese economy.

THE CHINESE INSTITUTE OF CERTIFIED PUBLIC ACCOUNTANTS

The Chinese Institute of Certified Public Accountants (CICPA) is the national association of certified public accountants (CPAs). It was established on 5 November 1988 during the course of a rapid expansion of public accounting in China. Later, various provinces set up local institutes of CPAs. Establishment of the CICPA is a cornerstone in the development of public accounting in China, since it was the first step made towards self-discipline of the accounting profession.

Under the fifth article of the *Certified Public Accountant Law of the People's Republic of China* (the CPA Law), which was introduced in 1993, Chinese CPAs are allowed to organize institutes of CPAs to protect the rights of the profession, to share practising experience and to promote professional exchanges with professional bodies in other countries. In addition, this law authorizes the CICPA to formulate auditing standards which, upon approval by the Ministry of Finance, will become authoritative guidelines that are binding on all CPAs. Since its formation, the CICPA has issued a series of practical rules and auditing standards, which have contributed significantly to the growth of the public accounting profession and represented the institute's initial response in its role as a monitor of public accounting practice in China.

Structure and objectives of the CICPA

The CICPA is a national organization composed primarily of independent CPAs in China. It came into being because CPAs are independent professionals when performing their duties, whereas public accounting firms are business entities which are responsible for their own profit and loss. With the rapid growth in the number of public accountants and public accounting firms, the CICPA was set up to coordinate the performance of CPAs and public accounting firms, to share accounting working experience among CPAs, to supervise compliance with accounting and auditing regulations and to regulate public accounting practices in China.

From its inauguration, the CICPA has been under the direct control of the Ministry of Finance. The following factors have contributed to this situation.

1   China's socialist economic system and business administrative systems are very different from those in other countries, therefore the CICPA is not supposed to follow completely the pattern or structure of the professional accounting bodies in western countries.
2   The CICPA and public accounting profession have been growing for a short period of time only and there is a lack of experience in managing them.
3   The CICPA is more relevant as a non-profit-making unit; it has to rely upon the government's budgetary appropriations or financial support and so it is subject to the government's control.

The following primary objectives have been stated in the by-laws of the CICPA:

●   to guide CPAs to perform their duties by closely following the related laws and government regulations;
●   to continuously improve self-development of CPAs, and to protect the legal rights of the accounting profession;
●   to share work experience and communicate professional knowledge among professional accountants, to speed up public accounting growth in China;
●   to increase interchanges with professional accounting bodies in other countries; and
●   to fulfil other tasks assigned by the government, particularly in performing supervision of public accounting practice.

As discussed in Chapter 7, the CICPA was reorganized in late 1995, after the merging of the CICPA and the former Chinese Association of Certified

Public Auditors. Currently, the CICPA is subject to the joint supervision of the Ministry of Finance and the NAA.

Responsibilities of the CICPA

According to Chapter 5 of the CPA Law, the responsibilities of the CICPA are as follows.

1 To act as liaison between the government and professional accountants (CPA firms and individual CPAs) and to provide channels of communication between the two parties.
2 To express opinions and suggestions of CPAs.
3 To inform or educate members regarding the government's economic and business policies, laws and regulations.
4 To assist or facilitate the government in administration of public accounting within China, including annual performance review and renewal of CPA's practising licences.

More specifically, the CICPA is responsible for performing the following four areas of duties.

1 To exercise self-discipline of self-management of the CPA profession under delegation of authority from the Ministry of Finance, for example,
   - to be in charge of certification of CPAs and approval of the formation of CPA firms, and to conduct annual review and renewal of practising licences for CPA firms and individual CPAs;
   - to formulate and implement the code of professional ethics of CPAs;
   - to draft general and practical auditing standards for public accounting;
   - to monitor compliance with professional ethics and auditing standards by CPA firms and individual CPAs;
   - to administer national CPA examinations, including handling candidate registration and organization of the CPA examinations.

2 To offer services for CPAs and promote the legitimate interest of its members; for example,
   - to initiate professional development programmes for members, especially the continuing professional education (CPE) programmes;
   - to protect CPAs' legal rights and interests; to handle enquiries and reasonable demands of members;

- to organize professional exchanges among members or their CPA firms, aiming at encouraging sharing of work experience and increasing the quality of public services offered by members.

3 To provide coordination among members, CPA firms and government authorities; for example,
   - to establish proper relations with corresponding government authorities, including consultation on the registration of CPA firms with industrial and business administrative bureaux and with state taxation bureaux about the tax issues regarding CPA firms;
   - to coordinate mutual exchanges among public practitioners and to offer arbitration to CPA firms involved in business disputes or other conflicts;

4 To develop exchange ties with foreign professional bodies. For example, the CICPA is responsible for building up professional links with international or regional professional accounting bodies. In addition, the CICPA is authorized by the Ministry of Finance to carry out supervision of foreign CPA firms operating within China: in particular,
   - to review the application of foreign CPAs or CPA firms to establish representative offices, joint ventures and temporary practising permits in China;
   - to evaluate business activities of foreign CPAs or CPA firms which have operated in China with approval from the Chinese government; and
   - to monitor the implementation of government regulations governing operations of foreign CPAs and CPA firms within China.

Organization structure of the CICPA

The CICPA structure includes the assembly of member representatives, the council and the secretariat.

The assembly of member representatives

The assembly of member representatives consists of representatives from individual members and institutional members. The assembly is the highest authority of the CICPA in accordance with its by-laws. The following actions are usually within the scope of responsibility of the assembly: (1) to formulate and revise the Institute's by-laws and other internal administrative rules, (2) to develop strategic policies for the institute, (3) to elect and dismiss the council members of the institute, (4) to review and approve the performance reports of the institute's council, and (5) to approve other policies or decisions with great significance for the institute.

The assembly of member representatives holds its general member meeting once every three years and, if necessary, the meeting can either be convened earlier or postponed.

The council

The council is the CICPA's leading body. Council members must be elected at the Assembly's general meeting. Council members, consisting of government officials in charge of public accounting, representatives of practitioners and academics, usually serve a three-year term, with possibility of re-election. The council must report to the Assembly of Member Representatives to discharge its duties. The primary responsibilities of the council are as follows: (1) to organize the general meeting of the Assembly, and submit a performance report to the Assembly, (2) to implement the resolutions and other decisions adopted by the Assembly, (3) to co-ordinate activities between the CICPA and government authorities in charge, and (4) to oversee the performance of the secretariat on behalf of the Assembly.

The council's membership include ordinary members and standing committee members. Usually, the senior executives of the CICPA, that is, its president, vice-presidents and secretary-general, must be selected from the standing committee members.

The secretariat

The secretariat is the executive body of the CICPA. It is located in Beijing and consists of one secretary-general, a few deputy secretary-generals, and other staff. The secretariat is responsible for administering the daily activities of the CICPA. Several functional divisions are established under the secretariat to be in charge of (1) CPA certification, (2) practising licensing for CPA firms, (3) discipline of professional conduct and (4) setting independent auditing standards, and liaising with governments and professional bodies abroad.

In addition, the CICPA is authorized by the Ministry of Finance to set up an Office on National CPA Examinations to administer the national CPA examinations. The Office is the executive body of the National Committee on Uniform CPA Examinations which is headed by a deputy minister of the Ministry of Finance. The basic duties of the Office are as follows: (1) to draft and analyse the policies or rules on national CPA examinations, (2) to organize preparatory training programmes for candidates, including drafting the outlines of preparation and study materials for the examinations, (3) to prepare the examination papers, (4) to organize and administer the examinations nationwide, and (5) to organize marking and evaluation of the examination results and to determine the passing grades for the examinations.

Independent auditing standards

One of the CICPA's most significant achievements in recent years is to study and draft the independent auditing standards for CPAs. The framework of the *Chinese Independent Auditing Standards*, which were drafted in the light of the CPA Law by the CICPA's task force on standard setting, consists of four elements: the standards on independent auditing, the standards on professional ethics, the standards on quality control of independent auditing and the standards on professional continuing education.

Regarding formulation of auditing standards, the *Chinese Independent Auditing Standards* promulgated by the CICPA are classified into three levels.

Level 1   General auditing standards

These standards act as an overall framework for setting specific auditing standards and practical guidelines. They consist of the basic principles governing auditing in public practice.

Level 2   Practical auditing standards

There are two subgroups of practical auditing standards. The first group set out the principles and essential procedures which auditors are required to comply with in performing audits of a general nature (that is, financial statement audits). The other group sets out the principles and essential procedures which auditors are required to comply with in performing audits of specialized industries, or audits for special purposes.

Level 3   Practical guidelines

These standards provide guidelines for independent auditors to apply the practical auditing standards with further detailed operational procedures.

According to official planning, the CICPA will complete the establishment of the *Chinese Independent Auditing Standards* before the end of this century. The whole standards project includes about four general auditing standards, 30 practical standards, ten special auditing standards and ten practical guidelines. Up to June 1997, two batches of 27 pieces of the independent auditing standards have been completed and released jointly by the Ministry of Finance and the NAA. The preparation of the third batch of these standards is currently under way.

THE CHINA SOCIETY OF AUDITING

The China Society of Auditing (CSA) is the national association of auditing practitioners (mainly involved in governmental auditing) and educators or researchers. It was founded in the mid-1980s. Under the Audit Law, the CSA is under the supervision of the NAA. The primary objective of the CSA is to promote the studies of auditing theories and practices, with an emphasis on governmental auditing. As indicated in its by-laws, the CSA's responsibilities include the following.

1   To study auditing issues or practical problems and organize special investigations, to provide input of relevant data and information for policy making by government authorities in charge of auditing affairs.
2   To organize forums, seminars and exchanges among government auditors, and to summarize and popularize the successful experience of audit work in China.
3   To study and draft the rules of professional ethics on auditing – governmental auditing in particular.
4   To study and promote education in auditing and training of auditing personnel.
5   To encourage members to participate actively in auditing research and the upgrading of knowledge.
6   To exercise certain auditing administrative duties under delegation of authority from the NAA, such as:
   • administering the professional grading system for auditing personnel,
   • preparing and organizing national auditing qualification examinations, and
   • reviewing the applications for professional auditing titles or ranks.

The CSA is organized in a structure fairly similar to that of the ASC, consisting of the member assembly, the council and the secretariat. There is an overlap in membership of the CSA and that of the ASC and the CICPA, since auditing is actually a branch of accounting. The headquarters of the CSA is located in Beijing. The council members of the CSA, including its senior executive officials, are selected by the annual general member conference, although the nomination of its senior executive officials must be approved by the NAA in advance. The CSA has made substantial efforts to promote the restoration and expansion of auditing in China since the early 1980s.

THE CHINESE ACCOUNTING PROFESSORS' ASSOCIATION

The Chinese Accounting Professors' Association (CAPA) was inaugurated at an international accounting symposium held in Shanghai in July 1995. It was the first national association for accounting professors or educators in China. The CAPA is an institutional member of the ASC.

Although the CAPA is a very young accounting association, with a relatively small number of members, it has maintained a very high profile in accounting research in China. The members of the CAPA are academics and very active in pursuing accounting and auditing research. The CAPA holds its annual conference in July every year, the centre of focus being presentation and discussion of academic research papers. The CAPA conferences have been well received in China and have attracted accounting scholars from abroad. For example, numbers of accounting professors from the United States, Australia, the United Kingdom, Canada, Korea, Taiwan and Hong Kong have attended the CAPA conference over the last three years. The foreign guest speakers at the last three CAPA conferences included the past president, president and president-elect of the American Accounting Association (AAA). The academic link between CAPA and its counterparts in other countries has been expanded remarkably. It is expected that the CAPA will play a leading role in upgrading accounting education and research, thus promoting the growth of accounting practice in China.

ACCOUNTING RESEARCH AND PUBLICATIONS

The general status of accounting research

Accounting research has boomed in China since 1980. Along with the reform of the national economic structure, accounting reform has grown rapidly. A great number of new accounting issues have emerged in practice, for which no solutions could be found from the traditional accounting models derived from the planned economy originally adopted in China.

274 Accounting and Auditing in China

New accounting theories and practices were thus urgently needed. Accounting research was required to study the new accounting issues or problems and to develop solutions to the reform of Chinese accounting.

Accounting research in China before 1980 had long been underdeveloped. Under an economic system with highly centralized governmental accounting control, accounting research was restricted to a mechanical interpretation of the mandatory accounting regulations formulated by the government. Greatly diversified study interests surfaced, however, after 1980, when the economic and accounting reforms were in full swing. Both the quantity and quality of the research output have been considerably enhanced in the last fifteen years. The main characteristics of accounting research in China can be highlighted as follows.

1 The primary focus of most research projects was placed on practical accounting issues. Many practitioners pursued studies of concrete accounting problems encountered in real life and developed practical solutions based on field investigations or analysis.
2 The topics relating to strategic development of accounting and auditing development have been studied mostly by accounting academics or accounting associations under the auspices of the government. The establishment of Chinese accounting and auditing standards and the conceptual framework of Chinese accounting, for example, has been a dominant theme in accounting research in the last decade.
3 A substantial part of accounting research is the study and introduction of accounting theories and practices in other countries, mainly in the form of direct translation or adaptation of the teaching and research materials from the western countries, including a systematic introduction of the standards published by International Accounting Standards Committee (IASC). The study results in this area have helped to promote the development of accounting reform and accounting internationalization in China.
4 The research methodologies applied in China, however remained relatively poor, judging by the standards adopted in the West. For example, the descriptive approach has been dominant in accounting research. Most studies completed were lacking empirical data and theoretical analysis. The empirical or positive research approach emerged, however, in very recent years, thanks to the efforts initiated by newly trained graduate students or returning scholars who have visited academic institutions in the West. The application of the empirical research approach in China, nonetheless, is at a stage of early development. The main constraints upon conducting empirical research in China include the resistance of traditionally trained researchers and the lack, or unavailability, of empirical data at the moment.

Accounting publications

Most research results have been disseminated through various accounting journals and magazines, both professional and academic. Accounting publications have flourished in recent years in step with the rapid growth in Chinese accounting. There are hundreds of accounting magazines and journals in circulation at present, their focus and quality differing substantially. In general, the Chinese accounting publications can be grouped into four categories.

National academic journals

This is the first tier of accounting publications in China, consisting of a small number of leading academic accounting journals. Among them, *The Accounting Review* is the most prestigious. This journal was first published jointly by the ASC and the Cost Accounting Research Society of China in January 1980. The journal was originally a quarterly, but has been a monthly since 1990. This journal provides a forum for developing accounting theories and concepts, with the target readership mainly academic accountants and educators. The hundredth issue of *The Accounting Review* was published in February 1996. The publisher of the journal held a ceremony to celebrate this significant event. At present, *The Accounting Review* is the most influential academic accounting journal in China.

National professional publications

This group consists of accounting journals or magazines with emphasis upon practical dimensions of accounting and auditing. *The Financial Management and Accounting*, the *Journal of CPA* and *China Auditing* are just a few examples in this category. They are prepared mainly for accounting and auditing practitioners and most articles published are closely associated with practical accounting problems and exchange of work experience.

Industry-specific and local magazines

The third group of accounting publications comprises a large number of accounting magazines published by industry-specific accounting associations or accounting associations at the level of local government, such as *Finance and Accounting in Electronic Industry, Budgetary Accounting, Shanghai Accounting, Fujian Finance and Accounting*, and so on. They are numerous and greatly diversified in content. These professional magazines are practice-oriented with a strong slant towards a particular industry or local influence. In general, the quality or reputation of these publications is lower than that of the national publications.

Research journals of higher educational institutes

Most leading universities in China publish research journals regularly. These journals are not specifically designed as accounting journals, but some of them may carry research papers prepared by their accounting faculty members. Thus the research journals from a few top universities with leading accounting programmes in China, such as *Forum on China Economic Issues* (Xiamen University), the *Journal of Shanghai University of Finance and Economics, Economics and Management* (Renmin University of China) and *Economics Sciences* (Peking University), have been very influential in accounting research. The quality of these academic journals is relatively high since they are aimed mainly at academic readers.

13 The Environment of Business Regulation

Since 1979, China has opened up its purely socialist, state-run economy to include elements of the free-market system. By doing so, China is paving the way towards becoming an economic superpower. Nowadays, an increasing number of foreign investors are conducting business either with or in China. To do this successfully, foreign businessmen and professionals must prepare themselves by learning about the business environment in China. In addition, business regulations affect accounting work directly. Anyone learning accounting development cannot ignore the related business regulations. An overview of the Chinese business environment is therefore presented in this chapter. The emphasis is then placed on a brief elaboration of the major business laws or regulations that are currently in effect in China.

OVERVIEW OF THE BUSINESS ENVIRONMENT

Many western companies have now invested heavily in China. The rapid economic growth, coupled with the Chinese government's steadfast endeavours to improve the environment for foreign investment, has made China an attractive target for foreign investors. However, some bad signs, such as sociopolitical instability, high inflation, tense labour–capital relations, inadequate energy supply, underdeveloped infrastructure, limited local financing and low labour productivity, still intimidate many foreign investors. Nevertheless, the desire to join the World Trade Organization (WTO) will force China to liberalize its trade policies and establish more business laws or regulations which are compatible with those of Western nations. As we can see, China has, in recent years, already made great strides in transforming its economy from a command economy to one that is market-driven.

Forms of Chinese enterprises

Chinese enterprises can be broadly classified into four categories in terms of business accounting: state-owned enterprises, collectively owned enterprises, privately owned enterprises and foreign invested enterprises. State-owned enterprises may belong either to the central government (under the administration of various ministries by different lines of industry) or to the local governments at different levels. Theoretically, the state-owned enterprises are considered to be the 'enterprises owned by the whole people'. The prime minister, governors and mayors are all managers, however, because they are responsible for multiple administrative functions and duties as heads of the government. They usually delegate managerial power to subordinate and specialized ministries or departments. Two of the biggest state-owned enterprises are state-owned farms and army-run enterprises.

Collectively owned enterprises are the second important category of enterprises in China. They are administered by local governments, and their assigned production targets have been incorporated into the state plan. Most local governments have set up a Bureau of Light Industry with supervisory authority over operations of the collectively owned enterprises. Nonetheless, fewer government controls are exercised over the collectively owned enterprises than over the state-owned enterprises.

On the government's interpretation, a privately owned enterprise is a business entity, with fewer than eight employees, owned by an individual citizen or citizens; thus it is also called an 'individual economic household' in China. Privately owned enterprises can be established in one of three legal forms: solo proprietorship, partnership or a company with limited liability. Only a company with limited liability is entitled to register as a legal entity. Privately owned enterprises in China are also subject to certain governmental control, especially in the areas involving foreign investment and international trades.

The state-owned and collectively owned enterprises are typically more reliable than the non-government-owned enterprises in terms of financial stability because they have been created under government sponsorship and are consequently more likely to obtain financial support in the event of serious economic difficulties. On the other hand, privately owned enterprises possess more flexibility in business operations than the state-owned and collectively owned enterprises.

Foreign invested enterprises are business entities affiliated with foreign capital, which came into existence in China only after implementation of the 'open door' policy that was adopted by the government in the late 1970s. Various types of foreign invested enterprises are now operating in China. Among them the joint ventures, with Chinese and foreign partners, both equity ventures and contractual ventures, account for a great proportion, while a relatively small proportion are solely foreign-owned enterprises such as subsidiaries or branches of foreign companies. According to existing government regulations, formation of foreign invested enterprises in China must be approved by the government authority in charge. In addition, the proposed foreign invested enterprises must be equipped with advanced technology and equipment, or must export all or most of their product produced in China. These two basic requirements are designed to block the entry of foreign firms that intend to share the domestic markets with Chinese manufacturers without bringing in any technology. In general, wholly owned foreign invested enterprises should reflect more government control than the joint ventures, because no Chinese partners are involved.

Sources of business financing

The securities markets are a new source of corporate funding in China. Under the traditional planned economy, the majority of enterprises were state-owned and funded by the government through direct appropriations from the government's finance department or by loans from the state-owned banks. Changes have taken place, however, during the course of economic reform. For example, many state-owned enterprises have now been reorganized into share-capital companies while direct financing from the government has been reduced. Nowadays, in order to raise enough capital, business financing usually involves the use of capital market instruments and commercial bank loans. Besides the original investment made by the government, three additional sources are available for business financing: (1) contributed capital by shareholders, or other types of equity holders, (2) short-term borrowings from commercial banks, and (3) utilization of the retained profits (earnings) by enterprises, in accordance with the related government regulations.

At present, government funding is the main source of financing for state-owned enterprises, but contributed capital and retained profits are the two major sources of capital for non-state-owned enterprises including all foreign invested enterprises. In addition, all types of enterprises have to rely upon borrowing from the commercial banks, particularly for short-term financing and operating needs. As a result, assets of most enterprises are financed by liabilities and equity contributed by owners (either the state, various government bodies or stockholders/equity holders).

SUMMARY OF BUSINESS REGULATIONS IN CHINA

Investment in China holds attractive potential for foreign investors. Cost-effective Chinese labour, together with the preferential treatments specified in Chinese business laws and regulations, have been encouraging to many foreign investors. In particular, the Chinese government has made substantial efforts to establish a legal framework for business regulation since the late 1980s. A series of business laws and regulations have been enacted and enforced by the government. The newly introduced business regulations include the Enterprise Law, the Law for Joint Ventures, the Corporation Law, the banking laws, the Economic Contract Law, the Foreign Exchange Regulation, the Insurance Law, the Advertisement Law, the Trademark Law and the Antitrust Law.

The main content or requirements of selected business laws and regulations are briefly examined below, in turn.

The State-owned Enterprise Law

This is the state law governing administration of the state-owned enterprises. The main provisions included in this law are as follows.

Basic principles

The basic principles codified in the Enterprise Law include the following:

- ownership and management are separable, this is consistent with the goal of economic reforms that aim at enabling the government to reduce direct involvement in business administration;
- management of enterprises are responsible for operations of individual enterprises;
- instead of managing enterprises directly, the government will focus on the monitoring function at macro-level;
- the Communist Party committee within enterprises will monitor the implementation of business decisions made by management and make sure that business decisions and plans have been carried out properly;
- management should encourage employees' responsibility for production, enthusiasm and creativity.

Rights and responsibilities of an enterprise

According to the law, the rights of an enterprise include autonomy in the areas of producing, pricing, purchasing, investing, exporting/importing, administering, labouring, and so on. Correspondingly, a state-owned enterprise is required to bear the following responsibilities associated with its rights:

- fulfilment of the required projects and contracts;
- protection and maintenance of the properties or fixed assets entrusted by the state;
- compliance with government regulations and supervision governing business financing and pricing;
- improvement of the quality of product;
- reduction in the consumption of production elements (cost saving); and
- protection of the environment.

Formation, reorganization and dissolution of an enterprise

Several criteria for establishing an enterprise are stated in the law, including the following:

- the products of an enterprise should be needed by the society;
- the labour, material, energy and transport facilities required by an enterprise's production should be available;
- an enterprise must have a name and a place to operate its business;
- an enterprise should have a sufficient amount of legally stated capital;
- compliance with laws and regulations governing business activities.

An enterprise will be dissolved if one of the following events has occurred:

- its product does not satisfy the required government standard or does not have a market;
- the enterprise has incurred a huge amount of losses or debts;
- business merger or split.

The internal management system of an enterprise

The law addresses not only management's power and responsibilities, but also the rights and responsibilities of employees in a state-owned enterprise, such as participation in decision making and supervision of management's performance, through functioning of the 'Employees' representative board', which must be set up in every enterprise.

The relationship between enterprise and government

A state-owned enterprise belongs to the state and is owned by the people. The government maintains the right to oversee or redirect an enterprise's operations. Nevertheless, an enterprise has power to make its own operating decisions in terms of the government's guidelines and other regulations.

The Privately Owned Enterprise Law

The main provisions included in this law are listed below.

Forms of privately owned enterprise

Three types of business are allowed to form a privately owned enterprise: sole proprietorship, partnership and a limited liability company.

Formation and termination

In order to establish a privately owned enterprise, applicants must properly file the registration forms to the State Administration of Industry and Commerce (SAIC), stating explicitly the location of the business, the amount of capital and names of owners, and specifications. Likewise, if a privately owned enterprise intends to close its business, filing with the SAIC is required. Termination can be made on a voluntary or involuntary basis (such as bankruptcy or court order).

Rights and responsibilities

A privately owned enterprise can enjoy rights such as hiring workers, setting the levels of wages and the profit-sharing scheme, applying for trademark or patent, entering business contracts, and so on. Its responsibilities include paying taxes, complying with the government's regulations and establishing a sound accounting system.

Management and supervision

The law requires management of a privately owned enterprise to exercise duties of enhancing the productivity of its employees, setting proper wages and benefits for employees, prohibiting child labour (employees under 16 years old), filing business registration and applying for an operating licence, and so on.

The Corporation Law

This law was enacted in the early 1990s to accommodate the need to reorganize some state-owned enterprises into limited liability companies or stock companies. The major provisions of this law include the following.

Overview of corporations

A corporation is a profit-driven legal entity that is separated from its share-holders or owners. The Corporation Law formalizes the rules and procedures for company operations in China.

Limited liability corporations

The law specifies that shareholders have limited liability on corporation debts and losses. The number of shareholders for a limited liability company, however, cannot exceed 50. No stocks can be issued or publicly traded for limited liability companies.

Corporations limited by shares

Differing from limited liability corporations, a share-capital company can issue stocks and bonds to the public. No restriction is specified on the number of shareholders, so it will be easier for a share-capital company to raise capital.

Corporate financing and accounting

Corporations may go public to obtain financing for their operations. Issuing stocks and corporate bonds is the major means of corporate financing. In order to protect the interest of shareholders and bondholders, the Corporation Law requires that corporations establish sound accounting systems and make appropriate disclosures according to the requirements laid down by the appropriate government authorities.

Consolidation, bankruptcy, dissolution and liquidation

Business consolidation is the event in which two or more corporations join together to become a completely new corporation. The original corporations cease to exist and the new corporation assumes all assets and liabilities of the original corporations. Sometimes, dissolution may occur when a corporation has terminated its business activities, or by special resolution of shareholders. Under the Corporation Law, transactions involving consolidation, bankruptcy, termination and liquidation must be reported to the responsible government authorities in advance. Audit of financial statements is also required.

Legal responsibility

Shareholders should contribute the amount of capital that has been stated in the constitution of the corporation. The Corporation Law states clearly that any acts involving false registration or business frauds conducted by a corporation will be penalized in accordance with the provisions specified in the law and other government legislation or regulations.

The banking laws

There are two state laws governing the banking industry; one applies to commercial banks operating in China, while the other is applied exclusively to China's central bank. Currently, quite a few commercial banks are in operation: some are state-owned, some are collectively owned (in a share-capital format) and the rest are foreign capital affiliated. The main provisions of the Chinese banking laws are summarized below.

Overview of banks

The overall rights and responsibilities of banking institutions have been specified in the banking laws. In addition, the customers' interests or rights have also been addressed, such as freedom of deposit and withdrawal from bank accounts and confidentiality of customer bank accounts.

The Central Bank Law

The People's Bank of China is designated as the central bank in China. Under the law, the duties of the central bank include (1) setting monetary policy and interest rates, (2) regulating the circulation of currency (*Renminbi*),

(3) administering the applications for offering banking services in China, (4) setting minimum reserve requirements for all commercial banks, (5) monitoring or inspecting the performance of banking institutions, and (6) acting as the state treasury for the central government. The relative independence of the central bank from the executive branch of the central government is also defined.

The Commercial Bank Law

Commercial banks in China include specialized banks, mixed-function banks and other financial institutions. Under the Commercial Bank Law, all forms of commercial banks should be independent business entities. They can offer a great variety of banking and non-banking financial services. The operations of commercial banks are, however, subject to the banking regulations or monetary policies and rules formulated by the central bank on behalf of the central government. Reserves in terms of the minimum level specified by the central bank must be maintained for bank loans issued at all times.

The Economic Contract Law

This law is enacted and enforced to promote order in business life. Some provisions of this law follow.

Overview

The law defines economic contracts as the agreements reached between legal persons and which specify the contractual relationship with regard to mutual rights and duties of the economic parties involved.

Formation of contract

Enterprises are permitted to enter into contracts in terms of their own needs and purposes. The principle of equality, mutually beneficial agreement through consultation, and corresponding economic rewards must be followed as a guide to contract formation.

Guarantee of contract

Any economic contract can be guaranteed in three forms: security deposit, personal guarantee or through the vehicle of lien enforcement.

Contract modification and termination

According to the Economic Contract Law, a contract may be modified or terminated if one of the following conditions is satisfied:

- the parties involved have mutually agreed to modify or terminate the contract through consultation;
- the state economic plans upon which the economic contract is based have been revised or terminated;
- one contracting party finds it impossible to perform the contract because of business closures, or suspension of production, but consultation with another party is required;
- the performance of the contract by any contracting party is prevented by force;
- continuation of the contract performance becomes unnecessary because of the failure of performance by another contracting party.

Liability for breach of contract

In the case of contract breaching, the non-breaching party has the right to collect payment derived from liquidated damages. Other remedies such as damages compensation, specified performance and personal responsibility are also available under the Economic Contract Law.

Control of contract formation and performance

Statutory provisions concerning contract control and management are a distinctive feature of China's centrally administered economy. The Economic Contract Law delegates the power of contract control to the relevant supervisory authorities overseeing the contracting parties and to the SAIC at various levels.

The Insurance Law

The Insurance Law maintains the following main provisions.

Overview of insurance

Insurance is a way to transfer risk to a guarantor by paying a certain fee (premium). Some insurance is involuntary, for example airline passenger insurance, which is required by the government. Other types of insurance, such as estate insurance, health insurance or unemployment insurance, are voluntary in nature.

Insurance institutions

There are several types of insurance institutions: state-owned insurance companies, insurance corporations, corporate insurance organizations, and individual insurance entities. The law allows a great variety of insurance services to be offered by various forms of insurance institutions in China.

Insurance contracts

Insurance contracts should be used to specify the obligations and responsibilities of the insurers and insurees. The contract can be a fixed value, non-fixed value, estate or life insurance contract. In particular, the format to determine premium payments, claim process and settlement compensation should be clearly stated.

Reinsurance

Under the law, a reinsurance transaction is allowed. An insurance company may transfer some of its responsibilities (or risks) to other participating insurance companies. The reinsurance can be a temporary arrangement, but sometimes it can be a fixed arrangement between insurance companies.

The Advertisement Law

The Chinese government enacted and enforced the Advertisement Law in the early 1990s, aimed at strengthening control of commercial advertisements appearing in the public media. The main provisions of this law are given below.

Overview of advertisements

In China, an advertisement can be economic (for promotion of merchandise), cultural (for art, films or science), social (for example, welfare, lost and found notes) and governmental (public announcements). The Advertisement Law addresses the purpose, principles and content limit of advertisements. Furthermore, it states the legal liability or penalties for people who breach advertising regulations or who violate the law.

Advertisement regulation

The law specifies the principles governing the regulation of advertisement activities, including specific requirements on the design, content and means of public media to be applied for different types of advertisement.

Qualification of advertising agents

Under the law, advertising agents are required to possess knowledge of marketing research, advertisement design and editing, as well as certain knowledge in professional financing.

Permission for advertisements

The law specifies that only eligible organizations are permitted to advertise publicly. For instance, only legally formed business entities with business licences issued by the SAIC can make commerce-related advertisements.

Conditions of issuing advertisements

The content of the advertisement must not be in violation of the Chinese laws and government regulations. Advertising of products with a sexual content is not permitted. In addition, a permit is required for advertising through the public media. Application for the permit should be addressed to the relevant governmental authorities. For instance, manufacturers of food products must apply to the Department of Public Health for permission to advertise their products.

Violation and penalty

If an organization violates the Advertisement Law, for example using fraudulent advertising to attract customers, it will be punished by a fine of a specific sum, or may even lose its business licence if the violation is severe in nature.

Appeal process

If an advertising firm does not agree with the verdict laid down by the government authority in charge of advertisement administration, the firm can apply for retrial within 15 days of the verdict being served. If it is not satisfied with the result of the retrial, it can appeal its case to the administrative authority at a higher level of government within 30 days of the retrial decision being notified.

The Trademark Law

The provisions of Trademark Law are as follows:

Overview

Under the Trademark Law and its implementing regulations, foreign businesses seeking to obtain protection for their trademarks must retain an agent authorized by the SAIC. The Trademark Law is designed to protect the right of the individual who owns trademarks, and to punish those who violate the law.

Monopoly of trademark

The law states that a holder has an exclusive right to use the trademark, and no one can use it unless he or she receives permission from the owner. The trademark also specifies the usage in terms of time and geographic area.

Subject and object of trademark

The person who registers the trademark and those who get permission to use it are the subjects of trademark. Then, after a trademark has been registered by the State Administration of Trademark, its name and logo become the objects of trademark.

Application for trademark registration

An applicant is allowed to use the same registered trademark on different products. If there is any change needed regarding the applicant, such as the address of the applicant, or the trademark itself, for example the word or logo, the applicant should reapply for registration.

Life of trademark

The life of a registered trademark is ten years. However, it can be renewed six months prior to the expiry date. As a result, the life of a trademark can be extended indefinitely.

Transferability

A holder has the right to transfer the registered trademark to other parties. However, filing with, and permission from, the State Administration of Trademark are required.

Contract

A holder can allow other people to use a registered trademark by entering a legally binding contract. Both parties must be bound by the specified rights and responsibilities. For instance, the party who receive the permission cannot use the trademark outside the assigned area.

Cancellation

A trademark will be cancelled in one of three situations: registering an illegal trademark, breaching the Trademark Law or other regulations, or where a dispute regarding trademark cannot be reasonably resolved.

The Antitrust Law

Starting on 1 December 1993, the Antitrust Law has been put into effect in China. The law aims at protecting trade and commerce from unfair competition, unlawful restraints, price discrimination, price fixing and monopoly. Some provisions of this law follow.

Definition of anti-competition activity

According to the law, anti-competition activities include using fraudulent trademarks, packaging and names, acting as a monopoly, stealing trade secrets, offering or receiving bribery and destroying other competitors' reputation by the spreading of fraudulent 'facts'.

Supervision and regulation

This law empowers the central government with the right to examine, inquire, investigate and punish companies that are involved in anti-competition activities.

Legal liabilities of offenders

Violators of the Antitrust Law may face a forfeiture of the profits that have been earned from the anti-competition activities. Government authorities may redirect the forfeited profits to compensate the companies which have experienced damages in the operations. Offenders may even lose their business licences if the violation of the law is severe in nature.

BUSINESS LAWS FOR ENTERPRISES WITH FOREIGN INVESTMENT

As mentioned earlier, direct foreign investment in China mainly takes one of three forms: (1) equity joint ventures between Chinese and foreign partners, (2) contractual joint ventures (also called 'Sino-foreign cooperative enterprises'), and (3) wholly foreign-owned subsidiaries. Over two-thirds of the foreign invested enterprises in China are currently in the form of equity joint ventures. In addition, foreign investors were permitted, in 1991, to invest in listed companies for the first time through the vehicle of B shares, which are registered shares denominated in RMB ¥ (Chinese currency) listed on the stock exchanges in China and offered exclusively to foreign investors for purchase and sale using foreign currency (in US or Hong Kong dollars).

The Chinese government has made great efforts to attract foreign investment since the beginning of the 1980s. For example, it has enacted legislation and regulations applicable exclusively to foreign-affiliated business entities, with certain special provisions or treatments being granted. The two major pieces of business law governing foreign invested enterprises are *The Law of the People's Republic of China on the Joint Ventures with Chinese and Foreign Capital* and *The Income Tax Law of the People's Republic for Enterprises with Foreign Investment and Foreign Invested Companies*.

The Chinese–Foreign Joint Ventures Law

This Joint Ventures Law is one of the most important pieces of business legislation in China, since it was the first state legislation laying down a legal foundation to deal with foreign investment. The law was originally enacted and enforced in the early 1980s, and has contributed significantly to the huge inflows of badly needed foreign capital in the last 15 years. The law contains the following main provisions.

Overview of joint ventures

Under the law, a joint venture is defined as a form of partnership between Chinese and foreign investors. The joint venture can be organized in the form either of a contractual venture or of an equity venture. A venture should be mutually beneficial to Chinese and foreign investors.

Formation of joint ventures

Applications for the establishment of a joint venture with Chinese and foreign partners must include copies of the venture agreement, text of the contract, articles of joint venture and other relevant documents signed by both Chinese and foreign partners. The application forms should be submitted to the government department authorized by the State Council, that is the Ministry of Foreign Trade and International Cooperation, or its designates at the provincial level, for review and approval.

Capital contribution to joint ventures

The contributed capital can be made in the form of cash, physical assets, technology or industrial know-how, investment loans, leased properties in the name of the joint venture or utilization of a third party's assets. There is, however, a restriction on the maximum proportion of investment contributed in the form of intangibles. In addition, all capital contributed to a joint venture must be verified by CPAs registered with the Chinese government.

Management and profit sharing of joint ventures

Each joint venture is required to set up a board of directors to hold ultimate authority over operations of the venture. President, vice presidents and directors are responsible for handling strategic and operating decisions. After its financial statements have been audited by certified public accountants in China, the after-tax net profits can be distributed in accordance with the preset formula specified in the venture agreement.

Solutions to disputes

If disputes occur, they can be solved either through consultation among the venture's partners or their sponsoring entities, or through arbitration by external authorities, or by court settlement.

Termination

A joint venture may be dissolved in the following ways: (1) expiration of its contractual term, (2) inability to continue operation as a result of heavy operating losses, (3) inability to continue operation because of a breach of contract agreement or articles of venture, (4) inability to continue operation resulting from unforeseeable factors caused by force, such as war or natural disasters, (5) failure to achieve primary business objectives, and (6) other causes for dissolution that are prescribed in the contract agreement of the venture. Winding up of a joint venture must be filed with the government authorities who originally approved the joint venture and the liquidation accounts must be audited by Chinese CPAs.

The Income Tax Law for Foreign Invested Enterprises

Before 1990, the Chinese government adopted business administrative systems segregated by different business ownership. Thus there were separate income tax laws or regulations governing income taxes of the domestic and foreign invested enterprises. Even for foreign capital affiliated business entities, separate income taxes were applied to the three different forms of foreign invested enterprises, that is, equity joint ventures, contractual joint ventures and wholly foreign-owned subsidiaries, although there was no substantial difference among these three sets of income tax regulations.

In order to harmonize the income tax system, and to stimulate more foreign investment, China's National People's Congress enacted *The Income Tax Law of the People's Republic of China for Enterprises With Foreign Investment and Foreign Enterprises* in summer 1993. The new law imposes a uniform income tax system for all foreign invested enterprises in China. The law identifies two general classes of taxpayers: foreign enterprises and domestic enterprises with foreign investments. A foreign enterprise is taxable only on income derived in China, while a domestic enterprise is taxable on all of its income, including the income earned from foreign sources. In most cases, foreign invested enterprises are eligible for certain preferential tax treatments, such as tax reduction and exemptions. Varied conditions however, have been applied to the preferential tax treatments for foreign invested enterprises following the tax reforms adopted by the Chinese government in recent years. Readers may revisit Chapter 8 to obtain more detailed information on current tax policies governing foreign invested enterprises.

Appendix A

THE ACCOUNTING LAW OF THE PEOPLE'S REPUBLIC OF CHINA

(ADOPTED ON 21 JANUARY 1985 AT THE NINTH SESSION OF THE STANDING COMMITTEE OF THE SIXTH NATIONAL PEOPLE'S CONGRESS. AMENDED ACCORDING TO THE 'RESOLUTION ON THE AMENDMENT OF THE ACCOUNTING LAW OF THE PEOPLE'S REPUBLIC OF CHINA' ADOPTED ON 29 DECEMBER 1993 AT THE FIFTH SESSION OF THE STANDING COMMITTEE OF THE EIGHTH NATIONAL PEOPLE'S CONGRESS)

Chapter I   General provisions

Article 1

This law is enacted to strengthen accounting work, to ensure that accounting staff exercise their duties and rights according to the law and to bring into full play the role of accounting in upholding the order of the socialist market economy, in strengthening economic management and in improving economic efficiency and benefits.

Article 2

Government agencies, social organizations, enterprises, non-business units, private industrial and commercial entities and other organizations shall abide by this law in handling accounting affairs.

Article 3

Accounting offices and accounting staff shall abide by the laws and regulations in handling accounting affairs, doing accounting calculation and

295

exercising accounting supervision, in accordance with the stipulations of this law.

Article 4

Administrative officers of each unit shall lead their accounting offices, accounting staff and other personnel in implementing this law; ensure the legitimacy, truthfulness, accuracy and completeness of accounting information; and shall ensure that the functions and rights of accounting staff are not infringed upon. Nobody shall be allowed to attack or retaliate against accounting staff.

Moral and material rewards shall be given to the accounting staff who make notable achievements in conscientiously implementing this law and who are devoted to their duties.

Article 5

The public finance department of the State Council shall regulate the accounting work of the entire country.

The public finance departments of local people's governments at each level shall regulate the accounting work of their respective jurisdictions.

Article 6

A State uniform accounting system shall be formulated by the public finance department of the State Council according to this law. The public finance department of the people's government of each province, autonomous region and municipality directly under the central government, the industrial regulatory departments of the State Council and the General Logistics Department of the Chinese People's Liberation Army may formulate the practical rules or supplemental stipulations to implement the state uniform accounting system, which must be submitted to the public finance department of the State Council for examination and approval or for the record, as long as this law and the state uniform accounting system are not contravened.

Chapter II   Accounting calculation

Article 7

Accounting treatment and accounting calculation shall be done for the following transactions:

(a) receipts and disbursements of cash holdings and securities;
(b) receipts, issuance, additions, deductions and uses of assets;
(c) formations and settlements of debts and claims;
(d) increases and decreases of funds, receipts and outlays of appropriations;
(e) computations of revenue, expenses and costs;
(f) computations and treatments of financial results;
(g) other transactions that may require accounting treatment and accounting calculation.

Article 8

The fiscal year shall run from 1 January to 31 December of the Gregorian calendar year.

Article 9

Accounting books shall be kept with *Renminbi* as the bookkeeping currency unit.

Entities with operational receipts and disbursements mainly denominated in foreign currencies may choose a foreign currency as the bookkeeping unit; however, all accounting statements must be expressed in *Renminbi*.

Article 10

Accounting documents, books of account, accounting statements and other accounting information must be consistent with the stipulations of the state uniform accounting system. The accounting documents and books should be free of falsification, and no false accounting statements shall be reported.

Entities adopting computerized accounting systems shall ensure their application software and all accounting documents, books, statements and other accounting information generated therein be in accordance with the relevant regulations stipulated by the public finance department of the State Council.

Article 11

Source documents shall be filled out and filed in a timely manner to the accounting office, for handling the transactions as specified in Article 7 of this law.

Accounting offices must examine the source documents and prepare accounting vouchers based on the examined original documents.

Article 12

Each unit shall set up its chart of accounts and books of account in accordance with the stipulations of the state uniform accounting system.

Accounting offices shall record their books on the basis of the examined source documents and accounting vouchers in accordance with the stipulations specifying the bookkeeping rules in the state uniform accounting system.

Article 13

Each unit shall set up its physical inventory system and ensure that the accounting records conform with physical assets and cash holdings.

Article 14

Each unit shall prepare its accounting statements using records in accounting books as the basis and in accordance with the stipulations of the state uniform accounting system. The accounting statements shall be reported to the public finance department and other departments concerned.

Accounting statements shall be signed or sealed by the unit administrative officer and the accounting staff in charge. The leader, the chief accountant or the controller in a unit which has established the position of controller shall also sign or seal the accounting statements.

Article 15

Accounting documents, books of account, accounting statements and other accounting information shall have files established and properly maintained as required by the relevant state regulations. The stipulations on the retention period and the destruction procedures shall be formulated jointly by the public finance department of the State Council and other relevant government departments.

Chapter III Accounting supervision

Article 16

Accounting offices and accounting staff shall exercise accounting supervision in their respective units.

Article 17

Accounting offices and accounting staff shall not accept any source document that is not faithful or not legitimate. Source documents with inaccurate and incomplete records shall be returned for correction and supplementation.

Article 18

Accounting offices and accounting staff who have found that the records in accounting books do not conform to the physical assets and cash holdings shall resolve the issue in accordance with relevant stipulations. If they have no authority to handle the discrepancy by themselves, they shall report immediately to the administrative leaders of their units to request an investigation of the cause and a settlement of the issue in question.

Article 19

Accounting offices and accounting staff shall not handle any receipts or disbursements that violate the state regulations.

Accounting offices and accounting staff shall stop and correct the operating receipts and disbursements that they believe are in violation of the state regulations. They shall report in writing to the administrative leaders of the units to request corrective action, if they are unable to stop or correct the irregularities by themselves.

Accounting offices and accounting staff may be liable for the receipts or disbursements that violate the state regulations if they do not take action to stop or correct the irregularities, or fail to report in writing to the administrative leaders of their units.

Accounting offices and accounting staff shall report to the superior administrative units or the government departments of public finance, auditing and taxation any unlawful receipts and disbursements that have caused severe damage to the interests of the state and the general public. The superior administrative units or the government departments who receive the report shall take action to handle the issue.

Article 20

Each unit must, in accordance with the state laws and other relevant regulations, accept supervision exercised by the auditing agency, public finance agency and tax agency; and must truthfully provide the government agencies with accounting documents, books of account, accounting statements, other accounting information and relevant data. No rejection of supervision, concealment of information, or falsification of reporting shall be allowed.

Chapter IV   Accounting offices and accounting personnel

Article 21

Each unit shall install an accounting office or set up in a relevant office positions for accounting staff with designated accounting staff in charge, subject to the needs of its accounting work. Those units which are short of the accounting resources may contract out their bookkeeping task to the accounting or business consulting agencies that are organized under the approval of government authorities. Large and medium-sized enterprises, non-business units and business administrative departments may establish positions of controllers. The position of a controller shall be held by a person with the technical title of accountant or a senior professional title.

Accounting offices shall establish in themselves an internal cross-checking system. A cashier should not work concurrently as transaction verifier, accounting file keeper or bookkeeper in charge of revenue, expenses, claims and liability accounts.

Article 22

The main functions of accounting offices and accounting staff are:

(a)   accounting calculation pursuant to Chapter II of this law;
(b)   accounting supervision pursuant to Chapter III of this law;
(c)   formulation of specific procedures to handle accounting affairs in their respective units;
(d)   participation in formulating economic plans and examination and analysis of the results of the execution of budget and financial plans; and
(e)   conducting other accounting affairs.

Article 23

Accounting staff shall possess the necessary professional knowledge. The appointment or removal of chief accounting officers and accounting staff in charge in the state-owned enterprises or non-business units shall be approved by their superior administrative units. Casual removal or dismissal of these accounting personnel is not allowed. If an accounting staff member who is loyal to his or her duties and adheres to principle is mistreated, the superior administrative unit shall instruct the unit in which he or she works to correct the treatment. If an accounting staff member proves himself or herself unsuitable for accounting work owing to negligence or betrayal of principle, the superior administrative unit shall instruct the unit in which he or she works to dismiss him or her.

Article 24

Accounting staff who are changing or leaving their working positions must clear their handing over procedure with the staff who are assuming those positions.

The chief accounting officer and accounting staff in charge shall supervise such transitions for general accounting staff. The unit administrative leader shall supervise such transitional procedures for the chief accounting officer and accounting staff in charge and the superior administrative unit may send a delegate in to participate in the supervision of transfers of accounts, when necessary.

Chapter V   Legal liability

Article 25

Administrative discipline shall be taken against those unit administrative leaders and accounting staff who seriously violate the stipulations on accounting calculation in Chapter II of this law.

Article 26

Those unit leaders, accounting staff and other personnel who have counterfeited, deceptively altered or deliberately destroyed accounting documents, books of account, accounting statements and other accounting information, or have committed tax evasion or caused severe damage to the interests of the state and the general public, shall be sanctioned by the public finance agency, auditing agency, taxation agency, or other administrative authorities, in accordance with the stipulations of the state laws and other administrative regulations. Criminal liability shall be determined in cases where the violation of the state laws is evident.

Article 27

Administrative sanction shall be taken against those accounting staff who have accepted and processed source documents that they clearly know to be not faithful or not legitimate; against those accounting staff who do not report in writing the unlawful operating receipts or disbursements to the administrative leader of the unit; against those accounting staff who do not report to the superior administrative unit or the government's public finance agency, auditing agency or taxation agency the unlawful receipts and disbursements that have caused severe damage to the interests of the state and the general public. Criminal liability shall be determined in cases where violation of the state laws, or grave loss to public or private properties, is evident.

Article 28

Administrative sanction shall be taken against those unit administrative leaders who have, upon receiving the written reports from the accounting staff pursuant to the second paragraph of Article 19 of this law, insisted on the processing of the unlawful receipts and disbursements, or failed to take action against the reported irregularities within the stipulated period without adequate reason. Criminal liability shall be determined in cases where violation of the state laws, or grave loss to public or private properties, is evident.

Article 29

Administrative sanction shall be taken against those unit administrative leaders and other personnel who attack or retaliate against accounting staff who perform their functions and duties pursuant to this law. Criminal liability shall be determined if the violation of laws is evident.

Chapter VI   Other provisions

Article 30

This law shall be implemented on and after 1 May 1985.

[Appendix. *The Resolution on the Amendment of 'The Accounting Law of the People's Republic of China'*, adopted on 29 December 1993 at the Fifth Session of the Standing Committee of the Eighth National People's Congress (omitted). The Resolution shall go into effect immediately.]

Appendix B

THE AUDIT LAW OF THE PEOPLE'S REPUBLIC OF CHINA

(ADOPTED AT THE NINTH MEETING OF THE STANDING
COMMITTEE OF THE EIGHTH NATIONAL PEOPLE'S CONGRESS
ON 31 AUGUST 1994, PROMULGATED BY ORDER NO. 32 OF THE
PRESIDENT OF THE PEOPLE'S REPUBLIC OF CHINA ON 31
AUGUST 1994 AND EFFECTIVE AS OF 1 JANUARY 1995)

Chapter I   General provisions

Article 1

This law is formulated in accordance with the Constitution, with a view to strengthening the state supervision through auditing, maintaining the financial and economic order of the country, promoting the building of an incorruptible government and ensuring the healthy development of the national economy.

Article 2

The state shall practise a system of supervision through auditing. The State Council and the local people's governments at or above the county level shall establish audit institutions.

Revenues and expenditures of various departments of the State Council, of the local people's governments at various levels and their departments, revenues and expenditures of state-owned monetary organizations, enterprises and institutions, as well as other revenues and expenditures subject to auditing according to this law, shall be supervised through auditing in accordance with the provisions of this law.

Audit institutions shall, according to law, supervise through auditing the authenticity, legality and effectiveness of the revenues and expenditures specified in the preceding paragraph.

Article 3

Audit institutions shall conduct supervision through auditing in accordance with the functions, powers and procedures prescribed by the law.

Article 4

The State Council and the local people's governments at or above the county level shall annually present to the standing committees of the people's congresses at the corresponding levels the audit reports prepared by audit institutions on budget implementation and other revenues and expenditures.

Article 5

Audit institutions shall independently exercise their power of supervision through auditing in accordance with the law, subject to no interference by any administrative organ or any public organization or individual.

Article 6

Audit institutions and auditors shall, in performing their audit items, be objective and fair, practical and realistic, upright and honest, and not divulge confidential information.

Chapter II   Audit institutions and auditors

Article 7

The State Council shall establish the National Audit Office to take charge of the audit work throughout the country under the leadership of the premier of the State Council. The auditor general shall be the administrative leader of the National Audit Office.

Article 8

Audit institutions of the people's governments of provinces, autonomous regions, municipalities directly under the central government, cities divided into districts, autonomous prefectures, counties, autonomous counties, cities not divided into districts and municipal districts shall be in charge of the audit work within their respective administrative areas under the respective leadership of governors of provinces, chairmen of autonomous regions,

mayors, prefectural heads or heads of counties and districts as well as under
the leadership of audit institutions at the next higher level.

Article 9

Local audit institutions at various levels shall be responsible for and report
on their work to the people's governments at the corresponding levels and to
audit institutions at the next higher levels, and their audit work shall be
directed chiefly by the audit institutions at the next higher levels.

Article 10

Audit institutions may, as required by work, designate resident audit officers
to areas under their jurisdiction.

Resident audit officers shall, according to the authorization of audit institutions, conduct audit work in accordance with the law.

Article 11

Funds required by audit institutions for performing their functions shall be
listed in the budgets of and guaranteed by the people's governments at the
corresponding levels.

Article 12

Auditors shall possess the professional knowledge and ability suited to the
audit work they engage in.

Article 13

Auditors shall withdraw from performing audit projects if they have an
interest in the auditees or the audit projects.

Article 14

Auditors shall have the obligations to guard state secrets and the auditees'
trade secrets they have come to know in performing their functions.

Article 15

Auditors shall be protected by law in performing their functions in accordance with the law.

No organization or individual may reject or obstruct auditors from performing their functions in accordance with the law, or retaliate against them.

Persons in charge of audit institutions shall be appointed or removed in accordance with legal procedures. None of them may be removed or replaced at will unless they are found guilty of illegal acts, or are negligent or no longer qualified for the appointment.

Chapter III   Responsibilities of audit institutions

Article 16

Audit institutions shall exercise supervision through auditing over the budget implementation, final accounts and management and use of extrabudgetary funds of departments (including their subordinate units) at the corresponding levels and of the people's governments at lower levels.

Article 17

The National Audit Office shall, under the leadership of the premier of the State Council, exercise supervision through auditing over the implementation of the budget of the central government and submit audit reports thereof to the premier.

Local audit institutions at various levels shall, under the respective leadership of the governors of provinces, chairmen of autonomous regions, mayors, prefectural heads and heads of counties or districts, as well as under the leadership of audit institutions at the next higher levels, exercise supervision through auditing over the budget implementation at the corresponding levels and submit audit reports to the people's governments at the corresponding levels and to the audit institutions at the next higher levels.

Article 18

The National Audit Office shall exercise supervision through auditing over the revenues and expenditures of the central bank.

Audit institutions shall exercise supervision through auditing over the assets, liabilities, profits and losses of the state-owned financial institutions.

Article 19

Audit institutions shall exercise supervision through auditing over the revenues and expenditures of the state administrative institutions.

Article 20

Audit institutions shall exercise supervision through auditing over the assets, liabilities, profits and losses of the state-owned enterprises.

Article 21

Audit institutions shall conduct audit in a periodic and planned way of the state-owned enterprises that are vital to the national economy and the people's livelihood, or state-owned enterprises that depend heavily upon government subsidies, or have a large amount of losses, and other state-owned enterprises designated by the State Council or the people's governments at the corresponding levels.

Article 22

Supervision through auditing over the enterprises with state-owned assets controlling their shares or playing a leading role shall be stipulated by the State Council.

Article 23

Audit institutions shall exercise supervision through auditing over the budget implementation and final accounts of the state construction projects.

Article 24

Audit institutions shall exercise supervision through auditing over the revenues and expenditures of the social security funds, public donations and other relevant funds and capital managed by governmental departments and public organizations authorized by the government.

Article 25

Audit institutions shall exercise supervision through auditing over the revenues and expenditures of projects with aids or loans provided by international organizations or governments of other countries.

Article 26

In addition to the audit items stipulated by this law, audit institutions shall exercise supervision through auditing over the items that shall be audited by audit institutions as stipulated by other laws, administrative rules and regulations, in accordance with the provisions of this law as well as relevant laws, administrative rules and regulations.

Article 27

With regard to the particular items relating to state revenues and expenditures, audit institutions shall have the right to carry out special investigations through audit from relevant localities, departments and units and report the results thereof to the people's governments at the corresponding levels and to the audit institutions at the next higher levels.

Article 28

Audit institutions shall determine their audit jurisdiction on the basis of the auditees' financially subordinate relations or the supervisory and managerial relations with respect to the state assets of auditees.

Where a dispute arises on audit jurisdiction between audit institutions, the matter shall be determined by an audit institution superior to both disputing parties.

Audit institutions at higher levels may authorize audit institutions at lower levels to audit the items under their jurisdiction as stipulated from paragraph 2 of Article 18 to Article 25 in this law. Audit institutions at higher levels may directly audit the major items under the jurisdiction of audit institutions at lower levels. However, unnecessary repetitive audits shall be avoided.

Article 29

Departments of the State Council and of the local people's governments at various levels, state-owned financial institutions, enterprises and institutions shall establish and improve their internal auditing systems in accordance with the relevant provisions of the state. Such internal auditing shall be subject to the professional guidance and supervision of state audit institutions.

Article 30

Public audit firms that independently conduct public audit according to law shall be guided, supervised and managed in accordance with relevant laws and provisions of the State Council.

Chapter IV   Rights of audit institutions

Article 31

Audit institutions shall have the right to require auditees to submit, in accordance with the relevant provisions, their budgets or plans for financial revenues and expenditures, statements about budget implementation, final accounts and financial reports, audit reports produced by public audit firms and other information relating to their revenues and expenditures. Auditees shall not refuse to do so, or delay the submission or make false reports.

Article 32

Audit institutions shall, in conducting audit, have the right to examine the accounting documents, account books, accounting statements and other information and assets relating to revenues and expenditures of the auditees, and the auditees shall not refuse to produce those materials.

Article 33

Audit institutions shall, in conducting audit, have the power to carry out investigations among units or individuals concerned into matters relating to audit items and to obtain relevant testimonial materials. The units and individuals concerned shall support and assist the audit institutions in their work by providing them with truthful information and relevant testimonial materials.

Article 34

When audit institutions conduct audit, the auditees shall not transfer, conceal, falsify or destroy their accounting documents, books of account, accounting statements or other information relating to their revenues and expenditures, and shall not transfer or conceal the assets that are in their possession but obtained in violation of the provisions of the state.

Audit institutions shall have the right to stop the ongoing acts of the auditees relating to the revenues and expenditures in violation of the provisions of the state. If they do not succeed in stopping such acts, they shall, with the approval of the responsible persons of audit institutions at or above the county level, notify the financial departments and the competent authorities to suspend allocating funds directly related to the acts in violation of the provisions of the state regarding the revenues and expenditures or to suspend the use of the funds already allocated. However, adoption of the above-mentioned measures shall not hinder the lawful business activities, production and operation of the auditees.

Article 35

If audit institutions consider that the regulations of the competent departments at higher levels on revenues and expenditures implemented by the auditees contravene the law or the administrative rules and regulations, they shall suggest that the competent departments concerned make corrections. If the departments concerned fail to make corrections, the audit institutions shall refer the matter to the competent authorities for disposition according to law.

Article 36

Audit institutions may issue circulars about their audit results to the relevant governmental departments or publish such results to the public.

Audit institutions shall, in circulating or publishing audit results, keep state secrets and trade secrets of the auditees in accordance with the law and observe the relevant provisions of the State Council.

Chapter V   Audit procedures

Article 37

Audit institutions shall form audit teams according to the audit project specified in the plans of the audit programmes and shall serve audit notifications on the auditees three days prior to the execution of audit.

The auditees shall cooperate with audit institutions in their work and provide necessary working facilities.

Article 38

Auditors shall conduct audit and obtain testimonial materials by means of examining accounting documents, books of account, accounting statements, and documents and data relating to the audit items, checking cash, negotiable securities and other property, and making investigations of the units and individuals concerned.

Auditors shall, in making investigations of the units and individuals concerned, produce their work attestations and a copy of the audit notification.

Article 39

Audit teams shall, after the completion of field audit, submit audit reports to the audit institutions. However, prior to the submission, they shall solicit opinions of the auditees. The auditees shall, within ten days from the date of receiving the audit reports, send their comments in written form to the audit teams or audit institutions.

Article 40

Audit institutions shall, after examining the audit reports, give an appraisal of the audit items and produce their audit opinions. They shall, within the sphere of their statutory functions and powers, make audit decisions on revenues and expenditures in violation of the provisions of the state, that must be dealt with or punished according to law, or they shall make suggestions concerning such disposition or punishment to the competent authorities.

Audit institutions shall, within 30 days from the date of receiving the audit reports, serve their audit opinions and audit decisions on the auditees and units concerned.

Audit decisions shall enter into effect from the date when they are duly served.

Chapter VI   Legal liability

Article 41

If an auditee, in violation of this law, refuses or delays provision of information relating to the audit items, refuses or hinders examination, the audit institution concerned shall order the auditee to make correction or may circulate a notice of criticism and issue a warning. Anyone refusing to make correction shall be investigated for responsibility in accordance with the law.

Article 42

When an audit institution discovers an auditee, in violation of the provisions of this law, transfers, conceals, falsifies or destroys accounting documents, books of account, accounting statements or other materials relating to the revenues and expenditures, the audit institution shall have the power to stop such acts.

If an auditee commits any of the acts specified in the preceding paragraph, and if the audit institution considers that the persons in charge and other persons held directly responsible shall be given administrative sanctions according to law, the audit institution shall put forward suggestions to this effect. And the auditee or its overseeing organ or the supervisory authority shall make decisions without delay in accordance with the law. If the offence constitutes a crime, the judicial organ shall investigate for criminal responsibility according to law.

Article 43

If an auditee, in violation of this law, transfers or conceals assets gained unlawfully, the audit institution, the people's government or the competent authorities shall have the power to stop such acts within the sphere of its statutory functions and rights or appeal to the court for adoption of preservative measures.

If an auditee commits any of the acts specified in the preceding paragraph, and if an audit institution considers that the persons in charge and other persons held directly responsible shall be given administrative sanctions according to law, the audit institution shall put forward suggestions to this effect. And the auditee or its overseeing organ or the supervisory authority shall make a decision without delay in accordance with the law. If the offence constitutes a crime, the judicial organ shall investigate for criminal responsibility according to law.

Article 44

Audit institutions, the people's governments or the competent authorities shall, within the sphere of their statutory functions and rights and in accordance with the laws, and administrative rules and regulations, deal with the acts violating the state budgets committed by departments (including their subordinate units) at the corresponding levels or the governments at lower levels or other acts in violation of the provisions of the state regarding revenues and expenditures.

Article 45

If an auditee commits any acts in violation of the provisions of the state regarding revenues and expenditures, the audit institution, the people's government or the competent authorities shall, within the sphere of its statutory functions and rights and in accordance with the laws, and administrative rules and regulations, order the auditee to turn over within a time limit the

part of the revenues that shall be turned over, to return within a time limit
the income gained unlawfully or the state-owned assets illegally seized, or
take other corrective measures, and may impose penalties on the auditee
according to law.

Article 46

With respect to the persons in charge and other persons held directly responsible for the acts committed by the auditee in violation of the provisions of
the state regarding revenues and expenditures, if the audit institution considers that they shall be given administrative sanctions according to law, the
audit institution shall put forward suggestions to this effect. The auditee or
its overseeing organ, or the supervisory authority shall make a decision
without delay in accordance with the law.

Article 47

If an auditee violates the provisions of relevant laws, or administrative rules
and regulations, in matters of its revenues and expenditures and if the
offence constitutes a crime, the auditee shall be investigated for criminal
responsibility according to law.

Article 48

Whoever retaliates or makes a false charge against auditors shall, if such an
act constitutes a crime, be investigated for criminal responsibility; if such an
act does not constitute a crime, he shall be given administrative sanctions.

Article 49

If an auditor abuses his functions and rights, engages in malpractices for
selfish ends, or neglects his duties, and if his act constitutes a crime, he shall
be investigated for criminal responsibility; if his act does not constitute a
crime, he shall be given administrative sanctions.

Chapter VII Supplementary provisions

Article 50

Regulations on audit in the Chinese People's Liberation Army shall be
formulated by the Central Military Commission in accordance with this law.

Article 51

This law shall enter into effect as of 1 January 1995. *The Audit Regulations of the People's Republic of China* promulgated by the State Council on 30 November 1988 shall be annulled therefrom.

Appendix C

THE CERTIFIED PUBLIC ACCOUNTANT LAW OF THE PEOPLE'S REPUBLIC OF CHINA

(APPROVED ON 31 OCTOBER 1993 AT THE FOURTH SESSION OF THE STANDING COMMITTEE OF THE EIGHTH NATIONAL PEOPLE'S CONGRESS OF THE PEOPLE'S REPUBLIC OF CHINA)

Chapter I General provisions

Article 1

This law is formulated in order to give full play to their function in examining and servicing socioeconomic activities of certified public accountants (CPAs), strengthen the administration of CPAs, safeguard social and public interests and legitimate interests of investors, and promote the healthy development of a socialist market economy.

Article 2

CPAs are persons who have obtained CPA certificates in accordance with the law and practise auditing, accounting consulting work and accounting services by accepting commissions.

Article 3

A public accounting firm is an organization composed of CPAs and established in accordance with the law to render CPA services. A CPA shall become a member of a public accounting firm to practise his/her profession.

Article 4

A certified public accountants' association is a social organization composed of CPAs. The Chinese Institute of CPAs (CICPA) is the national organization of CPAs and CPAs' associations of the province, autonomous region, or directly administered municipality are the local organizations of CPAs.

Article 5

CPAs, public accounting firms and CPAs' associations will be given supervision and guidance by the Ministry of Finance of the State Council and the Finance Department of the people's government of the provinces, autonomous regions or directly administered municipalities in accordance with the law.

Article 6

CPAs and public accounting firms must abide by the law and administrative regulations to practise their profession. CPAs and public accounting firms shall practise their profession on an independent and fair basis and shall receive the protection of the law.

Chapter II   Examination and registration

Article 7

The state will implement the National Uniform Certified Public Accountant Examination (NUCPAE) system. The procedures of the NUCPAE will be formulated by the Ministry of Finance, and organized and enforced by the CICPA.

Article 8

Any Chinese citizen who is a college graduate, or has held an intermediate or higher professional grade in accounting or related fields, may apply to sit for the NUCPAE. Persons who have held senior professional grades in accounting or related fields may be exempted from certain subjects of the examination.

Article 9

A candidate who has passed the NUCPAE and has two or more years' auditing experience, may apply for registration to CPAs' associations of the province, autonomous region or directly administered municipalities. Except for the situations listed in Article 10 of this law, the CPAs' association which has accepted an application shall approve for registration.

Article 10

In the event of any of the following situations, the CPAs' association, which has accepted an application, shall not approve for registration:

(1)   the applicant's civil right has been impaired;
(2)   the application date for registration of an applicant is less than five years from the last day of implementation of penalty due to the applicant's past criminal conduct;
(3)   the application date for registration of an applicant is less than two years from the decision date of imposing penalty or punishment on him/her due to the applicant's past serious mistake made in finance, accounting, auditing, business administration or other economic administration work resulting in administrative penalty or discharge from his/her job;
(4)   the application date for registration of an applicant is less than five years from the decision date of penalty on him/her to revoke his/her CPA certificate;
(5)   other situations under which registration will not be approved by the regulations of the Ministry of Finance of the State Council shall be included.

Article 11

The CPAs' association shall file with the Ministry of Finance the name list of the applicants who have been approved for registration. Should the Ministry of Finance find the approval of a certain candidate to be inconsistent with regulations of this law, it shall notify the related CPAs' association to dismiss the registration. The CPAs' association shall notify in writing the applicant who is not approved for registration in accordance with the provisions in Article 10 of this law within 15 days of the decision date.

In case the applicant has an objection, he/she can appeal for reconsideration to the Ministry of Finance of the State Council or the finance department of the people's government of the province, autonomous region or directly administered municipality.

Article 12

The CPAs' association shall issue the CPA certificates prepared by the Ministry of Finance to the applicants who have been approved for registration.

Article 13

Registration of the persons who have obtained CPA certificates, under any of the following situations in addition to the situations in paragraph 1 of Article 11, will be dismissed and their CPA certificates will be recalled by the CPAs' association.

(1) a person who has lost his civil rights;
(2) a person who is under criminal penalty;
(3) a person who is under administrative penalty or is discharged from his/her job due to his/her past serious mistake made in finance, accounting, auditing, business administration or other economic administration work;
(4) a person who has not been in accounting practice of his/her own will for one year.

The person whose registration has been revoked can apply for reconsideration to the Ministry of Finance of the State Council or the finance department of the people's government of the province, autonomous region or directly administered municipality within 15 days of the date of receipt of the notification of revocation of registration and recall of CPA certificate, in the event that he/she has an objection.

A person whose registration has been revoked in accordance with the provision in paragraph 1 of Article 11 may reapply for registration, but the application shall conform to the provisions of Articles 9 and 10 of this law.

Chapter III   Scope and rules of business

Article 14

CPAs handle the following auditing work:

(1) auditing accounting statements of enterprises and issuing audit reports;
(2) verifying the assets of an enterprise and issuing asset verification reports;
(3) the audit work in merger, separation and liquidation of enterprises and issuing related reports;
(4) other auditing work stipulated by the laws and administrative regulations.

The reports issued by CPAs when practising audit work in accordance with the law have an attestation effect.

Article 15

CPAs can handle accounting consulting work and accounting service work.

Article 16

The public accounting firms for which the CPAs work shall accept business from clients and sign contracts with clients. The public accounting firm shall have civil responsibility for the work conducted by its CPAs in accordance with the regulations set forth.

Article 17

CPAs may review a client's related accounting material and documents, inspect a client's business location and facilities, and request a client to provide other necessary assistance as appropriate.

Article 18

Should there be a conflict or interest between a CPA and the client, the CPA shall withdraw from the case. The client has the right to request his/her withdrawal.

Article 19

CPAs shall have the obligation to maintain strict confidentiality in respect of confidential information acquired in the process of their professional work.

Article 20

Should a CPA discover any of the following situations during the course of his/her work, he/she shall refuse to issue related reports:

(1)   any suggestion from the client that a false or improper testimony be given;

(2)   failure of the client to provide related accounting material and documents on purpose;

(3)   failure to make correct statements on the important financial accounting subjects in the audit report issued by the CPA due to the unreasonable requirements of the client.

Article 21

CPAs shall issue audit reports in accordance with work procedures stipulated by regulations and rules of performing professional services when conducting professional work. Any of the following conduct by a CPA in the course of practising professional work and issuing audit reports is disallowed:

(1)   failure to point out, when known by the CPA, the client's handling of certain important subjects in financial accounting which is in conflict with the state's related regulations;

(2)   concealing, or issuing false reports on, the client's handling of certain important subjects in financial accounting which will endanger the interests of report users or other persons concerned, when known by the CPA;

(3)   failure to point out the client's handling of financial accounting which will mislead report users or other persons concerned, when known by the CPA;

(4)   failure to point out the false content in important subjects in the client's financial accounting reports, when known by the CPA.

The provisions set forth shall apply to conduct by the clients when known by the CPA in accordance with regulations and rules of their professional work.

Article 22

Any of the following conduct by a CPA is disallowed:

(1) purchase or sale of the stocks or bonds of the company being audited or purchase of the assets belonging to a company being audited or an individual, during the time limit that stocks or bonds of such company being audited cannot be purchased or sold or the assets of such company being audited or of such individual cannot be purchased, which is stipulated by the law and administrative regulations in the course of his/her audit work;

(2) asking for or accepting money or other asset beyond the contract price or seeking other improper interests by taking advantage of conducting profession;

(3) accepting a commission to press for payment of debt;

(4) allowing other persons to conduct audit work by using his/her name;

(5) practising at two or more public accounting firms at the same time;

(6) conducting advertisements for his/her capability to attract clients;

(7) other conduct which is against the law and administrative regulations.

Chapter IV Public accounting firms

Article 23

Public accounting firms can be formed by a CPA partnership. Liability of a public accounting firm formed by partnership shall be agreed upon by partners in accordance with the proportion of investment or agreement and shall be guaranteed by the partners' own assets. The partners shall be responsible for the related liability of their public accounting firm.

Article 24

A public accounting firm that meets the following requirements shall be qualified as a legal person with limited liability:

(1) having not less than RMB ¥300 000 registered capital;

(2) having a certain number of professional personnel, among whom shall be at least five CPAs;

(3) being within the scope of business and other requirements stipulated by the Ministry of Finance of the State Council.

A public accounting firm with limited liability shall have limited responsibility on its liability for all its assets.

Article 25

The establishment of a public accounting firm should be approved by the Ministry of Finance of State Council or the Finance Department of the people's government of the province, autonomous region or directly administered municipality.

When applying for establishment of a public accounting firm, the applicant shall submit the following documents to the examination and approval authority:

(1) application statement;
(2) name, organizational structure and business location of the public accounting firm;
(3) articles of the public accounting firm, partnership agreement if a partnership agreement exists;
(4) name, résumé and related certificate documents of CPAs,
(5) name, résumé and related certificate documents of the person in charge or principal partners of the public accounting firm;
(6) capital contribution certificate for a public accounting firm with limited liability;
(7) other documents required by the examination and approval authority.

Article 26

The examination and approval authority shall decide whether to approve or disapprove such application within 30 days of the date of receipt thereof. The applications of public accounting firms approved by the finance department of the people's government of the province, autonomous region or directly administered municipality shall be filed with the Ministry of Finance of the State Council. Should the Ministry of Finance of the State Council find the approval of a certain application to be inappropriate, it must notify the original examination and approval authority to carry out a re-examination within 30 days of date of receipt of such filing report.

Article 27

The establishment of a branch of a public accounting firm should be approved by the finance department of the people's government of the province, autonomous region or directly administered municipality in which the branch is located.

Article 28

Public accounting firms shall pay tax in accordance with the law. Public accounting firms shall set up a professional risk reserve in accordance with the regulations of the Ministry of Finance of the State Council and purchase professional insurance.

Article 29

Public accounting firms can conduct business beyond the limit of the administrative region and field, except under the specific regulations of the law and administrative regulations.

Article 30

No organization or individual is permitted to interfere in the client's contracting with the public accounting firm to perform professional services.

Article 31

The provisions of Articles 18 to 21 shall apply to public accounting firms.

Article 32

The conduct listed in items 1 to 4 and items 6 and 7 in Article 22 of this law is disallowed for public accounting firms.

Chapter V   Certified public accountants' association

Article 33

A CPA shall become a member of a certified public accountants' (CPAs') association.

Article 34

The articles of the CICPA shall be prepared by the national CPAs' congress and filed with the Ministry of Finance of the State Council. The articles of the CPAs' association of the province, autonomous region or directly administered municipality shall be prepared by CPAs' congress of the province, autonomous region or directly administered municipality and filed with the finance department of the people's government of the province, autonomous region or directly administered municipality.

Article 35

The CICPA will draft the business rules and regulations for CPAs. These rules and regulations will be implemented after approval of the Ministry of Finance of the State Council.

Article 36

The CPAs' association shall support the CPAs' practising profession in accordance with the law, maintain their legitimate interests and make comments and suggestions to related parties.

Article 37

The CPAs' association shall annually inspect the qualification and business situation of the CPAs.

Article 38

The CPAs' association shall be a social organization and a legal entity within the definition of the laws.

Chapter VI Legal liability

Article 39

Should a public accounting firm violate the provisions of Articles 20 and 21 of this law, the finance department of the people's government of the province may give a warning, confiscate the illegal proceeds and impose a fine which is more than one time but less than five times the amount of the illegal proceeds. In case of serious violation, the finance department of the people's government of the province may impose penalties such as suspension from practice or a dismissal order.

Should a CPA violate the provisions of Articles 20 and 21 of this law, the finance department of the people's government of the province may give a warning to him/her. In case of serious violation, the finance department of the people's government of the province may impose penalties such as suspension from practice or revocation of the CPA certificate.

Should a public accounting firm or a CPA violate the provisions of Articles 20 and 21 of this law, such as issuing a false audit report or a false asset verification report, which constitutes a criminal offence, the judicial organ will impose punishment in accordance of the law.

Article 40

Should an organization, without approval, handle the CPA services stipulated in Article 14 of this law, the finance department of the people's government of the province may force the organization to terminate its illegal activity, confiscate the illegal proceeds and impose a fine which is more than one time but less than five times the amount of the illegal proceeds.

Article 41

In case the parties concerned have an objection, they can apply for reconsideration to the superior authority of the organ which has made the penalty decision within 15 days of the date of receipt of the notification of penalty. The parties concerned can directly bring a suit in the people's court within 15 days of receiving the notification of penalty.

The authority in charge of reconsideration shall make the reconsideration decision within 60 days of the date of receipt of such reconsideration application. In case the parties concerned have an objection to the reconsideration decision, they can directly bring a suit in the people's court within 15 days of the date of receipt of such reconsideration decision. If the authority in charge of reconsideration has not made any decision after the time limit, the parties concerned can bring a suit in the people's court within 15 days from the date of the reconsideration period expiring.

In the event that the parties concerned have neither applied for reconsideration within the time limit, nor brought a suit in the people's court, nor carried out the penalty decision, the authority which has made the penalty decision may ask for the people's court to enforce the penalty.

Article 42

Should a CPA violate the provisions of this law, resulting in loss to the client or other related persons, he/she shall compensate for the loss in accordance with the law.

Chapter VII Supplementary provisions

Article 43

A certified public auditor who has been practising audit work and has met the qualifications of a CPA by confirmation, may practise business stipulated by this law. The confirmation of the qualification and the ways of supervising, guiding and controlling certified public auditors will be stipulated by the State Council.

Article 44

In case a foreigner applies to sit for the NUCPAE and registration, this will be handled in accordance with the principle of mutual benefit.

Foreign CPA firms can establish representative offices in China upon approval of the Ministry of Finance of the State Council. Application for the establishment of the joint venture CPA firms formed by a foreign CPA firm and a Chinese CPA firm should be examined by the department in charge of foreign economic relations and trade under the State Council or by other organs authorized by the State Council and by the people's government of the province, and shall be thereupon submitted to and approved by the Ministry of Finance of the State Council.

In addition to the situation in the above paragraph, a foreign CPA firm shall obtain approval by the related people's government of the province, autonomous region or directly administered municipality before it can conduct business temporarily within the territory of China.

Article 45

The State Council may formulate implementation regulations in accordance with this law.

Article 46

The present law shall become effective from 1 January 1994.

The Regulations of the Certified Public Accountants in the People's Republic of China promulgated on 3 July 1986 shall simultaneously be repealed.

Appendix D

ACCOUNTING STANDARDS FOR BUSINESS ENTERPRISES

(APPROVED ON 30 NOVEMBER 1993 AND PROMULGATED BY THE MINISTRY OF FINANCE, THE PEOPLE'S REPUBLIC OF CHINA)

Chapter I General provisions

Article 1

In accordance with *The Accounting Law of the People's Republic of China*, these standards are formulated to meet the needs of developing a socialist market economy in our country, to standardize accounting practice and to ensure the quality of accounting information.

Article 2

These standards are applicable to all enterprises established within the territory of the People's Republic of China. Chinese enterprises established outside the territory of the People's Republic of China (hereinafter referred to as enterprises abroad) are required to prepare and disclose their financial reports to appropriate domestic regulatory authorities in accordance with these standards.

Article 3

Accounting systems of enterprises are required to comply with these standards.

Article 4

An enterprise shall accurately account for all its transactions having actually taken place in order to provide reports of reliable quality on the economic and financial activities of the enterprise itself.

Article 5

Accounting and financial reports should proceed on the basis that the enterprise is a continuing entity and will remain in operation into the foreseeable future.

Article 6

An enterprise shall account for its transactions and prepare its financial statements in distinct accounting periods. Accounting periods may be a fiscal year, a quarter or a month, commencing on first days thereof according to the Gregorian calendar.

Article 7

The *Renminbi* is the bookkeeping base currency of an enterprise. A foreign currency may be used as the bookkeeping base currency for enterprises which conduct transactions mainly in foreign currency. However, in preparing financial statements, foreign currency transactions are to be converted into *Renminbi*. This latter requirement applies to enterprises abroad when reporting financial and economic results to concerned domestic organizations.

Article 8

The debit and credit double entry bookkeeping technique is to be used for recording all accounting transactions.

Article 9

Accounting records and financial reports are to be compiled using the Chinese language. Minority or foreign languages may be used concurrently with the Chinese language by enterprises with foreign investment, and by foreign enterprises.

Chapter II General principles

Article 10

The accounting records and financial reports must be based on financial and economic transactions as they actually take place, in order to reflect objectively the financial position and operating results of an enterprise.

Article 11

Accounting information must be designed to meet the requirements of national macroeconomy control, the needs of all concerned external users to understand an enterprise's financial position and operating results, and the needs of management of enterprises to strengthen their financial management and administration.

Article 12

Accounting records and financial statements shall be prepared according to stipulated accounting methods, and accounting information of enterprises must be comparable and convenient to be analysed.

Article 13

Accounting methods used shall be consistent from one period to the other and shall not be arbitrarily changed. Changes and reasons for changes, if necessary, and their impact on an enterprise's financial position and operating results, shall be reported in explanatory notes to the financial statements.

Article 14

Preparation of accounting and financial reports must be conducted in a timely manner.

Article 15

Accounting records and financial reports shall be prepared in a clear, concise manner to facilitate understanding, examination and use.

Article 16

The accrual basis of accounting is to be adopted.

Article 17

Revenue shall be matched with related costs and expenses in accounting.

Article 18

The principle of prudence should be followed in reasonably determining the possible loss and expense.

Article 19

The values of all assets are to be recorded at historical costs at the time of acquisition. The amount recorded in books of account shall not be adjusted even though a fluctuation in their value may occur, except when state laws or regulations require specific treatment or adjustments.

Article 20

A clear distinction shall be drawn between revenue expenditures and capital expenditures. Expenditure shall be regarded as revenue expenditure where the benefit to the enterprise is only related to the current fiscal year; and as capital expenditure where the benefits to the enterprise last for several fiscal years.

Article 21

Financial reports must reflect comprehensively the financial position and operating results of an enterprise. Transactions relating to major economic activities are to be identified, appropriately classified and accounted for, and separately reported in financial statements.

Chapter III   Assets

Article 22

Assets are economic resources, which are measurable by monetary value, and which are owned or controlled by an enterprise, including all property, rights as a creditor to others, and other rights.

Article 23

For accounting treatment, assets are normally divided into current assets, long-term investments, fixed assets, intangible assets, deferred assets and other assets.

Article 24

Current assets refer to those assets which will be realized or consumed within one year of their acquisition, or within an operating cycle longer than a year. They include cash, cash deposits, short-term investments, accounts receivable, prepayments, and inventories, and so on.

Article 25

Cash and all kinds of deposits shall be accounted for according to the actual amount of receipt and payment.

Article 26

Short-term investments refer to various marketable securities, which can be realized at any time and will be held less than a year, as well as other investment with a life of no longer than a year.

Marketable securities shall be accounted for according to historical cost as obtained.

Income received or receivable from marketable securities in current period and the difference between the receipt obtained from securities sold and book cost shall be all accounted for as current profit or loss.

Marketable securities shall be reported at their book values (book balance) in the accounting statements.

Article 27

Receivables and prepayments include: notes receivable, accounted receivables, other receivables, account prepaid and prepaid expenses, and so on. Receivables and prepayments shall be accounted for according to actual amount.

Provision for bad debts may be set up on accounts receivable. The provision for bad debts shall be shown as a deduction item of accounts receivable in the financial statement.

All receivables and prepayments shall be cleared and collected on time, and shall be checked with related parties periodically. Any accounts receivable proved to be definitely uncollectible according to state regulations, shall be recognized as bad debts and written off against provision for bad debts, or charged to current profit or loss, if such provision is not set up.

Prepaid expenses shall be amortized according to period benefiting, and the balance shall be shown separately in the accounting statements.

Article 28

Inventories refer to merchandise, finished goods, semi-finished goods, work-in-process, and all kinds of materials, fuels, containers, low-value and perishable articles and so on that are stocked for the purpose of sale, production or consumption during the production or operational process.

All inventories shall be accounted for at historical cost as obtained. Those enterprises which keep books at planned cost or norm cost in daily accounting shall account the cost variances and adjust planned cost (or norm cost) into historical cost periodically.

When issuing inventories, the costs of inventories are determined based on the following methods: first-in, first-out (FIFO), weighted average, moving average, specific identification, last-in, first-out, (LIFO) and so on.

A physical inventory shall be taken periodically. The inventory shortage and surplus, and the losses from inventory obsoleteness, deterioration and damage shall be recognized in a timely manner and charged to current profit or loss.

All the inventories shall be disclosed at historical cost in the accounting statements.

Article 29

Long-term investment refers to the investment impossible or not intended to be realized within a year, including shares investment, bonds investment and other investments.

In accordance with different situations, shares investment and other investments shall be accounted for by cost method or equity method, respectively.

Bonds investment shall be accounted for according to actual amount paid. The interest accrued contained in the actually paid amount shall be accounted for separately.

Where bonds are acquired at a premium or discount, the difference between the cost and the face value of the bonds shall be amortized over the periods to maturity of the bonds.

Interest accrued during the period of bonds investment and the difference between the amount of principal and interest received on bonds sold and their book cost and interest accrued but not yet received shall be accounted for as current profit and loss.

Shares investment, bonds investment and other investments shall be shown separately in accounting statements at book balance.

Bonds investment matured within a year shall be shown in the accounting statements separately under the caption of current assets.

Article 30

Fixed assets refer to the assets whose useful life is over one year, whose unit value is above the prescribed criteria and where the original physical form remains during the process of utilization, including building and structures, machinery and equipment, transport equipment, tools and implements, and so on.

Fixed assets shall be accounted for at historical cost as obtained. Interest on loans and other related expenses for acquiring fixed assets, and the exchange difference from conversion of foreign currency loans, if incurred before the assets have been put into operation or after being put into operation but before the final account for the completed project is made, shall be accounted as the value of fixed assets, if incurred after that, they shall be accounted for as current profit or loss.

Fixed assets coming from donations shall be accounted through evaluation with reference to market price, wear and tear degree or the value determined with relevant evidence provided by contributors. Expenses incurred on receiving these donated fixed assets shall be accounted for as the value of fixed assets.

Fixed assets financed by leasing shall be accounted with reference to the way fixed assets are accounted and shall be explained in notes to the accounting statements.

Depreciation on the fixed assets shall be accounted according to state regulations. On the basis of the original cost, estimated residual value, the useful life of the fixed assets or estimated working capacity, depreciation on the fixed assets shall be accounted for on the straight line method or the working capacity (or output) method. If approved or conforming to relevant regulations, the accelerated depreciation method may be adopted.

Fixed assets' original value, accumulated depreciation and net value shall be shown separately in the accounting statements.

The actual expenditures incurred in the course of acquiring or technically bettering the fixed assets before available to the users shall be shown separately as construction in progress in the accounting statement.

An inventory of the fixed assets must be taken periodically. The net profit or loss incurred in discard and disposal, and also surplus or shortage of fixed assets shall be accounted as current profit and loss.

Article 31

Intangible assets refer to assets that will be used by an enterprise for a long term without physical state, including patents, non-patented technology, trademark, copyrights, right to use sites, goodwill, and so on.

Intangible assets obtained through purchase shall be accounted for at actual cost. Intangible assets received from investors shall be accounted for at the assessed value recognized or the amount specified in the contract. Self-developed intangible assets shall be accounted at actual cost in the development process.

All intangible assets shall be averagely amortized periodically over the period benefiting from such expenditures and be shown with unamortized balance in the accounting statement.

Article 32

Deferred assets refer to all the expenses that could not be accounted as current profit or loss totally but should be periodically amortized in future years, including organization expenses, expenditures incurred in major repair and improvement of the rented fixed assets, and so on.

The expenses incurred in an enterprise during its preparation period shall be accounted for as organization expenses except those which should be accounted into related property or material value. The organization expenses shall be averagely amortized in a certain period of years after the operation starts.

Expenditures incurred on major repair and improvement of the rented fixed assets shall be averagely amortized by years in the period of leasing.

All deferred assets shall be shown separately in accounting statements by their balance not yet amortized.

Article 33

Other assets refer to the long-term assets, except all items mentioned above.

Chapter IV   Liabilities

Article 34

A liability is debt borne by an enterprise, measurable by monetary value, which will be paid to a creditor using assets or services.

Article 35

Liabilities are generally classified into current liabilities and long-term liabilities.

Article 36

Current liabilities refer to the debts which should be paid off within a year or an operating cycle longer than a year, including short-term loans payable, notes payable, accounts payable, advances from customers, accrued payroll, taxes payable, profits payable, dividends payable, other payables, provision for expenses, and so on.

All current liabilities shall be accounted for at actual amount incurred. Liabilities incurred but with the amount needing to be estimated shall be accounted for at a reasonable estimate, and then adjusted after the actual amount has been given.

Balance of current liabilities shall be shown by item in accounting statements.

Article 37

Long-term liabilities refer to the debts which will be redeemed after a year or an operating cycle longer than a year, including long-term loans payable, bonds payable, long-term accounts payable, and so on.

Long-term loans payable include the loans borrowed from financial institutions and other units. It shall be accounted independently according to the different characters of the loan and at the amount actually incurred.

Bonds shall be accounted for at par value. When bonds are issued at a premium or discount, the difference between the amount actually obtained and the par value shall be accounted independently, and be written off periodically by adding or subtracting interest expenses of every period until the bonds mature.

Long-term accounts payable include accounts payable for importing equipment and accounts payable for fixed assets financed by leasing. Long-term accounts payable shall be accounted at actual amounts.

Long-term liabilities shall be shown by item of long-term loans, bonds payable and long-term accounts payable in accounting statements.

Long-term liabilities to be matured and payable within a year shall be shown as a separate item under the caption of current liabilities.

Chapter V   Owners' equity

Article 38

Owners' equity refers to the interest of the investors remaining in the net assets of an enterprise, including capital of the enterprises invested in by investors, capital reserve, surplus reserve, undistributed profit retained in the enterprise and so on.

Article 39

Contributed capital is the capital fund actually invested in the enterprise by its investors, whether it be in form of cash, physical goods or other assets for the operation of the enterprise.

Contributed capital shall be accounted for at the amount actually invested.

Amount of shares issued by a corporation shall be accounted for as capital stock at the face value of the shares issued.

Special appropriation allocated by the government to an enterprise shall be accounted for as government investment unless otherwise provided.

Article 40

Capital reserve includes premium on capital stock, legal increment of property value through revaluation and value of donated assets accepted, and so on.

Article 41

Surplus reserve refers to the reserve fund deriving from profit, set up according to relevant government regulations.

Surplus reserve shall be accounted for at the amount actually established.

Article 42

Undistributed profit refers to the profit reserve for future distribution or not yet distributed within the current period.

Article 43

Contributed capital, capital reserve, surplus reserve and undistributed profit shall be shown by item in the accounting statements. Deficit not yet made up, if any, shall be shown as a deduction item of owners' equity.

Chapter VI   Revenues

Article 44

Revenue refers to the financial inflows to an enterprise as a result of the sale of goods and services, and other business activities of the enterprise, including primary operating revenue and other operating revenue.

Article 45

Enterprises shall rationally reorganize revenue and account for the revenue on time. Enterprises generally recognize revenue when merchandise is shipped or service provided, as well as cash collected or the claim of collecting cash established.

Revenue of a long-term project contract (including labour service) shall be reasonably recognized, in general, according to the percentage of completion method or the completed contract method.

Article 46

Return of sales, sales allowances and sales discount shall be accounted for as deduction items of operating revenue.

Chapter VII   Expenses

Article 47

Expenses refer to the outlays incurred by an enterprise in the course of production and operation.

Article 48

Expenses directly incurred by an enterprise in production and service provision, including direct labour, direct materials, purchase price of commodities and other direct expenses, shall be charged directly into the cost of production or operation; indirect expenses incurred in production and provision of service by an enterprise are to be allocated to the cost of production and operation, according to certain criteria of allocation.

Article 49

General and administrative expenses incurred by an enterprise's administrative sectors for organizing, managing, producing and operating, financial expenses, purchase expenses on commodities purchased for sale, and sales expenses for selling commodities and providing service, shall be directly accounted for as periodic expenses in the current profit and loss.

Article 50

The expenses paid in current period but attributable to the current and future periods shall be allocated and accounted for in current and future periods. The expenses attributable to the current period but not yet paid in the current period shall be recognized as accrued expenses and charged to cost of the current period.

Article 51

Enterprises shall generally calculate products cost every month. Costing methods shall be decided by the enterprise itself according to the characteristics of its production and operation, type of production management and requirements of cost management. Once they are decided, no change can be made arbitrarily.

Article 52

Enterprises shall calculate expenses and costs on actual amounts incurred. Those adopting norm costing or planned costing in accounting for daily product costing shall reasonably calculate the cost variances, and adjust them into actual cost at the end of the month when preparing accounting statements.

Article 53

Enterprises shall convert the cost of commodities sold and service provided into operating cost accurately and timely, then account current profit and loss together with periodic expenses.

Chapter VIII Profit and loss

Article 54

Profit is the operating results of an enterprise in an accounting period, including operating profit, net investment profit and net non-operating income.

Operating profit is the balance of operating revenue after deducting operating cost, periodic expenses and all turnover taxes, surtax and fees.

Net investment profit is the balance of income on external investment after deducting investment loss.

Net non-operating income is the balance of non-operating income after deducting non-operating expenses. Non-operating income and expenses have no direct relation to the primary operations of an enterprise.

Article 55

Loss incurred by an enterprise shall be made up according to the stipulated procedure.

Article 56

Items that constitute the profits and the distribution of profits shall be shown separately in the financial statements. A distribution of profit plan which is not yet approved at time of publication of the financial statements is to be identified in notes to the financial statement.

Chapter IX Financial reports

Article 57

Financial reports are the written documents summarizing and reflecting the financial position and operating results of an enterprise, including a balance sheet, an income statement, a statement of changes in financial position (or a cash flow statement) together with supporting schedules, notes to the financial statements and explanatory statements on financial condition.

Article 58

A balance sheet is an accounting statement that reflects the financial position of an enterprise at a specific date.

Items of the balance sheet should be grouped according to the categories of assets, liabilities and owners' equity, and shall be shown item by item.

Article 59

An income statement is an accounting statement that reflects the operating results of an enterprise within an accounting period, as well as the distribution of profit.

Items of the income statement should be arranged according to the formation and distribution of profit, and shall be shown item by item.

Items of the profit distribution part of the income statement may be shown separately in a statement of profit distribution.

Article 60

A statement of changes in financial position is an accounting statement that reflects comprehensively the sources and application of working capital and its changes during an accounting period.

Items of the statement of changes in financial position are divided into two groups: sources of working capital and application of working capital. The difference between the total sources and total applications is the net increase (or decrease) of the working capital. Sources of working capital are subdivided into profit sources and other sources; applications of working capital are also subdivided into profit distribution and other applications; all shall be shown item by item.

An enterprise may also prepare a cash flow statement to reflect the changes in its financial position.

A cash flow statement is an accounting statement that reflects the condition of cash receipts and cash disbursements of an enterprise during a certain accounting period.

Article 61

Financial statements should include comparative financial information for the corresponding previous accounting period, when so required. If the classification and content of statement items of the previous accounting period are different from those of the current period, such items should be adjusted in conformity with those of the current period.

Article 62

Accounting statements should be prepared from the records of account books, completely recorded and correctly checked, and other relative information. It is required that they be true and correct in figures, complete in content and issued on time.

Article 63

Consolidated financial statements shall be prepared by the enterprise (acting as a parent company) which owns over 50 per cent of the total capital of the enterprise in which it invested (acting as subsidiary) or otherwise owns the right of control over the enterprise invested in. Financial statements of an invested enterprise of a special line of business not suitable for consolidation may not be consolidated but should be submitted together with the consolidated financial statements of the parent company.

Article 64

Notes to the financial statements are explanatory of related items in the financial statements of the enterprise concerned so as to meet the need to understand the contents of the statements. These should include mainly:

(1) the accounting methods adopted for the current and previous accounting periods;
(2) changes in accounting treatments between the current and prior periods, including the reasons for, and impact on, the financial performance and status of the enterprise of such changes;
(3) description of unusual items;
(4) detailed information relating to major items listed in the accounting statements; and any other explanations necessary to provide users with a clear view and understanding of the financial statements.

Chapter X   Supplementary provisions

Article 65

The explanation of these standards is the charge of the Ministry of Finance.

Article 66

These standards will be effective as of 1 July 1993.

Appendix E

GENERAL RULES ON FINANCIAL AFFAIRS FOR BUSINESS ENTERPRISES

Chapter I   General provisions

Article 1

The captioned rules are formulated in an effort to meet the needs of developing a socialist market economy in our country, and to normalize the financial behaviours of the enterprises so as to be conducive to fair competition among enterprises, and strengthen their financial management and economic calculation.

Article 2

The general rules are principles and norms that must be observed in all the financial activities of various enterprises established within the territory of the People's Republic of China.

Article 3

An enterprise should, within 30 days of completing business registration or its modification, submit to the responsible governmental finance agencies the duplicated copy of such documents or their modification as the approval certificate of the establishing enterprise, the business licence and statutes.

Article 4

The fundamental principles guiding an enterprise's financial management are to establish and improve the enterprise's internal financial management system, effectively accomplish the basic work of financial management, truthfully reflect the enterprise's financial situations, calculate and turn over tax revenue to the state according to the laws, and ensure the investors' rights and interests against violation.

Article 5

The basic tasks and methods of an enterprise's financial management are to accomplish effectively the work relating to the planning, control, calculation, analysis and examination of the financial revenue and expenditure, reasonably raise funds according to the laws, effectively utilize the enterprise's assets and actively improve economic efficiency.

Chapter II   Fund raising

Article 6

The authorized capital is needed for establishing an enterprise. The capital refers to the fund registered by the enterprise in the business administration agency.

In terms of the investors, the capital can be classified as the capital of the state, the capital of the legal entity, the capital of the individual and the capital of the foreigner, and so on.

Article 7

An enterprise can, according to the laws and regulations of the state, adopt various measures to raise capital, such as state investment, contribution capital from various parities or issuing stocks. The investors can invest in the enterprise in the forms of cash, physical goods or intangible assets.

The enterprise and the other investors can, according to the laws, ask for compensation for losses caused by the non-compliance of the investor who fails to contribute funds according to the investment contract or agreement.

Article 8

The surplus of the fund contributed by the investors over the stated capital (including the stock premium) in an enterprise's operations of raising the capital, the increment of property value through revaluation according to the laws and the donated property accepted by the enterprise are all written into the capital reserve.

The capital reserve can be transferred into the capital according to the relevant stipulations by government authority.

Article 9

An enterprise enjoys, according to the laws, the management right over the capital it raised and, during the period of the enterprise's operation, the investors cannot withdraw their capital investment in any form except transferring according to the laws. If the laws and government regulations have other specific stipulations, these stipulations should be observed.

Article 10

The liabilities of an enterprise include long-term liability and current liability.

The long-term liability refers to the debt, the maturity period of which is over one year or over an operating cycle longer than one year, including long-term borrowings, long-term bonds payable and long-term accounts payable, and so on.

The current liability refers to the debt, the maturity period of which is within one year or within an operating cycle longer than one year, including short-term borrowings, short-term bonds payable, provision for expenses and the accounts payable or received in advance, and so on.

Article 11

The accrued interest expenses of the long-term liability are charged respectively into the organization expenses during the construction preparation period, into the financial expenses during the operation period and into the liquidation profit and loss during the liquidation period. Among these, the expense connected with building or purchasing a fixed asset or intangible asset is charged into the value of the built or purchased asset before the asset is delivered and put into operation or before the final account of the completed project is made even though the asset has been delivered and put into operation.

The accrued interest expenses of current liabilities are charged into financial expenses.

Chapter III   The current assets

Article 12

Current asset refers to the asset that can be realized into cash or utilized within one year or within an operating cycle longer than one year, including cash, deposits, inventories, receivable and prepayments, and so on.

Article 13

An enterprise can set up the provision for bad debt according to the stipulations of the state. The bad debt loss incurred should be written off against the bad debt provision. If the bad debt provision is not set up, the bad debt loss incurred is written into the current expenses.

The bad debt loss refers to the account receivable that cannot be collected even after the liquidation is made with the liquidated property or the legacy of the bankrupt or dead obligor, or the account receivable that remains uncollectible after three years when the obligor has failed to comply with the debt-redeeming obligation.

Article 14

The inventory refers to the materials reserved by an enterprise for the purpose of sale and consumption in the process of production and operation, including supplies, fuels, low-value and perishable articles, work in process, semi-finished goods, finished goods, outside-produced parts and merchandise, and so on.

The low-value and perishable articles and the turnaround reusable containers used for revolving purpose, after being put into use, can be charged to expenses in current period or deferred and amortized over certain periods.

The net gain or loss deriving from the inventory surplus, shortage or damage is written into the current profit and loss. Among these, the extraordinary loss of inventory damage is written into the current loss.

Chapter IV   The fixed assets

Article 15

The fixed assets refer to the asset, the service term of which is over one year, the unit value of which is above the prescribed criteria, and the original physical form of which remains in the process of utilization, including buildings and structures, machinery equipment, transport equipment, tools and implements, and so on.

Article 16

The difference between the revenue deriving from the sale of a fixed asset deducting the clearing expenditure and its book value, and the net gain or loss deriving from the inventory surplus, shortage or damage of the fixed asset are both written into the current profit and loss.

Article 17

The expenditures of the construction in progress refer to the incurred expenditure for building or purchasing a fixed asset or making technical innovation before the fixed asset is delivered and put into operation, including special materials such as equipment and supplies to be used for project construction, the project prepayments and the expenditures for the non-completed project.

The expenditure caused by the trial operation before the completion of the project and its related operation revenue are generally to be charged into or deducted from the cost of construction in progress.

Article 18

The fixed asset's classified depreciation life and the depreciation methods as well as the scope of calculating depreciation are determined by the Ministry of Finance. An enterprise, according to the stipulations of the state, may select specific depreciation methods and determines the extent of accelerating depreciation.

Starting from the next month after its operation, the depreciation of a fixed asset is to be calculated on a monthly basis. Starting from the next month after the fixed asset is out of utilization, the calculation of the depreciation stops.

Article 19

The repair expense for fixed assets is charged to costs or expenses in the current period. The repair expense, when irregular or relatively large, can be allocated over a number of periods through either amortization or accrual procedure.

Chapter V   Intangible assets, deferred assets and other assets

Article 20

Intangible assets refer to those assets which are used by enterprises for a long time but do not have concrete physical forms they include patents, trademarks, copyright, land-use rights, non-patented technology, goodwill and so on.

Starting from the day of first being used, the costs of intangible assets should be amortized periodically within the time specified by regulations. Those intangible assets which do not have a regulated time period should be amortized according to the expected life of service or within a period of no less than ten years.

Article 21

Deferred assets refer to those expenses that cannot be entirely written into the current year's profit and loss, and need to be amortized in the following years, including organization expenses, amelioration expenses for rented fixed assets and so forth.

The organization expenses should be amortized periodically within a period of no less than five years beginning from the day when the operation starts.

Article 22

Other assets include specially chartered reserve resources and so on.

Chapter VI   External investment

Article 23

The external investment refers to those investments in other enterprises carried out by an enterprise in the forms of cash, physical goods and intangible assets through buying such marketable securities as stocks and bonds, including both short-term and long-term investments.

Short-term investments refer to the marketable securities that can be readily converted into cash and are owned less than one year, as well as the other forms of investment with a life of no longer than one year.

Long-term investments refer to the marketable securities that are not intended to be converted into cash in a short period and are owned more than one year, as well as the other forms of investment with a life of longer than one year.

Article 24

For those external investments which are made by enterprises with physical property or intangible assets, the difference between the current value recognized by revaluation and the net book value should be recognized as the capital reserve.

With respect to those external investments in the form of purchasing bonds, the differences between the actual payments and the bond's face value should be recognized as the premiums or discounts of the bonds, and both of them should be amortized or be written off after transferring them into other accounts periodically before maturity.

With regard to those external investments in the form of purchasing stocks, when the actual payments include announced dividends, the actual payments after deducting the dividends receivable are recognized as the actual value of the external investments.

Article 25

Both profit and dividend deriving from an enterprise's external investment should be written into investment returns and are subject to the payment of income taxes according to the stipulations of the state.

The difference between the value of the external investment realized by an enterprise and the book value of the investment should be recognized as the current profit and loss.

Chapter VII   Costs and expenses

Article 26

All those payments of an enterprise for producing or dealing in commodities and providing services, including direct wages, direct materials, purchase price of commodities and other direct payments, should be charged directly into production and operation costs. Those indirect expenses for producing or dealing in commodities and providing services should be proportionally allocated to production and operation costs.

Article 27

Selling, administrative and financial expenses incurred by an enterprise are directly written into the current profit and loss.

The selling expenses include such expenses as transport expense, loading–unloading expense, packing expense, insurance expense, product exhibition expense, travel expense, advertisement charge and the staff wages of specially established selling institutes, and other expenses, all of which the enterprise should bear when selling products or providing services.

The administrative expenses refer to the expenses that the enterprise should unilaterally bear, including general office expense, labour union outlays, staff training expenses, labour insurance fee, unemployment insurance fee, board of director meeting expense, consulting fee, legal fee, tax payment, land-use fee, land deterioration recovery fee, technology transfer fee, technology innovation expense, amortization of intangible asset, amortization of organization expense, business entertaining expense, bad-debt loss, the administration fee handed over to higher level authorities, and other administrative expenses.

The financial expenses include the net expenditure for interest payment, the net exchange loss and the bank's service charge within the enterprise's operational period.

Article 28

The following outlays by enterprises should not be written into the cost or expense: expenses for purchasing and constructing fixed assets, payments for intangible assets and other assets, external investment outlays, confiscated assets, various kinds of fines, sponsorship contributions and donations, and some other outlays that cannot be treated as a product cost or expense item as stipulated by the state regulations.

Chapter VIII   Operating revenues, profits and their distribution

Article 29

Operating revenues refer to revenues an enterprise obtains from selling goods and providing services in its production and operation.

The sale return, sales allowance and sales discount are to be deducted from the current operating revenue of the enterprise.

Article 30

The total amount of an enterprise's profits includes operating profit, net investment profit, and the net amount of non-operating income and expenses.

Operating profits refer to the amount of operating revenue after deducting costs, expenses, various kinds of turnover taxes, and other additional taxes and fees.

Net investment profit refers to the remainder of investment profit after deducting investment loss.

The net non-operating income refers to the remainder of non-operating income after deducting non-operating expenses.

Article 31

The incurred current year's loss of an enterprise can be covered with the next year's profits; if the next year's profits cannot make a full covering, the enterprise can use its pre-income tax profits to do the covering continuously within a five-year period; if the loss still cannot be totally covered by pre-income tax profit in five years, the enterprise can use its post-income tax profit to cover.

Article 32

After adjusting the profits according to the state stipulations, an enterprise should pay the income tax according to the law.

Unless the state has other stipulations, the profit after income tax should be distributed in the following order:

(1) loss incurred by expropriation, fine and penalty for delayed tax payment in violation of tax law;
(2) compensation for operation loss of previous years (limited to five years);
(3) retention for a legal reserve fund earmarked for loss compensation and capital increase in accordance with state regulations;
(4) retention for a public welfare fund earmarked for expenditures on welfare facilities for the enterprise's employees;
(5) profit distribution to the investors. The undistributed profit of the previous years can be incorporated into distribution in the current year.

Chapter IX   Foreign currency transactions

Article 33

Foreign currency transactions refer to all the transactions conducted in currencies other than the bookkeeping base currency, including, among others, cash receipts and payments, settlement of current accounts, and asset valuation.

Reminbi is the bookkeeping base currency for an enterprise. Those enterprises conducting operational receipts and payments mainly in foreign currencies may choose one foreign currency as the bookkeeping base currency.

Article 34

The closing balance of various foreign currency items (excluding those recorded separately at the exchange rates in the foreign exchange swap centres) should be translated into bookkeeping base currency at the official exchange rate prevailing at the end-of-period, unless regulated otherwise by the state. The difference between the amount of the bookkeeping base currency translated from foreign currency at the official exchange rate and the book amount stated in bookkeeping base currency should be carried forward into the current profit and loss as gain and loss on exchange.

Article 35

The net gain and loss on exchange incurred by an enterprise during the preparation and construction period should be carried into organization expenses and amortized in a period of no less than five years starting from the operation of the enterprise, or be retained to compensate for the loss incurred by the enterprise during the operation period, or be retained and incorporated into liquidation gain and loss. The exchange gain and loss incurred during the production and operation period should be carried into financial expenses and, during the liquidation period, into liquidation gain and loss. The exchange gain and loss associated with purchase and construction of fixed assets and intangible assets should be carried into the value of the purchased and constructed assets prior to the delivery to their users or prior to the final account for completed project after the delivery to the users.

Article 36

In case of foreign exchange swap transactions of an enterprise, the difference between the amount of bookkeeping base currency translated from the foreign currency at the swap rate and the book amount stated in bookkeeping base currency should be carried forward into the current profit and loss.

Chapter X   Enterprise liquidation

Article 37

When an enterprise is disbanded or goes bankrupt in accordance with its Articles of Association, or is closed because of other reasons, a liquidator should be established to clear its assets, claims and obligations in a thorough manner, to compile a balance sheet, general inventory and statement of claims and debts, to work out the rules for asset valuation and treatment of claims and obligations, and to process appropriately all the remaining issues.

Article 38

The wages, travelling expenses, office expenses and announcement fees of liquidation during the liquidation period should be carried into liquidation expenses and be covered as the first priority by the enterprise with its current assets.

Gain and loss derived from inventory surplus or shortage, disposal of property, insolvent obligations and non-recoverable claims, and operating income and loss incurred during the liquidation period should be carried into liquidation gain and loss.

Article 39

After the disbursement of liquidation expenses out of the enterprise's property, the debts and obligations should be liquidated according to the following order:

(1)   staff wages and labour insurance payable;
(2)   unpaid tax payable;
(3)   other obligations payable.

If the enterprise fails to liquidate all the items according to the above order, the liquidation should be made proportionately.

Article 40

Income tax should be paid according to the law on the net liquidation gain after the completion of the liquidation. The remaining after-tax property should be distributed in proportion to the equity contributions of investors or in accordance with the provisions of contracts and Articles of Association.

Chapter XI   Financial reports and financial assessment

Article 41

Financial reports, including balance sheet and income statement, statement of changes in financial position (statement of cash flows), relative reporting schedules and explanatory statements on financial condition are written documents summarizing and reflecting the financial position and operation results of an enterprise.

An enterprise is required to submit at regular intervals the financial reports to its investors and creditors, government agencies and other users.

Article 42

The explanatory statements on financial condition mainly illustrate:

— the status of production and operation of the enterprise, realization and allocation of profit, increase and decrease and turnover of funds, tax payment and changes in the condition of assets and properties;
— the issues which have a key impact on the current and future financial position;
— the issues which may substantially affect the financial position of the enterprise after balance sheet date and prior to the submission of financial reports; and
— other issues which need to be explained.

Article 43

Financial indexes (ratios) summarizing and assessing the financial position and operation results include liquidity ratio, quick ratio, accounts receivable turnover, turnover of inventories, assets–liabilities ratio, profit–costs ratio, profit (and tax) operating revenue ratio and so on.

Chapter XII   Supplementary provisions

Article 44

The explanation and implementation of the General Rules is in the charge of the Ministry of Finance.

Article 45

The enterprise financing systems of different industrial sectors will be formulated by the Ministry of Finance in accordance with the General Rules specified herein.

Article 46

The General Rules will be effective as of 1 July 1993.

Index

Note: Page references to figures and tables are shown in *italic*

'A shares' 75–6
accelerated depreciation 12
account payable 55, 228, 230
account receivable 55, 228, 230
accountant, qualifications of 37–8, 139, 242, 253–5
accounting administrative system 47, 53
accounting associations *see* professional associations
accounting calculation, regulations on 296–8, 300
accounting clerk, qualifications of 37, 38, 242, 252–5
Accounting Law of the People's Republic of China (1985, 1993), 11, 24–6, 27, 31–2, 39–40, 52, *53*, 53–4, 327
  English translation 295–302
    accounting calculation 296–8, 300
    accounting offices and accounting personnel 300–1
    accounting supervision 298–300
    general provisions 295–6
    legal liability 301–2
    other provisions 302
accounting period *60*, 61, *64*, 297, 328, 340
accounting personnel
  computer specialists 221, 222, 230, 231
  dismissal of 40, 41, 158, 270, 300–1, 306, 317, 318

number of 28, 36, 38, 103, 241
  CAuPs 131
  CPAs 87, 139, 143, 145
  internal auditors 128
obligations of 40–1, 53
  CPAs 148–51
  supervision 41–2, 129, 298–300
quality of 103, 109, 128, 265
responsibilities and rights of 39–40, 53, 129–30, 300–1
Accounting Reform and Development Outlook (1995) 241
Accounting Regulations for Enterprises Adopting the Share-capital System (1992) 10, 86
Accounting Regulations on Joint Ventures Using Chinese and Foreign Investment (ARFJV) (1985) 10, 246
Accounting Review 275
Accounting Society of China (ASC) 20, 49 n.2, 227, 261, 262–6, 273, 275
  Accounting Education Reform Committee (1993) 247
  founded (1980) 263
  member conferences 264
  objectives 263–4
  planning of accounting research 265–6
  structure 263
  Task Force on Developing Accounting Software (1987) 217

accounting standards 12, 13, 14, 18, 20,
27, 30, Ch. 3
    and accounting regulation system
        51–4
    *Accounting Standards for Business
        Enterprises* (ASBE) (1993) 10,
        12, 15, 33–4, 35, 44–8, 52–3,
        53, 57–8, 218, 247
    accounting element standards *60*,
        63–7, *67*, 330–9
    conceptual structure 59–63, *64*
    accounting assumptions 59–61, *60*,
        64, 328, 341
    basic accounting principles *60*, 61–3,
        64, 328–30
        costs and expenditures provisions
            90, 92–3, 97, 337–8
        English translation 327–42
            assets 330–4
            expenses 337–8
            financial reports 339–41
            general principles 328–30
            general provisions 327–8
            liabilities 334–5
            owners' equity 335–6
            profit and loss 339
            revenues 337
            supplementary provisions 341–
                2
        financial reporting and disclosures
            62, 67–9, 339–41
        implications of 69–70
        objectives 59, 70
    *Accounting Standards on Related
        Party Transactions* (1997) 34,
        57
    for budgetary accounting *53*, 54,
        58, 212, 247
    and business financing rules 48–9
    computerized accounting software
        218, 226, 228, 229
    development of 54–8
    enforcement of 15, 28, 30, 35
    general standards 46, *47*, 55, *56*
    implementation guidelines *56*, 57–
        8
    International Accounting Stand-
        ards (IAS) 12, 14, 65, 274
    practical standards 46–7, *47*, 55–6,
        56, 57
        financial statements standards
            47, *56*, 56
        general transaction standards
            46, 55, *56*
        special transactions standards
            46–7, 55, *56*
    process of standard setting 557–8
    rationale for 52
    research on 265, 266, 274
    structure of 55–7, *56*
    Study Group on Accounting
        Standards 55, 57, 212
*Accounting System for Aggregated
    Accounts by Government* 58
*Accounting System for Governmental
    Entities* 58
*Accounting System for Manufacturing
    Enterprises* 228
*Accounting System for Master Fiscal
    Budgets* 199
*Accounting Systems for Non-profit
    Organizations* 58
accounting work, organization of 39,
    53, 300
accounts payable 335, 345
accounts receivable 64, 331, 345
accrual accounting 12, *60*, 61, 62, *64*,
    91, 92, 174, 204, 209, 213, 329,
    338, 347
*Administration of Computerization
    Accounting* (1994) 218
Administration of State-owned Proper-
    ties 75, 77
administrative expenses 66, 68, 91, 92,
    349–50
*Administrative Rules on Accounting
    Certificates* (1990) 241
Advertisement Law 287–9
Advisory Group of Domestic Experts
    154
Advisory Group of Foreign Experts
    154

aggregate budgetary units 197, *200*
  financial reporting for 208
agricultural (grains and food) industry
  35, 46
aid, foreign 122, 124, 307
American Accounting Association
  (AAA) 273
American Institute of Certified Public
  Accountants (AICPA) 151
amortization period 65–6
Anhui Institute of Finance and Trade
  251
Antitrust Law (1993) 290–1
Anyi-Tong yong (easypack) finance
  and accounting software 227–8
Army-run enterprises 278
  see also military units
Asia Development Bank 122
Assets 43, 55, 59, *60*, 63, 64–6, *67*, 82,
  85, 93, 146, 203, 213, 297, 298,
  299, 306, 307, 319, 330–4, 340,
  352, 353
  see also current assets; deferred
      assets; fixed assets; intangible
      assets; long-term investments
assistant accountant, qualifications of
  37, 38, 242, 253–5
assistant auditor, qualifications of 256–
  7, *257*, *258*
Association of Chinese Asset Appraisers 261
Audit Law of the People's Republic of
  China (1994) 11, 114, 117, 119,
  121, 122, 126, 127, 131–3, 154,
  272
  English translation 303–14
    audit institutions and auditors
      304–6
    audit procedures 310–11
    general provisions 303–4
    legal liability 311–13
    powers of audit institutions 309–
      10
    responsibilities of audit institu-
      tions 306–8
    supplementary provisions 313–14

auditing
  of annual reports 85
  computerized programmes for 221
  education and training in 116, 119,
      120, 237, 242, 246, *248*, *249*,
      249–50, 252, *255*, 255–8, *258*,
      272
  firms *see* certified public accountants
      (CPAs)
  governmental *see* governmental
      auditing
  institutional internal *see* institutional
      internal auditing
  nature and purpose of 111
  non-governmental *see* public ac-
      counting
  overview of Chinese auditing system
      114–14
    establishment of state audit system
      112–13
    system structure of state audit
      supervision 113–14, 115
  regulatory environment of state
      supervision 114–18
    accounting standards and guide-
      lines formulated by profes-
      sional bodies 118
    regulations formulated by the
      NAA 118
    regulations stipulated by the State
      Council 117–18, 314
    regulatory authority over auditing
      114–17
    state laws enacted through legisla-
      tive procedures 117
    see also Audit Law of the
      People's Republic of China
      (1994)
  restoration of auditing system 11
  standards 12, 16, 19, 20, 118, 151–6,
      266, 268, 271–2, 274
auditing clerk, qualifications of 256,
  257
Auditing Regulation of the People's
  Republic of China (1998) 118,
  314

auditor
  qualifications of 256, *257*, 257–8, *258*
  resignation or replacement of 85
Auditor-General 119, *120*, 304

'B shares' 8, 75–6, *76*, 291
bachelor degree programmes *236*, 236,
  239, *240*, 254, *257*, 257
  curriculum of 244–50
    accounting core courses before
      mid-1980s 244, *245*
    accounting curriculum after 1993
      246–50
      core courses 247, *248*
      textbooks 247–9, *249*
    dual-core curriculum (mid 1980s–
      1992) 245–6
bad debts 12, 55, 62, 64, 85, 331, 346,
  350
balance sheets 62, 68, 70, 84, 339–40,
  354
banks/banking
  accounting for master fiscal budgets
    by 197
  accounting regulations for 26, 33, 35
  accounting standards for 55
  central bank *see* People's Bank of
    China (PBC)
  commercial banks 51, 113, 279, 285
  courses in *245*, 255
  'financial checking' by 112
  laws 284–5
    Central Bank Law 284–5
    Commercial Bank Law 285
  taxes on 171, *172*, 173
Beihai 189
Beijing 29, 50 n. 7, 57, 114, 137, 138,
  156, 165, 211, 227, 229, 230, 232,
  263, 264, 266, 270, 273
  University of 238, 248, *249*
Beijing AnYi Computer Company
  (*formerly* Research and Development Centre for Computerization
  of Accounting) 227–8
Beijing Engineering and Construction
  Company 229

Beijing Institute of Business Administration 238, 251
Beijing Institute of Economics *see*
  Capital University of Economics
  and Trade (*formerly* Beijing
  Institute of Economics)
Beijing Tianchiao Department Store 73
Blake, J. 21 n. 3
bookkeeping 239
  computerized 221, 228, 229
  double-entry 5, 204, 205, 207, 213,
    264, 328
  fund receipt-disbursement 204–5,
    213
    features of 205–7
    interrelation of journal entries
      under *206*
borrowing costs 55
brokerage firms 78
*Budget Law of the People's Republic of
  China* (1994) 201, 210
Budgetary Accounting 275
budgetary accounting Ch. 9
  accounting standards for *53*, 54, 58,
    212, 247
  administrative structure 193–9
    components of budgetary account-
      ing 197–9, *200*
    system of governmental budgetary
      administration 194–5, *196*
  characteristics of 202–7
    bookkeeping method 204–7, 213–
      14
    cash-based accounting 204, 213
    fund accounting 6, 203, 213
    objectives 202
    system of accounts 202–3
  courses in *245*
  need for reform 17, 210–11
  proposed changes 19, 211–14
    bookkeeping method 213
    centralization of standard-setting
      process 212
    modified accrual accounting 213
    redefinition of 'budgetary account-
      ing' 211–12

redesigning structure of financial
statements 213
uniform accounting standards 54,
58, 212
regulations for 58, 199–201, 212
*Budgetary Accounting System for
Administrative and Institutional
Organizations* (BASFAIO) 199,
201, 209
*Budgetary Accounting System for
Health Care Institutions* 201
*Budgetary Accounting System for
Scientific Research Institutes* 201
*Budgetary Accounting System for
Universities and Colleges* 201
budgetary costing system 92
Bureau of Auditing 112
Bureau of Light industry 278
Bureaux of Local Taxation 166
business combination 9, 47, 55, 61, 85,
146, 186, 284
business income tax *see* income tax
Business Income Tax Law 173
business organization costs 65–6
business regulation 20, 47
  Advertisement Law 287–9
  Antitrust Law (1993) 290–1
  banking laws 284–5
  Corporation Law 148, 149–50, 283–
  4
  courses in 252
  Economic Contract Law 285–6
  for enterprises with foreign invest-
    ment 291–3
    Income Tax Law (1993) 164, 291,
    293
    Joint Ventures Law (1979, 1990)
    245–6, 291–3
  Insurance Law 286–7
  overview of business environment
    277–9
    forms of Chinese enterprises 278–9
    sources of business financing 279,
    344–5
  Privately-owned Enterprise Law
    282–3

State-owned Enterprise Law 280–2
Trademark Law 289–90

capital construction 33, 35, 46, 55, 63,
122, 124, 171, *172*, 173, 197, 229,
245, 307, 347
capital reserve 66, 336, 344
capital stock 66, 336
Capital University of Economics and
Trade (*formerly* Beijing Institute
of Economics) 238, 251
capitalism 5, 63, 207
cash 331, 344, 345, 348, 352
cash-based accounting 204, 213
cash flow statement (SCFP) 62, 68–9,
84, 339, 340, 354
catering industry 35
Central China Institute of Engineering
238
Central Institute of Finance and
Banking 238, 249, 251
Central Military Commission 313
certified public accountants (CPAs) 85,
114, 122, 123, 138, 219–20, 292,
293
certification programme for 19, 50 n.
8, 133, 139–44, 156, 262, 268,
270, 316–18
continuing professional education
(CPE) 144, 242–3, 268
education 139, 242, 259
CPA specialization programme
251–2
qualification examination 50 n. 9,
139–43, 156, 242, 258–9,
268, 270–1, 316–17, 326
evaluation approach 140–3
pass rates 140, *141*
pass rates for overseas candidates 140, *142*
work experience 143, 259
CPA Law (1993) *see CPA Law of the
People's Republic of China*
(1993)
formation and administration of CPA
firms 144–8, 321–3

business scope 146–7, 318–19
financial management 147, 323
foreign CPA firms 145, 269, 326
procedures for setting up 145–6,
    322
requirements for formation 144–5,
    321
staffing 148
legal obligations 148–51
number of 87, 139, 143, 145
professional ethics and auditing
    standards 151–6, 266, 268, 270
*Regulations of the Certified Public
    Accountants in the People's
    Republic of China* (1986) 31,
    32, 138, 326
see also Chinese Institute of Certi-
    fied Public Accountants
    (CICPA)
Changchun Institute of Taxation 251
Changcun city 215
Chatfield, M. 21 n. 3, 133 n. 1
chief accountants 31, 39, 148, 298, 300,
    301
child labour, prohibition of 283
China Auditing 275
China Centre for Sciences and Technol-
    ogy Consultation Services 228
China Securities Regulatory Committee
    (CSRC) 75, 77, 78–9, 79, 80, 81–7
    passim, 147, 150
China Society of Accountants 216
China Society of Auditing (CSA) 119,
    261, 272–3
Chinese Academy of Sciences 201
Chinese Accounting Professors'
    Association (CAPA) 20, 263, 273
Chinese Association of Accountants in
    the Electronic Industry 261
Chinese Association of Accountants in
    the Grains and Food Industry 261
Chinese Association of Certified Public
    Auditors (CACAuP) 116–17, 118,
    119, 131–3, 267–8
Chinese Association of Cost Account-
    ing Research 261

Chinese Association of Science and
    Technology 227, 228
Chinese Budgetary Accountants
    Association 261
*Chinese Independent Auditing Stand-
    ards* (CIAS) 12, 16, 151, 152–6,
    271–2
Chinese Institute of Certified Public
    Accountants (CICPA) 20, *115*,
    116–17, 118, 131–3, 139, 140,
    143, 144, 146, 147, 149, 151–4,
    156–8, 242, 251, 258, 261, 262,
    263, 266–72, 316–18, 324–4
*Chinese Independent Auditing
    Standards* (CIAS) drafted by
    see Chinese Independent
    Auditing Standards (CIAS)
disciplinary action by 152, 157–8,
    270
founded (1988) 266
merger with Chinese Association of
    Certified Public Auditors (1995)
    117, 132, 267–8
organization structure 269–71
Task Force on Independent Auditing
    Standards 152, 154, 271
Chinese Institute of Internal Auditing
    115, 119, 261
Chinese Society of Auditing (CSA) 20
Chongqing 74, 138
Chuangjian (creative) 123 accounting
    software 230
Chuangjian Electronic Technology
    Research Institute 230
civil aviation industry 35
coastal economic developing areas
    (CEDAs) 189–90
Code of Professional Conduct (AICPA)
    151
collective ownership 8, 161, 278
colleges 10–11, 50 n. 5, 102–3, 139,
    199–201, 216, 231, 232, 235, *236*,
    236–9, 242, 256, 259
offering CPA specialization pro-
    gramme 151
see also under names of degree

programmes, e.g. bachelor
degree programmes; master
degree programmes
commodity markets 16
Communist Party 73, 112, 125, 280
completed method 63, 68
compliance audits 124
comprehensive cost control system 107
computerized accounting 19, 32, Ch.
10, 265
characteristics of 218–22
appraisal of computerized accounting system 219–20
constraints 221–2
current status 218–20
major characteristics 220–1
requirements for installation 219
education and training in 12–13, 216,
219, 221, 230–2, 246, *248, 249,*
252
evolution of 12–13, 215–18
prospects for 232–3
software
applications 216, 219, 220, 221,
229–30
auditing programmes 221
commercialized 12, 19, 216, 217,
220, 227–30
dealerships 219
regulation of 19, 217–18, 222–7
appraisal of accounting software
developed abroad 226–7
appraisal of accounting software
developed in China 223–6
regulatory requirements 223–3,
297
standardization of 218, 226, 228,
229
supportive systems for 220–21
Confederation of Asian-Pacific Accountants (CAPA) 13, 157
conglomerates 45
conservatism (prudence convention) *60,*
63, *64,* 65, 330
consistency principle 91
consolidation of financial statements 47

Constitution (1982) 113, *115,* 303
construction operations 33, 35, 46, 55,
63, 122, 124, 171, *172,* 173, 197,
229, *245,* 307, 347
consumption tax 164, 167, 169–71
continuing (going concern) assumption
59, *60, 64,* 328
continuing professional education
(CPE) 16, 235, 241–3
for certified public accountants
(CPAs) 144, 242–3, 268
definition of 241
for general accountants 241–2
for government auditors 242
contract law 285–6
contracting 9, 176, 177
controllers 298, 300
Corporation Law 148, 149–50, 283–4
cost accounting 18, 68, 89
computerized 219, 228, 229, 230, *249*
courses in 246, *248, 255*
in governments and NPOs 204, 213
practices 97–102
enterprise economic accounting
97, 99–102, 105
responsibility system of cost
control 97, 98–9
principles of 89–97
cost classification and measurement 91
product costing (practices) 93–7
product costing (principles and
requirements) 91–3
regulation of cost management
89–91
Cost Accounting Research Society of
China 275
cost centres 199
cost control system, comprehensive 107
cost controllability 105
cost effectiveness 62–3, *64*
cost management *see* cost accounting
cost planning 107–8
cost-volume profit (CVP) analysis 16
*CPA Law of the People's Republic of
China* (1993) 11, 32, 138–9, 144,

145, 148–9, 157, 242, 259, 266, 268, 271
English translation 315–216
certified public accountants' association 323–4
examination and registration 316–18
general provisions 315–16
legal liability 324–5
public accounting firms 321–3
scope and rules of business 318–21
supplementary provisions 326
CPA specialization programme 251–2
cultural and recreational facilities 198, *200*, 201
Cultural Revolution (1966–76) 5–6, 7, 31, 262
current assets 330, 331–2, 345–6, 353
customs tariffs *see* tariffs and duties
CVP (cost-volume-profit) analysis 16

DacEasy Company (USA) 227
Dalian 189
damages compensation 286
decentralization of economic administration 7
deferred assets 330, 334, 348
Deloitte Touche Tohmatsu International 57
Department of Accounting Affairs (DAA) (*formerly* Department of Accounting Systems) 25, *26*, 27, 54–5, 57, 263
Department of Budgetary Administration *25*, 58, 199
Department of Public Health 288
deposits 331, 345
depreciation 5, 12, 46, 55, 204, 333, 347
Detailed Rules for Enforcing the Income Tax Law for Enterprises with Foreign Investments and Foreign Enterprises (1992) 164
Detailed Rules on the Enforcement of the Provisional Regulations on

Income Taxes for Business Enterprises 164
Detailed Rules on the Enforcement of the Provisional Regulations on Value-added Taxes 164
Detailed Rules on the Information Disclosure of Publicly Listed Companies 47, 80
diploma programmes *236*, 236, 239, *240*, 241
direct costs 92, 96
directors 83, 84, 85, 148, 292, 350
disclosures *see* information
dismissals 40, 41, 158, 270, 300–1, 306, 317, 318
diversified business ownership 7–8, 23, 29, 32, 42, 104, 109
dividends *81*, 173, 176, 177, 185, 189, 335, 349
doctorate programmes *236*, 236, 239, *240*, 250, 254, *257*
donations 55, 93, 333, 350
double-entry bookkeeping 5, 204, 205, 207, 213, 264, 328
dual obligation, dilemma of 41–2

earned surplus 66, 336
Economic Contract Law 285–6
economic growth 1
Economics and Management 276
Economics Sciences 276
education and training in accounting 14, 15, 19–20, 26, 43, 87, Ch. 11
auditing 116, 119, *120*, 237, 242, 246, *248*, *249*, 249–50, 252, *255*, 255–8, *258*, 272
computerized accounting 12–13, 216, 219, 221, 230–2, 246, *248*, *249*, 252
continuing professional education (CPE) *see* continuing professional education (CPE)
CPA specialization programme 251–2
see also certified public accountants (CPAs); examinations; qualifications in accounting

curriculum for graduate programmes 250

curriculum for undergraduate programmes 244–50

institutional education 235–41

at college and university level 237–9

components of 235–7, *236*

definition of 235

full-time v. part-time accounting curricula 239–41, *240*

at polytechnic schools 239

restructuring of (1952) 237, 238

structure of *240*

managerial accounting 10–11, 102–3, 246, *248*, *249*, 252, *255*

vocational accounting programmes 243

Education and Training Systems for Certified Public Accountants (1992) 158 n. 4

educational institutions 198, 199–201, *200*, 235–41

see also colleges; polytechnic schools; schools; universities

employees' benefits 55

employees' representative boards 282

enforcement of accounting standards 15, 28, 30, 35

engineering colleges 238

enterprise economic accounting 97, 99–102

centralized approach 100, 101

decentralized approach 100–2

economic accounting system 99–100

Enthoven, A. 2

entity assumption 59, *60*, *64*, 341

ethics, professional 19, 38, 87, 118, 148, 151–6, 241, 243, 268, 271, 272

examinations

CPA *see* certified public accountants (CPAs)

for government auditors 242, 255–8, 272

content of *258*

national accounting examinations 26, 38, 241–2, 252–5

content before 1996 *253*

regulations after 1996 254–5

regulations before 1996 253–4

subjects before 1996 *255*

national entrance examination 237, *240*

training for professional qualification examinations 259–60

exchanges, international 13, 116, 238, 267, 269

expenses 5, 55, 59, *60*, 63, 66, *67*, 337–8, 349–50

administrative 66, 68, 91, 92, 349–50

budgetary 122, 195, 199, 202, 204

exports 168, 169, 171, 190

duties 178, 180

external investment 348–9, 350

'factory costs' 91

farms, state-owned 278

Finance and Accounting in Electronic Industry 275

'financial and taxation examination' 112

'financial checking' 112

financial conditions, explanatory statement on 62, 68, 69

financial indexes 354

financial institutions 35, 114, 119, 122, 124, 171, *172*, 173, 286–7, 306, 308

see also banks/banking

Financial Management and Accounting 275

financial statements *see* reporting financial

fines 93, 127, 149, 150, 187, 288, 325, 350, 351

First Automobile Manufacturing Plant 215–16

fiscal policies, violation of 4, 123, 125, 126–7, 129, 130, 131

fiscal year 61, 297, 328

fixed assets 55, 61, 65, 93, 204, 228,

229, 230, 330, 333, 335, 345, 346–7, 350, 352
fixed-norm costing 16
fixed-quota costing system 16, 66–7, 92, *94*, 95–6
flexible budgeting 16, 105
foreign currencies 47, 55, 59–61, 76, 129, 291, 297, 328, 351–3
foreign investment 1–2, 8, 51, 52, 104, 113, 131, 132, 138, 139, 145, 221, 227, 277, 278–9
   accounting regulations for 10, 11, 33, 47, 61, 147, 246
   business laws for enterprises with foreign investment 291–3
   Income Tax Law (1993) 164, 291, 293
   Joint Ventures Law (1979, 1990) 245–6, 291–3
   computerized accounting for 228
   formulation of foreign invested enterprises 279
   CPA firms 145, 269, 326
   shares 8, 75–6, *76*
   taxation of 19, 161–2, 163, 164, 168, 173, 175, 180, 181, 183–5
   income tax 164, 184–5, 189, 190, 291, 293
   regional development policies 188–91
   uniform industry and commerce tax (UICT) 184, 188, 189, 190
   see also joint ventures
foreign trade 35, 245–6
   Ministry of 145, 292
Forum on China Economic Issues 276
Fourth National Conferences on Accounting Affairs (Beijing, 1995) 29, 211, 214, 232, 266
Fudan University 238, 248, 251
Fujian Finance and Accounting 275
full-amount budgetary units (FABUs) 198–9, 199, *200*, 204, 213
   financial reporting for 209
fund accounting 6, 203, 213
fund applications 6

fund raising 279, 344–5
'fund sources' 6
futures contracts 55
Fuzhou 145, 189

gain and loss *67*, 345–9 *passim*, 352, 353
Gao, S. 21 no. 3
Ge, Jiashu 214 n. 4
General Logistic Department, People's Liberation Army 24, *25*
General Rules on Financial Affairs for Business Enterprises (1993) 34–5, 44, *45*, 48, 65, 90–1, 97
   English translation 343–55
   costs and expenses 349–50
   current assets 345–6
   enterprise liquidation 353
   external investment 348–9, 350
   financial reports and financial assessment 354
   fixed assets 346–7
   foreign currency transactions 351–2
   fund raising 344–5
   general provisions 343–4
   intangible assets, deferred assets and other assets 347–8
   operating revenues, profits and their distribution 350–1
   supplementary provisions 354–5
General Rules on Financing for Administrative and Institutional Units (1996) 201, 210–11
General Standard on Continuing Professional Education (1996) 144
General Standards on Professional Ethics (1996) 151
Generally Accepted Accounting Principles (GAAP) 18
Generally Accepted Auditing Standards (GAAS) 12, *67*, 154
government grants 55
governmental accounting 4, 5, 11, 13, 17, 19, 24, *25*, 36, 37, 39, *53*, 54, 58, 199, 211–12

see also budgetary accounting
governmental auditing 11, 18–19, 42,
    113, *115*, 116, 118–27
    forms of governmental auditing 123–
      5
      rotative audit 124
      routine audits 124
      special-case audits 125
    grading system for government
      auditors 256, *257*, 272
    organizational structure 119–21, *120*
    procedures of governmental auditing
      125–7, *128*
    qualification examination for govern-
      ment auditors 242, 255–8, 272
    content of *258*
    responsibilities of state audit offices
      121–2
    rights of state audit offices 122–3
    see also China Society of Auditing
      (CSA)
gross domestic product (GDP) 1
group companies 9
growth rate 1
Guangdong province 263
Guangzhou 74, 113, 138, 166, 189
*Guidelines for Non-governmental
    (Social) Auditing* 118

Hainan 188
Harbin Industry University 238
high school graduates 236–7, 239, *240*,
    253, 257
historical cost principle *60*, 61, *64*, 65,
    66–7, 91, 330, 331, 332, 333, 338
Hoepen, M.A. 21 n. 3
Hong Kong 74, 140, 145, 188, 226,
    230, 265, 273
    Exchange Commission 81
    Stock Exchange 8, 76
hospitals 198, 199–201, *200*
Hunan Institute of Finance and Eco-
    nomics 251

ideological influence 5–6, 63
implementation constraints *60*, 62–3, *64*

imports 168, 169, 186, 188
    tariffs 178, 179, 188
income determination 5, 43, 63, 66–7,
    67, 209
income statements 62, 68, 84, 210, 339,
    340, 354
income tax 55
    agricultural 167
    business 162, 164, 167, 173–4, 349,
      351, 353
      for foreign invested enterprises
        164, 184–5, 189, 190, 291,
        293
      tax base and tax payers 173
      tax calculation 174
      tax rates 173–4, 189, 190
      tax returns 186–7
    personal 162, 164, 167, 174–8
      tax base 176
      tax calculation 176–7
      tax deduction and exemption 178
      tax rates *177*, 177–8, *178*
      tax returns 187
      taxpayers (resident and non-
        resident) 175–6
*Income Tax Law of the People's
    Republic of China for Enterprises
    with Foreign Investments and
    Foreign Enterprises* (1993) 164,
    291, 293
indirect costs 92, 96
individual economic households *see*
    private businesses
industry-specific accounting regula-
    tions 26–7, 33, 34, 35, 42–7, 51,
    53, *53*, 54, 58, 68, 201, 212, 218,
    220, 228
    cost and expenditures provisions 90–
      5 *passim*, 97
inflation 61, 74, 277
information
    disclosure 56, 62, *64*, 67–9, 339–41,
      354
    and securities market 18, 47, 49,
      73, 78, 79–88
    see also securities markets

managerial accounting and 104, 109
relevance 60, 61, 91, 329
institutional budgets 195, *196*, 197–9,
  200
institutional internal auditing 113, 114,
  115, 116, 118, 122, 127–31, 308
  number of internal auditors 128
  procedures of internal auditing 130–
  1
  responsibilities of internal auditors
  129
  rights of internal auditors 130
insurance companies
  accounting regulations for 35
  Insurance Law 286–7
intangible assets 12, 55, 65–6, 93, 171,
  172, 292, 330, 333–4, 344, 345,
  347–8, 349, 350, 352
interim reports *81*, 83, 85, 195, 208,
  209
internal auditing *see* institutional
  internal auditing
International Accounting Standards
  (IAS) 12, 14, 65, 274
International Accounting Standards
  Committee (IASC) 13, 157
international aid 122, 124, 307
International Conference on Chinese
  Economic Reforms and Liberalization of Chinese Accounting
  Systems (Beijing, 1997) 50 n. 7
International Federation of Accountants
  (IFAC) 13, 157
International Monetary Fund (IMF) 122
internationalization of Chinese accounting 11–12, 43, 44–45, 52, 59,
  67, 213
inventories 5, 12, 46, 55, 63, 64–5, 66–
  7, 217, 219, 220, 228, 229, 230,
  331, 332, 345, 346, 353
investment 55, 82, 93
  centres 106
  consulting agencies 87
  external 348–9, 350
  foreign *see* foreign investment
  invested capital 336

long-term 330, 332
sources of business financing 279,
  344–5

Jiang Zeming 179
Jiangxi Institute of Finance and Eco-
  nomics 251
Jilin University 238, 251
Jiling Province 215
Jinan University 238, 251
job-order costing 95
joint ventures 1, 4, 8, 10, 47, 61, 104,
  145, 146, 180, 181, 185, 227, 228,
  245–6, 269, 278–9, 293, 326
  Joint Ventures Law (1979, 1990)
  245–6, 291–3
Journal of CPA 275
*Journal of Shanghai University of
  Finance and Economics* 276
journals, accounting 20, 275–6
Jun Lin, Z. 214 n. 4

Kang, Jun 135 n. 16

land 65
  land appreciation tax 164, 167, 182
  land usage taxes 167, 181, 350
*Law of Personal Income Tax of the
  People's Republic of China* (1993)
  164
*Law of Tax Levy and Administration of
  the People's Republic of China*
  (1991) 164
*Law of the People's Republic of China
  on Joint Ventures with Chinese
  and Foreign Capital* (1979, 1990)
  245–6, 291–3
leasing 9, 47, 55, 65, 176–7, 333, 335
legal liability
  accountants 301–2
  auditors 311–13
  CPA firms 324–5
Li, Jinghua 135 n. 16
liabilities 55, 59, *60*, 63, 66, *67*, 203,
  213, 306, 307, 334–5, 340, 345
Lianyungang 189

Liaoning University 251
limited liability entities 144–5, 278, 282, 283, 321
liquidations 9, 55, 59, 86, 146, 282, 284, 293, 319, 345, 346, 352, 353
listed companies, number of 8, 74, *75*, 76, *76*
litigation 83, 84, 85
London Stock Exchange 8, 76
long-term investments 330, 332
'lower of cost or market' (LCM) 63, 65

Macao 140, 226, 265
managerial accounting 89
  application of 16
  computerized 221
  practices of 105–8
    comprehensive cost control 107
    cost planning 107–8
    economic responsibility and responsibility budgeting 106
    economic responsibility and responsibility costing 105–6
  prospects of, in China 109–10
  rise of 10–11, 102–4
    educational development 10–11, 102–3, 246, *248*, *249*, 252, *255*
    functions and organizations 104
    practical aspects 103–4
Manila 179
manufacturing costs 66, 91, 93, *94*
manufacturing enterprises 33, 35, 91, 110 n. 1, 168, 169, 173, 191, 216, 220, 228
marginal budgetary units (MBUs) 198–9, *200*, 204, 205, 213
  financial reporting for 209
marine petroleum resources, taxation of 166, 180
Marxism 65
master degree programmes *236*, 236, 239, *240*, 250, 254, *257*, 257
master fiscal budgets 195, *196*, 197, 199, *200*
matching principle *60*, 62, *64*, 91, 92

materiality *60*, 62, *64*, 65, 91
measurement unit 59–61, *60*, *64*
merchandising 26, 33, 35, 90, 168, 244, *245*
mergers 9, 55, 281, 319
Middle-Young-Aged Society of Finance and Cost Research of China 261
military units *25*, 168, 181
  see also army-run enterprises
mineral products, taxation of 180–1, *181*
Ministry of Civil Affairs and Social Welfare 262
Ministry of Finance 4, 12, 24, *25*, 26–7, 29, 30, 33, 34, 35, 37, 38, 39, 44, 51, 52, 53, 54–5, 57–8, 77, 86, 90, 97, *115*, 116–17, 131, 132, 133, 138–9, 140, 145, 147, 149, 152, 154, 156, 164, 190, 195, *196*, 199, 201, 208, 211, 212, 215–16, 217, 218, 222, 223, 225, 226, 227, 228, 229, 231, 241, 242, 246, 247, 250, 251, 253, 254, 259, 262, 263, 266, 267, 268, 269, 270, 272, 316, 317, 318, 321, 322, 323, 326, 327, 341, 347, 354, 355
Ministry of Foreign Trade and International Cooperation 145, 292
Ministry of Labour and Human Resources 37, 242, 253, 254, 256
Ministry of Machinery 216
Ministry of Public Health 201
monetary unit 59–61, *60*, *64*
monopolies *see* Antitrust Law (1993)
multiple ownership 8

Nanjing Institute of Auditing 249
Nankai University 238
Nanking University 238
Nantong 189
National Audit Office 304, 306
National Auditing Administration (NAA) 12, 113, 114–17, *115*, 118–21, 126, 127–8, 129, 130, 131–2, 152, 154, 156, 242, 249, 251, 256, 262, 268, 272, 273

National Committee on Academic Accreditation 250
National Committee on Uniform Examinations 259, 270
National Conference on Accounting Affairs (Beijing, 1995) 22, 211, 214, 232, 266
National Fair of Accounting Software and Application Programs (Beijing, 1994) 227
National People's Congress (NPC) 30, 31, 32, 52, 113, 117, 119, 150, 164, 195, 208, 245–6, 293, 295, 202, 315
National Uniform Certified Public Accountant Examination (NUCPAE) 139–43, 156, 242, 258–9, 268, 270–1, 316–17, 326
Nationalist Party (*Guomindang*) 112
net assets 203, 113
New York Stock Exchange 8, 76
newspapers, national 83, 84, 85
Ningbo 189
non-governmental auditing *see* public accounting
non-profit organizations (NPOs) 4, 5, 13, 17, 19, 194, 195, *196*, 197–8, 199, *200*, 204, 205, 207, 211–12, 261–2, 267
    auditing of 112, 114, *115*, 116, 122, 124, 125, 127, 131
    financial reporting for *see* reporting, financial
    regulation of accounting for 11, 24, 25, 36, 37, 39, *53*, 58, 199–201, 212
    taxation of 168, 181
    see also budgetary accounting
Northeastern University of Finance and Economics 237, 248, 250, 251
Northern University of Communication and Transportation 238

objectives, accounting 3
    modification of 9–10
objectivity principle 91

obligations of accounting personnel 40–1, 53
    CPAs 148–51
    supervision 41–2, 129, 298–300
off-budget funds 134 n. 8, 202–3, 208, 209, 210, 211, 213
on-budget funds 134 n. 8, 202–3, 208, 209, 210, 211, 213
operating reserves, statement of 210
operation (business) tax 164, 167, 171–2
operation costing 95
Oracle Company (USA) 227
organization of accounting work 39, 53, 300
Osaka 179
owners' equity 55, 59, *60*, 63, 66, *67*, 68, 279, 335–6, 340

partial market economy 9, 14, 33, 43, 51, 52, 69, 77, 104, 106, 161–2, 207, 211, 246, 277, 327, 343
partnerships 144–5, 168, 173, 176, 177, 187, 278, 282, 321
payroll accounting 217, 219, 220, 228, 229, 230
Peking University 276
People's Bank of China (PBC) 74, 77, 78, *79*, 83, 114, 122, 124, 133 n. 3, 197, 284–5, 306
People's Liberation Army 24, *25*, 296, 313
People's Republic of China (founded 1949) 3, 18, 23, 89, 112, 193, 237
percentage-of-completion method 63
performance effectiveness audits 124
performance variance, disclosure of 81
period costs 66, 91, 92, 93
political parties 197–8, *200*
    see also Communist Party; Nationalist Party (*Guomindang*)
polytechnic schools 236–6, *236*, 239, *240*, 241, 253–4, *257*, 257
population 1
post and communication enterprises 35
post-doctorate programmes *236*, *240*

prepayments 331, 345
primary business revenues 66
private businesses 8, 48, 161–2, 168,
173, 176, 177, 185, 187, 278
see also Privately-owned Enterprise
Law
Privately-owned Enterprise Law 282–3
Procedures for Appraisal of Commer-
cialized Accounting Software
(1994) 218, 223
Procedures on Product Costing for
State-owned Industrial Enterprises
(1973) 90
process costing 95
product-based costing 95
product costing 5, 18, 30, 35
computerized 219, 228, 229
practices of 93–7
cost accounting system 97
designing product costing accounts 93–5, *94*
methods of product costing 95–6
procedures of cost accounting 96–
7
principles and requirements of 91–3
product costs *see* manufacturing costs
professional associations 20, 26, 49 n.
2, *115*, 116–17, 118, 119, *120*,
131–3, 156–8, Ch. 12
nature of 261–2
self-discipline by 29–30, 262, 266,
268
self-regulation by 29, 54, 87
see also under names of individual
professional associations e.g.
Accounting Society of China
(ASC); Chinese Association of
Certified Public Auditors
(CACAuP); Chinese Institute of
Certified Public Auditors
(CICPA)
profit and loss 59, *60*, *67*, 68, 92, 306,
307, 339
profit centres 106, 199
profits 350–1
distribution of 351

forfeiture of 291
of joint ventures 292
retained 279, 336, 351
property and real estate development
enterprises 35
property taxes 164, 167, 182, 186
prospectuses 18, *81*, 82–3
Provisional Regulation on Business
Income Tax of the People's
Republic of China (1993) 164
Provisional Regulation on Business Tax
of the People's Republic of China
(1993) 164
Provisional Regulation on Consump-
tion Tax of the People's Republic
of China (1993) 164
Provisional Regulation on Land
Appreciation Tax of the People's
Republic of China (1993) 164
Provisional Regulation on Resources
Tax of the People's Republic of
China (1993) 164
Provisional Regulation on Value-added
Tax of the People's Republic of
China (1993) 164
Provisional Regulations on Issuance
and Trading of Securities 80
prudence convention (conservatism) *60*,
63, *64*, 65, 330
public accounting 11, 16–17, 32, 42,
111–12, 113, 114, *115*, 118, 122,
Ch. 7
CPA Law (1993) 11, 32, 138–9, 144,
145, 148–9, 157, 242, 259, 266,
268, 271
historical evolution of, in China 137–
9
professional associations 20, *115*,
116–17, 118, 119, 131–3, 156–8
see also Chinese Association of
Certified Public Auditors
(CACAuP); Chinese Institute
of Certified Public Auditors
(CICPA)
see also certified public accountants
(CPAs)

public utilities 181
publications, accounting 20, 275–6

Qingdao 189
Qinghuangdao 189
qualifications in accounting 26, 28
    certification programme for certified
        public accountants *see* certified
        public accountants (CPAs)
    examinations *see* examinations
    government auditors 242, 255–8,
        258, 272
    grading system 31, 36–8, 242, 252–
        3
    government auditors 256, *257*, 272
Quan-Bu (overall) 110 n. 4

railways 27, 35
realization principle 61–2, *64*
regional tax policies 188–91
    special economic zones (SEZs) 188–
        90
    state high-tech industrial districts
        (SHTIDs) 190–1
registration statements *81*, 82
*Regulation for the Installation of Chief
    Accountants* 31
regulation of accounting 18, Ch. 2
    accounting standards and 51–4
    administrative system 23–30
        deficiencies of existing pattern 28–
            9
        Department of Accounting Affairs
            (DAA) *25*, 26–7, 54–5, 57,
            263
        main elements 24
        self-discipline by accounting
            profession 29–30, 262, 266,
            268
        statutory requirements 24–6
    budgetary accounting regulations 58,
        199–201, 212
    computerized accounting regulation
        19, 217–18, 222–7, 297
    cost management regulation *see* cost
        accounting

for foreign investments 10, 11, 33,
    47, 61, 147, 246
future development 15
historical 4
legal framework 11, 30–6
    Accounting Law (1985, 1993) 11,
        24–6, 27, 31–2, 39–40, 52,
        53, 53–4, 295–302, 327
    *Accounting Standards for Business
        Enterprises* (ASBE) (1993)
        see accounting standards
    CPA Law (1993) 11, 32, 138–9,
        144, 145, 148–9, 157, 242,
        259, 266, 268, 271, 315–26
*General Rules on Financial Affairs for
    Business Enterprises* (1993) 34–5,
    44, *45*, 48–9, 65, 90–1, 97, 343–
    55
    industry-specific *see* industry-
        specific accounting regula-
        tions
    qualifications and obligations of
        accounting personnel 36–42
    obligations of accounting person-
        nel 40–2, 53, 129, 148–51,
        298–300
    organization of accounting work
        39, 53, 300
    qualifications of accounting
        personnel 36–8
    responsibilities and rights of
        accounting personnel 39–40,
        53, 129–30, 300–1
reform of setting accounting regula-
    tions 42–9
    phase I: dual system of accounting
        regulations (since 1993) 44–5
    phase II: domination of transac-
        tion-based accounting
        standards 45–8
    relationship between general
        financing rules and account-
        ing standards 48–9
supplementary regulations and rules
    36, 80
system of, in China *53*

taxation regulations 4, 19, 47, 49,
184–5
see also business regulation
regulation of auditing *see* auditing
regulation of securities markets *see*
securities markets
Regulation on Public Accountants
(1930) 138
*Regulation of the Certified Public
Accountants in the People's
Republic of China* (1986) 31, 32,
138, 326
*Regulation on Cost Management for
State-owned Enterprises* (1984) 90
*Regulations on the Responsibility and
Rights of Accounting Personnel* 30
relevance principle *60*, 61, 91, 329
Renmin University of China 237, 248,
249, 250, 251, 276
Renminbi 1, 59, 75–6, 284, 291, 297,
328, 352
repair costs 65, 347
reporting, financial 18, 33, 47, 55, *56*,
59, 61, *81*, 83–6, 129, 354
ASBE requirements 62, 67–9, 339–
41
computerized accounting used in
219, 228, 229, 230
for governments and non-profit
organizations 207–10
aggregate budgetary units 208
FABUs 209
MBUs 209
redesigning structure of financial
statements 213
SFBUs 209–10
*Requirements for Basic Functions of
Accounting Software* (1994) 218,
222–3
*Requirements on CPA Education and
Training System* 242–3
research and development 55, 65, 197,
198, *200*, 201, 216, 227–8, 230,
232, 250
see also research in accounting and
auditing

Research and Development Centre for
Computerization of Accounting
(*later* Beijing AnYi Computer
company) 227–8
research in accounting and auditing
119, *120*, 265–6, 272, 273–4
publications 20, 275–6
Research Institute of Finance Sciences
228, 250
'reserve for bad debts' 64
*Resolution on Discipline of Criminal
Acts that Violate the Corporate
Law* (1995) 150
resources tax 164, 167, 180–1, 186
responsibilities of accounting personnel
39–40, 53, 129, 300–1
responsibility accounting 16, 98, 100,
101, 105–6, 246, *249*
responsibility system of cost control 97,
98–9
retained profits 279, 336, 351
revenue centres 199
revenue-sharing system 163, 166, 167,
210
revenues 5, 12, 43, 46, 55, 59, *60*, 61–
2, 63, *64*, 66, *67*, 337
budgetary 63, 89, 122, 163, 166, 167,
174, 195, 197, 202, 204, 210
operating 350
see also revenue centres
rights of accounting personnel 40, 130,
300–1
rotative audit 124
rule-based accounting 5
*Rules of Cost Management for State-
owned Merchandising Enterprises*
90
*Rules of Professional Ethics for
Chinese Certified Public Accountants* (1992) 151
*Rules on Field Audit Work Performed
by State Audit Offices* 118
*Rules on Product Costing in Manufac-
turing Enterprises* 30
*Rules on Regulation of Social Account-
ing* 133

*Rules on Supervision over Internal
     Auditing by State Audit Offices*
     127–8

S-K regulations 81
S-X regulations 81
Sales 228, 229, 230
Santou 188
schools *200, 236*
securities markets
     characteristics of 75–6
     growth of 8, 73–4, *75*
     listed companies (number of) 74, *75,
          76, 76*
     marketable securities 331, 345, 348–9
     problems of disclosure 86–7
          solutions to 87–8
     prospectus disclosure 18, *81,* 82–3
     regular disclosures *81,* 83–6
     regulation of 18, 77–82
          characteristics of Chinese disclo-
               sure requirements 81–2
          cheating and swindles 150
          regulatory authorities 77–9, *79*
          regulatory framework of disclo-
               sure for publicly listed
               companies 47, 49, 79–80, *81*
     securities trading centres 74, 77
     share-capital system 8, 73–4, 75, 77,
          86, 279, 283
     stock exchanges 8, 51, 74, 76, *76, 79,*
          81, 83, 86, 291
self-discipline, professional 29–30,
     262, 266, 268
self-financed budgetary units (SFBUs)
     198–9, *200,* 204, 205, 213
     financial reporting for 209–10
'self-regulation' 29, 54, 87
selling and administrative expenses 66,
     68, 91, 92, 349–50
senior accountant, qualifications of 38,
     140
senior auditor, qualifications of 256
separations 146, 186, 281, 319
Shanghai 74, 113, 138, 145, 166, 189,
     273

Jiaotong University 238
Stock Exchange 8, 51, 74, 76, *76, 79,*
     81
University of Finance and Econom-
     ics (SUFE) 237, 248, *249,* 250,
     251, 276
Shanghai Accounting 275
share-capital systems 8, 73–4, 75, 77,
     86, 279, 283
shareholders
     major 84
     maximum number of 283
Shehui Shenji see public accounting
Shenxi Institute of Finance and Trade
     251
Shenyang 74
Shenzhen 86, 145, 188, 230
     Stock Exchange 8, 51, 74, 76, *76, 76,*
     81
Shenzhen Yuanjian Science and Tech-
     nology Development Company
     230
Shuo, W. 133 n. 1
Sichuan United University 238
significant events reports 81, *81,* 85–6
social auditing *see* public accounting
social security funds 122, 307
socialist market economy *see* partial
     market economy
software *see* computerized accounting
Southwestern University of Finance and
     Economics 238, 248–9, 250, 251
special economic zones (SEZs) 86,
     163, 230
     tax policies for 188–90
speculation 8, 182
spending allowances 35
staffing
     CPA firms 148
     government agencies 28, 117, 119
     see also accounting personnel;
          accounting work, organization
          of
stamp tax 167
standard costing *see* fixed-quota
     costing system

Standard Procedures on Product Costing 97

standards *see* accounting standards; auditing

State Administration of Customs (SAC) 164, 169, 179

State Administration of Industry and Commerce (SAIC) 282, 286, 288, 289

State Administration of Trademark 289, 290

state audit supervision *see* auditing

State Commission on Reform of Economic Structure 75, 77, 86

State Council 4, 24, 25, 30, 31, 32, 37, 57, 77, 80, 90, 114, 117–18, 119, 132, 138, 145, 157, 164, 165, 169, 195, 208, 250, 251, 292, 296, 298, 303, 304, 306, 307, 308, 310, 316, 317, 318, 321, 322, 323, 326

State Council Securities Commission (SCSC) 77–8, 79, 83, 151

State Economic Commission 75, 77

State Education Commission 201, 251

state high-tech industrial districts (SHTIDs) 190–1, 230

State-owned Enterprise Law 280–2

State Planning Commission 251

state secrets 305

State Taxation Bureau (STB) 77, 164, 165, 166, 169, 179

stock markets *see* securities markets

Stone Computer Company 229

Stone finance and accounting software package 229

subsidies, government 122, 124, 168, 178, 307

supervision function 41–2, 129, 298–300

Supplementary Notices on the Policy on Issuing New Shares 80

supplementary regulations and rules 36, 80

supply and tools software 229

surplus reserve 66, 336

Symposium on the Application of Computers in Financial Management, Accounting and Product Costing (1981) 216

Taiwan 81, 140, 145, 188, 226, 265, 273

takeovers *81*, 85, 86

tariffs and duties 167, 178–80, 188

taxation 19, Ch. 8

administrative agencies 165–6

audit supervision 121–2

behaviour (activity) taxes 167

bilateral treaties 165, 179

centralized system (1949–93) 161–2, 194

consumption tax 164, 167, 169–71

courses in 252

CPA examination in 140, *141*, *142*

'financial and taxation examination' 112

of foreign investments 19, 161–2, 163, 164, 168, 173, 175, 180, 181, 183–5, 188–91, 291, 293

income tax 55

agricultural 167

business 162, 164, 167, 173–4, 184–5, 186–7, 189, 190, 291, 293, 349, 351, 353

personal 162, 164, 178–8, 187

land usage taxes 167, 181, 350

marine petroleum resources 166, 180

operation (business) tax 164, 167, 171–2

property taxes 164, 167, 180–1, 186

regional development policies 188–91

regulations 5, 19, 47, 49, 164–5

resources tax 164, 167, 180–1, 186

revenues 63, 89, 122, 163, 166, 167, 174, 195, 197, 202, 204, 210

services and consultation 146

State Administration of Customs (SAC) 164, 169, 179

State Taxation Bureau (STB) 77, 164, 165, 166, 169, 179

tariffs and duties 167, 178–80, 188

tax evasion 41, 187, 301
tax penalties 187
tax reform (1994) 162–3, 201, 210, 211
tax registration 185–6
tax returns 186–7
types of taxes 166–82
   see also under names of individual taxes e.g. consumption tax; value-added tax
value-added tax 164, 167–9
Taxation Bureau for Marine Petroleum Resources (TBMPR) 166
team accounting 16
Temporary Methods for Administration of the Resident Offices of Overseas Accounting Firms (196) 145
Temporary Regulation on the Administration of Qualification Examinations (1992) 242, 256
Temporary Rules on the Administration of Accountant Qualification Examinations
   (1993) 242
   (1996) 254
Tentative Measures on Preventing Cheating and Swindles in Securities Listing and Trading (1993) 150
Tentative Procedures for Administration of Accounting Software (1989) 217
Tentative Procedures for Administration of Training Programmes on Knowledge of Accounting Computerization (1995) 231
Tentative Rules for Public Accountants (1919) 137
terminology, technical 87
textbooks 11, 102–3, 219, 247–9, *249*, 250
three-overall cost control *see* comprehensive cost control
Tianjin Institute of Finance and Economics 237, 249, 250, 251
Tianjing 74, 138, 166, 189
Top financial software 229

tourist industry 35
Trademark Law 289–90
transport 27, 33, 35, 171, *172*, 173, 191, *245*, 350
trial balancing 206–7
Tsinghua University 238, 248, 251

underwriters 83
Unified Procedures on Product Costing Chart of Accounts for State-owned Industrial Enterprises (1953) 90
uniform accounting systems (UAS) 4–5
uniform industry and commerce tax (UICT) 184, 188, 189, 190
United Systems Ltd (UK) 227
universities 10–11, 102–3, 139, 199–201, *200*, 216, 231, 235, *236*, 236–9, 248–9, *249*
   journals published by 276
   offering CPA specialization programme 251
   offering doctorate programmes 250
   open universities 243
   see also under names of degree programmes e.g. bachelor degree programmes; master degree programmes
University of International Business and Economics 238
US Financial Accounting Standards Board (FASB) 62
US Securities and Exchange Commission (SEC) 81

value-added tax 164, 167–9
vocational accounting programmes (social accounting education) 243
voucher verification 96

Wangneng (general-purpose) financial accounting software 228
Wenzhou 189
word processing 223, 227
work experience 37–8, 143, 253–4, 256–7, 259, 264, 267, 269, 275

work-in-progress 93, *94*, 97, 332, 346
working capital, sources and uses of
    68–9, 340
Working Rules for Accounting Person-
    nel 39
Working Rules on Institutional Internal
    Auditing 118, 129, 130
World Bank 1, 34, 52, 57, 122, 162
World Trade Organization (WTO) 179,
    277
Wuhan 138
    University of 251

Xiamen 188
    University of 237, 248, *249*, 250,
    251, 276
Xi'an Jiaotong University 238, 251
Xiangfeng Accounting Computeriza-
    tion Company 229
Xiangfeng (pioneers) accounting
    software 229

Xie Ling 137

Yam, S.C. 133 n. 1
Yantai 189
Yongyou EDP Financial Technology
    Company 228–9
Yongyou (users' friends) financial
    accounting software 228–9
Yuanjian (vision) finance and account-
    ing software 230

Zhang, W.G. 214 n. 5
Zhang Youcai 50 n. 7
Zhanjiang 166, 189
Zhao, J.Y. 214 n. 5
Zhao dynasty 133 n. 1
Zhongnan University of Finance and
    Economics 237, 250, 251
Zhongshan University 251
Zhuhai 188
Zi-Jin-Ping-Heng-Biao 70